The World's Wine Markets

Globalization at Work

Edited by

Kym Anderson

Professor of Economics and Executive Director,
Centre for International Economic Studies,
University of Adelaide, Australia

Edward Elgar
Cheltenham, UK • Northampton, MA, USA

Published by
Edward Elgar Publishing Limited
The Lypiatts
15 Lansdown Road
Cheltenham
Glos GL50 2JA
UK

Edward Elgar Publishing, Inc.
William Pratt House
9 Dewey Court
Northampton
Massachusetts 01060
USA

Paperback edition 2005

This book has been printed on demand to keep the title in print.

A catalogue record for this book
is available from the British Library

Library of Congress Cataloguing in Publication Data
The world's wine markets : globalization at work / edited by Kym Anderson.
       p. cm.
   Includes bibliographical references and index.
   1. Wine industry. 2. International trade–Case studies. 3. Globalization–
Economic aspects–Case studies. I. Anderson, Kym.

   HD9370.5. W67 2004
   382'.456632–dc22   2004046991

ISBN 978 1 84376 439 7 (cased)
       978 1 84542 514 2 (paperback)

Typeset by Cambrian Typesetters, Frimley, Surrey
Printed and bound in Great Britain by
Marston Book Services Limited, Didcot

Contents

v

PART IV   OTHER EMERGING MARKETS

Figures

Tables

Contributors

Luis Miguel Albisu is a senior economist with Unidad de Economía Agraria SIA-DGA in Zaragoza, Spain.

Julian M. Alston is a professor in the Department of Agricultural and Resource Economics at the University of California, Davis, USA.

Kym Anderson is a professor of Economics and Executive Director of the Centre for International Economic Studies at the University of Adelaide, and a non-executive director of Australia's Grape and Wine Research and Development Corporation.

Emmanuelle Auriol is an economist with ARQADE and IDEI, Université des Sciences Sociales de Toulouse, Toulouse, France.

Jan Bentzen is an associate professor in Economics at the Aarhus School of Business in Denmark.

Helene Bombrun is a postgraduate researcher at the Agricultural Issues Center of the University of California, Davis, USA.

Chunlai Chen was a CIES Research Fellow at the University of Adelaide when this project began but is now a lecturer at the Asia Pacific School of Economics and Government at the Australian National University in Canberra.

Alessandro Corsi is an associate professor of Agricultural and Environmental Economics at the University of Turin in Italy.

Roger Farrell is an economist with the Asia Pacific School of Economics and Government at the Australian National University in Canberra.

Christopher Findlay is the APEC Economies Professor in the Asia Pacific School of Economics and Government at the Australian National University in Canberra.

William Foster is a professor of Economics at the Catholic University of Chile in Santiago, Chile.

Dale Heien is a professor in the Department of Agricultural and Resource Economics at the University of California, Davis, USA.

Mathilde Hulot is a freelance journalist working for *Le Figaro Economie*, *La Revue du vin de France* and *L'Amateur de Bordeaux*, *La Revue vinicole internationale*, *La Vigne* and *Wine Business Monthly*.

Klaus Kilov is the Wine Research Librarian for the Wine Marketing Research Group of the University of South Australia, Adelaide.

Johann Kirsten is a professor and Chair of the Department of Agricultural Economics, Extension and Rural Development at the University of Pretoria in South Africa.

Jean-Baptiste Lesourd is an economist with GREQAM, Université de la Méditerranée et Université de Droit, d'Economie et des Sciences d'Aix-Marseille in France.

Larry Lockshin is an associate professor and director of the Wine Marketing Research Group at the University of South Australia, Adelaide.

Mia Mikić is a senior lecturer in the Department of Economics at the University of Auckland in New Zealand.

Nivelin Noev is a researcher with the Policy Research Group (PRG-Leuven) and a Ph.D. student at the Department of Agricultural and Environmental Economics of the Katholieke Universiteit in Leuven, Belgium.

David Norman was an Honours economics student at the University of Adelaide when this project began and is now an economist in the Adelaide office of the Reserve Bank of Australia.

Eugenio Pomarici is an associate professor of Food Marketing and Management at the Federico II University in Naples, Italy.

Roberta Sardone is a researcher at INEA in Rome and collaborates with the Ministry for Agriculture in Italy.

Günter Schamel is an Economics lecturer with the Humboldt University of Berlin, Germany.

Steven G.M. Schilizzi is a senior lecturer in the School of Agricultural and Resource Economics at the University of Western Australia in Perth.

Valdemar Smith is an associate professor in Economics at the Aarhus School of Business in Denmark.

Tony Spawton is the International Director of the Wine Marketing Research Group at the University of South Australia, Adelaide.

Sally Stening is a researcher with the Wine Marketing Research Group at the University of South Australia, Adelaide.

Karl Storchmann lectures in the Economics Department of Yale University, New Haven, USA.

Daniel A. Sumner is the Frank H. Buck, Jr Professor in the Department of Agricultural and Resource Economics and Director of the Agricultural Issues Center at the University of California, Davis, USA.

Johan F.M. Swinnen is an associate professor at the Department of Economics and Director of PRG-Leuven (Policy Research Group on Food and International Development) at the Katholieke Universiteit, Leuven, Belgium.

Alberto Valdés has been an economist with the World Bank and is now a consultant to the Food and Agriculture Organization, Rome.

Nick Vink is a professor and Chair of the Department of Agricultural Economics at the University of Stellenbosch in South Africa.

Dewen Wang is an economist with the Asia Pacific School of Economics and Government at the Australian National University in Canberra.

Gavin Williams is a Fellow of St Peter's College at the University of Oxford, United Kingdom.

Glyn Wittwer is a Research Fellow at the Centre of Policy Studies and IMPACT Project, Faculty of Business and Economics, Monash University, Melbourne, Australia.

Preface

The idea for this book arose when the University of Adelaide's Centre for International Economic Studies (CIES) decided to sponsor a wine economics workshop as part of the 11th Australian Wine Industry Technical Conference. That conference was held in Adelaide 7–11 October 2001, immediately preceding the 26th World Congress of the Office Inernational de la Vigne et du Vin, Adelaide, 11–18 October, both of which coincided with Tasting Australia (a biennial food and wine extravaganza). Half of the CIES wine economics workshop was devoted to technical economic papers, many of which have since been accepted for publication in academic journals; the other half was set aside to review wine market developments in the major wine-producing and/or -consuming regions of the world. Following the workshop, authors of the latter set of presentations revised their papers. They have since been further updated for this volume with the aim of providing a comprehensive and contemporary picture of the impacts of globalization on the world's wine markets.

While many of the chapters provide a brief historical overview by way of background, the main focus of the book is on the dramatic changes since the late 1980s, during which time the share of wine production that is traded internationally has nearly doubled globally, and the New World's share of those export earnings has risen like a phoenix from its historical level of less than 2 per cent to 20 per cent.

Thanks are due to the Australia Research Council for a grant that made the workshop and book preparation possible, as well as to Australia's Grape and Wine Research and Development Corporation for providing earlier seed money to begin to compile a statistical compendium of global wine markets. That compendium has been revised and updated during the course of this project, and is used as a basis for cross-country comparisons in several of the chapters. Nick Berger, David Norman and Pierre Spahni especially are to be thanked for the time they gave to helping to compile those data into a usable format.

As always, thanks are also due to the people who helped to organize the workshop (particularly Pip Anderson and Sallie James) and to copy-edit the text itself (particularly Sudesh Mahadoo, Peta Marshman and Wendy Zweck). And finally, my thanks to the authors not only for their chapters but also for the energy and enthusiasm they put into the entire project.

Kym Anderson
Adelaide

Abbreviations

AOC	Appellation d'origine contrôlée (of France)
AWBC	Australian Wine and Brandy Corporation
CAP	Common Agricultural Policy (of the EU)
CMO	Common Market Organization (of the EU)
DO	Denominaciones de Origen (of Spain)
DOC	Denominazione di Origine Controllata (of Italy)
DOCG	Denominazione di Origine Controllata e Garantita (of Italy)
DWI	German Wine Institute
EC	European Commission
EEC	European Economic Community
EU	European Union
FDI	Foreign direct investment
GI	Geographical indication
IGT	Indicazione Geografica Tipica (of Italy)
INDO	Instituto Nacional de Denominaciones de Origen (of Spain)
ISO	International Standards Office
OIV	Office International de la Vigne et du Vin
ONIVINS	Office National Interprofessionelle des Vins
SAWIS	South Africa Wine Information and Systems
VDQS	Vin Délimité de Qualité Supérieure
VQPRD	Vin de Qualité Produit dans une Région Déterminée
WFA	Winemakers' Federation of Australia
WIC	Wine Institute of California
WINZ	Wine Institute of New Zealand
WSA	Wine and Spirit Association (of the United Kingdom)
WSET	Wine and Spirit Education Trust (of the United Kingdom)
WTO	World Trade Organization

PART I

Overview

1. Introduction[*]

Kym Anderson

Why does the wine industry attract so much attention? After all, it accounts for just 0.4 per cent of global household consumption, and vines cover only 0.5 per cent of the world's cropland (of which barely one-third produce wine grapes). Moreover, globally it is not a growth industry in that world wine production has been declining slightly over the past two decades. But to millions of investors and hundreds of millions of consumers, this industry provides a far more fascinating product than its shares of GDP or global expenditure might suggest. More than that, it provides an intriguing case study of globalization at work: since the late 1980s the share of wine production that is traded internationally has nearly doubled, there has been a surge of foreign investment and mergers and takeovers in the industry, and the phenomenon of 'flying winemakers' has emerged as viticulturalists and oenologists seek to widen their experience, particularly by changing hemispheres in their off-season.

Wine's globalization has brought major economic gains to participants in the expanding countries, but pain to many traditional producers. In the past 30 years, wine producers in France, Italy, Portugal and Spain have watched per capita consumption halve in their domestic markets, so they have received low prices despite having reduced their combined grapevine area from 5 million hectares in the late 1960s to 4 million in the late 1980s and to barely 3 million today. For those growers it adds insult to injury to see wines from New World upstarts suddenly invading the export markets they have used to soak up their surplus wine. Meanwhile, for Eastern European producers that New World onslaught has come just as they have had to adjust to the transition from communism.

Those less able or willing to adjust are understandably upset by the emergence of New World exporters. For example, Maurice Large, a winemaker and President of the Union Interprofessionelle des Vins du Beaujolais, has likened Australian wine to Coca-Cola and called the consumers who purchase it 'philistines'. And a report commissioned by the French Ministry of Agriculture in 2001 concluded 'Until recent years wine was with us, we were the centre, the unavoidable reference point. Today, the barbarians are at our gates: Australia, New Zealand, the USA, Chile, Argentina, South Africa.'

Even winemakers in the USA are beginning to worry. In the late 1980s, less than 4 per cent of wine imports to the USA came from the southern hemisphere. Today that figure is around 30 per cent, more than half of which is from Australia alone (which surpassed France in the volume of sales in the USA in 2002). Those (former) dotcom millionaires who bought Napa Valley land for more than $100 000 per acre in the late 1990s to establish vanity vineyards now wonder if they will ever see a return on their investment, as the price of grapes and wines from there and Sonoma County began falling in 2002.[1] The change has been even more dramatic in California's warmer central valley. There the price of bulk varietal wines fell to as little as 50 cents per litre on the wholesale market in 2002. That stimulated the development of a new label by Charles Shaw known as 'Two-buck Chuck' because he retailed it at $1.99 a bottle in California (and $2.99 in other states). In the first few months of 2003 it is reputed to have captured 20 per cent of the Californian market, eating into the market for Mondavi's popular Woodridge table wine label whose sales in that state fell by one-quarter. Even if Californian grape prices recover, such labels may well continue to thrive if they are able to import bulk wine from Chile and Argentina at less than 50 cents per litre.

Traditional consumers of premium wines are concerned too. They worry that what for centuries has been characterized as largely a cottage industry – with colourful, passionate personalities and a wide variety of wines that differ across regions from year to year because of the vagaries of weather or the vigneron's experimentation – will soon be difficult to distinguish from any other globalized industry. With this fear come similar concerns for ancillary industries such as wine tourism, since boutique wineries are the lifeblood of such tourism.

This is an industry whose consumption mix has also changed dramatically, with commercial premium bottled wine sales growing rapidly while jug wine sales have plummeted and super-premium wine sales have been rather static. And it is that change in demand patterns that has driven the changes in the fortunes of Old World versus New World producers.

Will the New World really send wine the way of colas and hamburgers? Will a small number of large winemaking firms dominate the global market by churning out ever-larger volumes of standardized products under their own brand or that of large supermarkets and discount chains? If so, will that drive small producers and boutique wine retailers out of business?

What first triggered the growth in export demand for New World wine was a change in British liquor licensing laws in the 1970s allowing supermarkets to retail wine to baby boomers. The new upwardly mobile middle class that arose from Margaret Thatcher's economic reforms was eager to experiment with products like wine that had hitherto been the preserve of the upper class. By the mid-1980s, supermarkets – dominated by Sainsbury's, Marks and

Spencer, Waitrose and Tesco – accounted for more than half of all retail wine sales in the UK, and were supplying wines with their own brand alongside (sometimes identical) winery-branded bottles. (Wal-mart in early 2003 began offering its own brand in the USA too, using Gallo wine, and now the German chain, Aldi, is seeking liquor licences for some of its 600+ stores in the USA.)

Given Australia's close historical ties with Britain, it is not surprising that Australian companies recognized and responded to this new market opportunity first. The timing of the initial export surge was helped by a significant devaluation of the Australian dollar in the mid-1980s. Rampant food-safety scares helped accelerate the swing away from Old World wines. Austrian wines, for example, were banned in the USA in 1985 when Austrian wine-makers used diethylene glycol, a deadly chemical found in antifreeze, as an artificial sweetener. Chernobyl caused further scares in April 1986. And when it was discovered in 1986 that methanol had been used in Italian wines to raise their alcohol content, exports of Italian wine plummeted 38 per cent in one year.

Australian success in the UK market, where per capita wine consumption has doubled each decade since 1960 to 16 litres per capita compared with just 3 litres a generation earlier, is now legendary. So dominant was the New World expansion that during the 1990s only one-quarter of the UK's increase in wine imports came from Europe. The trebling of wine consumption from the early 1990s in the booming economy of Ireland likewise has mostly been fuelled by New World suppliers.

Competition from other New World producers was slow in coming. South Africa initially posed little threat because of over-regulation domestically and anti-apartheid sentiment abroad. Argentina and Chile, because their domestic and trade policies discriminated against exportable agricultural products, were also slow to penetrate the British market. Nor did the USA emerge as rapidly as Australia. Its viticultural land was more expensive and its currency stronger. In any case, the US domestic market was growing faster than domestic supply. This consumer trend was accelerated in the USA (and in Asia) following a 1991 report by CBS television's investigative programme *60 Minutes* on the so-called 'French paradox' – the apparent health benefits of (especially red) wine consumption in moderation. Having accounted for only 8 per cent of US alcohol consumption in the 1960s and 12 per cent in the early 1990s, wine's share had climbed to 16 per cent by 2001 (8 litres per capita, still only half the UK consumption level and so offering great potential for continuing growth, particularly in the under-$10 per bottle range where most young wine drinkers begin to experiment).

Despite the growth in US and UK demand, European suppliers failed to respond due to myriad regulations such as restrictions on which grape varieties can be used in each appellation, on maximum yields and alcohol content, and on vine density and vine training systems. In addition, producers were insulated from market forces by price supports in Western Europe and (until recently) socialist planning in Eastern Europe.

To exploit the rapidly growing markets requires large volumes of consistent, low-priced, easily approachable (fruity) premium wine, and mass marketing. The large wine companies in Australia had the capacity to supply both. And the export growth prospects – highlighted in a highly publicized 1996 vision statement called Strategy 2025, released by the Winemakers' Federation of Australia – stimulated a boom in new plantings that has doubled the acreage since the mid-1990s. These developments, together with low Australian domestic prices for red grapes in the mid-1980s (due to a local fashion swing to whites), increased substantially the incentive for wine companies to consolidate to reap the economies of scale necessary to invest in developing mass markets abroad. A number of mergers and acquisitions followed, including Pernod Ricard's 1989 purchase of Orlando Wyndham Wines, creating the Jacob's Creek label. Jacob's Creek's production has trebled since 1995, with sales growing at double-digit rates. In 2003 Orlando Wyndham sold more than 220 000 bottles of wine worldwide under the Jacob's Creek label every day.

For some, the result of greater competition from the New World is devastating. In Italy a 15 per cent fall in domestic wine sales in 2001 left an excess stock of 37 million litres that was much harder to dispose of internationally than it would have been in the past. Producers in Beaujolais also found they had 10 million litres of unsaleable wine from the 2001 vintage, and had to turn it into vinegar. That same vintage saw the selling price of ordinary wine grapes fall by as much as 30 to 40 per cent in southern France, prompting violent protests there in early 2002. Nor are the French and Italians alone in their frustration. Producers in Central and Eastern Europe, despite market reforms, have watched their wine export sales grow no faster than Western Europe's over the 1990–2001 period (4 per cent per year, compared with 20 per cent for the New World).

To make matters worse for small European producers, both Old World and New World wine companies are internationalizing their production and distribution. Wineries are forming alliances with foreign companies to reap economies of scale and scope, including through vertical integration with distributors. Western European firms are investing in Eastern Europe, South America, Australia, New Zealand and China (see the Annex to Chapter 3). US firms are investing in France, Italy and South America. And Australian firms are investing in North America and Europe. For example, Australia's Mildara Blass (part of the Foster's brewing company) in 2001 acquired the Californian firm Beringer to became Beringer Blass, which also has vineyards in Tuscany and Chianti, while BRL Hardy had a major winery (Domaine de la Baume) in the south of France, has a big joint venture in Sicily, signed in mid-2002 a distribution agreement with Dragon Seal in China – and then in 2003 it integrated with the US giant Constellation to form the world's largest wine company.

One might consider wine to be not very highly traded across national borders, since only one-quarter of global wine production was exported in 2001 in volume terms. But that compares with just 15 per cent in 1990 and less than 10 per cent in the 1960s. More significantly, in value terms the share of global wine production exported is around 40 per cent (since most of the low-quality wines are sold domestically).

Moreover, the pace of wine's globalization shows no signs of abating. With supermarketing of wine becoming more and more common, and concentration of ownership of supermarkets also increasing, the competitiveness of firms able profitably to supply large shipments to such markets is only going to strengthen relative to that of the smaller wineries. The supermarket chains' increasing domination of retailing is not only altering the sharing of profits along the supply chain, but is also starting to alter where firms sell. In Australia, for example, where the two main supermarket chains (Coles and Woolworths) have raised their share of domestic wine sales to more than 40 per cent, wineries have begun to look even more to export markets because their margins are being trimmed so much on the home market. But, because Southcorp was heavily discounting on the UK market during 2002, that market also became less lucrative, so Australian wineries focused more on other markets. With the low AUD/US$ exchange rate at the time, the most obvious market was the USA, where Australia managed to expand its wine sales by a massive 53 per cent by volume and 64 per cent in value in 2002.

Chile and South Africa are similarly becoming more nimble in accessing foreign markets. Both are emulating Australia in upgrading the quality and export marketing of their product range, and both are seeking to over-deliver in terms of value for money in key markets. For example, according to AC Neilsen data as reported by Wines of South Africa, during 2002–2003 that country raised its retail wine sales value in the UK by one-quarter, increasing its value share to 9.5 per cent compared with 8.1 per cent the previous year. Its value share now almost matches its volume share of 9.9 per cent in that market. Its performance in the Netherlands is even more impressive: the value share in 2002–2003 was 16.1 per cent (up from 14.4 per cent a year earlier), ahead of its volume share of 14.7 per cent (up from ·12.7 per cent in 2001–2002).

In the face of declining demand in European markets and increasing market pressure from the New World, Old World producers are looking for prospective markets elsewhere. So too will New World producers as their exportable volumes grow. The Middle East has the affluence but not the inclination to drink wine, thanks to Mohammed's decree against alcohol. Most Africans and South Asians are still too poor to provide mass markets any time soon. But do rapidly rising incomes elsewhere in Asia offer prospects? Sceptics question whether wine goes with Asian food, yet élites in China and India have consumed wine from grapes for centuries. China produced, consumed and traded wine with Persia as early as the first century BC, and Marco Polo noted that excellent wines were produced in China's Shansi province for exporting all over Cathay. The Mogul empire in sixteenth-century India, meanwhile, was supplied with wine from the High Indus Valley and Afghanistan. Can that interest of the élites be a springboard for converting the middle classes in Asia to this European product?

As incomes rise, and with them access to refrigeration, a gradual expansion in wine promotion into food-revering Asia could well yield a high long-term payoff. Recent efforts by wine marketers in Japan and Southeast Asia to match food with wine have been highly successful, with both Old and New World suppliers hosting promotional tastings and the like. And a speech by Chinese Premier Li Peng in 1997 affirming the health virtues of red wine helped consumption sky-rocket in cities on China's eastern seaboard. In Asia as a whole, wine sales have more than doubled over the past ten years, with Japan and China responsible for 80 per cent of this growth.

Sales growth in Asia will accelerate further if/when wine import and consumption taxes on wine are lowered. Indeed, that is already beginning to happen. Following China's recent accession to the WTO (World Trade Organization), its import tariffs are scheduled to come down from 65 to 14 per cent by 2004, during which time the regulation of its distribution and retail channels is to be eased. And India succumbed in March 2003 to pressure from the EU to lower its wine import tariff, albeit only from 200 to 166 per cent.

Meanwhile well-targeted information and promotion efforts will alter sales patterns over time, especially while per capita consumption is still low (still below 3 litres per year in Japan and less that half a litre on average in Asia's developing countries, or less than 3 per cent of total alcohol consumption in the region). It may even lead eventually to Chinese élite consumers refraining from the practice of diluting ultra-premium wines with soft drinks such as 7-Up to make the beverage sweeter!

But who will supply this emerging market? Unfortunately for exporters elsewhere, the chances are that China will remain close to self-sufficient, since its vineyard area and winery capacity have grown in parallel with domestic consumption demands in recent years. Scope remains for joint ventures, however. Currently there are more than 20 such activities in China. Of the imports that do get in, all but one-fifth of the volume has come from France in recent years (even though France supplies only one-quarter of global exports and is further away than Australia or California). It may be that French wines are preferred initially for snobbery reasons, but as the market attracts new consumers they are more likely to be seduced by the up-front, fruit-driven (and lower-priced) wines of the New World – although that might be imported not so much in branded bottles as in bulk for blending with Chinese wine for local labels.

In Japan, the high price of cropland means that imports will continue to dominate. But most imports come in as bulk wines for blending with local wines that are then sold as 'Product of Japan'. This practice is possible only because of arcane labelling laws that allow such a claim even if only a small fraction is derived from domestically produced grapes. The main beneficiary of that regulation is the domestic producer whose poor-value-for-money product may be otherwise unsaleable as a stand-alone product. As for unblended imported wine, France has held a 40–45 per cent share for more than a decade, while Germany's share has shrunk from a quarter to a tenth. This latter fact is mainly because of Italy's success in expanding its sales in restaurants there, but also because Australia and Chile have made efforts to break into this market.

If regulatory quirks have been used to bolster local producers in Japan, they have been employed even more heavily in Europe, ostensibly to preserve a cultural heritage. After successfully securing protection for geographical indication (GI) terms such as champagne (France), sherry (Spain), and port (Portugal), the EU is also proposing to introduce a new regulation in late 2003 that demands recognition for so-called 'traditional expressions'. Despite their everyday use in all English-speaking countries, France wants terms such as tawny, ruby, vintage, classic and cream to be usable only on EU wine labels for wines sold in the EU. Since these measures could provide another technical barrier to imports of wine from the New World (adding to the sea of paperwork currently required before wine is imported into some EU countries), New World countries have taken the matter up in the current WTO trade negotiations. Meanwhile, the USA has put forward the Stealth Bill by way of retaliation. That bill, if implemented as proposed by end-2003, would require all countries not signatories to a Mutual Acceptance Agreement with the USA (the New World wine producer/exporters are signatories but the EU is not) to be subject to similarly onerous paperwork requirements when exporting to the USA.

Other recent threats to New World wine exports to the Old World have included calls for the former to be labelled 'industrial wine' because of the use of modern R&D-inspired production techniques, and more specifically to indicate if oak chips were used it its production (in lieu of the more expensive practice of leaving it in oak barrels). Still another threat is the request in July 2003 from the Chiani Classico Consortium's Director, Guiseppe Liberatore, for the European Union to investigate claims that Australian wine is being 'dumped' in Germany at below its cost of production by a cartel of Australia's 20 largest wineries. Incredible though such claims are, they are none the less symptomatic of the threat the New World is perceived to be to the interests of Old World producers.[2]

Recent subsidies to wine producers in EU countries to help upgrade their wine industry are worth more than 400 million euros per year. If such subsidies encouraged structural adjustment toward producing and marketing what consumers want, and if France follows Spain in allowing blending of wine grapes from across the country,[3] then the Old World might gradually claw back some of its lost market share.

So far, the increasing globalization of the wine trade has not resulted in homogenization of wine. After all, firm concentration within the global wine market started from a very low base, at least compared with other beverage industries. The world market share of the three largest wine firms in the late 1990s was just 6 per cent, compared with 35 per cent for beer, 42 per cent for spirits, and 78 per cent for soft drinks. This decentralization alone suggests that wine is a very long way away from being homogenized – despite significant wine industry concentration within some New World countries. True, New Zealand's largest wine company – Montana – is responsible for producing more than two-thirds of that country's wine. But its volume is still small, and concentration is lower in other New World countries, where the share of national wine production held by the five biggest producers is around three-quarters in the USA and Australia and just half in both Chile and Argentina. In Europe it is of course far lower, even where large cooperatives operate.

While French and other Old World winemakers are right in claiming that the New World's low-end commercial wines sold in supermarkets are not very sophisticated, they ignore two key points. First, New World commercial premium wines are certainly more in demand than the low-end wines produced by myriad cooperatives in southern Europe. Hence, they will continue to take market share from the Old World in the bottom segments of the market. And second, Old World producers need to be aware that an increasing range of sophisticated wines is being produced in the New World. While volumes are not yet sufficient to take over the Old World's shelf space in the fine wine outlets of Europe, North America and Japan, by 2010 top-end New World wines may well overtake Old World rivals in some of the upper segments of the market.

With increasing affluence comes an increasing demand for many things, including product variety, the spice of life. Certainly, homogeneous wines like those produced under the Jacob's Creek label – which retail for about $5 in the USA and leave South Australian shores in whole container shiploads at a time – are wonderfully easy to mass-market to newcomers to wine. Over time, however, many of those new wine consumers will look for superior and more varied wines. Consumers will begin to differentiate between grape varieties, and between not just countries of origin, but regions within them. With the help of wine critics such as Hugh Johnson in the UK and Robert Parker in the USA, the 'philistine' consumers will increasingly discriminate between brands and labels within brands, reinforced by travel to their favourite wine regions. The preference for differentiated products, and the infinite scope for experimentation by vignerons, will continue to ensure that there will always be small- and medium-sized brands (like California's Ridge Wines and Australia's Petaluma) alongside the few large corporate labels such as Gallo, Mondavi and Orlando (the producer of Jacob's Creek).

The forces of globalization, together with the expansion in premium wine grape supplies as growers upgrade, may lead to more mergers, acquisitions, or alliances among wineries across national borders. This will be further encouraged by recent bilateral trade agreements, such as the EU providing South Africa with duty-free access for 42 million litres of wine per year and the USA phasing down its 12.5 per cent MFN (most favoured nation) import duty to zero over the next decade for Chile. But since the two largest wine firms (Constellation and Gallo) together account for less than 5 per cent of global wine sales (in contrast to the two largest soft drink manufacturers, Coke and Pepsi, which account for about 80 per cent of global sales), the world is a long way from having a cola-type homogeneity in wine markets.

Furthermore, the success of corporate wine labels in the global marketplace is likely to provide a slipstream in which astute smaller operators can also thrive. There are plenty of examples of New World wines from small wineries fetching fantastic prices after receiving high tasting ratings from Robert Parker, including Screaming Eagle from California and Duck's Muck from Australia's Barossa Valley. One of the two best-known icon red wines in Australia (Henschke's Hill of Grace) is from a small family winery in the Adelaide Hills that crushes well under 1000 tons per year.

The popularity of such small wineries in the ultra-premium and icon price brackets does not mean that the concerns of producers like Maurice Large in Beaujolais are overblown. On the contrary, the New World's strength is in the commercial premium range ($6–$10) and, increasingly, just above that price bracket.[4] This means that to do well in the age of supermarketing and consolidated winemaking giants, small and medium enterprises must work ever harder on marketing and distribution to ensure that their differentiated product is in demand. Possessing generations of traditional knowledge and being good at grapegrowing and winemaking are necessary and admirable, but not sufficient for survival in the new international wine marketplace. Mastering the formation of alliances with quality marketers and distributors is also essential, as is searching out and developing new markets in such places as East Asia.

Who will get all those ingredients right? At a 2001 conference in Italy,

Australian wine critic James Halliday was asked: What country will dominate the world's wine markets in 2100? Leaving aside the fact that, in a world of multinational corporations, the more pertinent question might be which *firms* will dominate. Halliday answered that Australia could well be in a similar position then to that of France today. Given that Australia has been exporting wine in commercial quantities for barely a century, his answer is consistent with Madame Rothschild's oft-quoted claim that winemaking is easy once you learn how; it is just the first 200 years that are difficult.

MOTIVATION FOR AND OUTLINE OF THE BOOK

What the above recent history makes clear is that the wine industry's fortunes can change very quickly, and can be simultaneously lucrative in some parts of the world while depressing in others.[5] If producers (and governments!) are to respond appropriately rather than over-react to each swing in the market, they need more accurate information on and analyses of market prospects that are well informed by not just current trends but also past experience – including recognition of the fact that so many past government interventions have exacerbated rather than reduced the adjustment problem. And with the ongoing globalization of wine markets, such assessments need a perspective that is not only historical but also global rather than just regional or national.

It is with those thoughts in mind that the authors have contributed the remaining chapters of this book. The next chapter provides a more detailed global overview of recent developments and offers some projections for the medium term using a new economic model of the world's wine markets. This is followed by six chapters on Western Europe, one on Eastern Europe's transition economies, five on New World countries, and a final one on East Asia's emerging markets.

In terms of becoming more export-oriented, it was found that the motivations of the Old World's four key exporting countries were very different from those in the New World. In the former, where wine is a declining industry, they were driven by the need to get rid of surplus production of low-quality wine induced by price-support policies of their Common Agricultural Policy in an environment where domestic demand was shrinking. In the New World countries, by contrast, wine production and export growth are the result of conscious business strategies aimed at exploiting new comparative advantages in commercial premium wine that resulted from the growth of wine super-marketing and the like.

Notwithstanding that generalization, there are many wine market differences between countries within the Old World, and also within the New World. There are rapidly emerging consumer markets within Europe (the UK, Ireland,

and the Nordic and Low Countries) but also in the New World (the USA and Canada); and there is a major country in the New World – Argentina – whose wine market evolution has looked more like that in southern Europe over recent decades but has the potential to become another wine export growth success in the years ahead. Diversity is what characterizes the world's wine markets more than anything else. But what the following chapters also reveal is that producers in all countries are becoming ever-more affected by the forces of globalization.

NOTES

* The first part of this chapter draws on Anderson (2003). The author is grateful to Mike Boyer of the Carnegie Endowment for International Peace for very helpful comments on an earlier draft.
1. Prices for wines from those valleys that were $40 a bottle in 2002 were selling for $25 in 2003 (sometimes disguised in a second label). Wine grape prices for California as a whole were 17 per cent lower in 2002 than for the 2001 vintage, but only 5 per cent lower in Sonoma and 4 per cent higher in Napa.
2. Europe is not alone in lashing out against southern hemisphere wines. A *Los Angeles Times* article on 1 May 2003 reported its panel of experts' views on wines imported from Australia. The second-lowest score went to Yellow Tail 2002 Chardonnay, described as 'reminiscent of pineapple juice' and 'excellent lighter fluid'. US consumers clearly disagree: Yellow Tail was launched in the USA in 2002 with its producer, Casella Estate Wines from the Riverina region, hoping to sell 25 000 cases at $6.99 a bottle. It turned out that they sold 1.5 million cases in that first year without even advertising, and were on target to sell around 4 million cases in 2003.
3. The proposed scheme, provisionally entitled Vins de Cépage de France, may yet be moth-balled because of fierce opposition from producers in Languedoc in the south of France who see it as a direct threat to the improving reputation of their varietal wines sold under the label Vin de Pays d'Oc.
4. More than half the vines in Australia, New Zealand and South Africa are less than five years old, and all of those new ones are premium varieties. Since wine quality tends to improve with vine age, other things equal, those new vines can be expected to deliver a much higher ratio of commercial to super premium bottles and a wider range of styles over the next decade.
5. This is familiar to historians of wine markets. The eruption of Vesuvius in AD 79, which destroyed the Roman Empire's prime vineyard area and caused wine prices to rise sharply, was followed by over-investment in new plantings in Italy and its colonies, just as happened in France following the freezing winter of January 1509 which killed vines and burst wine barrels. In both cases the government felt compelled to intervene a decade or so later and order the uprooting of many of the new plantings (Phillips 2000, pp. 180–81).

REFERENCES

Anderson, K. (2003), 'Wine's New World', *Foreign Policy*, **136** (May/June), 47–54.
Phillips, R. (2000), *A Short History of Wine*, London: Penguin.

2. The global picture[1]

Kym Anderson, David Norman and Glyn Wittwer

Globalization is not new to the world's wine markets, but its influence on them over the past decade or so has increased significantly. One indicator of that is the growth in the volume of exports as a percentage of global production, which rose from 15 to 26 per cent between 1988–90 and 2001.[2] For the big four European wine exporters that ratio rose from 20 to 33 per cent, which was impressive by historical standards; but for the New World exporters (North and South America, South Africa and Australasia), the ratio rose from just 3 per cent in the late 1980s to 20 per cent by 2001. That dramatic entry on to the international stage by New World producers has presented and will continue to present some serious challenges to producers in the Old World in both Western and Eastern Europe. Moreover, following a dramatic expansion in their vineyard plantings in the later 1990s, New World regions too face challenges as the grapes from those recent plantings add significantly to the stocks of wine available for sale.

This chapter's review of recent developments points in particular to the dramatic increase in the industry's export orientation and quality upgrading in the New World and the consequent competitive pressures on the Old World in key import markets. The chapter draws on a new model of the world's wine markets that distinguishes non-premium, commercial premium and super-plus premium wines in each of 47 countries or country groups spanning the world. It projects developments to 2005, based on trends in income, population and preferences on the demand side, and vine acreage and productivity trends on the supply side, of each market. The effect of a slowdown in the global economy in the medium term is also considered. Implications of recent and prospective developments on the key wine-exporting regions are exposed by the model's results. Finally, we explore the prospect that, in the case of wine, the forces of globalization and consequent market responses could well be such as to please both pro- and anti-globalization groups, while at the same time allowing the industry to prosper.

BRIEF HISTORY OF WINE INDUSTRY GLOBALIZATION

Virtually all industries and households are affected by the latest wave of global-ization, even though the term connotes different things to different people. On the one hand, economists think of it rather clinically as simply the lowering of transaction costs of doing business across space, and therefore a 'good thing' because it conserves resources. In the more specific case of business across national borders, economists refer more precisely to 'internationalization': to the growth in international trade in goods, services and the various forms of capital (human, physical, knowledge) relative to national output or expenditure.

For a vocal minority in many countries, on the other hand, one or more of the perceived consequences of globalization is considered a 'bad thing'. People in those anti-globalization groups may be concerned about such things as homogenization of marketed products, a growing dominance of multina-tional corporations, or the disappearance of small firms with their individual-istic goods or services. When applied to wine, they worry that what for centuries has been characterized as largely a cottage industry, with its colour-ful personalities and wide variety of wines that differ from year to year because of the vagaries of weather or the vigneron's experimentation, will soon be difficult to distinguish from any other high-tech industry with a small number of large firms churning out standardized products for distant markets rather than idiosyncratic products for local markets.

An important aspect of globalization is the movement of crucial inputs and know-how from established to new areas of application. The first systematic cultivation of grapevines for wine probably took place between and to the south of the Black and Caspian Seas at least six thousand years ago (Unwin, 1991). Production knowledge and cuttings of the best sub-species, *Vitis vinifera*, grad-ually spread west to Egypt, Greece and perhaps southern Spain by 2500 BC. The Etruscans began vine cultivation in central Italy using native varieties in the eighth century BC, which is also when the Greek colonists began to take cuttings to southern Italy and Sicily. Viticulture was introduced to southern France by the Romans around 600 BC, and was spread north in the second and first centuries BC. It took only until the fourth century AD for wine grape culti-vation to be well established in what we refer to now as the Old World of Europe, and in North Africa (Robinson, 1994, pp. 697–8). Meanwhile, the drinking of wine in the Middle East went into decline, following Mohammed's decree against it in the seventh century AD (Johnson, 1989, pp. 98–101).

The first explorers of the New World took vine cuttings and know-how with them first to South America and Mexico in the 1500s and then to South Africa from 1655. Attempts to export the same technology and varieties to the east-ern part of North America from as early as 1619 were unsuccessful, and it took until the Spanish–Mexican Jesuits moved north from Baja California in the early nineteenth century before cultivation began to flourish in what is now the US State of California. The first grape cultivation in Australia began with cuttings imported by the earliest British settlers in 1788, while for New Zealand it was three decades later (Robinson, 1994, p. 666). In Australia most of the production up to the 1840s was for own consumption or local markets (Osmond and Anderson, 1998).

International trade in wine itself was limited initially from the 1300s to relatively short distances within Europe via three networks: the Mediterranean trade by sea and by land to Poland and the Baltic countries; the southern German trade via the Rhine to northern Germay, Scandinavia and the Baltics; and western France's exports to England and Flanders (Phillips, 2000, p. 92). It was only after glass bottles were standardized and able to be stoppered – from the mid-nineteenth century – that fine wines could be shipped longer distances without risk of spoilage.

Government policies have had profound influences on the globalization of wine markets over the centuries. Up until recent times wine export taxes were common. The Greek island of Thasos in the second millennium BC, for example, allowed exports of wine only if they were sealed with the name of the magistrate not only as a guarantee of authenticity but also in order to tax exports (Robinson, 1994, p. 465). Along the Rhine river in the fourteenth century, there were no less than 62 customs points to tax wine trade.[3] Taxes on Bordeaux exports were so high in the dark ages that, when they were lowered in 1203, tax revenue actually increased (and allowed consumption by 1308 to rise to 4.5 litres of claret per capita in Britain – Johnson, 1989, p. 142). Fluctuations in relations between Britain and France were reflected in changes in export or import taxes on wine such that Bordeaux exports to Britain fluctuated from an annual average of 79 million litres during 1303–37 to 14 in 1337–56 to 29 in 1356–69 and back to 11 for 1440–53. Total French exports to Britain fell from around 10 million litres in the seventeenth century to an average of just 1 million litres from 1690 to 1850 when British preferences allowed Portugese exports to grow from 0 to 12 million litres and Spain's from 4 to 6 million litres p.a. (Francis, 1972, Appendix). The biggest policy influences on wine's globalization post-World War II have been the European Union's Common Agricultural Policy (CAP) and the COMECON arrangements within the communist bloc. With the break-up of the latter and the imminent expansion eastwards of the EU, it will be the wine policy within the CAP of an enlarged EU that matters most over the next few years. Also important, though, are wine consumption taxes, which in many of the non-producing countries are extremely high (Berger and Anderson, 1999).

What is globalization doing to the extent of firm concentration within the global wine market? Certainly concentration has been high in the past: at the time of Nero soon after the birth of Christ, for example, there were only six proprietors operating in the whole of Roman North Africa (Johnson, 1989, p. 59). Currently, however, wine is the least concentrated of the beverage and tobacco industries. According to Rabobank, the world market share of the three largest firms in the late 1990s was just 6 per cent in the wine industry compared with 35 per cent for beer, 42 per cent for spirits, and 78 per cent for soft drinks (Anderson and Norman, 2001, Chart 21). Mergers and acquisitions within the global wine industry are happening almost daily at present, though, as firms brace themselves for the increased competition expected over the next few years as new plantings come into production.

Perhaps more significant than the extent of firm concentration in the global market is the extent to which wine companies are becoming multinational in terms of their production and distribution and/or are forming alliances with foreign companies to reap economies of scope, especially with distributors and retail chains. While Western European firms are investing in Eastern Europe, South America, Australia, New Zealand and China, Australian firms are investing in North America and Europe (East as well as West) and US firms are investing in France and South America. This should not be surprising, given the huge growth reported above in cross-border mergers and acquisitions in other sectors,[4] but it is none the less a significant development for the wine industry. It has been happening much more in the New World than in the Old World, though, which shows up in the industry concentration statistics (Table 2.1). Presumably this is because in EU countries the dominant form of

Table 2.1　Firm concentration within the wine industry, selected Old World and New World countries, 2000

	Top 5's share of national wine production (%)	Average wine sales of top 5 firms (US$ million)
Old World		
France (excl. Champagne)	13	330
Italy	5	125
Spain	10	190
New World		
United States	73	750
Australia	68	310
New Zealand	80	na
Argentina	50	97
Chile	47	90

Source:　Rabobank.

Table 2.2   Prevalence of wine cooperatives in the European Union, 2000

	Number	Members ('000s)	Market share	Sales (euro million)	Sales per coop. (euro million)
France	870	121	52	4570	5.3
Italy	607	208	55	na	na
Spain	715	167	70	650	0.9
Portugal	90	55	49	220	2.4

Source: Rabobank.

industrial organization is the producer cooperative, most of which are very small and yet they produce the majority of output (Table 2.2). This difference adds to the challenges facing the Old World currently, which in Central and Eastern Europe include transitions from communism and towards accession to the EU.

One final point on globalization trends has to do with international technology transfer. This is accelerating not only with the spread of multinational firms but also through individual viticulturalists and winemakers exporting their services through spending time abroad as consultants (Williams, 1995). Those individuals and firms so engaged may be spreading abroad ideas developed in their home country, but they are also bringing back new ideas, so producers and consumers both at home and abroad benefit. In the process they are squeezing in an extra vintage each year – and that is more than doubling their experience, because the differences in production and market conditions are far greater across hemispheres than within a country.

RECENT DEVELOPMENTS

For many centuries wine has been very much a European product. It still is in that more than three-quarters of the volume of world wine production, consumption and trade involve Europe, and most of the rest involves just a handful of New World countries settled by Europeans (Table 2.3). In the late 1980s, Europe accounted in value terms for all but 4 per cent of wine exports and three-quarters of wine imports globally. Since then, however, the world's wine markets have been going though a period of spectacular structural change. In particular, California and several southern hemisphere countries (Australia, Argentina, Chile, New Zealand, South Africa and Uruguay) are beginning to challenge that European dominance in international markets.

Table 2.3   Shares of major regions in world wine production and consumption volume and in value of exports and imports, including and excluding intra-European Union trade, 1988 and 2001 (%)

	Prod'n volume	Cons'n volume	Exports	Imports	Exports	Imports
			Incl. intra-EU-15		Excl. intra-EU-15	
West. European exporters[a]						
1988	52.4	43.0	82.5	7.4	70.4	0.6
2001	53.6	34.7	71.9	6.1	54.0	1.0
Other Western Europe						
1988	7.1	16.6	8.5	62.8	7.2	25.0
2001	6.7	19.3	6.1	57.8	4.4	30.7
Europe's transition econs[b]						
1988	16.5	15.2	5.3	3.7	13.3	9.1
2001	10.9	15.8	2.9	3.4	5.4	6.5
North America						
1988	6.7	9.4	1.1	18.5	2.7	46.0
2001	8.8	10.1	3.7	19.8	7.0	37.5
Latin America						
1988	11.0	10.6	0.4	1.1	1.1	2.8
2001	9.5	8.4	5.9	2.6	11.1	5.0
South Africa						
1988	3.1	1.3	0.1	0.0	0.4	0.1
2001	2.7	2.2	1.6	0.1	3.1	0.1
Australia and New Zealand						
1988	2.0	1.6	1.4	0.9	3.6	2.2
2001	3.5	1.9	7.0	0.8	13.3	1.5
China and Japan						
1988	0.5	0.8	0.0	3.2	0.1	8.1
2001	2.3	5.6	0.0	5.9	0.1	12.0
World total (%)						
1988	100.0	100.0	100.0	100.0	100.0	100.0
2001	100.0	100.0	100.0	100.0	100.0	100.0
World total (billion litres or US$)						
1988	27.6	24.7	6.7	6.7	2.7	2.7
2001	27.5	24.7	14.0	14.0	7.4	7.4
Growth rate (% p.a.)	–0.0	0.0	6.1	6.1	8.1	8.1

Notes:
[a] France, Italy, Portugal and Spain.
[b] Central and Eastern Europe and the former Soviet Union.

Source: Anderson and Norman (2001 and 2003).

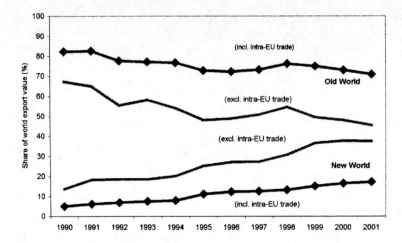

Source: Anderson and Norman (2003, Chart 9).

Figure 2.1   Old World and New World shares of value of global exports, 1990–2001

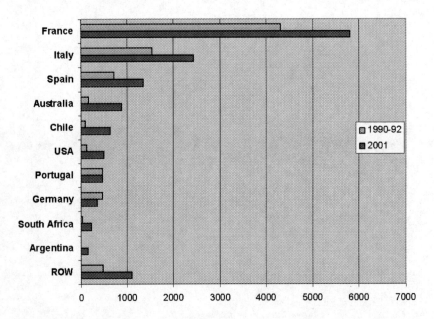

Source: Anderson and Norman (2003, Table 124).

Figure 2.2   Wine export values, top ten countries, 1990 and 2001

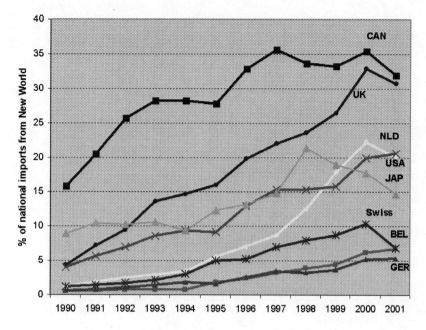

Source: Anderson and Norman (2003, Chart 16).

Figure 2.3 New World exporters' share of key import markets, by value, 1990–2001

Between 1988 and 2001, this New World group's combined share of global wine exports grew from 3 to 18 per cent in nominal US dollar terms (Figure 2.1, where the Old World is defined as France, Italy, Portugal, Spain, Greece, Bulgaria, Hungary and Romania). When intra-EU trade is excluded, Europe's decline in dominance is even more dramatic: from 91 per cent to 64 per cent, while the New World's share grows from 8 to 35 per cent (Table 2.3).

Of the world's top ten wine exporters, which account for 90 per cent of the value of international wine trade, half are in Western Europe and the other half are New World suppliers. Europe's economies in transition from socialism account for much of the rest. Of those top ten, Australia is the world's fourth largest exporter of wine, after France (alone accounting in 2001 for more than 40 per cent), Italy (17 per cent) and Spain (10 per cent) – see Figure 2.2. The share of France has dropped 11 percentage points since the late 1980s, which with smaller drops for Italy and Germany has ensured that the shares of New World suppliers have risen substantially in key import markets (Figure 2.3).

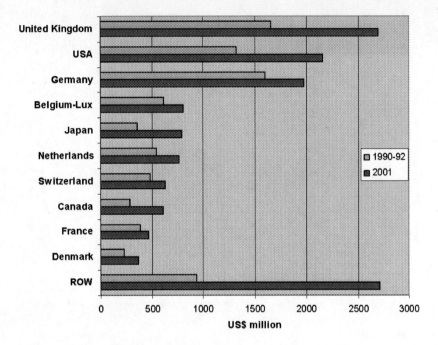

Source: Anderson and Norman (2003, Table 125).

Figure 2.4   Wine import values, top ten countries, 1990 and 2001

Just as wine exports are highly concentrated, so too are imports. The ten top importing countries accounted for all but 14 per cent of the value of global imports in the late 1980s. That 14 per cent residual had risen to 17 per cent by 2001, due mainly to Germany's reduced import share, indicating considerable growth of new markets (Figure 2.4). But in 2001, half the value of all imports continued to be bought by the three biggest importers: the UK (with 19 per cent), Germany (with 15 per cent) and the USA (with 14 per cent). In volume terms, Germany is the largest importer of wine (19 per cent of the world total), followed by the UK (17 per cent), France (8 per cent) and the USA (8 per cent). Note that the ten top exporters are quite different in their penetration of those and other import markets: the Old World has greater dominance in neighbouring countries in continental Europe whereas the New World has been much more successful in penetrating the growing markets of the UK and elsewhere in the world (Figure 2.3 and Table 2.4).

If the EU is treated as a single trader and so intra-EU trade is excluded from

Table 2.4   Shares of exports of major wine exporters going to various wine-importing regions, by value, 2001 (%)

Exports to: Exports from:[a]	Western European exporters[b]	Other Western Europe	North America	Australia and New Zealand	Asia (incl. the Pacific	World
1. France (42)	4	62	20	1	9	100
2. Italy (17)	6	57	27	1	4	100
3. Spain (9.6)	13	66	10	0	3	100
4. Australia (6.4)	1	56	32	5	6	100
5. Portugal (3.4)	32	43	16	1	2	100
6. Germany (2.6)	7	60	13	1	9	100
7. Chile (4.7)	3	44	28	0	7	100
8. United States (3.7)	2	62	16	0	17	100
9. South Africa (1.6)	2	80	8	1	2	100
10. Argentina (1.1)	2	37	29	0	10	100
CEF[c] (2.9)	2	26	3	0	2	100
World (100)	6	58	20	1	8	100

Notes:
[a] The country's 2001 share (%) of the value of global wine exports is shown in parentheses.
[b] France, Italy, Portugal and Spain.
[c] Central and Eastern Europe and the former Soviet Union.

Source: Anderson and Norman (2003, Table 101).

the EU and world trade data, Australia moves to number two in the world and its share of global exports rises from 3 per cent in 1988 to 12 per cent in 2001. It is this fact, in spite of Australia's small share of global production, that has made Australia suddenly a much more significant player in the global wine market. Meanwhile, the share of the other main New World exporters

*Table 2.5 Growth in vine area and wine production, consumption and
export volume and value, major regions, 1990–2001 (% per year,
from log-linear regression equations)*

	Export volume	Export value	Vine area	Prod'n volume	Cons'n volume
Western European exporters[a]	4.7	4.7	−1.5	−0.5	−1.3
Other Western Europe	0.3	3.5	−1.2	−0.3	1.3
Europe's transition economies[b]	3.4	4.0	−2.6	−2.3	1.3
North America	15.1	16.8	3.2	3.9	2.0
Latin America	16.5	22.7	0.8	1.1	−1.8
South Africa	26.8	26.2	1.6	2.0	3.5
Australia	15.6	17.9	9.0	7.7	2.4
New Zealand	13.6	18.2	8.3	2.6	2.0
China	9.1	11.9	7.2	6.3	6.9
World total	5.4	6.1	−0.8	0.2	0.4

Notes:
[a] France, Italy, Portugal and Spain.
[b] Central and Eastern Europe and the Former Soviet Union.

Source: Anderson and Norman (2003).

(Argentina, Chile, New Zealand, South Africa and the USA) rose even faster, from 4 per cent to 22 per cent (Figure 2.5). That is, while Australia has done very well as an expanding wine exporter, it is not alone: the world wine market as a whole is becoming more internationalized and far more competitive, and most key New World suppliers are expanding their export sales (albeit from a lower base) nearly as fast as or even faster than Australia, as is clear from Figure 2.5.

The rapid growth in wine exports over the past decade is ironic, in that it contrasts with the zero growth in world wine production and consumption from 1988 to 2001 (Table 2.3). Yet global wine trade rose by 5.4 per cent per year in volume terms and 6.1 per cent in nominal US dollar value terms over that period (Table 2.5). As a result, the trade orientation of the industry has increased substantially, and with speed.

Traditionally the countries producing wine were also the countries consuming it, with less than one-tenth of global sales being across national borders before 1970. The proportion traded rose to one-eighth in the 1970s and one-seventh in the 1980s, reflecting the fact that both Western and Eastern Europe were increasing their export orientation steadily from the early 1960s. While that in itself is remarkable by the standards of other agri-

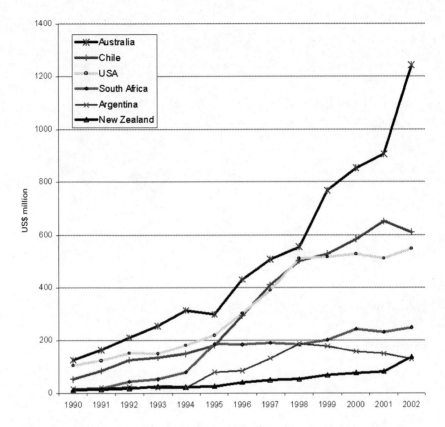

Source: Updated from Anderson and Norman (2003, Chart 10).

Figure 2.5 Value of wine exports, various New World countries, 1990–2002

cultural products, the pace of that increase has been far exceeded by the New World since the late 1980s (Figure 2.6). Now more than one-quarter of the volume and an even higher share of the value of global wine production is traded internationally.[5] For Europe's five major wine-exporting countries that percentage in 2001 was in the 25–35 per cent range, whereas it had climbed to 25, 36, 41 and 50 for South Africa, New Zealand, Australia and Chile, respectively. That is, despite per capita wine consumption falling by 1.0 per cent per year over the 1990s globally, wine is becoming much more of an internationally traded product as consumption shrinks in the traditional producing countries (from a high base) and consumption expands in non-producing countries in Europe and East Asia (from a low base – see Figures 2.7 and 2.8).

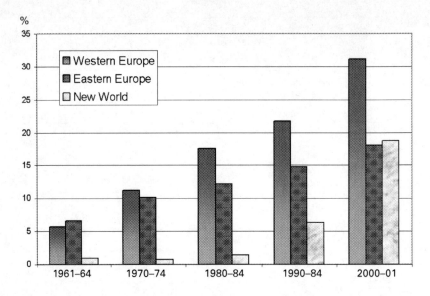

Note: [a] New World is defined as Argentina, Australia, Canada, Chile, New Zealand, South Africa, United States and Uruguay.

Source: Anderson and Norman (2003, Table 79).

Figure 2.6   Shares of wine production exported, Old World and New World,[a] 1961–2001 (%)

The factors contributing to these high rates of export growth are various but, as is evident by comparing Figures 2.9 and 2.10, there is a clear difference in the pattern among the four key West European exporters and that among the four New World countries whose wine exports are growing fastest. In the former group of countries, wine is a declining industry, and export growth has been driven by the need to get rid of surplus production of low-quality wine induced by price-support policies of their Common Agricultural Policy in an environment where domestic demand has been shrinking. In the four southern hemisphere countries, by contrast, wine production and export growth are the result of conscious business strategies aimed at exploiting new comparative advantages in commercial premium wine that resulted from the growth of wine supermarketing and the like.

More specifically, in the Old World, the area of vineyards has shrunk as part of structural adjustment pressures in both Western and Eastern Europe, caus-ing production also to fall; but in the key exporting countries domestic consumption has fallen even more than production, requiring them to export more. Within the New World, Australia's exports grew rapidly because its

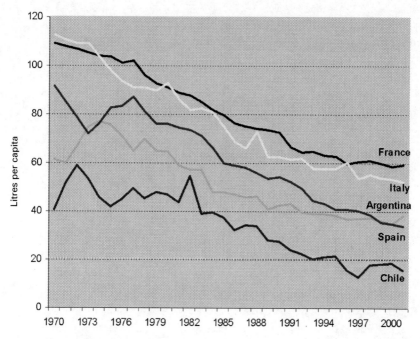

Source: Anderson and Norman (2003, Chart 7).

Figure 2.7   Wine consumption per capita, traditional markets, 1970–2001

grapevine area expansion led to production growth being much faster than its consumption growth. By contrast, in North America slower vine area and production growth accompanied even slower growth in the aggregate volume of consumption. Meanwhile, in the southern cone of Latin America vine area and production grew little but declines in domestic consumption allowed exports to boom (Table 2.5). Volumes of consumption per capita have become a little more equal across regions as a result but, as column 2 of Table 2.6 shows, there is still a wide variance.

Column 6 of Table 2.6 provides changes in an index of 'revealed' comparative advantage from the late 1980s, measured as the share of wine in a region's export earnings as a ratio of the share of wine in the value of global merchandise exports.[6] It shows virtually no change in that index for the key Western European exporters, from a very high level of 6.3, but a dramatic convergence to that same high level by Australia (a five-fold increase from 1.2 to 6.3), and an even larger proportional increase – from a lower base – for New Zealand (from 0.4 to 2.7). More dramatic still was Chile's increase in competitiveness, its index of comparative advantage rising from 1.2 in 1988–90 (the

Table 2.6   Volume of wine production and consumption per capita, trade orientation, and price of exports, by region, 1988–90 and 2001

	Volume of prod'n per capita (litres p.a.)	Volume of cons'n per capita (litres p.a.)	Exports as % of prod'n volume	Imports as % of cons'n volume	Prod'n as % of cons'm volume	Index of wine comp. adv.[d]	Export unit value (US$/l)
Western European Exporters[a]							
1988–90	98	63	21	7	156	6.34	1.88
2001	89	52	33	11	172	6.35	2.06
Other Western Europe							
1988–90	10	19	20	64	53	0.25	1.48
2001	8	21	25	87	39	0.22	1.83
Europe's Transition Economies[b]							
1988–90	9	8	5	11	108	0.36	0.77
2001	7	10	19	15	77	0.58	0.70
North America							
1988–90	7	8	3	19	89	0.08	1.75
2001	8	8	12	33	97	0.23	1.81
Latin America							
1988–90	5	6	2	2	96	0.17	0.73
2001	5	4	16	8	126	1.04	1.96
South Africa							
1988–90	24	9	1	1	267	0.18	1.13
2001	25	9	15	1	201	3.46	1.39
Australia							
1988–90	28	19	10	3	149	1.16	2.17
2001	47	21	41	4	228	6.26	2.40
New Zealand							
1988–90	15	14	7	16	102	0.39	2.61
2001	14	17	36	33	97	2.67	4.33

China							
1988–90	0.1	0.1	1	0	101	0.02	1.80
2001	0.5	0.5	1	2	98	0.01	1.45
World total							
1988–90	5.4	4.6	15	18	117[c]	1.00	1.67
2001	4.5	4.0	26	29	111[c]	1.00	1.93
Growth rate (% p.a.)	-1.2	-1.0	5.3	5.0	na	na	0.7
Memo item: EU-15							
1988–90	49	38	20	22	130	2.08	1.84
2001	44	34	32	37	127	2.09	2.04

Notes:
[a] France, Italy, Portugal and Spain.
[b] Central and Eastern Europe and the former Soviet Union.
[c] Production exceeds consumption globally because consumption is net of distillation and other industrial uses and sales are not the same as production because of cellaring in the winery prior to sale.
[d] The index of comparative advantage is defined as the share of wine in a region's merchandise exports divided by the share of wine in global merchandise exports, measured in value terms.

Source: Anderson and Norman (2001 and 2003).

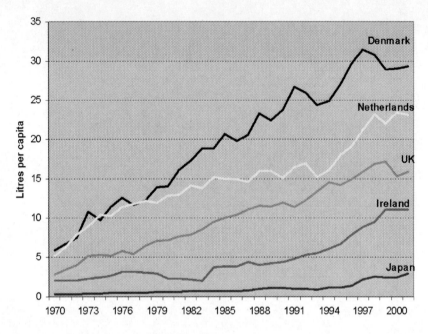

Source: Anderson and Norman (2003, Chart 8).

Figure 2.8 Wine consumption per capita, emerging markets, 1970–2001

same as Australia then) to 16.5 by 2001, to give it the highest value of any country other than the former Soviet republics of Georgia and Moldova (Anderson and Norman, Table 48).

What is happening to the quality of the wine being traded? A crude index of the quality of a country's wine exports is the average export price. To see how different exporting countries are faring relatively, Figure 2.11 shows each exporter's average price as a percentage of the global average, minus 100, for the year 2001 compared with the early 1990s. While France's strong position has changed little, New Zealand has dramatically raised its quality and is now ahead of France in terms of average export price. Chile and Argentina have improved even more, albeit from a much lower base, and Australia has improved to some extent too and was just 50 cents per litre behind France in 2001. Meanwhile, the average prices of exports from Bulgaria, Germany, Spain and South Africa have all dropped relative to the global average (which rose 0.7 per cent p.a. over that period in nominal US dollar terms). In short, most New World exporters have been successful in striving to raise the quality of their exports, albeit from different bases, while the average export price for Europe's big four exporters has remained static over those dozen years.

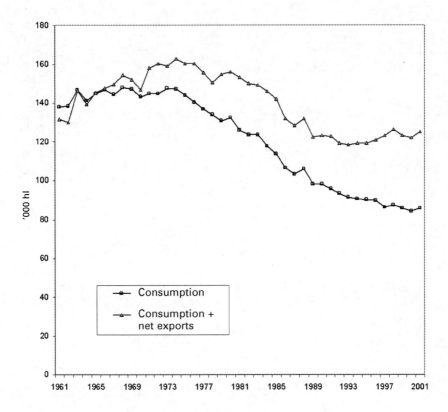

Source: Anderson and Norman (2003, Tables 67 and 78).

*Figure 2.9   Volume of domestic consumption and net exports of wine,
France, Italy, Portugal and Spain, 1961–2001 ('000 hl)*

Needless to say, the quality of wine imported varies a great deal across countries too, although much less so now than in the late 1980s (Figure 2.12). Japan, the USA and Switzerland stand out a long way ahead of Canada and EU countries. In particular, Germany – the world's biggest importer in volume terms – imports relatively low-quality wine (averaging just $1.48 per litre in 2001 which, even in nominal terms, is below its 1990 average of $1.79).

PROSPECTS TO 2005 AND BEYOND

What are the physical (physiological/climatic, agronomic, water) limits on the future expansion of premium wine grape production in the various regions of

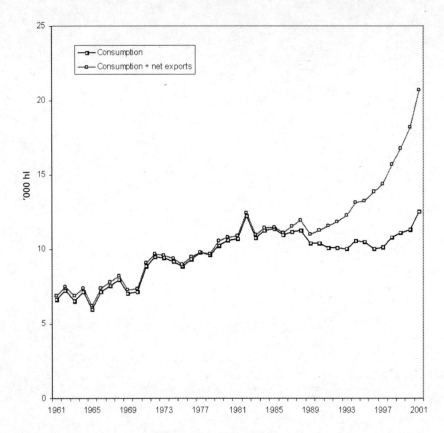

Source: Anderson and Norman (2003, Tables 67 and 78).

*Figure 2.10   Volume of domestic consumption and net exports of wine,
             Australia, Chile, New Zealand and South Africa, 1961–2001
             ('000 hl)*

the world? The greatest influence on wine quality is the climate for grape-
growing. Virtually all wine grapes are the sub-species *Vitis vinifera* which,
over ten millennia ago, grew wild in much of Europe, North Africa and the
Middle East (but not in the Americas or the southern hemisphere). They can
be grown successfully only between 30° and 50° north and south of the equator where their distinctive annual cycle can be accommodated.[7] That cycle
involves winter dormancy when temperatures can be below freezing, but the
mean daily temperature has to reach 10°C in spring before shoots grow and
20°C in summer for flower clusters to bloom. Frosts in spring can cause severe
damage, as can rain before the autumn harvest. Hence the idealness of a

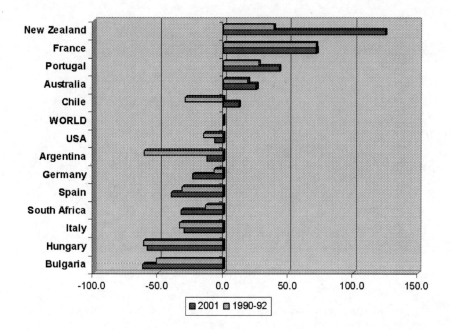

Note: ^a The relative quality index is defined as the unit value of a country's exports expressed as a percentage of the unit value of total world exports, minus 100. Note that the unit value of world exports rose over the 1990s, so it is possible for a country's unit value to have risen while its relative quality index as measured here falls (e.g. Spain).

Source: Anderson and Norman (2003, Chart 19).

Figure 2.11   Relative price of wine exports,^a top exporting countries, 1990 and 2001

winter-rain Mediterranean climate, with the addition of local or meso-climatic features that include the right combination of access to sunlight, shelter from wind, freedom from spring frosts, sufficient irrigable water in case of a summer drought,[8] and so on. Given that, it is not surprising that the world's top 30 wine-producing countries are all in the temperate zone. The next most important influence is the soil, which should preferably be gravelly and well drained, and not overly fertile. Beyond those features, the skills of the viticulturalist and winemaker are what matter. Those can be passed down through the generations and/or improved through adopting and adapting the findings from judicious investment in research and development.

Even among the temperate countries there is a huge variance in the vine intensity of cropping. At one extreme are the traditional producing countries of France, Spain, Italy and Portugal with 5, 6, 8 and 10 per cent of their

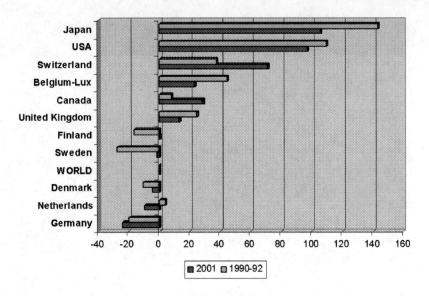

Note: a The relative quality index is defined as the unit value of a country's imports expressed as a percentage of the unit value of total world imports, minus 100. Note that the unit value of world imports rose over the 1990s, so it is possible for a country's unit value to have risen while its relative quality index as measured here falls.

Source: Anderson and Norman (2003, Chart 20).

Figure 2.12   Relative price of wine imports,a top importing countries, 1990 and 2001

cropped area under vines, respectively. Nearly as extreme (2–6 per cent) are the Balkan states of Southeastern Europe and also the Caucasus. Having had the opportunity there to cultivate grapes for more than two millennia, and given the financial supports provided by the EU in recent decades, it is likely that virtually all suitable land in Western Europe is already under vines. Hence future development there will need to come in the form of quality improvement, that is, expanding premium wine grapes at the expense of non-premium and improving the management of existing vines. If that means lowering vine yields, such quality upgrading would lower the aggregate volume of wine produced, which in turn would lower the price of premium relative to non-premium grapes and wine. Over the 1990s, however, vine yields per hectare rose by 2.0 per cent p.a. in the EU, adding to, rather than reducing, the EU's surplus of grapes.

At the other extreme are the New World wine producers, with the USA and Australia each having less than 0.3 per cent of their crop area under vines –

barely above China's 0.19 per cent. Argentina, Uruguay and South Africa also have vines accounting for low shares of their crop area (around 0.8 per cent – see Anderson and Norman, 2003, Table 6). Hence in those countries, which have ample land with suitable climates for expansion, the main influence on vineyard area is the expected long-term profitability of grapes relative to that of alternative uses for the land.

With both sets of regions in mind, what might be the net effect on global wine markets of recent and prospective trends in grape and wine supply and demand? The trend towards premium and away from non-premium wine production and consumption, together with the data on new plantings (the most recent of which will take 3+ years to produce significant crops), provide enough information to attempt to project wine markets a few years into the present decade.

A Model of Global Wine Markets

To make such a projection requires a global model of grape and wine markets that differentiates not only according to country of origin but also as between premium and non-premium segments of each market and each bilateral trade flow. A prototype model for that purpose was first built by Berger (2000) and improved by Wittwer et al. (2003) before being updated and expanded for this exercise. The algebra of the latest version can be found in the appendix to Anderson et al. (2003). The model's database draws on 1999 data for the 47 countries/country groups shown in Anderson and Norman (2001), but goes further in that it divides wine into three classes: non-premium, commercial premium and super-premium classes, with the dividing lines between the three classes being somewhat arbitrarily set at US$1 and US$4 per litre at the wholesale pre-tax level in 1999 (equivalent to about AUD3 and AUD12 per 750 ml at the tax-inclusive retail level in Australia in that year). The model's database has half the volume of global wine consumption in the non-premium category and one-sixth in super-premium (following Geene et al., 1999), while the value shares are one-fifth and two-fifths; the residual is commercial premium (one-third by volume, two-fifths by value). These proportions vary by country though, again following Geene et al. (1999).

The projections model is based on perfectly competitive microeconomic theory. As detailed in Wittwer et al. (2003) and Anderson et al. (2003), in each region market demands and supplies reflect utility- and profit-maximizing behaviour, with supplies equalling demands globally for each grape and wine product. Competitive prices are set equal to unit costs. While the model has several commodities it is partial equilibrium in the sense that the prices of intermediate inputs, other than grapes used in production of wine, are taken as given.

On the demand side, households consume 'other' products in addition to grapes and wine, where 'other' is a composite of all other goods and services. The theory of household demand employed is based on the Stone–Geary utility function. A consumption function allows the user to tie changes in household expenditure to changes in income. The comparative-static welfare calculations in the model, assuming constant preferences, are based on that utility function. We impose Armington (1969) elasticities of substitution in consumption between domestic and imported wine of 8.0, slightly higher than for beverages within the GTAP model's database (Hertel, 1996) because of the greater possibilities for substitution the more disaggregated is a product category. For substitution between different sources of wine imports, we chose 16.0. The expenditure elasticities in the initial database are 1.5 for premium wine and 0.6 for non-premium, based on estimates for Australia (CIE, 1995). The Frisch parameter is initially –1.82 in Australia, the EU and North America, and a slightly larger (absolute) value elsewhere, reflecting the latter's lower per capita incomes.

On the supply side, each region's wine is differentiated from the wine of each other region, so no region's domestically produced wine is a perfect substitute for wine imported from other regions. The model assumes that most factors used in grape and wine production are fixed. This is reasonable for the short to medium term, given the large fixed costs and partly irreversible nature of vineyard and winery investments. Labour is a mobile factor within each region but human capital is fixed, and all factors are assumed to be immobile internationally. Each industry within the model uses intermediate goods that, together with a primary factor composite, are proportional to total output for a given production technology. The degree of mobility in the version of the model used here implies that in response to external shocks, comparative-static adjustments are mostly through price (including changes in factor rewards) rather than output changes. The elasticity of substitution between primary factors is set at 0.5. Were we to allow for endogeneity of primary factors other than labour, supply within the model would be more price-responsive.

In its present form the model's database includes six intermediate input commodities (chemicals, water, premium grapes, multipurpose grapes, non-premium wine and other), six endogenous outputs (premium wine grapes, multipurpose grapes, super-premium wine, commercial premium wine, non-premium wine and non-beverage wine) and 47 countries/residual regions. Given the importance attached to distinguishing between the expanding premium and shrinking non-premium segments of the world wine market, a crucial part of database preparation is to estimate this split for each country. The appendix to Anderson et al. (2003) discusses this and other issues associated with putting together the 1999 data, which is the base from which the model projects the world's wine markets to 2005. The GEMPACK software used allows us to undertake systematic sensitivity analysis to examine the influence of parameter, growth and policy uncertainty on modelled outcomes (Arndt and Pearson, 1996).

Projecting the Database to 2005

New World producers have planted unprecedented areas to premium wine grapes since the mid-1990s. These are modelled to translate into substantially increased premium wine grape supplies by the early years of the new millennium and, after allowing for lags associated with wine maturation, much larger volumes of sales by 2005. Assumptions about aggregate expenditure growth and population growth are based on World Bank projections as used by Hertel et al. (2004). Their total factor productivity growth assumption for the manufacturing sector is assumed to apply also to winemaking. For the primary activity of wine grape production, we assume a small decrease in total physical factor productivity, because growers are seeking to reduce yields and chemical and water applications in order to increase wine grape quality. Growers will be rewarded for upgrading their quality in the form of effective demand growth, since we also assume a continuation of the movement in consumer preferences away from non-premium and towards premium wines.[9] We also assume that there is a preference swing in Germany towards imported wines, due to growing domestic preferences for premium red wine (not produced in Germany) over premium white wine. Growth in primary factor use is based on available plantings data. We assume that the wine industry attracts an accommodating increase in other factor supplies to match the new plantings, and that there are no changes in consumer or import taxes on wine. Also as part of that base case, we assume that, between 2001 and 2005, consumers show an increasing preference for Australian wines over those from other regions in response to the major marketing strategy launched by the Australian industry in November 2000 (WFA and AWBC, 2000). The extent of that shift is enough to reduce the projected decline in the producer price of Australian commercial premium grapes between 1999 and 2005 from 10 per cent to 2 per cent (while having little influence on producer prices in other countries). The resulting base case is examined in some detail below, before briefly looking at the implication of a slowdown in income growth in the medium term following the 11 September 2001 disaster in New York and Washington.

Given the growth assumptions in projecting the model from 1999 to 2005, the volume of world wine consumption is projected to grow at less than 1 per cent per year from 1999 to 2005, but the premium segments (44 per cent of global wine output in 1999) grow in aggregate at 3.7 per cent per year while output of non-premium wine declines slightly. The results for each country are too numerous to include, but trends to 2005 are shown in some of the graphs in Anderson et al. (2003). Key points are as follows:

- the share of global wine production that is exported rises from 25 per cent to 28 per cent by 2005 in volume terms, or from 37 to 39 per cent in value terms;
- the New World's share of global wine exports continues to grow, from 16 per cent in 1999 to 29 per cent in 2005, while the Old World's share falls further from 79 to 63 per cent;
- the value of wine exports from several of the New World countries continues to grow, roughly doubling from the southern hemisphere but growing considerably slower from the USA because their domestic market absorbs much of their increase;
- the New World matches the Old World's share of the UK market by 2005, having been only half as large in the late 1990s, and the gap closes in most other markets and especially the USA, where the New World's share of the value of wine imports rises from one-sixth to one-third as the Old World's falls commensurately;
- per capita wine consumption continues to fall slightly in traditional markets and grow in the emerging markets (see Figures 2.7 and 2.8); and
- the decline in per capita consumption of non-premium wine continues, from 2.1 to 1.8 litres per capita for the world as a whole between 1999 and 2005 as quality upgrading continues (with premium wine consumption growing in both the Old and New Worlds from 1.8 to 2.1 litres per capita).

What prices can producers expect to receive? For the world as a whole, the model's base case projects the 2005 price for non-premium wine to be the same as in 1999 in real terms. This comes about because the very slow growth in consumption is just matched by the change in projected supply as producers upgrade the quality of their vineyards and wineries. The global average producer prices of commercial premium and super-premium wines are projected to decline slightly over the 1999–2005 period (by 7 and 3 per cent, respectively), because projected supply growth outstrips growth in the demand for premium wines. Yet for all wine as an aggregate, the global average producer price rises 12 per cent. This reflects the fact that the average quality of the wine being produced around the world is rising, with global annual output expanding 13 per cent for commercial premium and 45 per cent for super-premium wine while shrinking 10 per cent for non-premium wine. The wine producer price effects differ by country, though. Table 2.7 presents results for a selection of key exporters. It shows super-premium prices falling less than commercial premium, particularly in the countries where commercial volumes are rising rapidly (the USA, Spain and Australia).

What have been the relative contributions of the different forces at work over the projection period to those price changes? Consider as an example the premium segment of the Australian industry. The base scenario projects that premium grape prices will hardly be any different in 2005 than in 1999 (a fall of just 0.9 per cent in real US dollar terms). It also projects little change in the producer price of commercial premium wines (–0.7 per cent), and a 9 per cent rise in super-premium prices (much of which has already happened during 1999–2001). How can that be, when we know there will be at least a doubling in premium grape and wine supplies as the large areas of newly planted vines come into full production in Australia over the next few years?

To answer that question the results are decomposed in Table 2.8 into six components. The first is the expansion in supply in Australia and other New World wine-exporting countries. On its own, this would depress premium grape prices by 31 per cent and premium wine prices by more than 40 per cent (row 1 of Table 2.8). The assumed upgrading of vineyards and wineries in the Old World further depresses international prices of premium relative to non-premium wines, which on its own would lower premium wine prices for

Table 2.7   Projected change in producer prices and output, selected countries, 1999–2005

	Commercial premium wine	Super-premium wine	Premium grapes
Price			
France	–5.7	–5.7	5.7
Spain	–12.0	–7.1	0.2
USA	–10.4	–1.3	–7.5
Chile	–5.4	–1.5	–3.8
Australia	–0.7	9.0	–0.9
World total	–6.7	–3.1	
Output			
France	–0	22	12
Spain	22	33	26
USA	36	57	45
Chile	99	136	115
Australia	99	136	115
World total	13	45	

Source: Authors' model results.

Table 2.8   Decomposition of the projected changes in producer prices and outputs in Australia's premium wine industry, 1999–2005 (% change over the period)[a]

	Commercial premium wine	Super-premium wine	Premium grapes
Producer price change (%) due to:			
• New World expansion in premium grape and wine supplies	−45.7	−41.6	−30.7
• Old World resource reallocation from non-premium to premium	−9.7	−11.8	−7.1
• Global growth in population and per capita expenditure	24.6	27.7	17.3
• Preference swing globally from non-premium to premium wine	7.2	9.1	5.4
• Preference swing in N. hemisphere towards New World fruit-driven wines	12.6	14.1	8.9
• Enhanced Australian promotion drive (shifts N. hemisphere preferences toward Australian wine)	10.9	11.8	7.5
Total	−0.7	9.0	−0.9
Production changes (%)	99	136	115

Note: [a] Numbers do not add up exactly because of rounding.

Source: Authors' model results.

producers in Australia by a further 10 per cent. However, there are four offset-ting forces at work. One is the assumed overall global economic growth, which on its own would be enough to lift premium wine prices in Australia by about one-quarter over this period. The second is an assumed continuation of the gradual preference swing globally away from non-premium and towards premium wine, which adds another one-twelfth. The third is an assumed continuation of the gradual preference swing in the northern hemisphere towards fruit-driven New World styles, which adds another one-eighth. Had they been the only influences, the producer prices in Australia would have been projected to fall by about 3 per cent for super-premium wine, 12 per cent for commercial premium wine and 8 per cent for premium grapes. But that would have been to ignore the campaign launched in November 2000 to boost substantially the promotion of Australian wines abroad (WFA and AWBC, 2000). We assumed that this campaign will be capable of shifting out the demand for Australian premium wines enough to boost their average price by about 11 per cent, which in turn raises the price of premium grapes by 7.5 per cent (row 6 of Table 2.8).

Those results are based on World Bank projections of overall economic growth in the various countries of the world as of early 2001. Since then, there has been a substantial downgrading of those forecasts. We therefore explored the effects of halving the assumed rate of growth for the 1999–2005 period. A sample of results is shown in Table 2.9, for producer prices of premium grapes and wines in several countries. The first five rows of columns 1 and 2 show the depressing effect of lower incomes on premium wine prices, and slightly more so for super-premium than for commercial premium wines (because of different income elasticities of demand). On average they would be dampened by about one-seventh, other things equal. But in fact other things would not be equal if there were such a downturn in the global economy. In particular, wineries could be expected to reduce their planned investments in processing capacity if their profit expectations were dampened. We assume that Australia would reduce its sizeable planned investments by wineries over the period to 2005 by 15 per cent, and that other countries would reduce their more modest expansions by 25 per cent. The second set of rows in Table 2.9 shows that such a scaling back has a considerable offsetting effect on wine prices, especially in the New World countries, where some major winery expansions would be delayed. However, such a postponement would depress New World grape prices, rein-forcing the direct effect of an economic downturn. This is particularly so in Australia, where premium grape supplies will be expanding fastest over the next four years. If the extent of slowdown in winery expansion is as great as modelled, the price of premium grapes in Australia in 2005 will be 28 per cent lower than they would otherwise have been, that is, 29 per cent instead

*Table 2.9 Decomposition of the additional effect on premium grape and
           wine producer prices of assuming slower global economic
           growth (which reduces household expenditure and causes
           wineries to expand processing capacity less), % difference in
           2005*

	Commercial premium wine	Super- premium wine	Premium grapes
Slower growth in household expenditure			
France	−13.7	−14.1	−18
Spain	−12.4	−14.4	−18
USA	−14.2	−16.2	−11
Chile	−13.6	−15.6	−8
Australia	−13.4	−14.9	−8
Slower growth in winery processing capacity			
France	4.4	4.4	5
Spain	4.7	4.6	2
USA	7.4	6.3	−8
Chile	8.6	8.2	−8
Australia	8.8	7.5	−20
Total effect			
France	−9.3	−9.7	−13
Spain	−7.7	−9.8	−16
USA	−6.8	−9.9	−19
Chile	−5.0	−7.4	−17
Australia	−4.7	−7.4	−28

Source: Authors' model results.

of just 1 per cent lower than in 1999 (see Table 2.8). Wine prices, however,
would be dampened much less because of that investment response by
wineries. In Australia's case the commercial premium price would fall 5
instead of only 1 per cent between 1999 and 2005, and the super-premium
price would rise by only 2 per cent instead of rising by 9 per cent.

CONCLUSION

What the above projection exercise demonstrates is that the answer to the question as to where grape and wine producer prices might be in a few years' time is the same as the answer to all such economic questions: it depends. But a global model such as that used here is able is give an indication of the relative importance of different contributing factors. In addition, when circumstances change, such as an unexpected economic downturn, the model can be rerun with just that change to see its likely effects.[10]

We cannot finish without one final comment on modelling the world's wine markets. Developing and using this model does not imply that we think wine is just another primary commodity whose heterogeneity can be ignored. On the contrary, in modelling these markets we have gone to considerable trouble to differentiate producers and consumers by country of origin and to subdivide wine into three different qualities. The constraint on doing more than that is unavailability of reliable data, but that is not the main point we want to stress. Rather, it is that the model can serve as an adding-up machine. Forces of supply and demand work as well for wine as for any other product, regardless of how much heterogeneity there is within the industry. Hence we can get a sense from the model of how prices might move on average, even if an individual producer, through his/her own actions, may be an outlier.

What, then, does globalization mean for small regions and boutique producers? With increasing affluence comes an increasing demand for many things, including product variety (the spice of life). Certainly homogeneous wines such as those in the basic Jacob's Creek family (which retail in Australia at just under AUD10 and which go abroad in whole shiploads at a time) are wonderfully easy to mass-market to newcomers to wine drinking through such outlets as supermarkets in the UK. However, over time, many of those consumers will look for superior and more varied wines. They will begin to differentiate between grape varieties, between not just countries of origin but regions within them, and, with the help of wine critics such as James Halliday in Australia, Hugh Johnson in the UK and Robert Parker in the USA, between brands and the various labels within a brand.[11] That preference for heterogeneity on the demand side, and the infinite scope for experimentation by vignerons on the supply side, ensures that there will always be small and medium producers alongside the few large corporations in the wine industry. Undoubtedly the forces of globalization together with the boom in premium wine grape supplies will lead to more mergers, acquisitions and other alliances among wineries within and across national borders, but their success in the global marketplace is likely to continue to provide a slipstream in which astute smaller operators can also thrive.

NOTES

1. This chapter is a revised and updated version of Anderson et al. (2003), and draws also on Anderson (2003). Unless otherwise stated, the data cited in this chapter are from Anderson and Norman (2003). A summary of those data for 1999–2001 is provided in Appendix Tables A2.1 to A2.4 of this chapter.
2. Note that this indicator is not the same as the share of exports in total sales, since produced wine spends anything from a few weeks to several years maturing in the winery before it is sold. For the many (particularly New World) countries that are expanding the proportion of red wines in their total production that require longer cellaring before sale, the change in the exports/production ratio understates the extent of increased export orientation of sales. In Australia, for example, exports/production volume in 2001–2002 was 34 per cent while exports/total sales volume was 52 per cent, even though those ratios were the same in the mid-1980s (just 3 per cent!) and were within three percentage points of each other in the early 1990s as Australia's recent red wine grape acreage expansion began (see Chapter 13 below). The understatement is even greater in value terms if the wine's quality is also rising.
3. Since an export tax is equivalent to the combination of a production tax and a domestic consumption subsidy (and because drinking water was unsafe), the volume of wine consumed per capita by the fifteenth century in Germany is estimated to have exceeded 120 litres or more than five times the current level (Johnson, 1989, p. 120).
4. The value of all cross-border mergers and acquisitions globally grew in US nominal dollars at 25 per cent per year from 1987 to 1995, and from 1995 to 2000 at an average of 44 per cent p.a. (UNCTAD, 2002, p. 337).
5. When expressed in *value* terms that share is considerably higher (37 per cent, according to our model discussed in the next section), because most non-premium wine is not traded internationally.
6. This index truly reveals comparative advantage only in the absence of distortions to trade patterns. In so far as government trade and subsidy policies assist grape and wine production more in Western Europe than elsewhere (see Berger and Anderson, 1999 and Foster and Spencer, 2002), then the index overstates Europe's true comparative advantage in wine.
7. In the tropics the vine is evergreen (no dormancy), but it tends to yield only a small crop of low-quality grapes. The key exceptions are in high-altitude areas where temperatures are more moderate. Genetic engineering may change this in the decades ahead, but not in the medium term.
8. Vines need relatively little water per year once they are established; yet having that water is essential for producing quality wine grapes every year over the long term in a drought-prone environment. That means the wine industry has been able to afford to pay much more than many other rural users for water rights in places such as Australia.
9. In the later 1990s, growers in New World countries such as Australia and the US received very high prices for wine grapes, with origin often mattering less than variety. Following the recent rash of plantings, the premiums that were being paid in response to wine grape shortages are now being replaced by higher premiums for quality. With the increase in wine grape supply and falling demand for non-premium wine, growers will find it more difficult to market low-quality, high-yielding grapes.
10. Two other examples of pertinent shocks are the recent devaluation of the US dollar and the prospective damage of a major outbreak of Pierce's Disease in Northern California. Both simulations are reported in Anderson and Wittwer (2001).
11. For empirical evidence of the growing extent of such discernment by consumers, see Schamel (2000) and Schamel and Anderson (2003).

REFERENCES

Anderson, K. (2003), 'Wine's New World', *Foreign Policy*, **136** (May/June), 47–54.

Anderson, K. and D. Norman (2001), *Global Wine Production, Consumption and Trade, 1961 to 1999: A Statistical Compendium*, Adelaide: Centre for International Economic Studies.

Anderson, K. and D. Norman (2003), *Global Wine Production, Consumption and Trade, 1961 to 2001: A Statistical Compendium*, Adelaide: Centre for International Economic Studies.

Anderson, K. and G. Wittwer (2001), 'US Dollar Appreciation and the Spread of Pierce's Disease: Effects on the World Wine Market', *Australian and New Zealand Wine Industry Journal*, **16** (2): 70–75.

Anderson, K., D. Norman and G. Wittwer (2003), 'Globalization of the World's Wine Markets', *The World Economy* **26** (5): 659–87.

Armington, P.A. (1969), 'A Theory of Demand for Products Distinguished by Place of Production', *IMF Staff Papers*, **16**, 159–78.

Arndt, C. and K. Pearson (1996), 'How to Carry Out Systematic Sensitivity Analysis via Gaussian Quadrature and GEMPACK', GTAP Technical Paper No. 3, Preliminary version, Purdue University, West Lafayette, May.

Berger, N. (2000), 'Modelling Structural and Policy Changes in the World Wine Market into the 21st Century', unpublished Masters' dissertation, Adelaide University, November.

Berger, N. and K. Anderson (1999), 'Consumer and Import Taxes in the World Wine Market: Australia in International Perspective', *Australian Agribusiness Review*, **7** (3).

CIE (Centre for International Economics) (1995), 'Generation of Demand Parameters for an Economy-wide Model of the Grape and Wine Industry', prepared for the Commonwealth Government Inquiry into the Wine Grape and Wine Industry, Canberra, February.

Foster, M. and D. Spencer (2002), *World Wine Market Barriers to Increasing Trade*, ABARE Research Report 02.6, Canberra: Australian Bureau of Agricultural and Resource Economics.

Francis, A.D. (1972), *The Wine Trade*, London: Adam and Charles Black.

Geene, A., A. Heijbroek, A. Lagerwerf and R. Wazir (1999), *The World Wine Business*, Utrecht: Rabobank International.

Hertel, T. (1996) (ed.), *Global Trade Analysis: Modeling and Applications*, New York: Cambridge University Press.

Hertel, T., K. Anderson, J. Francois and W. Martin (2004), 'Agriculture and Non-Agricultural Liberalisation in the Millennium Round', in M.D. Ingco and L.A. Winters (eds), *Issues, Interests and Options in the New WTO Trade Round*, Cambridge and New York: Cambridge University Press (forthcoming), Ch. 11.

Johnson, H. (1989), *The Story of Wine*, London: Mitchell Beazley.

Osmond, R. and K. Anderson (1998), *Trends and Cycles in the Australian Wine Industry, 1850 to 2000*, Adelaide: Centre for International Economic Studies.

Phillips, R. (2000), *A Short History of Wine*, London: Penguin.

Robinson, J. (1994), *The Oxford Companion to Wine*, London: Oxford University Press.

Schamel, G. (2000), 'Individual and Collective Reputation Indicators of Wine Quality', Discussion Paper 00/09, Centre for International Economic Studies, Adelaide University, March (www.adelaide.edu.au/CIES/wine.htm#other).

Schamel, G. and K. Anderson (2003), 'Wine Quality and Varietal, Regional and Winery Reputations: Hedonic Prices for Australia and New Zealand', *The Economic Record*, **79** (246), 357–70.

UNCTAD (2002), *World Investment Report 2002*, New York and Geneva: United Nations.

Unwin, T. (1991), *Wine and the Vine: An Historical Geography of Viticulture and the Wine Trade*, London and New York: Rouledge.

WFA (Winemakers' Federation of Australia) and AWBC (Australian Wine and Brandy Corporation) (2000), *The Marketing Decade: Setting the Australian Wine Marketing Agenda 2000 to 2010*, Adelaide: WFA.

Williams, A. (1995), *Flying Winemakers: The New World of Wine*, Adelaide: Winetitles.

Wittwer, G., N. Berger and K. Anderson (2003), 'A Model of the World's Wine Markets', *Economic Modelling*, **20** (3), 487–506.

Table A2.1   Summary of the world's wine markets,[a] 1999–2001

		Vine area ('000 ha)	Wine production ('000 hl)	Wine consumption ('000 hl)	Wine consumption (l/capita)	Wine exports ('000 hl)	Wine exports (US$ mill)	Wine imports ('000 hl)	Wine imports (US$ mill)	Wine exports (US$/litre)	Wine imports (US$/litre)
WEE	France	915	58740	35072	59.4	17125	5696.5	6618	483.9	3.32	0.73
	Italy	908	53125	30732	53.3	19336	2471.0	695	203.4	1.28	2.98
	Portugal	260	7189	5044	50.1	1845	487.8	2015	125.9	2.65	0.64
	Spain	1175	35514	14430	36.6	10237	1349.0	858	103.0	1.34	1.59
	Total WEE	3258	154567	85279	78.6	48544	10004.3	10187	916.2	2.06	0.90
WEN	Austria	50	2493	2415	29.8	409	40.9	592	116.3	1.04	1.97
	Belgium–Lux.	1	167	2575	24.1	242	87.1	3213	787.2	3.72	2.45
	Denmark	0	0	1552	29.1	159	41.8	1840	373.2	2.68	2.05
	Finland	0	0	387	7.5	2	0.7	439	88.9	3.80	2.04
	Germany	104	10292	19453	23.7	2492	393.8	13669	2050.5	1.58	1.50
	Greece	127	3946	2789	26.4	465	59.3	333	24.9	1.31	1.20
	Ireland	0	0	419	11.1	8	1.4	473	145.0	2.07	3.07
	Netherlands	0	0	3643	22.9	185	78.4	3997	786.1	4.24	1.98
	Sweden	0	0	1200	13.5	24	5.4	1320	272.6	2.56	2.08
	Switzerland	15	1254	2953	41.2	21	34.8	1956	635.8	17.94	3.25
	United Kingdom	1	14	9597	16.1	270	125.5	11365	2617.1	4.65	2.31
	Other WEN	20	548	581	9.3	259	13.0	691	165.8	0.50	2.40
	Total WEN	318	18713	47563	17.1	4536	882.2	39889	8063.4	1.95	2.02
CEF	Azerbaijan	46	335	402	5.0	24	0.4	2	0.3	0.19	1.71
	Bulgaria	112	2042	1748	21.4	854	76.7	18	1.4	0.88	0.76
	Croatia	59	2026	2013	45.7	107	9.8	33	3.3	0.92	1.12
	Georgia	66	1060	786	15.2	168	24.7	6	0.4	1.51	1.42

Table A2.1 Continued

		Vine area ('000 ha)	Wine production ('000 hl)	Wine consumption ('000 hl)	Wine consumption (l/capita)	Wine exports ('000 hl)	Wine exports (US$ mill)	Wine imports ('000 hl)	Wine imports (US$ mill)	Wine exports (US$/litre)	Wine imports (US$/litre)
	Hungary	103	3913	3028	30.0	803	66.8	38	3.9	0.83	1.05
	Moldova	130	1771	522	12.2	1874	123.3	21	0.8	0.66	0.58
	Romania	249	5655	7230	32.2	331	20.2	33	2.6	0.62	1.24
	Russia	68	2935	11067	7.6	13	1.0	2435	192.7	0.87	0.79
	Ukraine	116	673	413	0.8	125	14.8	100	11.7	1.18	1.66
	Uzbekistan	126	1354	1453	5.9	69	3.6	0	0.1	0.52	3.00
	Other CEF	273	6008	10821	8.4	550	30.9	2481	184.0	0.70	0.74
	Total CEF	1347	27772	39483	11.4	4918	372.3	5168	401.1	0.76	0.78
ANZ	Australia	137	9289	3868	20.2	3146	844.1	168	61.7	2.72	3.73
	New Zealand	13	578	639	16.7	183	75.6	315	60.1	4.12	1.93
	Total ANZ	150	9867	4508	19.6	3329	919.7	482	121.7	2.79	2.53
USC	Canada	7	465	2550	8.3	23	7.4	2344	577.3	3.38	2.46
	USA	407	22050	21486	7.7	2762	518.5	5195	2074.3	1.88	4.01
	Total USC	415	22515	24036	7.7	2784	525.9	7539	2651.6	1.89	3.53
LAC	Argentina	208	13507	12895	34.8	1092	161.6	139	20.0	1.52	1.49
	Brazil	61	3298	3293	1.9	74	4.2	297	88.8	0.56	2.99
	Chile	162	5742	2696	17.7	2703	588.3	51	5.4	2.18	1.23
	Mexico	40	51	187	0.2	48	5.5	227	55.7	1.14	2.52
	Uruguay	11	1070	1073	32.2	29	6.2	96	11.4	2.13	1.20
	Other LAC	20	236	966	0.5	9	1.6	922	184.3	1.81	2.00
	Total LAC	501	23904	21110	4.0	3955	767.4	1732	365.7	1.94	2.11

AME	South Africa	116	8326	3952	9.2	1487	224.7	81	10.5	1.53	1.31
	Turkey	566	313	246	0.4	50	6.2	6	3.0	1.28	5.47
	North Africa	204	1254	1198	1.0	180	16.0	47	8.5	0.92	2.07
	Middle East	6	115	1392	0.2	10	0.9	1458	121.1	1.62	0.85
	Other Africa	495	272	228	0.1	27	11.5	102	33.9	4.52	3.48
	Total AME	1386	10280	7016	0.7	1754	259.3	1695	176.9	1.50	1.06
APA	China	268	5717	5783	0.5	47	6.5	294	27.4	1.38	1.03
	Japan	22	1270	3295	2.6	7	2.3	2096	770.4	3.40	3.69
	Other NE Asia	36	0	344	0.5	10	6.3	322	113.9	6.07	3.55
	South east Asia	4	0	196	0.0	41	66.9	358	154.8	16.23	4.36
	Other APA	65	4	686	0.1	19	0.9	200	52.0	1.15	2.64
	Total APA	394	6991	10305	0.3	125	82.9	3271	1118.3	6.90	3.42
World		7769	274610	239300	4.0	69946	13813.9	69961	13815.1	1.98	1.98
Memo	EU-15	3541	171479	129309	34.4	52800	10838.7	47429	8178.1	2.05	1.72
	NWWG	1061	61027	49159	11.4	11425	2426.4	8388	2820.7	2.13	3.37

Note: [a] See note a of Table A2.4 for definitions of country groups.

Source: Anderson and Norman (2003).

49

Table A2.2   Other key indicators of the world's wine markets,[a] 1999–2001

		% of global prod'n	% of global cons'n	Wine as % of alcohol cons'n	Exports as % of prod'n	Imports as % of cons'n	Wine self-suff.	% of world export volume	% of world export value	% of world import volume	% of world import value	Index of comp. advant.	Index of I-I trade in wine
WEE	France	21.4	14.7	63.5	29.2	19	167	24.5	41.2	9.5	3.5	7.7	16
	Italy	19.4	12.8	78.7	36.4	2	173	27.7	17.9	1.0	1.5	4.6	15
	Portugal	2.6	2.1	58.3	25.7	40	143	2.6	3.5	2.9	0.9	8.9	41
	Spain	12.9	6.0	43.8	29.4	6	248	14.6	9.8	1.2	0.7	5.4	14
	Total WEE	56.3	35.6	62.8	31.4	12	181	69.4	72.4	14.6	6.6	6.3	17
WEN	Austria	0.9	1.0	36.3	16.8	25	103	0.6	0.3	0.8	0.8	0.3	52
	Belgium–Lux.	0.1	1.1	33.8	149.7	125	6	0.3	0.6	4.6	5.7	0.2	20
	Denmark	0.0	0.6	38.3	na	118	0	0.2	0.3	2.6	2.7	0.4	20
	Finland	0.0	0.2	13.4	na	113	0	0.0	0.0	0.6	0.6	0.0	2
	Germany	3.7	8.1	27.3	24.6	70	53	3.6	2.8	19.6	14.8	0.3	32
	Greece	1.4	1.2	46.0	11.8	12	142	0.7	0.4	0.5	0.2	2.6	59
	Ireland	0.0	0.2	12.7	na	113	0	0.0	0.0	0.7	1.1	0.0	2
	Netherlands	0.0	1.5	33.7	na	110	0	0.3	0.6	5.7	5.7	0.2	18
	Sweden	0.0	0.5	31.3	na	110	0	0.0	0.0	1.9	2.0	0.0	4
	Switzerland	0.5	1.2	54.6	1.7	66	42	0.0	0.3	2.8	4.6	0.2	10
	United Kingdom	0.0	4.0	24.6	na	119	0	0.4	0.9	16.2	18.9	0.2	9
	Other WEN	0.2	0.2	25.0	47.0	119	95	0.4	0.1	1.0	1.2	0.1	14
	Total WEN	6.8	19.9	29.2	24.4	84	39	6.5	6.4	57.0	58.3	0.2	20
CEF	Azerbaijan	0.1	0.2	na	7.1	1	83	0.0	0.0	0.0	0.0	0.1	78
	Bulgaria	0.7	0.7	41.9	41.9	1	117	1.2	0.6	0.0	0.0	7.4	4
	Croatia	0.7	0.8	na	5.3	2	101	0.2	0.1	0.0	0.0	1.0	50
	Georgia	0.4	0.3	na	17.3	1	136	0.2	0.2	0.0	0.0	36.0	3

		A	B	C	D	E	F	G	H	I	J	K	L
	Hungary	1.4	1.3	38.3	22.2	1	128	1.2	0.5	0.1	0.0	1.1	11
	Moldova	0.6	0.2	na	110.5	4	342	2.7	0.9	0.0	0.0	108.4	1
	Romania	2.1	3.0	36.2	5.9	0	79	0.5	0.1	3.5	0.0	0.9	22
	Russia	1.1	4.6	10.8	0.4	22	27	0.0	0.1	0.1	1.4	0.0	1
	Ukraine	0.2	0.2	na	19.2	33	192	0.2	0.1	0.0	0.1	0.5	78
	Uzbekistan	0.5	0.6	na	5.3	0	93	0.1	0.0		0.0	0.5	4
	Other CEF	2.2	4.5	12.5	9.1	23	56	0.8	0.2	3.5	1.3	0.1	27
	Total CEF	10.1	16.5	14.8	17.6	13	70	7.0	2.7	7.4	2.9	0.6	94
ANZ	Australia	3.4	1.6	30.6	33.8	4	240	4.5	6.1	0.2	0.4	6	14
	New Zealand	0.2	0.3	28.5	31.9	49	90	0.3	0.5	0.4	0.4	3	89
	Total ANZ	3.6	1.9	30.3	33.6	11	219	4.7	6.7	0.7	0.9	5.5	24
USC	Canada	0.2	1.1	15.4	4.8	92	18	0.0	0.1	3.3	4.2	0	3
	USA	8.0	9.0	14.9	12.6	24	102	3.9	3.8	7.4	15.0	0	40
	Total USC	8.2	10.0	14.9	12.5	31	94	4.0	3.8	10.8	19.2	0.2	33
LAC	Argentina	4.9	5.4	68.2	8.2	1	105	1.6	1.2	0.2	0.1	3	21
	Brazil	1.2	1.4	5.8	2.3	9	100	0.1	0.0	0.4	0.6	0	9
	Chile	2.1	1.1	43.1	47.3	2	214	3.9	4.3	0.1	0.0	15	2
	Mexico	0.0	0.1	0.8	94.2	121	28	0.1	0.0	0.3	0.4	0	18
	Uruguay	0.4	0.4	67.0	2.7	9	100	0.0	0.0	0.1	0.1	1	71
	Other LAC	0.1	0.4	1.7	3.6	95	24	0.0	0.0	1.3	1.3	0	2
	Total LAC	8.7	8.8	12.9	16.7	8	113	5.7	5.6	2.5	2.7	1.0	65

Table A2.2 Continued

		% of global prod'n	% of global cons'n	Wine as % of alcohol cons'n	Exports as % of prod'n	Imports as % of cons'n	Wine self-suff.	% of world export volume	% of world export value	% of world import volume	% of world import value	Index of comp. advant.	Index of I-I trade in wine
AME	South Africa	3.0	1.7	23.9	18.2	2	211	2.1	1.6	0.1	0.1	3	9
	Turkey	0.1	0.1	3.8	15.9	3	128	0.1	0.0	0.0	0.0	0	66
	North Africa	0.5	0.5	47.7	14.6	4	113	0.3	0.1	0.1	0.1	0	69
	Middle East	0.0	0.6	na	8.8	1.4	8	0.0	0.0	2.1	0.9	0	1
	Other Africa	0.1	0.1	na	10.0	46	120	0.0	0.1	0.1	0.2	0	51
	Total AME	3.7	2.9	25.6	17.3	24	147	2.5	1.9	2.4	1.3	0.3	81
APA	China	2.1	2.4	1.4	0.8	5	99	0.1	0.0	0.4	0.2	0	38
	Japan	0.5	1.4	6.2	0.5	64	39	0.0	0.0	3.0	5.6	0	1
	Other NE Asia	0.0	0.1	3.3	na	95	0	0.0	0.0	0.5	0.8	0	11
	South east Asia	0.0	0.1	0.2	na	183	0	0.1	0.5	0.5	1.1	0	60
	Other APA	0.0	0.3	2.6	478.3	29	1	0.0	0.0	0.3	0.4	0	3
	Total APA	2.5	4.3	1.8	1.8	32	68	0.2	0.6	4.7	8.1	0.0	14
World		100.0	100.0	15.9	25.5	29	115	100.0	100.0	100.0	100.0	1.0	100
Memo	EU-15	62.4	54.0	44.4	30.8	37	133	75.5	78.4	67.8	59.1	1.6	86
	NWWG	22.2	20.5	22.4	18.7	17	124	16.3	17.6	12.0	20.5	1.0	92

Note: [a] See note a of Table A2.4 for definitions of country groups.

Source: Anderson and Norman (2003).

52

Table A2.3 *Value of wine exports to various regions, 1999–2001^a (US$'000 per year)*

Exports to: Exporter:	WEE Sum	WEN Sum	CEF Sum	ANZ Sum	USC Sum	LAC Sum	AME Sum	APA Sum	Memo: NWWG	World
France	225810	3521016	59741	37586	1149363	85629	67395	549925	1196983	5696464
Germany	22458	241594	23313	1944	49407	9944	1000	44139	52330	393799
Italy	219425	1388116	53433	13865	621135	38049	11820	114190	637400	2471033
Portugal	140716	231969	609	2217	71219	18039	18138	7344	74358	490249
Spain	176173	889821	16597	3449	125940	43748	46255	47066	135644	1349050
Moldova	57	409	122331	0	374	0	123	32	374	123326
Bulgaria	1564	43463	22411	29	2641	2	356	6198	2671	76664
Hungary	2273	31865	17554	55	3092	94	134	1751	3146	66817
Australia	5814	485322	668	42184	253067	1260	2857	50600	295455	841772
New Zealand	289	45721	21	10149	14580	183	197	4476	24737	75617
United States	8103	308090	1056	701	88122	24686	1693	86054	90050	518506
Argentina	3065	60842	1539	602	40519	37502	1320	18492	50923	163879
Chile	14476	268440	2992	2672	166675	91077	3271	38736	182348	588338
South Africa	4583	181376	803	1459	17184	536	12261	6568	18651	224670
Total WEE	669290	5377733	140669	50097	1349865	137328	116186	565695	1415569	8406864
Total WEN	94101	539414	54458	4536	63965	23024	6895	124788	71203	911181
Total CEF	9010	167326	399780	336	14027	189	1598	12071	14535	604337
EU-15	853899	6541621	167325	61841	1043376	201688	151532	821096	2127480	10842378
NWWG	36714	1352076	7041	57770	584653	158879	21659	207566	666806	2426358
World	918707	8063425	401092	121735	2651645	365700	176926	1118349	2820743	13817580

Note: ^{a} See note a of Table A2.4 for definitions of country groups.

Source: Anderson and Norman (2003).

53

Table A2.4 Value of wine imports from various regions, 1999–2001 (US$'000 per year)

Imports from:	WEE	WEN	CEF	ANZ	USC	LAC	AME	APA	Memo: EU-15	NWWG	World
Importer:	Sum	Sum	Sum	Sum	Sum	Sum	Sum	Sum			
Belgium–Lux.	704644	32667	1720	8555	17151	10477	11778	206	733249	46005	787198
Denmark	295813	15887	2234	8988	10254	31975	7999	17	309997	58690	373168
France	355874	79844	3869	5484	6573	13846	17325	1088	427973	29308	483902
Germany	1786637	103592	56611	24870	14222	38634	25514	441	1874863	96361	2050529
Italy	188701	8628	1343	505	1321	1709	935	294	195909	4007	203435
Netherlands	528734	94704	4463	21576	74392	25166	36522	544	610820	156978	786101
Russia	43666	6333	139475	240	199	2405	407	16	48296	3178	192741
Sweden	182211	35264	6105	11622	8173	20060	9093	89	208449	48570	272616
Switzerland	560845	17688	1387	16395	18229	15213	5932	116	579307	54575	635805
United Kingdom	1633594	156971	38223	406392	147427	144016	88345	2141	1764013	782155	2617109
Canada	362349	15379	4812	49623	88122	48388	8620	33	375617	193622	577326
United States	1605307	64558	7459	218024	3954	161714	12426	877	1667176	391030	2074319
WEE	762124	97398	5691	6103	8345	18841	18344	1862	846813	36714	918707
WEN	6041922	531138	117239	531043	308405	333832	195687	4159	6501310	135076	8063425
CEF	131580	36601	225547	689	1056	4539	1014	67	164924	7041	401092
ANZ	57117	4803	150	52333	701	3279	1649	1703	61815	57770	121735
USC	1967656	79937	12272	267647	92075	210102	21045	910	2042793	584653	2651645
LAC	185464	16353	131	1443	24863	136427	614	405	198005	158879	365700
AME	143607	8320	1242	3054	1752	4745	13765	440	142177	21659	176926
APA	718525	107667	9998	55077	88708	57912	7136	73326	817622	207566	1118349

EU-15	6135057	583434	120101	514743	295187	320515	205961	5537	6634084	1306395	8180535
NWWG	2044385	87434	12422	320193	94042	236436	22824	30009	2126733	666806	2820743
World	10007996	882216	372269	917389	525907	769678	259254	82872	10775458	2426358	13817580

Note: Definitions of country regions:
WEE   Western European exporters (France, Italy, Portugal, Spain)
WEN   Western European non-exporters
CEF   Central and Eastern Europe and Former Soviet Union
ANZ   Australia and New Zealand
USC   United States of America and Canada
LAC   Latin America and Caribbean
AME   Africa and Middle East
APA   Asia and the Pacific Islands
NWWG ANZ, USC, Argentina, Brazil, Chile and South Africa

Source: Anderson and Norman (2003).

55

PART II

The Old World

AOC shecken constrain French competitiveness in world mkt

3. France

Emmanuelle Auriol, Jean-Baptiste Lesourd and Steven G.M. Schilizzi, with an annex by Mathilde Hulot

During the second half of the twentieth century, the demand for French wines has been characterized by a strong shift towards quality, a trend that is likely to continue during the twenty-first century. The present chapter examines this trend in an international market that is becoming more and more competitive, with complex quality attributes being a key factor.

Since at least the end of the nineteenth century, France has been arguably the most important wine producer in the world. The markets for French wines have traditionally been segmented into quality or fine wines, and ordinary table wines. The highest-quality French wines belong to regulated categories such as Appellation d'Origine Contrôlée (AOC, or controlled denomination of origin), or Vin Délimité de Qualité Supérieure (VDQS, or higher-quality wine from a given area). These certified quality labels guarantee that the wines in question have been produced in a traditional (and regulated) manner in one of the famous wine regions such as Alsace, Bordeaux, Burgundy, Beaujolais, Champagne, Côtes du Rhône, Languedoc, Loire and Provence. However, there are few VDQS wines, so that most of the French quality wines are AOC wines. Moreover, the two qualities are often merged into a third category, Vins de Qualité Provenant de Régions Déterminées (quality wines from specified regions, or VDQRD).

Similar denomination-of-origin schemes exist in most traditional European wine-growing countries, and also in comparatively more recent producers such as the USA with its American Viticultural Areas scheme. Recently a new segmentation has developed in France which includes, in addition to AOC wines and ordinary wines, *vins de pays* (country wines) and *vins de cépage* (variety-denominated wines). In practice, wines often belong to both of the latter categories, providing an intermediate quality class which, roughly speaking, can be defined as grape-variety-denominated wines coming from a specific region (that is, *pays*).

This chapter describes the French wine industry and its importance within today's international wine markets. It then surveys existing and expected features of French production, focusing on quality effects and on international trade.

THE FRENCH WINE INDUSTRY AND INTERNATIONAL MARKETS

From Table 3.1 it is clear that three European Union (EU) countries (France, Italy and Spain) are dominant players in the wine world. All have a long histor-ical tradition in viticulture. These three countries together accounted in 2001 for 51 per cent of global wine production, with the other EU member countries accounting for another 9 per cent. Currently the French wine industry is slightly ahead of Italy in terms of quantity, with a 21 per cent share of global output.

Many of the French wines are ranked in the highest-quality brackets, including some of the best Bordeaux and Burgundy wines. These wines are also ranked among the world's best wines, demand for which is strong. None the less, together with other traditional European wine suppliers, the French vineyard area is decreasing, suggesting excess supplies of at least the lower qualities. The numbers presented in Table 3.1 are aggregate data that hide the diversity of France's wine products, in terms of both regional origin and qual-ity. What follows is a more precise analysis of trends for the various French

Table 3.1   Vineyard and wine production, France and other wine-producing countries, 2001

	Area of vineyard ('000 ha)	Growth of vineyard area, 1999–2001 (% p.a.)	Wine production (million hl)	Share of world wine production (%)
France	870	–0.5	58.2	21
Italy	797	–1.7	51.3	19
Spain	1100	–2.7	31.1	11
Germany	102	–0.1	9.7	4
United States	425	3.2	23.8	9
Argentina	207	–0.0	15.8	6
Australia	148	9.0	9.1	3
South Africa	117	1.6	11.1	4
Romania	245	0.0	5.5	2
Chile	155	3.4	6.0	2

Source: Anderson and Norman (2003).

wine-producing regions, as well as for the various qualities of French wine products.

THE VARIOUS FRENCH WINE REGIONS

French vineyards can be classified into 14 main wine-producing regions. Ranked in terms of quantitative and qualitative importance, they are Bordeaux, Burgundy, Beaujolais, Champagne, Alsace, Jura, Savoie, Côtes du Rhône, Provence, Corsica, Languedoc, Roussillon, the Southwest of France, and the Loire Valley. All have a long historical tradition that, for many of them, dates back to Roman times. However, wine-making, grape varieties, and wine-drinking habits have changed throughout history. As shown by Tchernia and Brun (1999), winemaking and the very quality of wine were altogether different in Roman times from what they are today. The reputation of many of the important wine regions of France probably dates back to the Middle Ages. This is true, for instance, of the Bordeaux area, which developed and established a long-standing tradition of wine trade with England during the Hundred Years' War (1328–1453). Other important wine-producing regions developed later (during the eighteenth century in the case of Champagne sparkling wines). In the Middle Ages, and until the middle of the nineteenth century, European vineyards extended far beyond their present extent, due to the demand for sacramental (communion) wines.

The second half of the nineteenth century saw a break in the history of French vineyards. During that period, the development of railways (especially *1850 later* between the vine-growing regions of southern France and Paris) allowed greater competition from low-priced wines of both the Mediterranean provinces and some northern regions of France. Second, the phylloxera crisis almost entirely destroyed the French vineyards around 1880. As a result, grape varieties in French vineyards today are comparatively recent, based on phylloxera-resistant American grape varieties. Together these two shocks (railways and phylloxera) led to the demise of numerous vineyard areas, notably the Paris region (Ile de France) and Lorraine.

The present situation for regional wine production in France is summarized in Tables 3.2 and 3.3. Clearly, the disparity of prices across regions is enormous, even after the differences within regions is averaged out. Prices vary between 0.41 €/litre for ordinary table wines and 13.96 €/litre for Champagne sparkling wines (for pre-tax wholesale prices observed in September 2000 for 1999 vintage wines).

Within-region price variation is also very marked. This is true, for example, for one of the most important wine-producing regions in France, which is the region of Bordeaux (the Bordelais). The prices of red Bordeaux *vins classés*

Table 3.2 French regional red and rosé wine production, 2000

Region	Denominations	Area of vineyard ('000 ha)	Share of total French vineyard (%)	Grape varieties	Quality	Wholesale prices (€/litre)
Bordeaux	Bordeaux, Bordeaux Supérieur	58.5	6.6	Cabernet Sauvignon, Merlot, Cabernet France etc.	AOC	1.20
	Médoc	4.8	0.5		AOC	2.34
	Saint-Emilion	5.4	0.6		AOC	2.62
Burgundy	Beaujolais	10.5	11.8	Gamay	AOC	1.75
	Bourgogne Passetoutgrain	3.0	0.3	Pinot Noir, Gamay	AOC	1.53
	Bourgogne			Pinot Noir	AOC	2.57
Côtes du Rhône and Provence	Côtes du Rhône	45.0	5.1	Grenache, Mourvèdre, Shiraz	AOC	1.30
	Côtes du Rhône Villages	7.0	0.8		AOC	1.56
	Côtes de Provence rouge & rose	19.5	2.2		AOC	0.93
Languedoc	Corbières rouge	13.0	1.5	Mainly Carignan	AOC	0.90
	Coteaux du Languedoc	10.0	1.1	Grenache, Mourvèdre, Shiraz	AOC	0.88
	Minervois	5.3	0.6		AOC	0.89
	Vin de Pays d'Oc rouge	–	–	–	Vin de pays	0.68
	Vin de Pays d'Oc rosé	–	–	–	Vin de pays	0.58
Loire Valley	Bourgueil rouge	1.3	0.1	Cabernet Franc, Cabernet Sauvignon	AOC	1.41
	Chinon rouge	2.1	0.2		AOC	1.77
	Saumur Champigny	1.4	0.1		AOC	2.07
	Rosé d'Anjou	All Loire valley	–	Cabernet Franc, Cabernet Sauvignon	AOC	0.87
	Cabernet d'Anjou (Rosé)	2.8	0.3	Cabernet	AOC	0.96
Table wines	Red, rosé (11–12% alcohol by volume)	–	–	–	Table wines	0.41

Source: ONIVINS.

Table 3.3 French regional white and sparkling wine production, 2000

Region	Denominations	Area of vineyard ('000 ha)	Share of total French vineyard (%)	Grape varieties	Quality	Wholesale prices (€/litre)
Alsace	Alsace Gewürtztraminer	12.0	1.4	Gewürtztraminer	AOC + variety	2.70
	Alsace Riesling			Riesling	AOC + variety	1.44
Bordeaux	Bordeaux blanc	21.0	2.4	Sauvignon	AOC	0.56
	Entre-deux-mers	2.0	0.2	Sauvignon, Sémillon, Muscadelle	AOC	0.77
	Vin de pays des côtes de Gascogne	–	–	Various	*Vin de pays*	0.57
Burgundy	Bourgogne blanc	3.0	0.3	Chardonnay	AOC	1.93
	Bourgogne aligoté	1.6	0.1	Aligoté	AOC	1.79
	Chablis	2.8	0.3	Chardonnay	AOC	3.38
Loire valley	Muscadet de Sèvre et Maine	10.6	1.2	Melon de Bourgogne	VDQS	0.93
	Vin de pays jardin de la France	–	–	Miscellaneous	*Vin de pays*	0.63
Vins de pays/ vins de cépage	Vin de pays Chardonnay	–	–	Chardonnay	*Vin de pays + variety*	0.93
	Vin de pays Sauvignon	–	–	Sauvignon		0.76
	Vin de pays blanc 11–12°	–	–	Miscellaneous	*Vin de pays*	0.55
Champagne	All denominated as Champagne	31.0	3.5	Pinot Noir, Chardonnay Pinot Meunier	AOC	13.96

Source: ONIVINS.

(excluding Bordeaux and Bordeaux Supérieur), as observed in 2001 for the 2000 vintage year, vary between 9 and 36 €/litre for the top brands and denominations (Château Haut-Brion, Château Lafite-Rothschild, Château Latour, Château Margaux, Château Mouton-Rothschild). This means a dispersion factor of 4 for those wines – but the dispersion factor goes up to 30 when the best Châteaux of the Bordelais and plain Bordeaux wines are included.

QUALITY EFFECTS AND GLOBALIZATION

French regulations concerning quality date from the second half of the ninteenth century, with a decree of 1855 regulating the quality of the best Bordeaux wines (*grands crus classés*, or great classified vintages). The regulation establishing the AOC scheme came later, originating in a law of July 1935. A much more recent regulation, EEC regulation No. 822/87 of March 1987, applies to *vins de pays*. The AOC scheme captures the quality attributes of fine French wines that have been identified with traditional winemaking processes.

The AOC scheme is strongly related to the concept of *terroir*, a French word which is used worldwide in the wine industry. A *terroir* is an original, and sometimes unique, combination of natural factors such as the quality and nature of the soils, climate, and location and orientation factors such as the slope and sunshine exposure of vineyards. To these *terroir* quality attributes are added others that pertain to traditional winemaking processes. Under the French AOC scheme variety is not seen as a quality attribute as much as in other wine grape growing countries. Many French wines are made from a traditional blend (*assemblage*) of grape varieties. Bordeaux red wines, for example, are a blend of Cabernet Sauvignon, Merlot, Cabernet Franc and other varieties, while red wines of Burgundy are simpler blends that include mainly Pinot Noir and Gamay. Gamay is the traditional grape of Beaujolais, and it is also widely used in the neighbouring vineyards of the French-speaking regions of Switzerland. An exception is Alsace, whose wines are dominated by a single grape variety. These are grapes that are in wide use in German-speaking countries, in Central European countries such as Hungary, and also in the New World. They include Gewürztraminer, Sylvaner, Riesling, Tokay and Pinot Noir.

Thus the quality of the best categories of French wines (which are mostly AOC wines) is defined by a complex bundle of quality attributes, including *terroir*, a wine-making process usually involving a traditional blend of grapes and, for some famous denominations, a brand name. This brand effect is, for instance, observed for some famous châteaux of the Bordeaux region, such as Château Mouton-Rothschild, which is owned by the French branch of the Rothschild family.

This complex array of quality attributes is not specific to France. It is also observed in other traditional wine-producing countries such as Italy, Spain and Portugal. Moreover, it is a feature of some other traditional drinks. For instance, Scotch whiskies are characterized by being distilled exclusively in Scotland, produced with a traditional name. They are distilled under the supervision of the British government, just as the French AOC wines are produced under the supervision of French official agencies.

France's existing AOC scheme is a major constraint in a global market which is increasingly competitive, and there are concerns that the French wine industry is losing some of its competitiveness because of such regulations. *Vins de pays*, while regulated, are defined by simpler quality attributes, and are growing on international markets in terms of market share. *Vins de pays* and *vins de cépage* now represent about 30 per cent of all French wine exports to the UK, or 10 per cent of all wine sold there.

Concerns have been expressed about the loss of competitiveness of the French wine industry (for example Villard, 2001). France is still a major grape and wine producer in terms of volume, with a 12 per cent share of the world grapevine area, but its share of global wine exports has steadily declined since 1990 even though a growing proportion of its production is being exported (Tables 3.1 and 3.4). This has also been the case for other major European wine producers, including Italy, Portugal and Spain. Furthermore, the average price of French wine has risen only slightly over the 1990–2001 period in US dollar terms: 0.2 per cent p.a., compared with 0.9 per cent for Italy, and 0.5 per cent for Spain, and 0.7 per cent for the world as a whole (Anderson and Norman, 2003).

In response to the increasing competition from New World wine exports, quality attributes in France are beginning to depart from the traditional *terroir* focus and the AOC system. One indicator of this is the emergence of new

Table 3.4   Indications of French wine production and exports, 1990–2001

Year	1990	1995	2001
% of world grapevine area	11.2	11.7	11.9
% of world wine exports in value terms including intra-EU trade	51.9	42.3	41.5
% of world wine exports in value terms excluding intra-EU trade	46.8	35.6	32.3
% of wine production volume exported	20.0	23.1	30.0
Unit value of wine exports (US$/litre)	3.27	3.66	3.32

Source: Anderson and Norman (2003).

intermediate-quality classes in between ordinary wines and AOC wines, such as *vins de pays*, which indicates geographic origin but under less stringent regulations than in the AOC system. Variety-oriented qualities (*vins de cépage*), which traditionally were less prevalent in French wine production than elsewhere, also are developing and their markets are growing steadily. These new medium-quality categories are in line with trends in both the domestic market and English-speaking countries, Asian countries such as Japan, Korea and China, and several northern European countries where demand is growing for wines that are accessable to new consumers. Emerging producers such as the USA and Australia have responded quickly to this increasing demand, but they have also been able to supply more expensive, higher-quality wines in competition with many of the French AOC wines.

Finally, due to environmental concerns of an increasing proportion of consumers, the environmental attributes of wines have become part of what consumers are looking for (Lesourd and Schilizzi, 2001). In line with this emerging trend, the market for French organic wines (*vins biologiques*), including both *vins de pays/vins de cépage* and AOC wines, is also growing at a fast pace.

THE ACTORS IN INTERNATIONAL MARKETS FOR FRENCH WINES

While many French wine producers are still small, family-owned estates, often associated with winemaking cooperatives, there is clearly a trend towards more involvement of private and public joint stock. This trend is especially true of the best-quality wineries, in which large international public companies are paying an increasing rôle. Many of the châteaux of the Bordeaux region are now owned by either large private companies or large international corporations following a number of takeovers. Given the restrictive regulations that apply to the best French wines, external growth is often the only way French winemakers, including family-owned estates (*propriétaires*) and large private or publicly quoted companies, can expand. Such firms have been investing in emerging winemaking countries such as Australia, the USA, South Africa, Argentina, Chile and Uruguay. For instance, the Rothschild family (Château Mouton-Rothschild) is present in California, the Marnier family (famous for its Grand Marnier sweet liqueur brand) has invested in Chile, and the Cointreau family owns an estate in South Africa. French publicly quoted companies such as LVMH and Pernod Ricard also are heavily involved in Australia, in California and in South America.

Other actors of the French wine markets are *négociants* (literally traders, but usually translated in English as wine merchants or shippers). These are market intermediaries who are also traditionally involved in winemaking.

Table 3.5   Major multinational companies involved in international wine trade, 2000–2001

Company name	Turnover (€ million)
LVMH (France)	1783
E. & J. Gallo (USA)	1710
Foster's Group-Beringer class (Australia, USA)	915
Seagram (Canada)	899
Constellation Brands (USA)[a]	793
Southcorp-Rosemount (Australia)	747
Castel Brothers (France)	701
Diageo (UK)	656
Henkell and Söhnlein (Germany)	595
Mondavi (USA)	564

Note: [a] Constellation purchased Australia's BRL Hardy during 2003, which made it the world's largest wine company.

Source: Centre Français du Commerce Extérieur.

While family-owned private capital is still present, public companies (like LVMH or Pernod Ricard) are increasingly becoming involved in both wine production and marketing. As shown in Table 3.5, two French companies (LVMH and Castel Brothers) are among the world's leading wine merchants, but other international and especially American companies are also among these leaders. British merchants and shippers also have traditionally played an important rôle in the international markets for Bordeaux wines.

The next stage of the wine market is distribution, and here the purchasing divisions or branches of large distribution companies such as Carrefour in France, Metro in Germany and Sainsbury's in the UK play an important role in wine markets and are increasingly aware of the competition between various wine producers worldwide.

Innovations in the organization of markets also are worth mentioning. For instance, WINEFEX, a futures market for first-quality Bordeaux wines (*grands crus classés*) has been established by EURONEXT (the continental European stock exchange, which is a merger of the Paris Bourse, the Amsterdam and the Brussels stock exchanges). However, WINEFEX has so far disappointed in that it is attracting little liquidity. Other experiments in electronic spot markets, such as SpiritXchange, an online wine and spirit exchange operated by the Crédit Agricole, a leading French bank, have apparently been more successful.

SUMMARY

The wine market is increasingly globalizing and the ever-greater competition on world markets is quality-driven, which is altering the quality patterns of French wine production. The French wine market used to be divided into just two quality segments, namely, the complex traditional AOC and VDQS *terroir*-oriented top-quality wines, and ordinary table wines. However, a third intermediate, medium-quality category, composed of *vins de pays* (country wines) and/or *vins de cépage* (grape-variety-denominated wines), is emerging in response to demand trends in international wine markets. At the same time, ordinary table wines are becoming less and less important on both the French domestic market and in international markets.

REFERENCES

Anderson, K. and D. Norman (2003), *Global Wine Production, Consumption and Trade, 1961 to 2001: A Statistical Compendium*, Adelaide: Centre for International Economic Studies.

Lesourd, J.B. and S. Schilizzi (2001), *The Environment in Corporate Management. New Directions and Economic Insights*, Cheltenham, UK and Northampton, USA: Edward Elgar.

Tchernia, A. and J.P. Brun (1999), *Le Vin Romain Antique*, Grenoble, France: Glénat.

Villard, N. (2001), 'Vins: la suprématie française en danger', *Capital*, **120**, 52–72.

ANNEX: FRENCH WINE PRODUCERS ARE INVESTING WORLDWIDE[1]

Mathilde Hulot

'The French crisis partly comes from the fact that French producers went abroad to make wines in other countries. They took with them the techniques and the savoir-faire and now make wines that compete with our own production at home,' complained a Bordeaux producer whose sales had recently been going down. Very soon, the same producer asked a well-known (French) consultant to help him to make better wines to improve his sales. A healthy emulation, in the end.

French producers have always invested worldwide. It is not an exaggeration to say that they have contributed to the improvement of production in many countries. One of the most significant examples is what the Baron Philippe de Rothschild took overseas, to California. The association with Robert Mondavi, started in 1979, was considered at that time a crazy experiment, not certain to bear fruit. But the Baron not only invested in the vineyard. He also took with him a new winemaking style that could be called the 'grand cru à la bordelaise style'.

Opus One

The Baron's daughter, Philippine, has taken charge of a Chilean venture. 'Same approach, same principle, but also the idea of taking the notion of "grand cru" in a country that didn't have one.' Almaviva, the product of the joint venture with the Chilean family Gulisasti Tagle (Vina Concha y Toro), has proved, with other similar experiments, that the country can produce fabulous wines.

Other well-known producers who have been spreading quality out of France include the following: Eric de Rothschild (Château Lafite-Rothschild with Chalone in California, Los Vascos in Chile, Quinta do Carmo in Portugal, and so on), Edmond and his son Benjamin de Rothschild (Château Clarke, who created the Rupert–Rothschild partnership at Frederiscksburg in South Africa), the insurance company's subsidiary Axa Millésimes (in Porto (Casa do Noval) and Tokaj (Disznokö)), Château Margaux director Paul Pontallier and Bruno Prats (Vina Aquitana in Chile), Marnier Lapostolle (Casa Lapostolle in Chile), Joseph Drouhin (in Oregon), les domaines Boisset (Viña Progreso in Uruguay, Michel Chapoutier (in Australia), Christian Moueix (Dominus in California), not to mention the Champagne houses Moët et Chandon and Roederer, the huge Bordeaux *négociants* Castel, Benard Taillan and William Pitters. Even the consultant Michel Rolland started investing in Argentina, and recently in South Africa, and started to make some wines in Spain with Jacques and François Lurton, two other international French wine-makers and investors.

Different reasons drive the French producers and wine merchants abroad. The wine-producer Estelle Dauré, who already has three domaines in Roussillon, France, and has invested in Chile (Las Ninas), explained: 'In France, it's difficult to extend when you have a family business. For tax reasons, it's not worth it.' The price of the assets and the tax pressure encourage the French to look for areas where one can plant without restraint. Abroad, they suddenly feel free from administrative constraints and the complicated AOC system. Wine-growing techniques as well as winemaking and labelling are generally more open.

International investing can be for commercial and strategic reasons. To be a producer in a country helps target the right market, for both local and French wines. Moreover, there is a special reason for the Bordeaux owners to look for experiments elsewhere. They are getting tired of the Bordeaux habits, the special market systems of '*la place*', and the constraints. 'Bordeaux allows so few initiatives,' revealed Gérard Néraudau, Gam Audy's director, 'Compared to France, Argentina is paradise.'

A group of producers and winemakers found that freedom in Argentina, where they bought around 800 hectares offering space and promises of quality wines out of good yields. The Rothschilds (Benjamin), Laurent Dassault, the d'Aulans (who own Château Sansonnet in Saint-Emilion), Catherine Péré-Vergé (owner of 27 hectares in Pomerol) all have a contract with Vista Flores. The aim is to launch a common selection called Clos de los Siete under Michel Rolland's direction, which was first produced in 2002 (the planting programme is still in progress) and will be on the retail market between US$12 and $15 (150 000 bottles for the first year). Péré-Vergé, who has just built a winery on her site and produces her own brand (12 000 bottles of a super-premium called Linda Flor, US$30) in addition to the Clos de los Siete label, seemed confident. 'This operation will certainly be more rentable than my investments in Pomerol, as far as margins are concerned.' Still the investments are risky. 'It's very interesting to work with Michel Rolland, but you must be ready to spend money,' said Péré-Vergé.

The d'Aulans have the biggest plot at 220 hectares, and own about 100 ha beyond that. Besides the common brand, they produce Alta Vista, a 37 000-case production, with a total capacity of 250 000 cases when all the vines are planted. The three main markets d'Aulan targets are the USA (Rock Creek Wine Merchant), the UK and the Netherlands. The premium wine is sold for US$9.99, Cosecha for US$6.99, Grande Reserve (Malbec) costs US$19.99 and Alto (an 80 per cent Malbec and Cabernet blend) is US$55. The d'Aulans have also invested in Tokaj (Hungary) in a company and brand called Dereszla.

Chile also offers a lot of opportunities to French investors – probably the country where they invested the most. 'We couldn't find a better place,' admitted Cyril de Bournet, president of Marnier-Lapostolle (Grand Marnier). He and his wife, Alexandra Marnier-Lapostolle, decided to invest in 1994. They started with 120 ha, and now have 320 ha in Requinoa, Apalta and Casablanca. Today, they produce 150 000 cases of eight different wines (with a target of 200 000 cases maximum). They export into 26 countries with the strength of the Marnier-Lapostolle distribution network, but mainly to the USA, where 'Casa Lapostolle is sold for more than 40 per cent in the restaurants, which is a lot for a Chilean wine'. The sales increased in 2002 (up 9 per cent). The range begins with a US$7 wine, Cuvée Alexandre is US$18–$20, Clos Apalta is US$55. Looking forward to investing in other parts of the world, the couple still keep an eye on California and Australia (which they described as 'too expensive now'), and France (Bordeaux, Châteauneuf-du-Pape). They are also enthusiastic about Italy (Tuscany) and Spain, where there are 'greater opportunities than in Languedoc, where we can't stick to the French mentality'.

What about South Africa? A few French adventurers have started new vineyards since 1994. Anne Cointreau-Huchon was the first to buy an estate 15 months before the elections. For ten years now, she has been fighting to make out of Morgenhof (Stellenbosch, on Simonsberg) one of the best producers of South Africa. Another French producer, Alain Moueix (manager of Château Mazeyres in Pomerol and since 2001 of Château de Fontroque in Saint-Emilion), bought 25 ha in Sommerset West with some relatives. They have since baptized the purchase Ingwe. Since the vintage of 2002, they have been producing two brands: Amelho (65 000 bottles), an easy-to-drink Bordeaux blend with a touch of Shiraz, and Ingwe (20 000 bottles), a more classical, rich and elegant Bordeaux blend. The aim is 'To make beautiful red wines without too much extraction and with a nice length.'

Australia is an interesting place to go to for French investors, but certainly very far away. Even though a few French investors gave up their desire to make Australian wines (too far, too expensive, and 'too difficult to fight against the strong Australian groups', said William Pitters's general manager Bernard Magrez), there is great opportunity there. Michel Chapoutier started several joint ventures in the country – Tournon Estate, created in 1998 in the Mont Benson area, Cambrian Pty Ltd in Heathcote (Central Victoria), and FAA (France Australia America). Focusing on Rhône varieties (Syrah, Marsanne, Viognier, and so on), the aim for the next ten years is to build up in Australia the equivalent of the Maison Chapoutier in France (around 300 ha, cultivated 'biodynamically' with the same philosophy).

For Pernod Ricard (listed on the French stock market), Australia is the best opportunity they have ever found. 'We continue our strong growth of Australian, but also Californian, Argentinian and South-African wines,' said Tim Paech, marketing manager of the group, clearly taking advantage of the New World trend. 'The leading Australian brand Jacob's Creek (from Orlando Wyndham) grows more than 10 per cent every year, up to 5.9 million cases, one of the most successful wine brands in the world.' The range now counts ten wines with a philosophy of 'value for money' (five or six pounds sterling in the UK), a premium line and a super-premium portfolio. And Jacob's Creek sparkling wine is now 'the number one Australian sparkling wine in the UK'.

The USA is also a very strong market with high expectations. Pernod Ricard uses the same selling pitch for both its wines and spirits (the group recently concentrated on its main spirit brands and bought Seagram's brands Chivas Regal and Martell Cognac). Are they looking for new vineyards? 'We hope we can find good opportunities to increase the portfolio with the right brands and assets. But for now, we have our hands full,' said Paech.

After the New World and the New Old World, there the 'New' New World wines and countries. These countries are the new trend, launched by the number one French wine merchant, Castel (the company's turnover in 2001 was 724 million euros). The group invested in Morocco in 1994, replanted 1050 ha of vines in Meknes and Boulaouane. The success is continuously growing. 'The brand Boulaouane is the number one foreign wine brand in France and Atlas Vineyards has a great success in Netherlands,' said Franck Crouzet, in charge of marketing and sales of the Castel range. 'The New World time is over, now people want something new.' The next step is China, where two joint ventures have been created for a total investment of US$8 million. The ventures are Castel Changyu Winery Company, a bottling site, and Changyu Wine Village, an estate where red premium wines will be made for the Chinese market.

What about investing in Languedoc and Roussillon, the new place to consider? 'We could go back to Southern France,' said Paech, 'but France is now losing market share, which makes us less confident of being a producer in France.' Others are confident, and prefer betting on the biggest wine area in the world. For some Bordeaux investors, Languedoc is even a 'country inside a country', three hours' drive from their home. But it is not considered the easiest vineyard area in which to invest.

NOTE

1. This is an abridged version of an article published by the author in *Wine Business Online*, July 2003.

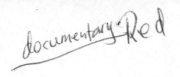
documentary Red

4. Italy

Alessandro Corsi, Eugenio Pomarici and Roberta Sardone

Wine-growing and winemaking have deep historical roots in Italy. Although ancient Greek settlers in southern Italy undoubtedly brought wine-growing with them, it is likely that the technology was already known by former populations. In the early Roman period, wine was not in much favour, except for religious purposes. However, the enlarging conquests led to greater grain imports, which reduced the price of wheat, and to more slaves, which reduced the cost of growing labour-intensive crops. This caused farmers in Italy to shift from wheat-growing to more profitable crops, including wine grapes, which utilized the skills of the many Greek and Asian slaves brought to Italy. At the same time, wine became more fashionable in Rome, and for the first time women were allowed to drink it.[1] Italian wines also started to be exported to France, Spain, western Africa and the Danubian area. The eruption of Vesuvius in AD 79 ruined vineyards near Naples (at that time the Bordeaux of the wine world), which caused a large rise in the price of wine, stimulating a rush of new plantings throughout the empire. So massive was that investment that at the end of the first century AD, emperor Domitianus promulgated an edict banning new plantings of vineyards in Italy and ordering the grubbing up of half the vineyards in the rest of the empire.

After the dark periods of the High Middle Ages, wine flourished again in Italy. Communes and signories often issued laws to protect wine-growing, most of which was for local consumption. Exports were even prohibited at times so as to ensure sufficient availability of food, of which wine was now considered an integral part (Cipolla, 1977).

In the following centuries, wine-growing gained importance, as did research on wine-growing techniques and the classification of existing varieties (Dalmasso, 1937). Production became predominantly market-oriented only during the eighteenth and nineteenth centuries, led in part by innovative landlords. For example, Cavour and Ricasoli, two important leaders of the Italian reunification, both produced wine. Also contributing to this trend were foreign entrepreneurs. Among them were two Englishmen, Woodhouse and Ingham, who started producing in Italy and exporting Marsala wine, following the examples of Porto and Madeira.

The division of Italy had delayed until the nineteenth century the creation of an integrated national market, but after Italian reunification in 1861, grape and wine production had a long period of expansion until the first decade of the twentieth century (Table 4.1). Wine production increased from 19 million hl in 1861 to a peak of 65 million hl in 1909 (ISTAT, 1976). The boom was partly in response to expanding domestic demand but also to growing export demand, and the share of production exported grew from 1 to 6 per cent between the 1860s and the 1890s. Trade policy reform helped exports in the 1860s but, even after the return to protectionism in the 1880s, wine exports still grew. When the 'customs war' with France closed that market to Italy, alternative markets were found in Switzerland, Austria and Germany (Castronovo, 1975). That redirection was possible in part because French production was sharply hit by phylloxera, a devastating disease that reached Italy only later.

The peak in production in the first decade of the twentieth century was followed by a long period of decline. Causes included World War I, the decline in exports to America because of prohibition during the 1920s, and the autarchic policy responses in the Great Depression of the 1930s which encouraged wheat production at the expense of grape growing.

After World War II, Italian wine production averaged 37 million hl in 1946–50, of which just 0.6 million hl were exported. Then the 1950s and 1960s saw a rapid increase in wine production, which reached 52 million hl in 1960 and 69 million hl in 1970. Both internal and export demand growth drove the increase in production. Per capita wine consumption, which was 83 litres in 1951, grew to 110 litres in the 1960s. The increase in exports, due to a further opening of the Italian economy and the formation of the European Economic Community (EEC), was even more dramatic: exports grew at 8 per cent per year during the 1950s and 4 per cent per year in the 1960s. As a result, the share of production exported – which had fallen to 1.7 per cent in 1946–50 – was back above 4 per cent in the 1960s. The growth in production was made possible by the increasing specialization in wine-growing: the specialized grape area rose by 20 per cent between 1950 and 1970, while in the same period the area of vineyards mixed with other crops decreased by 75 per cent.

EVOLUTION OF THE ITALIAN WINE SECTOR AFTER 1970

The period from the implementation of the Common Agricultural Policy (CAP) for the wine sector in 1970 to the present can be conveniently divided into three phases, roughly corresponding to the three decades involved. In the

Table 4.1 Wine grape and wine production, wine grape area and wine exports, Italy, 1861–2001

	Wine grape production (million q.)[a]	Wine production (million hl)	Wine grape area ('000 ha)		Wine exports (million hl)	Wine exports as % of production
			Total[b]	In production		
1861–70	40	24			0.3	1
1871–80	46	27			0.6	2
1881–90	54	31			2	6
1891–00	57	33			2	6
1901–10	77	44			1	3
1911–20	73	45			1	3
1921–30	72	45	854		1	3
1931–40	63	39	964		1	3
1946–50	61	37	994		1	2
1951–60	87	55	1082		2	3
1961–70	100	66	1154		3	4
1970–80	8	72	1213		12	17
1981	93	71	1216		19	27
1982	100	73	1201		19	27
1983	110	83	1057	1028	14	17
1984	93	71	1048	1021	16	22
1985	81	62	1022	993	17	27
1986	98	77	1013	982	11	14
1987	99	70	1003	973	11	16
1988	81	61	994	969	12	20
1989	81	61	985	959	14	23
1990	73	55	971	947	12	23
1991	81	61	943	915	12	20
1992	89	69	917	890	12	17
1993	81	63	896	867	13	20
1994	78	60	877	848	17	28
1995	72	56	851	825	18	31
1996	79	54	843	817	14	26
1997	73	49	839	811	14	30
1998	78	55	832	804	16	28
1999	79	56	836	807	18	33
2000	73	52		802		
2001		51				

Notes:
[a] Wine grapes in specialized areas only, actually harvested, excluding direct consumption; q. = hundred thousand tonnes.
[b] Survey criteria changed in 1983 so the two series are not directly comparable.

Sources: ISTAT (1976) for data up to 1970; ISTAT as elaborated by INEA for data from 1970.

first period after the implementation of the CAP for wine (the 1970s), the preceding expansion continued but with different characteristics. Grape and wine production increased by about one-third in the 1970s even though the area planted with wine grapes shrank by 8 per cent (Table 4.1).[2] The rapid

increase in yields was mainly due to a further increase in the share of specialized vineyards in the total area. Although the boom was mainly based on a
quantitative increase, some efforts were also directed to improving quality. In
particular, the number of appellation wines almost doubled during the 1970s,
when the first DOCG wines were created.[3]

Unlike in previous decades, domestic demand was decreasing and Italy's
per capita consumption fell by around 10 per cent in the 1970s. The boom was
therefore driven by exports, which more than trebled over the 1970s (Table
4.2). The share of exports in total wine production rose to 17 per cent in the
1970s.

Italian wine exports were to a large extent low-quality wines with their
competitiveness mainly based on price rather than on quality. They were
boosted by the devaluation of Italian lira versus the currencies of the main
countries of destination during the 1970s.[4] The largest part of the exports went
to France (bulk wine for reinforcing the alcoholic strength of French wines)
and to Germany, accounting in the 1970s for more than two-thirds of the
Italian wine export volume (Table 4.3). More generally, the EEC was the main
market for Italian exports. However, at the end of this period the USA
increased its imports from Italy. Wines for the US market were generally
higher priced, ensuring their share in Italy's total exports was much larger in
value than in volume terms.

By contrast, Italian wine imports stagnated (with some fluctuations) during
the 1970s. A large part of the import value consisted of French champagne,
which went out of favour during the economic crisis of the period. The devaluation of the Italian lira also dampened imports. Whilst export prices in real
terms fluctuated during the decade around a flat trend, real import prices
increased markedly.

A second, and new, component of the boom was the support provided by
the CAP for the wine sector, which dates back to 1970. Market interventions
were limited to table wines, in terms of aids to long- and short-term table wine
storage, and subsidies to distillation if the price decreased below the 'orientation price'. Few constraints were initially imposed on new plantings and
replantings, due to an optimistic view that a market equilibrium was reached
at the end of the 1960s (Scoppola and Zezza, 1997). A few years of good
harvests led to price decreases, large distillations, and to several episodes of
'wine wars' between Italy and France. These events persuaded the European
Commission to adopt from 1976 to 1979 measures to reduce wine grape
production, including a ban on new plantings and premiums for grubbing up
existing vines. At the same time, the EEC aimed at supporting farmers' income
through further measures such as voluntary and preventive distillations at a
minimum retirement price. Price support was large enough to stimulate the
production of low-quality wine grapes in high-yielding and low-cost farms.

Table 4.2 *Foreign trade in wine, Italy, 1870–1999*

	Import volume ('000 hl)	Export volume[a] ('000 hl)	Import value (bill. ITL)	Export value (bill. ITL)	Import price ('000 ITL/hl)	Export price ('000 ITL/hl)	Real import price[b] ('000 ITL/hl)	Real export price[b] ('000 ITL/hl)
1970	180	4 831	11	67	61	14	798	182
1971	338	8 468	18	107	54	13	672	158
1972	288	13 339	24	166	82	12	966	147
1973	1120	9 501	46	177	41	19	438	199
1974	470	9 544	34	203	72	21	641	190
1975	200	12 909	23	254	116	20	884	150
1976	211	12 873	33	338	156	26	1021	172
1977	235	10 716	42	386	178	36	986	199
1978	232	11 999	53	502	228	42	1122	206
1979	225	17 711	67	782	297	44	1263	188
1980	195	15 065	77	701	397	47	1394	164
1981	177	18 966	84	926	473	40	1402	145
1982	144	19 421	70	1116	485	60	1235	152
1983	171	13 725	63	1085	368	79	815	175
1984	146	15 751	77	1283	529	82	1058	163
1985	689	16 847	143	1532	207	91	382	168
1986	596	10 513	152	1137	255	108	443	188
1987	570	10 897	173	1183	304	100	504	180
1988	372	11 880	192	1358	516	114	817	181

Table 4.2 *Continued*

	Import volume[a] ('000 hl)	Export volume[a] ('000 hl)	Import value (bill. ITL)	Export value (bill. ITL)	Import price ('000 ITL/hl)	Export price ('000 ITL/hl)	Real import price[b] ('000 ITL/hl)	Real export export price[b] ('000 ITL/hl)
1989	876	13 827	244	1580	278	114	413	170
1990	731	12 489	262	1713	359	137	502	192
1991	784	12 268	282	1770	359	145	472	191
1992	723	11 636	265	1803	366	155	456	193
1993	458	12 925	194	2062	424	160	508	191
1994	314	16 983	214	2630	683	155	787	178
1995	297	17 627	259	3215	873	182	954	199
1996	349	13 913	234	3284	672	236	707	248
1997	704	14 450	271	3572	384	247	397	256
1998	1072	15 570	340	4100	317	263	322	268
1999	536	18 320	357	4467	666	244	666	244

Notes:
[a] Including vermouth until 1970.
[b] In 1999 ITL, deflated by the consumer price index.

Sources: ISTAT plus OIV for 1998–99 volumes.

Table 4.3 *Shares of major countries in wine exports, and export prices,
Italy, 1969–99*

	1969–71	1979–81	1984–86	1989–91	1993–95	1997–99
Shares in export volume (%)						
France	30	41	36	34	25	20
Germany	34	25	27	33	33	35
UK				9	9	9
USA	4	12	17	8	7	10
Shares in export value (%)						
France	24	25	17	15	10	6
Germany	30	26	23	31	33	33
UK				14	11	10
USA	13.5	25	34	19	17	19
Export prices (ITL/hl)						
France	10	29	43	56	68	77
Germany	13	47	78	125	169	231
UK				205	219	260
USA	50	94	190	306	394	484
Total	14	46	92	133	170	246

Sources: ISTAT, INEA.

This was particularly true for farms in the south of Italy. But with the decrease in domestic consumption, and notwithstanding the export boom, this created frequent excess supply (as elsewhere in Europe in these years). The attempt by the European Commission to reduce production by limiting the vineyard area alone was unsuccessful because of an increase in yields.

A peak in grape and wine production was reached in 1980, and in the following decade production fell by one-quarter, to a level lower than in the 1970s. Two-thirds of the reduction was due to a decrease in acreage, the rest to a drop in yields. The trend was the result of the reversal of the conditions that had supported the boom in the preceding decade: on the one hand, foreign and domestic demand both fell, while on the other hand, Europe's CAP was more successful in curbing production.

After peaking in 1982, the volume of Italy's wine exports declined during the rest of the decade, and particularly after 1986 when the 'methanol wine

[handwritten margin notes: export decrease since 1980 ① Methanol scandal ② world trend to higher quality wine ③ exchange rate]

scandal'[5] provoked a 38 per cent drop in one year. Two other reasons for the decline in Italian wine exports were the worldwide shift in consumption from lower- to higher-quality wines (when a large part of Italy's exports was based on bulk and cheap wine) and the joining by Italy in 1979 to the European Monetary System of fixed exchange rates. The Italian lira devalued slightly in nominal terms and was overvalued in the second half of the 1980s in real terms, given Italy's higher inflation rate relative to other countries.[6] Hence the decline in its wine exports, particularly to France (from 8.8 million hl in 1979 to 3.8 million hl in 1990). Exports to Germany performed better in volume, and during this period Germany became, and still is, the largest importer of Italian wines. Exports to the USA increased during the first half of the decade but declined during the second half. This partly reflected the strengthening of the US dollar and partly the change in tastes away from red sparkling wines, which had boomed in the previous decade. The decline in exports to other countries was only partially offset by an increase in exports to the UK. In this case price was not the main determinant as exports consisted of higher-quality wines (Table 4.3).

The second contributor to the boom of the 1970s, namely support by the EEC, was also reversed in the 1980s. The orientation of the Commission to discourage production, especially of low-quality wines, was reinforced in 1982. This was when it was decided that the compulsory distillation of a percentage of production would be triggered whenever supply exceeded consumption for some months.[7] The price for such wine was set at 60 per cent of the orientation price,[8] which made distilled wine production much less profitable than previously. A compulsory distillation was first implemented in 1985, and repeated in the following years. In addition, the ban on new plantings was extended, and premiums for the permanent abandonment of wine-growing were reintroduced.

On the demand side, domestic consumption strongly decreased during this period. The decline was focused on table wines as consumption of quality wines continued or even slightly increased. The decrease in production was not sufficient to compensate for the fall in demand, resulting in large market imbalances. It was thus necessary to withdraw large quantities of wine through distillation, amounting to more than 30 per cent of wine production in some years. Even then, wine prices declined over the decade.

Painful though these adjustments were in the 1980s, they did raise the average quality of Italian wine. The number of DOC wines kept increasing, and several new DOCG wines were created. Since quality wines were more saleable abroad, their share of Italy's exports increased, particularly to non-EEC countries, where that share rose from about one-third to about one-half over the decade (Table 4.4).

The improvement was even better in value terms because the currencies of

Table 4.4 Shares of different wine types in the volume of Italian exports, 1981–96

	Third countries				Within EU[a]				All destinations			
	VQPRD	Table wines	Other	Total third countries	VQPRD	Table wines	Other	Total within EU	VQPRD	Table wines	Other	Grand total
1981	36.9	61.7	1.4	100.0	13.1	85.3	1.6	100.0	19.6	78.8	1.5	100.0
1982	26.6	69.9	3.5	100.0	12.6	83.1	4.2	100.0	16.8	79.2	4.0	100.0
1983	32.8	62.0	5.3	100.0	13.3	81.3	5.4	100.0	19.3	75.3	5.4	100.0
1984	35.5	59.9	4.6	100.0	15.2	77.2	7.6	100.0	21.5	71.8	6.7	100.0
1985	37.9	57.8	4.3	100.0	12.6	81.0	6.4	100.0	19.3	74.9	5.8	100.0
1986	43.3	51.1	5.6	100.0	14.9	77.8	7.3	100.0	22.9	70.3	6.8	100.0
1987	54.6	45.0	0.4	100.0	17.1	82.1	0.8	100.0	26.9	72.4	0.7	100.0
1988	56.1	42.6	1.3	100.0	15.7	83.4	0.9	100.0	24.7	74.3	1.0	100.0
1989	48.7	50.7	0.6	100.0	13.4	82.8	3.8	100.0	20.5	76.3	3.2	100.0
1990	50.6	49.0	0.4	100.0	16.1	77.0	6.9	100.0	23.1	71.3	5.6	100.0
1991	56.6	42.9	0.4	100.0	21.7	75.9	2.4	100.0	28.2	69.7	2.0	100.0
1992	51.8	47.7	0.5	100.0	24.0	72.8	3.2	100.0	30.0	67.4	2.6	100.0
1993	51.4	47.9	0.6	100.0	22.1	74.5	3.3	100.0	28.8	68.5	2.7	100.0
1994	37.4	62.1	0.5	100.0	18.6	76.9	4.6	100.0	23.6	72.9	3.5	100.0
1995	39.6	59.9	0.5	100.0	18.2	77.5	4.3	100.0	22.2	74.2	3.6	100.0
1996	50.7	49.3	0.0	100.0	24.6	75.0	0.3	100.0	30.0	69.8	0.3	100.0

Note: [a] 1981–82: EU-10; 1983: EU-11; 1984–95: EU-12; 1996: EU-15.

Source: EC, DG VI, Bilanci vini, in ISMEA (1998, 2000).

the main importing countries strengthened relative to the lira: by 6–7 per cent in the case of the French franc and UK pound and by 50 per cent in the case of the DM and US dollar. That, combined with the quality improvement, meant that export prices almost trebled during the 1980s.

The decade of the 1990s was quite different again. Market balance was restored and mainly through market forces rather than government coercion. Production of table wine decreased in response to the fall in demand, and surpluses were eliminated via exports. Moreover, the expansion in exports was not driven by further devaluations but rather by a strong improvement in the quality of Italian wines, whose demand was rising.

From the supply side, grape and wine production decreased slightly over the decade and the area of wine grapevines dropped from 971 to 836 thousand ha, partly in response to the premiums for grubbing up vines.[9] Since the abandoned areas had been low yielding, average yields rose. There was also a reduction in the wine/grape transformation ratio, which contributed to raising the average quality of wine produced.

The fall in Italy's per capita domestic consumption of wine slowed down to 1.4 per cent per year in the 1990s, compared with 3.3 per cent in the 1980s, and consumption increasingly shifted from table to quality wines.

As compared to the situation in the 1970s and 1980s, another key difference concerns the Common Agricultural Policy. In the first years of the 1990s subsidized distillation was still an outlet for wine production, withdrawing from the market substantial quantities of wine, but its role was decreasing such that in the second half of the decade it amounted to no more than 10 per cent of total wine production. That is, the incentive to 'produce for distillation' had much reduced.

While domestic consumption and distillation were both decreasing, exports were booming. The export volume in the early 1990s averaged 11 and 13 million hl and by the end of the decade it was 18 million hl. By that time red VQPRD wines had become Italy's top agro-food export item.

This trend was partly the result of monetary events. Following an increase in stress in the European Monetary System, Italy quit the EMS in 1992 and a strong devaluation of the lira followed. However, restrictive macroeconomic policies, especially after Italy joined the European Monetary Union in 1996, curbed the inflationary pressure that in the past had progressively eroded the competitive advantage of the devaluations.

The increase in exports from the early 1990s was partly helped by the devaluation, but its role in pushing Italian wine exports was not the same as in the 1970s. First, the share of very low-quality wine had been much reduced. Exports to France, for the largest part bulk and cheap wine, had been decreasing such that their share in total wine exports fell from 34 per cent in 1989–91 to 20 per cent in 1997–99 in volume, and from 14.5 per cent to 6.2 per cent in value. Also, the share of VQPRD wines in exports increased, reaching 30 per cent by volume in 1996 (ISMEA, 2000). Most of that increase came from intra-EU sales, which accounted for four-fifths of all exports. Second, export prices in nominal Italian lire grew 87 per cent from 1989–91 to 1997 and also rose in real terms, especially in the latter years. Third, the rise in exports was not only to traditional importing countries (Germany, the UK, the USA and France), as an increasing share, in both volume and value terms, went to other countries.

These recent developments have repositioned the Italian wine sector in the international market. In the past Italy specialized in low-quality wines, involving large yearly fluctuations in volumes and prices depending on the French market situation. The main competitive element was price, with several devaluations helping to maintain the competitiveness of Italian exports. In the present situation, by contrast, with the euro now in place, the competitiveness of Italian wine is based on cost control and quality. Cost control is essential for commercial wines, where the competition is based on value for money.

Before examining these elements in more detail, note needs to be taken of the reform of the Common Market Organization (CMO), given the strong influence of the CAP on the sector. A new regulation concerning the CMO for wine, approved in 1999 and implemented in 2000, has three features that will affect the sector in the years ahead. First, while confirming the prohibition of new plantings until 2010, and reconfirming an abandonment premium scheme, it introduces several elements of flexibility: the creation of new planting rights (13 000 ha in Italy, plus a further reserve not yet divided among the states); the possibility to regularize unauthorized plantings; and financial subsidies for restructuring and converting vineyards so as to improve wine quality. All new plantings must be destined for VQPRD or IGT wines.

Second, aid schemes for private storage have been lowered and only voluntary distillations are now provided for. The latter are in two forms. One is automatically implemented every year up to a maximum quantity of wine (and at a price similar to the one provided for the old preventive distillation), and the other is a voluntary crisis distillation, to be adopted in case of market disturbances on request, even for VQPRD wines (the retirement price is not predetermined).

Third, a legal basis for producer organizations and interbranch organizations is now provided. In general, these reforms are aimed at eliminating the use of distillation as an artificial outlet for surplus production; at encouraging production of wines that have good market prospects; at helping the reorganization of the wine sector; and yet still guaranteeing a safety net for producers in case of market imbalances, even if at a lower level. In short, the sector is now more easily able to take advantage of emerging market opportunities, but it is also subject to higher risks.

STRUCTURE OF THE ITALIAN WINE SECTOR

Wine-growing

Italian wine-growing is characterized by small-sized family farms, most of which are not specialized in the cultivation of grapes alone. In 1997 there were about 770 000 farms growing wine grapes (ISTAT, 1999), with an area occupied by vineyards of about 772 000 hectares, mostly located in the south of Italy (Table 4.5). Grapes are a traditional crop for Italian farms, and they are grown on one-third of all farms. Two-thirds of the wine grape vine area is destined for the production of table wines and typical geographical indication wines (or IGT), while the area for DOC or DOCG wines accounts for just 36 per cent and is mainly concentrated in northern Italy, where about 60 per cent of the area devoted to the production of high-quality wines is to be found.

The 1990s saw a steady decrease in the number of farms in this sector, accounting for a contraction of over 9 per cent between 1993 and 1995, and a further reduction of about 7 per cent in the following two years. The wine grape vine area also decreased, although to a lesser extent (by about 4 per cent in each of the periods 1993–95 and 1995–97). Yet there has been a considerable increase of about 12 per cent in the area involved in the production of higher-quality wines (DOC and DOCG), mostly in northern Italy. The last few years have also seen the success of wines in the intermediate range (IGT), which represents a very important part of the sector, above all in regions of the northeast and the centre of the country.

However, this adjustment process (increasing specialization in production of medium- and high-quality wines) is not uniform across the various areas of the country, with the northern regions being more dynamic than the others. To this it should be added that the growth of vines for the production of DOC–DOCG wine in the north is based on a transfer of replanting rights from southern regions, a process of de-localization to the advantage of the north (Pomarici and Sardone, 2001).

The improvement in quality is also shown by the increasing number of DOC and DOCG wines, rising from little more than 290 in the mid-1990s to over 338 in 2000. Wines of intermediate quality also are increasing in importance: IGT wines were introduced in 1995 and by 2000 had reached 115. In addition, several IGT wines became DOC wines, indicating that IGT status can be a first step in a qualification process (Pomarici and Sardone, 2001). In 1999, VQPRD wines accounted for 29 per cent of the total volume of production and IGT wines for another 26 per cent (ISMEA, 2000). Their share in value terms is even larger, of course.

The changes in the number of farms and in the wine-growing area during the 1990s did not affect the average farm size, which is still extremely small.

Table 4.5   Wine-growing farms and wine grape area by region, Italy, 1997

	Farms		Area		1997/95 (% change)		1995/93 (% change)	
	('000)	(%)	('000 ha)	(%)	Farms	Area	Farms	Area
Italy, total	769 784	100	772	100	−6.9	−4.0	−9.5	−3.6
Northwest	84	11	98	13	9.6	6.3	−25.8	−4.1
Northeast	151	20	189	25	−4.0	7.9	−10.0	0.3
Centre	164	21	136	18	−0.6	−0.2	−12.6	−4.5
South	371	48	348	45	−13.4	−12.8	−4.3	−4.9

Grapes for DOC–DOCG wines

	Farms		Area		1997/95 (% change)		1995/93 (% change)	
	('000)	(%)	('000 ha)	(%)	Farms	Area	Farms	Area
Italy, total	154	100	278	100	15.0	11.7	−8.0	0.7
Northwest	41	27	71	26	40.2	28.1	−14.1	0.8
Northeast	51	33	94	34	9.4	9.3	−1.9	1.6
Centre	24	16	64	23	17.4	7.9	−28.6	−2.3
South	38	25	48	17	1.1	1.5	6.5	3.0

Source: Elaboration from ISTAT (1999).

weakness: small [handwritten]

Nationally, over three-quarters of farms have less than 1 hectare of grape vine area, while barely 3 per cent have over 5 hectares. In particular, in all regions the farms with vines producing table and IGT wines are less than 1 hectare in size on average. The average size of the vineyards for VQPRD wines is slightly larger: 57 per cent have less than 1 hectare of vine area and 7 per cent have more than 5 hectares.

In addition to the small size of farms, a further weakness of the Italian wine-growing industry is the ageing of farmers. Over half of the Italian grape-growing farms belong to farmers aged 60 or over, while the share of farms run by farmers under 44 is less than 15 per cent. This suggests that in the next ten years the number of farmers engaged in wine-growing could fall sharply, as could the wine grape area in so far as fragmentation of farms dampens the process of replacement or transfer of area to other farms. *what about now?* [handwritten]

Winemaking

Italian winemaking is characterized by the coexistence of three types of operators acting in different markets and characterized by widely different production conditions. They are on-farm winemakers, private companies, and cooperatives. The most numerous group, located in the centre and north, is represented by a large number of wine-growers/winemakers (about 60 000) accounting for 8 per cent of the overall number of wine-growers (Tables 4.6 and 4.7). These growers produce no more than 15 per cent and 17 per cent of table wines and IGT wines, respectively, but they account for over 35 per cent of DOC–DOCG wines.

The second group of operators comprises firms that only make industrial wine. Although there are only 2 000 of them, they are very important in terms of quantity, since they produce over 30 per cent of Italy's total table wine production. There are strong differences within this group, both with regard to

① on-farm producer most DOC/DOCG [handwritten]

② Industrial commercial wine [handwritten]

private companies Industrial [handwritten]

Table 4.6   Winemakers by type, Italy, 1998

	On-farm winemakers	Cooperatives	Other winemakers
Italy, total	60 768	861	1 925
Northwest	17 153	132	539
Northeast	13 533	203	387
Centre	20 873	135	288
South	9 209	391	711

Source: Elaboration from AIMA.

Table 4.7   Wine production by type, Italy, 1998 (%)

[handwritten: 8% of total (wine-growers) invest, more DOC/G wines]

	Table wines			IGT wines			DOC–DOCG wines		
	On-farm winemakers	Cooperatives	Other winemakers	On-farm winemakers	Cooperatives	Other winemakers	On-farm winemakers	Cooperatives	Other winemakers
Italy, total	12.5	56.2	31.3	17.6	69.1	13.3	35.4	48.7	15.9
Northwest	49.7	21.1	29.2	25.3	33.2	41.4	35.3	34.0	30.6
Northeast	18.1	55.6	26.3	16.3	74.4	9.3	31.7	57.1	11.2
Centre	33.8	35.6	30.6	36.5	51.5	12.0	52.6	39.5	7.9
South	5.9	60.9	33.2	8.7	70.7	20.6	18.7	62.5	18.7

[handwritten note: Coops concentrate in NE & South]

Source: Elaboration from AIMA.

87

size (many only have a local or regional focus, while few operate on the national and international markets), and to their efficiency and market orientation. In general, these private companies do not own vineyards of their own but rather purchase grapes or bulk wine on the open market. Only in a few cases (for example Moscato d'Asti grapes) are there agreements in which prices are decided in advance between producers of grapes and the wineries.

Cooperatives, though small in number, produce the largest quantities of wine, account for 56 per cent of table wine, almost 70 per cent of IGT wine and about 49 per cent of DOC–DOCG wine. Their members make up approximately 60 per cent of all wine grape-growers in Italy. Their significance is a result of legislation favouring them, and of support from farmers' unions striving to gain/retain bargaining power for small farms. They produce grapes for low-quality wine for mass consumption. Over 45 per cent of the cooperative wineries are in the south but the largest ones are in the northeast. In general, members are bound to give their whole grape production to the cooperative.

The above differences highlight two characteristics of the Italian winemaking sector: its dualistic structure, and its lack of concentration. While a great number of operators are very small in size, there is at the same time a small number of large-scale operators represented by big cooperatives and industrial winemakers. There is also a dualistic character in terms of efficiency and market orientation, and by production types: in the case of table wines, the national production system is dominated by the cooperatives and by companies of a purely 'industrial' nature, while for higher-quality wines, grape-grower winemakers play a decisive role.

In terms of concentration, the first ten companies (which also include five cooperatives) in 1998 accounted for one-fifth of total turnover (less than 1700 billion lire, of which half came from the top three – ISMEA, 2000). Nor has there been much interest in mergers. The few mergers and acquisitions that took place in recent years have been mainly oriented to horizontal synergies aimed at easing entrance into national and international markets.

Characteristics of Wine Consumption and Distribution

The slow but progressive move towards higher-quality products can be partly explained by the evolution of domestic wine consumption patterns. This has been characterized by a strong decrease in per capita wine consumption since the 1980s, and a change in consumers' shares of different types of wines.

The continuous decline in consumption also went on, though to a lesser degree, in the 1990s. During that decade, following an initial period of stabilization, a further decrease occurred in more recent years, with the level of consumption declining to 52 litres per capita in 2001, or half that of the 1970s. The same period saw alternative drinks – mineral water, soft drinks and fruit juices – grow in importance, but the most dramatic substitute is beer, whose per capita consumption has trebled since the early 1960s.

The second effect of the changes in consumer behaviour is the increasing success of higher-quality wines (DOC–DOCG). Their share in domestic consumption increased from 11 per cent in 1981 (ISMEA, 1997) to 15 per cent in 1991 and to 22 per cent in 1999 (Pomarici and Sardone, 2001). This orientation of national consumption towards higher-quality products has strong similarities with the other main wine-producing countries in the EU, although the extent of that in Italy is still barely half the EU average of 41 per cent. Another significant trend in the Italian market is the steady increase in the consumption of red wines at the expense of white wines, a trend driven by health concerns.

In addition, wine consumption in Italy still has a strong geographical character: the northeastern regions have the highest consumption levels, and the islands the lowest. This is partly due to climatic reasons, and partly to the link between consumption and production tradition. Because wine has a strong territorial specificity, the consumption of quality wines is larger in the zones specialized in their production. A similar correlation between consumption and production can also be found with respect to wine colour.

Important changes in consumption styles have also come about in recent years as regards the purchasing channels. On the basis of a recent survey, most purchases of wine by Italian households (67 per cent) take place in supermarkets (ISMEA, 2000). The success of these outlets is due to the enlargement of the range of wines on offer, in terms of both labels and prices: over 60 per cent of appellation wines are now marketed through supermarkets. By contrast, traditional shops are losing their importance, and their share is now less than one-quarter. This latter channel is important for the sale of bulk wine, in particular table wine. However, the specialized wine shops sell mostly high-quality wines. Sales through e-commerce channels are developing only slowly. There were barely 1700 sites for Italian wine-growers on the Internet in 2000, of which only a hundred or so directly sold wine on-line.

A further important change is represented by the increasing habit of consuming wine away from home. The HORECA sector (hotels, restaurants, bars and catering) has come to represent an extremely important consumption channel, and one that is already about one-third of the volume consumed at home. In 2000, HORECA consumption comprised 39 per cent appellation wines, 52 per cent table wines or IGT wines, and the remaining 9 per cent sparkling wines.

INTERNATIONAL COMPETITIVENESS OF ITALIAN WINE

Recent Performance

Since the late 1980s, Italian wine exports have grown slightly slower than world exports by volume, and at the same pace in terms of value (6.1 per cent – see Anderson and Norman, 2003). This is a fairly good performance for a traditional producing country, considering the large increase in New World wine trade during that period and the constraints on supply in the Old World.

Italy redirected the production no longer demanded in the domestic market to the international markets by upgrading export quality. During 1990–2001, the unit value of Italy's wine exports rose 0.9 per cent in US dollar terms, compared with the rest of the world's, which grew at less than 0.7 per cent (Anderson and Norman, 2003, Table 50). The famous wines from Piedmont, Veneto and Tuscany are now sold in the most important wine auctions, but wines from southern Italy are also being increasingly appreciated too.

A more detailed analysis of Italy's competitive performance in foreign markets can be carried out by considering the position of Italian wines in the markets of the main client countries (Table 4.8). France, Germany, the UK and the USA are the largest clients, absorbing around 80 per cent of Italy's wine exports in value and volume. Canada, Belgium, the Netherlands and Japan are other traditional clients. While exports to France are dominated by cheap wine, exports to the USA, Canada and Japan include a comparatively large share of high-quality wine. Italy has shown a fair capacity to defend its position against the increasing pressure of new competitors, which has been particularly strong in the UK and the USA and, from the late 1990s, in Germany. The data show that Italian firms concentrated their export efforts on Germany where, over the past decade, Italian shares in value and volume slightly improved. By contrast, Italy's shares in the UK fell, especially in volume terms, while falling only slightly in the USA. In France, too, the Italian share has been decreasing. Japan is the only client where market shares increased in volume more than in value.

In summary, Italy partly compensated for the reductions in its share in some traditional markets by improving its performances in several new countries, mainly European ones, by exporting better-quality wines. However, Italian premium wine exports are constrained by the available supply, given the strong demand also in domestic markets.

During the 1990s the sector performed well in domestic markets.[10] Along with the increase in quality wine consumption, consumption habits also changed for ordinary wines. It is becoming more and more common in urban areas to purchase wine in modern packages ('brik' or bag in box), identified by well-known producers' labels or private labels.

Table 4.8 Italy's shares in selected countries' wine imports, 1991–2000

| | \multicolumn{6}{c}{Shares on import value (%)} | | | | | |
	1991/1993	1996	1997	1998	1999	2000
France	40	42	31	29	41	n.a.[b]
Germany	32	34	34	32	35	33
UK	14	12	12	11	9	9
USA	29	28	27	26	25	27
Canada	15	17	16	16	16	17
Belgium	5	5	2	4	4	5
Netherlands[a]	6	6	7	–	–	–
Japan	6	14	13	14	12	12

| | \multicolumn{6}{c}{Shares of import volume (%)} | | | | | |
	1991/1993	1996	1997	1998	1999	2000
France	67	52	52	46	76	n.a.[b]
Germany	41	41	42	39	47	43
UK	20	13	12	13	13	12
USA	41	36	35	35	36	36
Canada	15	16	15	16	17	19
Belgium	11	8	9	7	9	8
Netherlands[a]	9	8	9	–	–	–
Japan	6	15	15	15	14	17

| | \multicolumn{6}{c}{Relative import price index[c]} | | | | | |
	1991/1993	1996	1997	1998	1999	2000
France	0.60	0.81	0.60	0.69	0.52	n.a.
Germany	0.78	0.834	0.81	0.83	0.75	0.77
UK	0.72	0.90	0.98	0.86	0.72	0.75
USA	0.71	0.79	0.77	0.73	0.69	0.75
Canada	1.00	1.06	1.05	0.98	0.92	0.90
Belgium	0.48	0.60	0.19	0.53	0.48	0.62
Netherlands[a]	0.67	0.78	0.80	–	–	–
Japan	1.07	0.91	0.87	0.94	0.84	0.71

Notes:
[a] No record in 1988–2000 because too small.
[b] Not available.
[c] Average price of Italian imported wine/average price of total imported wine.

Source: CFCE.

Performances on the domestic and foreign markets during the 1990s translated to fairly good performances for, at least, the largest Italian wine companies. The return on investment from 1995 to 1999 for 22 main wine companies, which account for 17 per cent of sector turnover, increased from 9.7 per cent to 10.2 per cent (a performance similar to that of the overall economy), and return on equity rose from 5.5 per cent to 9.7 per cent (compared with 12.6 per cent for the overall economy). During the same period, the average turnover increased from 310 000 to 376 000 euros and the average invested capital rose from 244 000 to 297 000 euros (increases of 20 and 22 per cent, respectively – see Mediobanca, 2000). These results are not representative of the whole Italian wine sector, though: a large number of private or cooperative firms, mainly in the south, are not very profitable, and several southern estates have been acquired by wineries based in the north or centre of Italy.

Contributive Factors

The competitive position of the Italian wine sector can be better understood by analysing the sector in terms of factor availability, the presence of related and supporting industries, the actions of public administrators, the nature of socioeconomic relations among industry agents, the role of domestic demand, and strategy, structure and rivalry (Traill and Pitts, 1998).

Labour and land are of course critical. In Italy widespread skills in viticulture and oenology exist, but a conservative attitude makes the diffusion of innovative practices and continuous improvement slow. Moreover, in many areas the replacement of older workers is difficult, and training programmes for qualified technicians are inadequate. Also, the land market is very rigid and the high prices of land in many areas – which are linked to CAP limits on new vineyard plantations – constrain farm size enlargement.

Many important suppliers of technical equipment and auxiliary products for grape-growing and winemaking are located in Italy. This ensures that producers have excellent access to technology, so the limitation is in embedding innovations into the farming systems.

As already mentioned, the CAP has been pervasive in market regulation and has had a strong impact on the sector's evolution. The new objectives of the CAP – driving producers to take advantage of expanding markets, enabling the sector to become more competitive in the longer term – require different tools and it is questionable whether Italian public administration is able to support the sector to fully exploit the new regulations. Almost all Italian regions are likely to be slow in taking the administrative steps required as prerequisites for implementing the new CAP, which dampens mobility of vineyard planting rights. In addition, programmes for local administrations seem completely absorbed by bureaucratic aspects and less focused on identifying the best options for vineyard restructuring and conversion. Local administrations also have been ineffective in driving and coordinating the development of the geographic indication system,[11] and in promoting research and experimentation of new oenological practices.

In the wine areas of Italy there exists an extremely rich collective endowment of knowledge, sustaining the network of socio-economic relations among wine firms, individuals and families, but tradition in a conservative sense often seems to prevail. As a consequence, this network does not support and stimulate innovations, help develop private and public extension services, or promote producer associations and interbranch organizations. That is, wine sector agents have been inadequate in stimulating administration and in developing collective action in promotion, research, education, training and lobbying.

Guanxi obstruction to innovation

Domestic demand, which represents one of the largest wine markets in the world, is becoming more selective, and Italian producers have direct contacts with customers, both traders and consumers. This could facilitate rapid product improvement, but consumer behavioural analysis is still very underdeveloped.

In terms of firm strategy, structure and rivalry, the Italian wine sector is far from homogeneous, since firm concentration is very low, and small company size makes it difficult to develop an appropriate organization and effective strategies. The largest firms, by contrast, have a very competitive industrial asset, high investment capacity and marketing behaviour similar to the most active of competitors in the international market (Gaeta, 2000). These leader companies, which are bringing strong competitive pressure to the domestic market, provide positive examples for medium and small firms.

Small Medium Producers are ineffective

Many wine firms are insufficiently market oriented in their business strategies (ISMEA, 2000; Esposito et al., 2001). This shows up as weak marketing activities and distribution policies. Many medium and small firms face difficulties in maintaining quality standard and differentiating their product. In Italy there are many different grape varieties available, and vines are located in many sites, which could be a great marketing opportunity. However, the existing limited research capability is scattered, and the necessary process of identifying the optimal wine profile in different districts is slow, so many wines do not have a specific personality. Communication is still traditional so new consumption motivations are often not exploited, including in the area of wine-tourism. As for distribution, only a few firms are trying to develop innovation and to integrate among producers and between producers and retailers (Gaeta and Pomarici, 2001).

Problems and Prospects

The Italian wine sector performed well over the 1990s. Undoubtedly there has

been an improvement in wine quality, and demand for Italian wine has grown
in the international market, partly stimulated in the early 1990s by the devaluation of the Italian currency. But the performance has not been totally determined by an intrinsic competitiveness, as there are still weaknesses in firms'
competitive processes. In particular, increasing competition from New World
countries is a serious threat to many Italian producers. Moreover, the evolution
of supermarket procurement strategies could extend this threat from the international to the domestic market in so far as that increases wine imports. It is
unlikely that the volume of Italian production will increase significantly,
although growth is still possible in terms of quality. But without substantial
productivity improvements, a severe consolidation by the largest and better-
equipped companies seems likely, together with an overall reduction in the
vine area and a reorientation toward higher-quality grapes in the remaining
vineyards.

An alternative scenario is also possible. If the sector were to be effective in
improving its competitiveness and reallocating its resources, it could take
advantage of international market trends and move towards a more differentiated set of products. Italian producers have much to offer in this respect, given
the variety, richness and complexity of Italian products, and this might allow
for growth of medium and small firms to be driven by internal and foreign
demand for quality wines. In this scenario, producers would face a demand
curve with a lower price elasticity, ensuring higher revenues. Achieving that
will require overcoming competition not only from the New World but also
from cheap wine from those East European countries that are soon to join the
EU.[12]

In order to enhance the sector's competitiveness, a necessary condition is
strengthening policy-making capacity and network relations within the sector.
This is a prerequisite to catch the opportunities offered by the new EU wine
Common Market Organization (CMO), by stimulating the improvement of
oenological practices and rationalizing the market for vine planting rights. The
last point is particularly important because Italy suffers from a scarcity of
wines suitable for export and yet some wine is still distilled, indicating that
some vine areas are misused.

The strengthening of network relations among private agents is also very
important. The new CMO requires that firms participate in the policy-making
process. Private involvement also is crucial for developing an effective education system, for experimenting and promoting new oenological practices, for
allowing extensive zonage plans, and for ensuring the evolution of Italy's
geographic indication (GI) system. In a competitive context where the problem of product identification is pervasive, and branding policies are extensively adopted by the largest companies, the competitiveness of the quality
wine produced by small and medium firms could depend on the existence of a

well-recognized GI system so that generic regional brands can be developed.
A rationalization of the GI system, making it easy for consumers to identify
the origin and the intrinsic value of regional wines, and a coordination of product policies, are required. Producers in each area may have to agree on rules
in winemaking, so as to develop a local wine profile that consumers can recog-
nize as distinctive.

The improvement in factor and policy conditions should ease the necessary
efforts of firms to improve their organization and management. The logistic
and retailing functions, the ability to activate efficient communication policies
(including the use of GI names, producers' brands, and distintive wine names),
and the capacity to manage efficient and effective quality and cost control
systems, are key elements for improving the market performance of firms. But
considering the great differences in terms of firm size and resources within the
sector, what is really critical for firms' success is for them to make clear and
realistic choices as they make strategies to develop their competitive advantage, choosing between differentiation and price leadership.

In the low-price wine segment where firm concentration is very high, firms
are operating efficient large-scale plants and are usually making very clear
market choices. But clear decisions in terms of production orientation are also
necessary for the large number of medium and small firms operating with a
wide range of quality products. These firms have to select their core business
and develop the necessary knowledge and skills to compete successfully.
Specific skills are needed not only in production but also in marketing and
distribution if such firms are to enter selective retailing channels. In the
premium segment it is price competition that is increasingly important to
suppliers, who have to be very competitive in terms of their costs. In wine-
growing, margins for reducing costs need to be exploited, especially via a
more extensive use of mechanical harvesting[13] and yield-stabilizing irrigation.
Reducing costs is possible in winemaking too, by adopting production
schemes and layouts optimized for premium wine production, based on
automation and on strict prevention of fermentation risks (Pomarici et al.,
1997). Marketing and physical handling are areas where reducing costs is also
crucial, even if difficult to achieve. Small producers and distributors need to
become integrated into complex marketing systems (which implies a business
style unusual in the Italian context), so as to be able to adopt better-integrated
promotion strategies, supply timeliness and flexibility, transport rationalization, and warehouse and communication automation.

The Italian wine sector is facing some difficult challenges. Now that Italy
is in the euro zone, exchange rate depreciations as in the early 1990s are less
likely to provide a boost to exports. Hence the competitiveness of Italian wine
will need to be based on quality and cost control. It is not easy to predict how
the Italian wine sector will evolve, and an intermediate scenario between the

two presented above (severe consolidation or evolution of the present industry structure) is also possible. How severe the selection will be depends on to what extent the current internal weaknesses are overcome and how domestic and foreign demands evolve. If a reasonable part of the internal problems can be solved and present market trends continue, it is conceivable that the sector will maintain its current structure and at least hold if not improve its international position.

NOTES

1. Before that it was illegal for women to drink wine. Pliny cites examples of cruel punishment of women breaking this law, and the curious habit of kissing them on the mouth to verify if they had drunk wine (Dalmasso, 1937).
2. Readers should be warned that available data on grape and wine production, as well as on foreign trade, vary according to the source and even from the same source when data are revised. This is also true for area coverage, which shows discrepancies, particularly between the annual estimates and those that result from periodic agricultural censuses or field surveys.
3. According to European rules, wines are divided into table wines, with or without a geographical indication, and 'quality wines produced in specified regions' (or VQPRD). According to the present Italian law (Law 164/1992), table wines are divided into *vini da tavola* and IGT (Indicazione Geografica Tipica) wines, corresponding to table wines without and with, respectively, a geographic indication. VQPRD wines include DOC wines (controlled denomination of origin) and DOCG wines (controlled and guaranteed denomination of origin). Each of these corresponds to a progressively higher-quality level, and the production of IGT, DOC and DOCG wines has to comply with increasingly strict production rules.
4. The French franc increased its value relative to the Italian lira by 78 per cent between 1970 and 1980 and the DM by 175 per cent. The increase was lower for the exchange rates with the UK and USA but still sizeable, at 32 and 36 per cent, respectively. Although the Italian inflation rate was larger than in competing countries, the Italian lira also lost value in real terms (Balcet, 1997).
5. Some cases of wine adulteration, which also caused some casualties, were discovered that year: low-quality wines were added with poisonous and cheap methanol to raise the alcohol content. The incident received wide media coverage both in Italy and abroad, resulting in a decrease in domestic consumption and exports. It induced the government to introduce tighter preventive controls against adulteration, and pushed many producers to strive to improve the quality of their wines.
6. The Italian lira devalued substantially only relative to the DM (and to a much lower degree than during the 1970s), but very little relative to the French franc and to the UK pound. The lira/US dollar rate reached a high value during the first part of the decade, followed by a decline in the second half.
7. In 1987 the conditions triggering the compulsory distillation became much wider, which made compulsory distillation more frequent.
8. This level was lowered to 50 per cent of the orientation price in 1987, and to 40 per cent for the distilled quantity larger than a threshold (further reduced to 7.5 per cent in 1988).
9. During 1988–99 about 93 000 ha were abandoned under the scheme (Pomarici and Sardone, 2001), 95 per cent of which was table wine quality (Scoppola and Zezza, 1997).
10. A comparison with wine imports is not very relevant, since consumption of foreign wine in Italy is still small and sporadic; the competition is rather with other beverages.
11. 'Understanding how Italian wines are classified is a daunting task' (Belfrage, 2001, p. 108).

12. The current levy on wine imports (32 euro/hl) has been so far quite effective in protecting EU-15 producers from imports of common wine from Eastern Europe and the New World.
13. Some reports suggest there are just 1000 wine harvesters in Italy, compared with 11 000 in France.

REFERENCES

Anderson, K. and D. Norman (2003), *Global Wine Production, Consumption and Trade, 1961 to 2001: A Statistical Compendium*, Adelaide: Centre for International Economic Studies.

Balcet, G. (1997), *L'economia italiana*, Milan: Feltrinelli.

Belfrage, N. (2001), 'A law unto itself', in *Italy 2001*, supplement to *Decanter*.

CFCE (various years), *Statistiques étrangères des vins et spiritueux*, Supplement au VIVS, Paris: Centre Français du Commerce Extérieur.

Castronovo, V. (1975), 'La storia economica', in *Storia d'Italia*, Vol. IV, Turin: Einaudi.

Cipolla, C.M. (1977), 'La penisola italiana e la penisola iberica', in M.M. Postan, E.E. Rich and E. Miller (eds), *Storia economica Cambridge*, vol. III, Turin: Einaudi.

Dalmasso, G. (1937), *Le vicende tecniche ed economiche della viticoltura e dell'enologia in Italia*, Milan: Arti Grafiche Enrico Gualdoni.

Esposito, P., A. Giordano, M.T. Gorgitano, E. Pomarici, R. Postiglione, S. Raia and M. Romano (2001), *Assetti aziendali e dei sistemi locali del settore vitivinicolo nelle regioni dell'Obiettivo 1 e azioni per la valorizzazione dei vitigni autoctoni* in *Atti del III Workshop POM B-35*, Università degli studi di Sassari.

Gaeta, D. (2000), *Il sistema vitivinicolo in cifre*, Milan: Editrice Unione Italiana Vini.

Gaeta, D. and E. Pomarici (2001), 'General trend in wine distribution and appropriate wine producers strategies in Italy and other old wine countries', in *Proceedings of the XXX OIV Congress*, Adelaide.

INEA (various years), *Annuario dell'agricoltura italiana*, Rome.

ISMEA (various years), *Filiera vino*, Rome.

ISTAT (1976), *Sommario di statistiche storiche dell'Italia 1861–1975*, Rome.

ISTAT (1999), *Struttura e produzioni delle aziende agricole: Anno 1997*, Rome.

Mediobanca (2000), *Focus on the main wine companies in Italy*, Milan: Ufficio studi di Mediobanca, mimeo.

OIV (2001), 'The State of Vitiviniculture in the World and the Statistical Information in 1999', supplement to *Bulletin de l'OIV*.

Pomarici, E., A. Rinaldi and F. Sallusti (1997), 'Quality and Process Reengineeering Patterns and Cost in Wine Production', in G. Schiefer and R. Helbig (eds), *Quality Management and Process Improvement for Competitive Advantage in Agriculture and Food*, Bonn: LIB.

Pomarici, E. and R. Sardone (eds) (2001), *Il settore vitivinicolo in Italia. Strutture produttive, mercati e competitività alla luce della nuova Organizzazione Comune di Mercato*, Rome: Studi & Ricerche, INEA.

Scoppola, M. and A. Zezza (1997), *La riforma dell'organizzazione comune di mercato e la vitivinicoltura italiana*, Rome: Studi & Ricerche, INEA.

Traill, W.B. and E. Pitts (1998), *Competitiveness in the Food Industry*, London: Blackie Academic & Professional.

5. Spain and Portugal

Luis Miguel Albisu

In Spain and Portugal, vineyards are integrated into the rural landscape. They mean more than a productive activity, because for centuries wine has been part of Iberian Peninsula culture and integral to the diet of its habitants. Nevertheless, distinctive features distinguish those two countries with respect to their grapes, to the kinds of wines, and to the types of businesses operating there. Even though they have been following the same policy rules since entering the European Community in 1986, and both have increased the promotion of their wines in the rest of Europe and elsewhere, they face different international market conditions.

This chapter examines those similarities and differences in the two countries by first providing a brief historical survey of pertinent developments to 1990, then examining trends during the past decade or so, and finally looking at the prospects for Spain and Portugal.

HISTORICAL DEVELOPMENTS UP TO 1990

There is no precise knowledge about when wines were introduced to Spain and Portugal. They might have been brought by the Greeks or the Carthaginians, in the fourth and fifth centuries before Christ. There were already vineyards on the Iberian Peninsula when the Romans arrived, but they spread this crop to many more geographical areas. At that time wine was exported to Rome to pay taxes. Other cultures that invaded the Peninsula also enjoyed the benefits of drinking wine, apart from the Arabs whose culture, which came to Spain in the eighth century, forbade alcohol. As a result many vineyards were uprooted at that time although some permissive attitudes prevailed among their judges and, fortunately for the wine sector, many hectares were left in production.

At the time when the Jews were expelled from Spain, wine traders from England replaced them. Sherry and Málaga wines started to become famous, especially in England, in the fourteenth century. These wines had high alcohol content, and so were able to last longer than the wines produced previously. After the discovery of the Americas in 1492, there were new demands from the other side of the Atlantic.

1700'

In the eighteenth century important English wine firms were operating in the southern part of Spain, as well as in Portugal with Port wines. In both countries extensive vineyards were producing for the English market as the main outlet. English traders, as the driving force behind these developments, were able to invest in vineyards and wineries in Spain and Portugal, launch new products in the English market, and create new markets in other European countries. These exported products were quite different from normal wines consumed in the Iberian Peninsula, which had a lower-alcohol content and were very unstable.

In the nineteenth century, biological and chemistry discoveries improved oenological processes, but then phylloxera had a devastating influence on wine production across much of Europe. It led to French entrepreneurs moving to Spain to start new businesses, which was the beginning of the flourishing of Rioja wines. This region was producing high-quality wines for the English market while Cataluña, Aragón and Levante were producing common wines that were exported to America, France and Switzerland.

The Spanish Civil War of 1936 to 1939 had profound negative effects because vineyards were neglected, but by the 1950s vineyards in Spain occupied almost 10 per cent of total cultivated land. Yields have been low on average (2 tonnes/ha), but they varied greatly from year to year because all vineyards were cultivated on dry land. In the 1960s, annual production was around 25 million hl, but it rose to around 35 million hl by the 1980s. With highly varying yields and little capacity to carry inventories, producers' prices fluctuated markedly from season to season. In Portugal, for example, between 1953 and 1962 average wine production was 11 million hl but ranged between 7.5 and 15 million hl.

In the early 1960s Portugal was producing 140 litres per capita, the highest in the Mediterranean area, in comparison with 130 litres in France, 120 litres in Italy and 80 litres in Spain. At that time it had about 290 000 hectares under vines, and wine represented 2.5 per cent of total GNP and 10 per cent of agricultural GNP. Between 1942 and 1961, the Portuguese Junta Nacional do Vino accounted for 62 per cent of total wine produced in the country and the DO (Deonominaciones de Origen) Vinhos Verdes accounted for another 21 per cent.

Spain created, in 1970, the INDO (Instituto Nacional de Denominaciones de Origen), which has been a crucial institution for regulating and controlling quality wines in Spain. Each DO has a Regulatory Council, which applies particular rules in that geographical area following the general rules set up by INDO. The INDO was part of the Ministry of Agriculture and each DO Regulatory Council takes into consideration the interests of wine producers, processors and traders.

The first DO was created in 1933 (Sherry), followed by Málaga, Montilla

and Moriles. Rioja was established in 1945 and it was followed by other qual-
ity wine areas, such as Tarragona, Priorato, Ribeiro, Valdeorras, Alella, Utiel-
Requena, Valencia, Alicante, Cariñena, Navarra, Penedés, Jumilla and Huelva.
Most historical DO were created before 1975 although some more have been
set up recently. In Portugal the most important DO regions were Vinhos
Verdes, Dáo, Colares, Bucelas and Carcavelos.

Spanish wines have been produced in geographical areas of diverse precipitation, ranging from 200 mm (Alicante and Murcia) to 1000 mm (Galicia),
and with diverse soil conditions. Some areas also face high summer temperatures aggravated by lack of water. Vines are cultivated on land stretching from
sea level up to 1200 metres. Harsh climatic conditions have had a great influence on wine quality and homogeneity across production seasons. There are
many local varieties which, even if they have not been fully developed tech-
nically, characterized each productive region and DO. In Portugal there is less
variation but conditions and hence wines do vary between the north and the
south.

TRENDS AND MAIN DEVELOPMENTS SINCE 1990

Production

Spain has the biggest vineyard area in the world with 1.1 million hectares
(down from 1.7 million in the 1970s and compared with 0.9 million in each of
France and Italy). Around 50 per cent is located in the central part of Spain,
Levante has around 10 per cent, and Extremadura 7 per cent. Around 90 per
cent of the total surface is cultivated on dry land and practically all cultivation
is undertaken on its own without mixing with any other crop. Since 1990, the
area under vines in both Spain and Portugal has diminished by about one-third.
Wine production has fallen less, but there has been great variations from year
to year (Table 5.1).

Irrigation was forbidden in Spain until 1995, a rule that has had a profound
impact on its viticulture. Now each DO Regulatory Council establishes irrigation practices and limitations in the area under its responsibility. Yields were
low before irrigation was allowed: 3.1 tonnes/ha in the 1970s, 3.6 in the 1980s,
but more than 4.0 during 1995–2001. Climatic conditions are semi-arid in
many areas and so irrigation is necessary to regulate the quality and quantity.

In Spain there is a clear distinction between quality wines, fully related to
DO, and common wines. The amount of wine sold by DO accounts for over
35 per cent of the total volume of wine produced in Spain and over 60 per cent
of consumer expenditure on wine. There are also strong differences among
DO wines, as there are 56 distinct DO areas.

Table 5.1 Area planted to vines, wine production and wine consumption, Portugal and Spain, 1990–2001

	1990	1991	1992	1993	1994	1995	1996	1997	1998	1999	2000	2001
Area planted ('000 ha)												
Portugal	379	371	360	267	360	261	259	260	260	260	261	247
Spain	1532	1513	1381	1281	1235	1196	1162	1169	1171	1180	1174	1100
Wine production ('000 hl)												
Portugal	11372	9826	7608	4607	4576	7255	9712	6124	3750	7859	6694	7015
Spain	38658	31390	33832	26507	18954	20876	31000	33218	31175	33723	41692	31127
Wine consumption ('000 hl)												
Portugal	5007	6196	5537	6000	5762	5760	5800	5223	5055	4980	5020	5132
Spain	16539	16810	15500	15236	15336	15000	14459	14589	14793	14249	13843	15199
Wine consumption per capita (litres)												
Portugal	51	63	56	61	58	58	58	53	51	50	50	50
Spain	43	43	40	39	39	38	37	37	38	36	35	38

Source: Anderson and Norman (2003).

The amount of bottles sold in the market defines quite precisely the strength of each DO. Recent data indicate that more than 10 million hl are sold in the market by all DO, more than 60 per cent of which is sold on the domestic market. Rioja is the biggest DO, both in terms of volume (around 12 per cent of the total volume of wine sold) and value (over 25 per cent of total value of the wine sold), followed by Valdepeñas, Penedés and Navarra. The latter areas produced between one-third and one-quarter of the volume usually produced in Rioja. The gap between the value of Rioja wines and the rest is even greater. Penedés, Ribera del Duero and Navarra each account for around 4–5 per cent of the total value of DO wines.

As the most important wine DO, Rioja deserves a short description of its position in the market. This DO has been the leader in quality wines in Spain throughout history, although the gap between Rioja and other DO has been narrowing in recent years. With more than 50 000 ha of cultivated vines, Rioja is divided into three areas: Rioja Alta, Rioja Baja and Rioja Alavesa. Each area has different precipitation, temperature range and soil composition. The best-known wines are in the first area, the second area provides bulk wines which are mixed with the rest plus a small percentage of bottled wine, while the third area has different kinds of wines mostly produced by small wineries. This variation creates a market problem because the region has to market its wines in many different price segments, which incurs image difficulties for the most expensive wines.

Tempranillo is the main variety, with over 50 per cent of the total Rioja vine area, followed by Garnacha. Rioja has been marketing its wine with four different denominations: *sin crianza or joven*, *crianza*, *reserva* and *gran reserva*. That distinction is based basically on age and technological accomplishments. Around 50 per cent is sold in the lowest category. Only exceptional years provide the highest-quality wines, known as *gran reserva*. The price range varies accordingly. Recent price rises have led to some important export markets being lost, however. This DO also suffered an important legal battle, as there was a request to bottle some of its wines outside the DO region, in fact in a different country. After several years at the International Court of Justice in The Hague, the region won the right for its wine to be bottled only in Rioja. The region has since made it compulsory to sell only bottled wine on foreign markets.

Penedés is a small area in the Cataluña region, well known for its white wines but specially names by its leading wine maker, the Torres family. Its approach departs quite drastically from a traditional DO in that innovation is a constant drive and its promotion is based on its own rather than on the DO Penedés name. It would like to put together all DO from the Cataluña region, under a unique DO name, so as to have a bigger wine volume to be able to better face global markets, and to improve wine homogeneity by mixing grapes from different geographical origins within the Catalonian region.

Somontano DO is worth mentioning as one of the newest and one that already has a solid reputation in the market. It has around 2000 hectares under vines and, since the very beginning, foreign varieties have been an important part of its production. Its origin was a consequence of several French families who left France and came to this area close to the Pyrenees. They planted some of the best-known French varieties such as Cabernet, Merlot, Chardonnay and Pinot Noir. There are only three big wine firms, and public investment from the region has helped to develop their businesses.

Navarra is another DO worth mentioning. Near Rioja, it has always had a good reputation for rosé wines. The DO tried to change that image by introducing red wines based on the variety Garnacha, the most popular variety in this DO. Cooperatives play an important role in the region but private businesses are the leading force. Their positioning in the domestic market is in the middle price range and, although exports have increased constantly during the past decade, they are positioned in the medium to low price segments.

Ribera del Duero is the most promising area that is catching up with Rioja's reputation. This area is host to Vega Sicilia, which is considered the best Spanish firm, but there are other firms that also have become prominent not because of size but because of their quality reputation in and outside Spain.

La Mancha is not well known for quality wines but it comprises around 50 per cent of the total area dedicated to DO in Spain (around 600 000 ha). Airen is the dominant white variety in this DO. Temperatures are as extreme in summer for Ciudad Real, at over 44 °C, and also in winter for Albacete, with 22 °C below zero. Cooperatives handle around 60 per cent of elaborated wine. However, plots average just 2 ha. The amount of La Mancha wines sold in bottles is very small.

Besides these traditional DO appellations, a new movement is rising with the creation in 1999 of *vinos de la tierra*. Their bottles are allowed to put the year, the varieties and the region on the label. Huge investments in the past few years might change Spain's basic production and marketing approach and have a significant impact on Spanish wines, in so far as these wines are successfully taken up by the big distribution chains.

Vinos de la tierra accounted for 2.2 million hl in the season 2000/01, and 42 per cent was produced in Castilla-La Mancha. It is a protected geographical indication (GI), which normally covers small areas that try to be reconverted, later on, to protected denomination of origin. Two-thirds of its total production is red wine. In the year 2001, the Ministry of Agriculture approved the possibility of elaborating those wines in several autonomous communities. Their prices stand normally below those of DO wines. Production in Castilla-La Mancha is above production in well-known DO areas such as Ribera del Duero, Rueda and Penedés. Castilla y Leon expects to produce 500 000 hl of 'vinos de la tierra', over and above the 300 000 hl which corresponds to its

DO. In this region they have made it compulsory to sell the wine in only one year. The same trend is happening in Extremadura, and Castilla-La Mancha expects to reconvert 100 000 ha by 2010.

Portugal has a favourable climate and excellent soils for vines. In the past decade production ranged between 6 and almost 10 million hl, with red wines accounting for almost 60 per cent of total production. In 2000 DO wines represented 49 per cent of total production and *vins de pays* accounted for 20 per cent. EU schemes to reconvert vineyards have had a positive impact in transforming common wines into quality wines.

Portugal has 32 DO under very different productive circumstances. The Douro region produces 22 per cent of total production and accounts for 85 per cent of DO production, followed by Estremadura and Ribatejo, which respectively account for 19 per cent and 11 per cent of national production, but with less than 5 per cent of DO wines. The regions in the centre of the country (Dáo, Bairrada and Beiras) have a balanced production of different types of wines, the Alentejo (in the south) and the Minho (in the north) producing almost exclusively quality wines (DO and *vins de pays*).

Consumption

The total quantity of wine consumed in Spain has been steadily decreasing. Since 1990, it has gone down from 16.5 million hl to less than 15 million hl (Table 5.1), or from 42 to 38 litres per capita. At the same time quality wine consumption has been increasing so that the total amount spent on wine has been decreasing only slightly. In Portugal the same trend can be observed, with total consumption going down from 16 to 15 million hl since 1993, or from 60 to 50 litres per capita (Table 5.1).

Quality wines are related to the type of containers in which they are sold, and there are price differentials also according to container type. Thus, any quality wine in the domestic market has to be sold in bottles containing 750 ml, regardless of whether they have a DO label. Ordinary wines are sold in bottles of one litre, or briks usually of one litre. Briks have been common containers for milk, so initially consumers had serious difficulties in accepting them. However, they are accepted now and several big firms sell their cheapest wine in briks.

Spain is a country where the quantity of wine sold in restaurants and bars almost equals the volume sold in retailing channels. Over the past decade, DO wines have increased their domestic market share from 24 to 36 per cent, while wines sold in the same kind of bottles but without DO have moved up from 17 to 25 per cent. The share of wine sold in briks and other containers has gone down commensurably, from 59 to 39 per cent.

In 2000, Spain's hypermarkets accounted for 24 per cent of all wine sales and 39 per cent of DO sales. For large supermarkets those shares were each one-third, while for smaller supermarkets (less than 400 square metres) those shares were 32 and 22 per cent, leaving 10 and 5 per cent, respectively, for traditional shops.

A recent survey indicates the percentage of the population who know the different DO: Rioja (94 per cent), Valdepeñas (50 per cent), Ribera del Duero (46 per cent), Ribeiro (45 per cent), Penedés (36 per cent), Cariñena (28 per cent), Jumilla (28 per cent), Navarra (24 per cent), Rueda (22 per cent), La Mancha (21 per cent), Toro (16 per cent), Rias Baixas (15 per cent), Somontano (12 per cent), Bierzo (11 per cent), Calatayud (10 per cent), Campo de Borja (10 per cent), Chacolí de Bizcaia (10 per cent) and Priorato (10 per cent).

Brands are even less well known among Spanish consumers. Only 5 brands are known by more than 10 per cent of the population: Marqués de Cáceres (15 per cent), Vega Sicilia (12 per cent), Faustino (11 per cent), Paternina (11 per cent) and Marqués del Riscal (11 per cent).

There is a current fashion to develop wines where the name of the variety is one of the most important assets, but the Spanish market is not yet accustomed to such an approach. Thus, in a survey undertaken in 1999, the proportion of consumers who knew some varieties were the following: Moscatel (69 per cent), Albariño (24 per cent), Tempranillo (24 per cent), Garnacha (18 per cent), Cabernet Sauvignon (17 per cent), Cariñena (13 per cent) and Chardonnay (9 per cent).

Internal and External Markets

In Spain, DO wine exports account for 30 per cent of total DO production and the main importing countries are the following: Germany, the UK, the Netherlands, France and Denmark within the EU; and Switzerland, the USA, Canada and Japan outside the EU.

Out of total DO sales in 1999, Rioja accounted for almost 35 per cent of the market, followed by Valdepeñas (11 per cent), Penedés (9 per cent), Navarra (8 per cent), Jumilla (6 per cent) and Mancha (4 per cent). Apart from Rioja wines and some of the top ten better-known DO, which are distributed nationwide, the rest are sold mainly in regional markets and are difficult to find in big distribution chains all over Spain.

It is difficult to differentiate business firms by the value of wine sales because the biggest ones are also in the business of other drinks as well. But two firms have sales of around 600 million euros, six firms between 200 and 400 million euros, and eight firms are selling between 100 and 200 million euros worth of wine. Of those 16 firms, only four are fully dedicated to the wine business and the biggest ones are selling around 200 million euros

(Bodegas y Bebidas and Arco Bodegas Unidas, although the first has been recently acquired by Allied Domecq).

In 2001, Spain and Portugal were the third and ninth largest wine-exporting countries. Spain and Portugal wine exports change according to their harvest seasons such that there is a close correspondence between volume produced and exports. In the past decade, Spain has doubled its exports (to 11.6 million hl), while Portugal's fluctuated between 1.6 and 2.7 million hl (Table 5.2).

The value of Spanish wine exports has risen from US$660 million in 1990 to $1.3 billion in recent years, while in Portugal it has fluctuated between $420 and $520 million. Their imports over the same period have fluctuated much more, but have grown on average at more than 20 per cent p.a. (Table 5.2).

Portugal's wines account for 1–1.5 per cent of the European market. Portuguese wines do not have an important presence on distribution shelves across Europe, and they are put together in the section of 'other wines', where many different origins can be found. France is the main importer of Portuguese wines, followed by the UK, Belgium, the Netherlands, Germany and Denmark. Dáo is by far the leading export area, with more than 50 per cent of total wine exports, followed by Bairrada and Douro. Most of the exports are still shipped in bulk. Exports account for about one-quarter of total production and in 2000 were made up of 45 per cent Port wines and 13 per cent VQPRD wines in volume (or respectively 68 per cent and 11 per cent in value).

Viniportugal deals with the promotion of Portuguese wines inside and outside the country. Promotion efforts are focused on the most important countries (Portugal, Germany and the UK) but also on the USA, Brazil and Ireland. Also, there is a so-called Group of Seven consortium made up of seven wine companies that together export around 80 per cent of Portuguese bottled wines (not including Port wines). This group is attempting through promotion to overcome the negative image linked to Portuguese wines. (Portuguese wines are linked to cheap rosés and *vinho verde* plus a limited amount of premium wines, and none have big brand names except for Mateus which specializes in rosés.) A new movement, based on Caves Aliança, is trying to sell wines from five different regions. Other projects include the Sogrape strategy to build up Portuguese varieties not so well known on the international markets.

Prices

Grape prices suffer great variations from year to year in DO regions. For example, in Rioja in the past few years, grape prices have been between 100 and 400 pts/kg but started at 60 pts/kg for red varieties in the early 1990s. An average price for quality varieties tends to be between 80 and 100 pts/kg.

Table 5.2 Wine exports and imports, Portugal and Spain, 1990–2001

	1990	1991	1992	1993	1994	1995	1996	1997	1998	1999	2000	2001
Export volume ('000 hl)												
Portugal	1613	1742	2584	2091	1988	1696	1964	2504	2260	1968	1876	1692
Spain	4127	6212	6547	8841	7695	6693	7403	10451	11738	9074	9975	11662
Export value (US$ million)												
Portugal	441	455	517	421	450	496	539	523	529	526	468	469
Spain	663	700	815	764	814	992	1164	1256	1373	1459	1262	1346
Import volume ('000 hl)												
Portugal	253	78	60	208	1355	1221	709	757	1849	1817	2189	2037
Spain	94	137	75	77	512	3215	733	199	1048	1439	827	309

Source: Anderson and Norman (2003).

There is no agreement between producers and winemakers on how to settle prices between seasons.

The average price for DO wines sold in retail shops in Spain was 470 pts per bottle in 2000. The average price, in pts, for the most qualified DO were: Rias Baixas (1221), Ribera del Duero (1200), Rioja (779), Somontano (767), Alella (630), Rueda (526), Penedés (431), Valdeorras (425), Calatayud (425), Navarra (415) and Campo de Borja (405). Most Spanish and Portuguese wine prices on international markets retail at less than US$6.

Policy Matters

A clear distinction should be made before and after the entry of Spain and Portugal into the European Union in 1986. Apart from EU policy, probably the most important national policy restriction in Spain was the ban on growing wine with irrigated water. Also, each DO has its specific rules that try to enhance quality. These relate to the productivity of vineyards, the varieties allowed in each area, the amount of money dedicated to promotion activities, and so on. In general, most rules are aimed at quality improvements and promotion. There is also an institution called ICEX (Instituto de Comercio Exterior), which depends on funds from the central government to promote Spanish wine in foreign markets.

FUTURE PROSPECTS

Spain and Portugal have not followed the same development path in the last decade, nor do they face the same future because of their different production structures. Both countries are firmly attached to DO products and are convinced that quality wines are linked to that sort of quality label. *Vinos de la tierra* will offer new opportunities for those regions that want to find a compromise between tradition and innovation. Wine firm agglomeration will continue, and the biggest firms will carry on with their investments in DO areas but will search for more international markets.

Joint promotion among firms belonging to a specific DO will be reinforced in the national market, but the main benefit will be in international markets. The amount of money spent to enhance the image of Spanish and Portuguese wines will increase considerably from both public and private sources.

The many small firms will have to concentrate on local markets where they will be fully recognized, and only family firms are likely to survive. Medium-sized firms will try to enter foreign markets but only those producing high-value wines will compete successfully for niche markets in various countries.

At the same time, wine producers in Spain and Portugal will have to compete with many foreign wines in their domestic markets, and consumers will become more familiar with other wine styles. While importers' market shares will not increase greatly, their presence in the domestic market will be more noticeable in the years ahead.

REFERENCE

Anderson K. and D. Norman (2003), *Global Wine Production, Consumption and Trade, 1961 to 2001: A Statistical Compendium*, Adelaide: Centre for International Economic Studies.

6. Germany

Karl Storchmann and Günter Schamel

Germany is the eighth-largest wine producer in the world and is well known for its white wines such as Riesling or Müller-Thurgau. For more than a decade, vineyard area and production levels have remained virtually unchanged. However, there have been significant structural changes in the industry. The proportion of red varieties planted in Germany has grown from 16 per cent to over 26 per cent, while mass-produced white varieties are declining, and production is increasingly focusing on premium quality.

Germany is also the world's fourth largest consumer market for wine. More than two-thirds of all households buy wine, which is the only alcoholic beverage with an increasing per capita consumption. However, as Germans consume more reds, the share of domestic wine in total sales keeps falling and, in 2000, red wine overtook white wine consumption.

Discount stores dominate wine retailing, capturing over 37 per cent of total wine sales and 75 per cent of foreign wine sales. The percentage of higher-priced wines sold in Germany is very low, with only about one-eighth of sales at prices above 7 euros per standard bottle size. Almost 40 per cent of all domestically produced wine is sold directly by producers or their cooperatives.

Germany now imports more than half of its domestic wine consumption. New World producers are gaining ground relative to traditional European suppliers. Only about 25 per cent of German production is exported, half of which goes to the UK. High-quality exports mostly go to the USA and Japan, while ordinary table wine is exported to other European countries.

BRIEF HISTORY

The German wine culture is more than 2000 years old. The wild vine, the *Vitis silvestris*, found in certain districts especially in the Rhine valley, existed from the time of the last Ice Age. Judging from seeds that have been found, it must have been in Germany more than 4000 years ago. Pips of the vine indicate that the population of these districts ate the bluish and greenish wild grapes as part of their diet. Long before the Romans entered Germany, German tribes must have produced some alcoholic beverage from the wild grapes. Whether or not they also tried to cultivate the vine cannot be confirmed, but some believe this to be so. Long before the Roman occupation, the Roman writer Posidanius (135–51 BC) wrote that the Germans drank a lot of undiluted wine (Hallgarten, 1976).

We know from Cicero (106–43 BC) that a decree of the Roman Senate prohibited viticulture in the provinces of the Empire so as to ensure of a Roman wine monopoly (Hallgarten, 1976). Emperor Domition passed a second decree prohibiting viticulture in AD 91. This was changed in the second century, when the Emperor Probus denounced Rome's monopoly in viticulture and the wine trade and did all he could to further viticulture in the occupied countries. From the first centuries AD, the Romans produced wines in many German districts, mainly in the valleys of the rivers Rhine and Mosel. This has been confirmed by many discoveries of old Roman wine presses and related tools (Matheus, 1997).

During subsequent centuries German viticulture was widely extended, even to Northern Germany and the Baltic provinces. This occurred mainly through the monasteries, which produced their own wines for celebrating Mass. For liturgical purposes, the Church preferred the wine to be red. Hence the production of red wine was much larger than that of white wine, even on the Mosel, where today virtually no red wine is to be found (Hallgarten, 1976).

In the early medieval times the area devoted to viticulture increased considerably, reaching an all-time maximum in the early fifteenth century. During this period wine was produced all over Germany, even above latitude of 54° North. This development was driven by increasing demand, extensive tariff systems and a remarkably warm climate at that time. According to the *Historical Climate Database*, the peak of wine production coincides with steadily increasing temperatures from the eleventh to the late fourteenth century, pushing the margin of wine production further north (Glaser, 2001). The peak of viticultural spread in the early fifteenth century is also the beginning of the so-called 'little Ice Age'. From the early fifteenth century average temperatures were decreasing until the late seventeenth century, during which time the area devoted to vines shrank to the regions most suited for wine production. Moreover, the formation of the Customs Union in Germany in 1834 and the resulting fall of protecting tariff barriers led to greater competition in the wine market. As soon as the wines from the important wine-growing districts (the Palatinate, Rheinhessen, the Rheingau and the Mosel) could be transported all over Germany, without paying duty from one principality to the next, the price of the very ordinary, mass-produced wines fell dramatically: from 250 thalers to less than 20 thalers per 1000 litres in 1850 (Hallgarten, 1976; Winter-Tarvainen, 1992). This intensified the pressure to enhance efficiency. Nowadays, all German wine production is located south of 50° latitude.

PRODUCTION

In 2000 there were about 68 000 estates growing vines in 13 defined wine-growing regions. With a total output of about 10 million hl, Germany was the world's seventh largest wine producer in 2001, just behind South Africa and slightly ahead of Australia. Table 6.1 shows the vineyard area, the must production and the main varieties by growing region. With the exception of the two eastern German regions Saale-Unstrut and Sachsen, the entire German wine production comes from the relatively mild climate of the valley of the Rhine and its tributaries, the Mosel, Main and Ahr. Since these regions are located at the northernmost frontier of wine production, vineyard attributes such as aspect and steepness are crucial in order to gather and optimize the scarce but critical sunlight. Therefore, most vineyards are located on steep slopes with a southern aspect. Like a solar panel, an optimally tilted vineyard in the Mosel valley can catch almost as much sun energy as a flat spot at the equator (Ashenfelter and Storchmann, 2001).

After a steady expansion from the 1950s until the beginning of the1990s, the total vineyard area in Germany has changed little during the past ten years, but there have been significant changes within the structure of varieties. First, low-quality varieties such as Müller-Thurgau and Kerner are in decline. The share of Müller-Thurgau dropped from 24 per cent in 1990 to 19 per cent in 2000, leaving Riesling again as the dominant variety (Table 6.2).

Second, and more important, following persistently changing consumer preferences, there has been a strong shift from white to red grape varieties. The fraction of red grape varieties increased in the 1990s from 16 to 26 per cent. This is mainly due to an expansion of two varieties: the Pinot Noir area grew from 5.5 per cent to 8.8 per cent of the total vineyard area, making it the third most important variety after Riesling and Müller-Thurgau; and the dark and colour-intensive mass grape Dornfelder has more than tripled, from 1.2 per cent to 4.2 per cent.

Since total vineyard area expansion is restricted by EU laws, replacement with different grape varieties is the main means of adjusting supply to changes in wine demand. Therefore, the trend to replace mass-producing white varieties with red grapes can be expected to continue unless and until fashions change again. The German wine industry did not allow the cultivation of non-indigenous grape varieties such as Chardonnay, Sauvignon Blanc, Cabernet Sauvignon, or Merlot, but rising global wine market competition has eased this restriction so that in most German wine regions 'new varieties' are advancing rapidly. For instance, the share of Chardonnay in Germany's total vineyard area has risen from 0.0 per cent in 1990 to 0.6 per cent in 2000.

Table 6.1 Vineyard area and yields, Germany, 2000

Wine-growing region	Vineyard area ('000 ha)	Yield ('000 hl)	Yield per ha (hl)	Main variety
Ahr	513	46	89	Pinot Noir
Baden	15 372	1 225	80	Pinot Noir, Müller-Thurgau
Franken	5 925	480	81	Müller-Thurgau, Silvaner
Hessische Bergstrasse	443	42	95	Riesling
Mittelrhein	540	45	84	Riesling
Mosel–Saar–Ruwer	11 042	1 128	102	Riesling
Nahe	4 428	361	82	Riesling
Pfalz	22 606	2 611	116	Riesling, Müller-Thurgau
Rheingau	3 144	275	88	Riesling
Rheinhessen	25 596	2 606	102	Müller-Thurgau, Silvaner
Saale–Unstrut	621	42	68	Müller-Thurgau, Pinot Blanc
Sachsen	415	23	56	Müller-Thurgau, Riesling
Württemberg	10 903	1 197	110	Trollinger, Riesling
Total	101 548	10 099	99	Riesling, Müller-Thurgau

Source: Deutsches Weininstitut (2001).

Table 6.2   Winegrape varieties, Germany, 1990–2000 (% of total vineyard area)

	1990	1995	1996	1997	1998	1999	2000
Total white grapes	83.8	80.9	80.0	78.8	77.3	75.9	74.0
Riesling	20.8	21.9	21.9	21.8	21.8	21.4	21.1
Müller-Thurgau	24.2	22.2	21.7	21.2	20.4	19.8	19.1
Silvaner	7.7	7.1	7.1	6.9	6.8	6.6	6.4
Kerner	7.5	7.1	7.1	7.0	6.7	6.6	6.2
Others	23.6	22.6	22.2	21.9	21.6	21.5	21.2
Total red grapes	16.2	19.1	20.0	21.2	22.7	24.1	26.0
Pinot Noir	5.5	6.8	7.1	7.4	7.9	8.3	8.8
Portugieser	4.0	4.2	4.3	4.5	4.5	4.7	4.8
Dornfelder	1.2	1.8	2.0	2.5	3.1	3.6	4.2
Others	5.5	6.3	6.6	6.8	7.2	7.5	8.2

Source: Deutsches Weininstitut (2001).

Table 6.3   Wine exports, Germany, 1970–2000

Year	Volume ('000 hl)	Value (million DM)	Unit value (DM/hl)
1970	319	99	312
1980	1727	584	338
1985	2727	982	360
1990	2588	727	281
1991	2321	665	286
1992	2721	745	274
1993	2450	547	223
1994	2333	581	249
1995	2392	633	265
1996	2360	689	292
1997	2178	680	312
1998	2137	703	329
1999	2145	679	317
2000	2254	659	293

Source: Deutsches Weininstitut (2001).

EXPORTS

Most of the domestically produced wine is consumed within Germany, with only one-quarter exported. The total volume of wine exported has changed little for over 15 years, fluctuating between 2.2 and 2.7 million hl per year (Table 6.3). The total annual value of German wine exports ranged between 550 and 700 million DM in the 1990s. Only in 1985 was it considerably higher, amounting to almost 1 billion DM. This was due to the high volume exported, as well as to higher unit values. The 1985 average price of 360 DM/hl has never been achieved since. After 1985, prices of exported wines dropped considerably and reached their trough in 1993 at 223 DM/hl. Since then prices have recovered somewhat, to more than 300 DM/hl in the late 1990s.

Table 6.4   German wine exports, by country of destination, 1999

Country	Volume ('000 hl)	Value (million DM)	Unit value (DM/hl)	Volume share (%)	Value share (%)
UK	982	240	245	45.8	35.4
The Netherlands	253	65	254	11.8	9.5
Japan	146	89	609	6.8	13.1
USA	114	62	546	5.3	9.2
Sweden	96	31	325	4.5	4.6
Denmark	87	18	205	4.0	2.6
France	86	22	256	4.0	3.3
Belgium/Lux.	50	14	283	2.3	2.1
Norway	43	15	340	2.0	2.2
Canada	39	16	403	1.8	2.3
Brazil	28	8	293	1.3	1.2
Ireland	27	7	261	1.3	1.0
Finland	23	8	326	1.1	1.1
Poland	23	7	303	1.1	1.0
Austria	22	18	811	1.0	2.6
Italy	16	2	141	0.8	0.3
Mexico	16	4	269	0.7	0.6
Latvia	9	6	718	0.4	0.9
South Korea	8	3	359	0.3	0.4
Switzerland	7	9	1268	0.3	1.3
Australia	5	2	467	0.2	0.4
Other countries	65	33	514	3.0	4.9

Source: Deutsches Weininstitut (2001).

This development is mainly driven by the structure of the export markets and economic growth in important consumer countries. As shown in Table 6.4, the UK is by far the most important export country for German wines: almost half of the entire exports go there. This is followed by the Netherlands, Japan and the USA. The last two are high-priced markets: whereas the average price of all German wine exports was 317 DM/hl in 1999, Japan and the USA imported wine worth 609 and 546 DM/hl, respectively. By contrast, countries such as Denmark (205 DM/hl) and Italy (141 DM/hl) import mainly inexpensive German wines. Overall, exports in non-EU countries (507 DM/hl) yield prices twice as high as exports into EU countries (259 DM/hl).

IMPORTS

Germany imports slightly more than half of its domestic consumption. Table 6.5 shows import figures for the year 2000 published by the German Wine Institute (DWI, 2001). In volume terms, Italy was by far the biggest source of imports, with a 44 per cent share, down from 50 per cent in 1999. In value terms, however, France's share is about equal to Italy's at 32 per cent, reflecting much higher prices being paid for French wines (438 DM/hl versus 222 DM/hl for Italian imports). Spain captures another sizeable fraction of the German import market, with a share of 12 per cent by volume and 15 per cent by value in 2000. Together, France, Italy and Spain supply all but one-fifth of German imports. Despite the recent success of New World wines in Europe, their share of German imports rose from just 2 per cent in the mid-1990s to 5.3 per cent by 2001, according to Anderson and Norman (2003, Table 102). However, these numbers might be somewhat understated as some wines may have been re-exported by the UK.

During the 1990s, the volume of wine imports to Germany increased by about 40 per cent to 14 million hl (Anderson and Norman, 2003). During the same period, the share of non-EU imports has stayed within a 10–12 per cent range. Before that, during the 1970s and 1980s, German imports fluctuated between 8 and 11 million hl, depending largely on yield variations in the source countries.

Changes in the source of wine imports to Germany began at the end of the millennium. Comparing the statistics for 2000 with those for 1999 shows relatively large changes in volume terms for Australia (+63 per cent), the USA (+50 per cent), South Africa (+46 per cent), Chile (+25 per cent) and New Zealand (up 51 per cent from a very tiny base). Losing ground are France (–10 per cent), Italy (–6 per cent) and Romania (–16 per cent). Imports from other EU countries are down about 5 per cent. Clearly the New World producers have begun to gain ground in Germany at the cost of more traditional

Table 6.5   German wine imports, by country of origin,[a] 2000

Country	Value (million DM)	Volume ('000 hl)	Unit value (DM/hl)	Value share (%)	Volume share (%)	Value change[b] (%)	Volume change[b] (%)
France	1 157	2 639	438	32.3	21.8	−11	−10
Italy	1 188	5 364	222	33.2	44.3	−8	−6
Spain	531	1 394	381	14.8	11.5	12	10
USA	129	206	628	3.6	1.7	51	50
Chile	90	212	426	2.5	1.8	36	25
Greece	57	201	283	1.6	1.7	1	0
Australia	73	130	560	2.0	1.1	61	63
Austria	43	255	170	1.2	2.1	5	12
Portugal	41	106	390	1.2	0.9	3	6
Macedonia	40	477	84	1.1	3.9	2	15
Hungary	48	246	195	1.3	2.0	25	22
South Africa	58	132	438	1.6	1.1	56	46
Bulgaria	29	196	145	0.8	1.6	−15	−8
Romania	17	132	125	0.5	1.1	−24	−16
Cyprus	10	157	65	0.3	1.3	−21	−20
Argentina	17	43	398	0.5	0.4	46	18
New Zealand	4	5	745	0.1	0.0	5	51
Other countries	57	204	278	1.6	1.7	26	5
EU countries	3 021	9 967	303	84.3	82.4	−6	−5
Non-EU countries	564	2 135	264	15.7	17.6	28	13
Total	3 585	12 102	296	100.0	100.0	−2	−2

Notes:
[a] Preliminary data.
[b] Changes relative to 1999.

Source: Deutsches Weininstitut (2000).

European suppliers in volume and 6 per cent in value terms from the previous year.

Table 6.6 differentiates German wine imports by quality, style and colour. The volume share of white wine imports was 36 per cent compared to a value share of only 23 per cent in 2000. The share of white wine imports is declining as Germans import and consume more and more reds. However, this switch is not reflected in a decline in higher-quality white wine imports, which are increasing. Germans seem to be moving towards higher-quality imports of white wines and red wines in general. Because white table wine imports were down substantially by 11.6 per cent in 2000, a decline in the overall volume of wine imports of 2.2 per cent results. In value terms, however, wine imports were up by 2.1 per cent. Liqueur and dessert wine imports are in decline, as well as aromatized and sparkling wines. Sparkling wine imports were down

Table 6.6   German wine imports, by quality, style and colour,[a] 2000

	Value ('000 hl)	Volume (million DM)	Unit value (DM/hl)	Volume share (%)	Value share (%)	Volume change[b] (%)	Value change[b] (%)
White wine	4 296	809	188	35.8	22.7	−8.6	−3.5
Quality wine	973	395	407	22.6	48.8	3.4	+0.5
Table wine	3 323	414	125	77.4	51.2	−11.6	−6.9
Red wine	5 967	1 914	321	49.7	53.6	4.9	+4.7
Quality wine	2 302	1 128	490	38.6	58.9	2.6	−1.2
Table wine	3 565	786	221	59.7	41.1	3.6	14.4
White and red total	10 163	2 723	268	84.6	76.2	−2.2	+2.1
Quality wine	3 275	1 523	465	32.2	55.9	2.8	−0.8
Table wine	6 888	1 200	174	67.8	44.1	−4.3	+6.0
Liqueur, dessert	108	47	435	0.9	1.3	−18.3	−13.8
Aromatised wine	523	47	90	4.4	1.3	29.4	−6.0
Sparkling wine	929	666	717	7.7	18.6	−13.0	−15.2
Other wine styles	290	91	312	2.4	2.5	13.8	+9.3
Total	12 011	3 573	298	100.0	100.0	−1.9	−1.8

Notes:
[a] Preliminary data.
[b] Changes relative to 1999.

Source: Deutsches Weininstitut (2000).

sharply in 2000, probably as expected after an increase of more than 20 per cent due to the millennium effect in the previous year. Total imports for all wine styles were down by 1.9 per cent volume and 1.8 per cent in value terms in the year 2000 following a slight increase of 1 per cent in the previous year.

CONSUMPTION

Germany is the world's fourth largest wine market in terms of volume consumed, after France, Italy and the USA. On a per capita basis its consumption is about 24 litres per year.

The relative importance of still wine consumption compared to other alcoholic and non-alcoholic beverages remained relatively constant during the 1990s, with a recent increase from about 18 to 19 litres per capita (Table 6.7). Between 1996 and 2000, the per capita consumption of all alcoholic beverages declined steadily (−4.3 per cent) while non-alcoholic beverage consumption expanded (+4.2 per cent). However, wine (and especially red wine) is the only alcoholic beverage type that showed an increase in per capita consumption.

Table 6.7   Beverage consumption, Germany, 1996–2000 (litres per capita)

	1996	1997	1998	1999	2000	% change 1996/2000
Alcoholic	161	160	156	156	154	−4.3
Beer	132	131	128	128	126	−4.9
Still wine	18	18	18	18	19	+3.8
Sparkling	5	5	5	5	4	−14.6
Spirits	6	6	6	6	6	−7.9
Non-alcoholic	502	506	509	520	523	+4.2
Total	663	666	665	677	677	+2.1

Source: Deutsches Weininstitut (2001).

According to Anderson and Norman (2003), German per capita wine consumption in 2001 is ranked fourteenth in the world, at less than half that of France, Italy and Portugal. The latter group's consumption has been falling, however, whereas Germany's has been rising slightly.

On a historical note, it is worth mentioning that per capita consumption of still wine has always been higher in the former West Germany, and this continues today. However, East Germans continue to consume more sparkling wine per capita (GfK, 2001). Consumption levels in the western part increased significantly in the late 1960s and early 1970s, but then stayed fairly constant at between 23 and 25 litres per capita (Anderson and Norman, 2003). At the time of reunification, overall per capita wine consumption declined, but it is now approaching the pre-unification levels observed in the western part.

A GfK[1] consumer survey for Germany shows that in the year 2000, 69 per cent of all households in Germany bought wine, a 2 per cent gain over the previous year (Table 6.8). This percentage is higher in the former East Germany, where 75 per cent of all households buy wine. The survey also shows that the market share for domestic wines was 49 per cent in 2000, ahead of French wines with 16 per cent and Italian wines with 13 per cent (GfK, 2001). However, domestically produced wine is rapidly losing favour with the Germans as their market share dropped by almost 10 per cent during the five years to 2000. So even though Germany's imports of French and Italian wines have been declining in volume and value over recent years, their market shares in volume terms actually increased because of the loss of interest in domestic wines.

Germany used to be a classic white wine country. In 1995, German consumers still clearly preferred white wine (54 per cent) to red wine (37 per

Table 6.8   Consumer buying trends, Germany, 1995–2000

	1995	1996	1997	1998	1999	2000	% change 1995/2000
Households buying wine (%)	62	65	63	67	67	69	6.5
Market shares (volume, %)							
German wine	59	55	52	49	50	49	−9.9
French wine	13	15	16	17	17	16	3.0
Italian wine	11	10	12	12	12	13	2.0
Others	17	20	20	22	21	22	4.9
White wine	54	52	49	48	47	43	−10.7
Red wine	37	40	43	44	45	48	11.4
Rosé	9	8	8	8	8	8	−0.7
German white wine	71	69	67	69	68	64	−7.0
German red wine	18	21	24	25	25	28	10.0
German rosé	11	10	9	6	7	8	−3.0
Average prices (DM/lira)							
Wine total	5.45	5.83	5.91	5.80	6.06	6.09	11.7
German wine	5.75	6.28	6.40	6.55	6.55	6.50	13.0
Imported wine	–	–	–	–	5.57	5.71	–
White wine	5.47	5.93	5.86	5.59	5.72	5.71	4.4
Red wine	–	–	–	–	6.49	6.57	–
Place of purchase (%)							
Wineries/cooperatives	19	21	21	20	19	19	−0.4
Supermarkets	24	24	23	23	24	24	−0.1
Specialty trade	8	8	8	6	7	7	−1.0
Discount	31	30	31	36	36	37	6.5
Other outlets	18	17	17	15	13	13	−5.0

Source: Deutsches Weininstitut (2001).

cent). However, for years consumers have increasingly favoured red wine. The latest GfK survey for 2000 revealed that about 48 per cent of wine consumption was red, 8 per cent rosé and only 43 per cent white wine (Table 6.8). Thus the year 2000 marks the first year that Germans drank more red wine than white wine. Overall, the share of white wine consumption has declined by more than 10 per cent during the five years to 2000 as the reds have taken over. Among German wines consumed, reds are also advancing, increasing by 10 per cent between 1995 and 2000.

The average retail price paid for German wine was 6.50 DM/litre, while imported wine sold for 5.71 DM/litre in 2000 (Table 6.8). The increasing popularity of red wine is also reflected in their price: on average a litre of red wine sold for 6.57 DM while a litre of white wine sold for only 5.71 DM. German red wine sold at an average price of 8.08 DM/litre, which was considerably more expensive than imported red wine, which sold for only 5.98 DM/litre.

Point-of-purchase statistics for wine are also revealing. In German retailing, discount stores have a predominant role, capturing over 37 per cent of total wine sales (typically selling wine-in-a-box). Recently, they have been capturing an extra percentage of the market each year, while supermarkets have been keeping a steady market share of about 24 per cent. About 40 per cent of all German wine is sold directly by the producer or their cooperatives (GfK, 2001). By way of contrast, three-quarters of all foreign wines are sold through discount stores. Aldi, the market leader among discount stores, alone sells one-quarter of all foreign wine. To a large extent, this also explains the price structure of wines sold in Germany. Only about 12 per cent of all wine is sold at prices above 10 DM, while 25 per cent sell for less than 3 DM per standard bottle size. For domestically produced wine this picture is somewhat more favourable, with a 13 per cent share costing 10 DM or more and only about 19 per cent selling for less than 3 DM per standard bottle size in 2000 (DWI, 2001).

SUMMARY AND PROSPECTS

Germany is the world's eighth largest wine producer, well known for its white wines such as Riesling and Müller-Thurgau. Vineyard area and production quantities have changed little for more than a decade. This is very different from more dynamic New World producers such as Australia, Chile and Argentina. However, there have been significant structural changes, reflecting changes in consumer demand: the portion of vineyard area planted with red wine varieties grew from 16 per cent to over 26 per cent in the 1990s, mass-producing white varieties are on the decline, and production is increasingly focusing on high-quality wines. Most of Germany's production is consumed domestically, with only about 25 per cent of total production exported, half of which goes to the UK. Whereas most European countries import only ordinary German table wines, high-price exporters rely almost exclusively on the USA and Japan. Exports to those countries achieve prices which are far higher than those commanded by exports to EU countries.

Germany is the world's fourth largest consumer of wine, with a per capita consumption of 24 litres of still and sparkling wine. Two-thirds of all households buy wine. It is the only alcoholic beverage that has been showing an increase in per capita consumption levels. However, German wine is growing out of favour with the Germans: as they consume more and more reds, the market share of domestic producers has been falling steadily. Germany now imports more than half of its domestic consumption, with New World producers strongly gaining ground relative to their European competitors.

Having always preferred white wine, German consumers have recently begun to favour red wine, and for the first time in 2000 Germans drank more red wine than white wine.

Discount stores have a predominant role in German retailing, capturing over 37 per cent of total wine sales. To a large extent, this explains why only about 12 per cent of all wine is sold at prices above 10 DM and 25 per cent sells for less than 3 DM per standard bottle size. Moreover, three-quarters of all foreign wines are sold at discount stores, while almost 40 per cent of all German wine is sold directly by producers or their cooperatives.

The prospects for the German wine market over the next decade will be largely determined by global developments. Whether the trend to export relatively highly priced German wines to the USA and Japan will continue is doubtful given recent economic developments, including the drop in wine prices in international markets. However, for German consumers, quality wine imports are likely to become cheaper and, given that, the importance of discount stores as a sales outlet especially for imported wine will continue to grow. Since German consumers are known for their price and quality consciousness, the anticipated price squeeze will make Germany a very competitive export market in the coming years. On the domestic production side, the trend to replace traditional, mass-produced white varieties with red grapes will persist as long as the trend towards more red wine consumption continues.

NOTE

1. Gesellschaft für Konsumforschung (GfK) is a private consumer research firm surveying 17 000 representative German households and their consumption habits annually.

REFERENCES

Anderson K. and D. Norman (2003), *Global Wine Consumption and Trade, 1961 to 2001: A Statistical Compendium*, Adelaide: Centre for International Economic Studies.

Ashenfelter, O. and K. Storchmann (2001), 'The Quality of Vineyard Sites in the Mosel Valley of Germany', in *Oenometrie VIII*, 8th annual meeting of the Vineyard Data Quantification Society in St Helena/California.

Deutsches Weininstitut – DWI (2001), *Deutscher Wein – Statistik*, various annual issues, Mainz.

Gesellschaft für Konsumforschung – GfK (2001), *Consumer Household Surveys*, Nürnberg. http://www.gfk.de

Glaser, R. (2001), *Klimageschichte Mitteleuropas, 1000 Jahre Wetter, Klima, Katastrophen*. Darmstadt: Primus Verlag.

Hallgarten, S.F. (1976), *German Wines*, London: Publivin.

Matheus, M. (1997), 'Weinbau zwischen Maas und Rhein in der Antike und im Mittelalter', Trierer Historische Forschungen, 23, Verlag Philip von Zabern, Mainz.

Winter-Tarvainen, A. (1992), 'Weinbaukrise und preussischer Staat', Verlag Trierer Historische Forschungen, Trier.

7. The United Kingdom

Sally Stening, Klaus Kilov, Larry Lockshin and Tony Spawton

The UK is a major market for many wine-exporting countries. Negligible local production and rising per capita consumption provide an expanding market for wine producers and shippers alike. Throughout the 1990s the UK market grew by nearly 4 per cent per year. Although consumption is lower than in southern European countries, the UK is one of the key countries where per capita consumption of wine continues to rise, signalling further growth prospects for successful exporters. At a time when many countries' wine production outstrips their consumption, markets such as the UK become increasingly important.

Not only is growth in market volume encouraging to exporters, but increases in the market value show that the average price paid for a bottle of wine also continues to increase. Euromonitor's 1999 report shows that over the 1998/99 period, when volume grew 5 per cent, market value grew at 6 per cent (at current prices). This is indicative of previous years, which have also seen growth in market value outpace growth in market volume.

Historically, UK wine merchants were instrumental in the development of wine regions such as Bordeaux and the Douro. UK consumer and merchant demands for a system of quality control have shaped wine laws in other parts of Europe, thereby influencing wine production in EU exporting countries. More recently, UK multinational drinks companies have come to influence the global wine industry through their acquisition of wine producers in numerous countries around the globe.

HISTORY

The Roman occupation has been widely credited with bringing the vine to England, and while wine had been imported into the UK from the second century BC, it was only after the Roman occupation that vineyards began appearing in southern England (Unwin, 1991a; Burnett, 1999). Towards the end of the fourth century AD and the decline of the Roman Empire, Christianity became instrumental in the proliferation of wine. Requiring wine for the Eucharist, monastic estates developed vineyards as far north as York (Burnett, 1999). Private vineyards were also being planted, and by the time of the Domesday survey in 1086, 78 of England's 130 vineyards were lay vineyards and the remainder ecclesiastical (Burnett, 1999; English Wine Producers, 2001). Wine had become a drink of status, consumed by nobles and courtiers, and with that domestic demand for wine the local wine industry flourished. Competition from Bordeaux and later Portugal undoubtedly affected viticulture in England, but may not be solely responsible for the decline of British viticulture. The dissolution of the monasteries and climatic changes also led to the decline of viticulture (English Wine Producers, 2001). Wine consumption continued to increase with the marriage of Henry II to Eleanor of Aquitaine in 1152. The marriage brought the area of Gascony (including Bordeaux) under the control of the crown and with it abundant supplies of wine. In addition to the abundant supply, Henry II, in order to win favour with the people of Gascony, ensured that Gascon wine was cheaper to buy for the English than any other wine, imported or home produced (Burnett, 1999; Unwin, 1991a).

Trade wars between France and the UK saw the importing of French wines prohibited, and in 1693 the bans were replaced by prohibitive duties (Robinson, 1994). Further treaties with the Portuguese shaped wine consumption in the UK, and duties were set on imported wine, which made French wines considerably more expensive than those from Portugal and Spain (Burnett, 1999). The War of the Spanish Succession saw British trade with France cease once again (Robinson, 1994). The Methuen Treaty cemented Portugal's position in the English wine market, stipulating 'tariffs on Portuguese wines would not exceed two-thirds of those on French [wines]'; in the 1700s 65 per cent of wine imported into the UK was Portuguese (Burnett, 1999, p. 145). Portuguese producers enjoyed the lower duties until 1813, when the Methuen Treaty was abandoned and all European wines were taxed at the one rate (Unwin, 1991a).

High consumption of alcohol, mostly in the form of spirits and ale, led to an increased presence of the temperance movement. In 1861 duties on all wines became based on alcohol content and excise duties were further lowered. Lowering of duties was in part to reduce the profitability of doctoring wines, but also responded to the growing temperance movement. Temperate views also saw licences become available to eating houses in order to encourage the consumption of wine with food (Burnett, 1999), a sentiment that is echoed in many of today's licensing laws.

Wine trade between Portugal and Great Britain not only shaped British laws but also Portuguese wine laws. Scandals arising from the adulteration and the overproduction of wine led to a fall in wine prices in the eighteenth century, threatening the prosperity of the Anglo-Portuguese wine trade

(Robinson, 1994). To protect the Portuguese wine industry, in 1756 regulations were introduced including the demarcation of Port-producing vineyards
to guarantee the quality and authenticity of wines sold to British merchants.
Similarly, regulations were imposed by Bordeaux vignerons. At the time, these
regulations provided a type of quality assurance, guaranteeing authenticity of
products for the merchants and future sales for vignerons.

In the late 1800s and early 1900s more temperate views saw the lower-alcohol French wines increase in popularity as a source of table wine, but
Portuguese and Spanish wines continued to dominate the market. Wine continued to be a part of British culture enjoyed by a widening range of consumers
despite a decline in per capita consumption. Gladstone, the then exchequer,
had introduced the first off-premise licences in 1861, which is when wine
retailing began to prosper. For example, one of the pioneers of the English
wine trade, The Victoria Wine Company (today part of the First Quench
group) was established in 1865.

Supplies of wine from France were severely affected by World War I,
resulting in a temporary resurgence in the more readily available Port. The
postwar economic climate was undoubtedly a major influence on production
of British wines, which re-emerged in this era. Made in the UK from imported
material, British wines were free of customs duties and subject to lower taxes
than imported finished wine. Import duties were also changed to favour wines
made in colonies of the British Empire. Australian wine entered the UK
market and was readily accepted by consumers. World War II similarly
stemmed wine consumption in the UK, when import duties on wine were
increased more than fivefold.

Wine retailing had begun to change its structure in the late 1800s and then
in the 1900s the modern wine merchant began to emerge. By 1911 Victoria
Wines had 96 branches selling a wide variety of wine styles (Unwin, 1991b).
A number of wine merchants that not only shipped but also sold wine emerged
in this period, such as Victoria Wines and Gilbeys. Wider selections of wines
necessitated the use of proprietary labelling of wines: wines previously
labelled under the name of the shipper were now sold under the label of the
producer (Unwin, 1991b).

Aided by the post-World War II reduction of duties on table wine and the
marketing efforts of wine producers, consumption of wine in the UK began
once again to rise (Unwin, 1991b). In the 1950s, while the wine sector had
been undergoing gradual changes, the beer sector had been undergoing a
period of consolidation (Figures 7.1 and 7.2). As a result, breweries began to
turn their attention toward the wine sector. As beer and spirits consumption
declined and wine consumption increased, brewing groups began to acquire
wine merchants, for example Allied's acquisition of Victoria Wine.

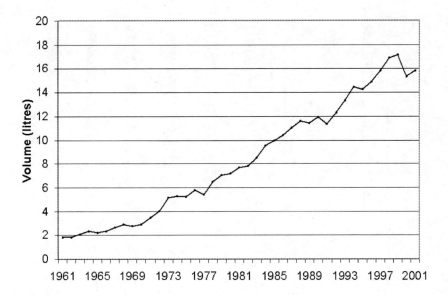

Source: Anderson and Norman (2003, Table 69).

Figure 7.1 Wine consumption per capita, UK, 1961–2001

Even though changes that have occurred in the UK market have been at a national level, their effects have been felt by the global wine trade. In some ways the fate of the UK wine industry has been tied to that of the UK breweries. Declining beer consumption in the post-World War II period coincided with major reshaping of the breweries. The result was a reduction in the number of breweries, from 1000 in 1937 to 160 in 1982. By 1989 the top six breweries had 75 per cent of the beer market in the UK (Unwin, 1991b). The 1980s and 1990s saw many breweries enter the wine market through acquisition. Declining consumption of both beer and spirits increased the appeal of wine-related enterprises within the alcoholic beverages sector. Acquisitions included wine retailers, wholesalers and producers. The philosophy behind these acquisitions was most likely to capitalize on apparent synergies within the alcoholic beverages market. Irrespective of whether or not that happened, the move has created multinational companies within the wine sector. The metamorphosis of Allied Brewing, a brewer with interests in wine retail, to the present-day Allied Domecq, a multinational wine and spirits company, illustrates the changing structures within the UK alcoholic beverages industry. In August/September 2001 Allied Domecq purchased Montana Wines (New Zealand's largest wine producer), Kuemmerling GmbH (a German bitters maker) and entered negotiations to purchase Bodegas y Bebidas (Spain's

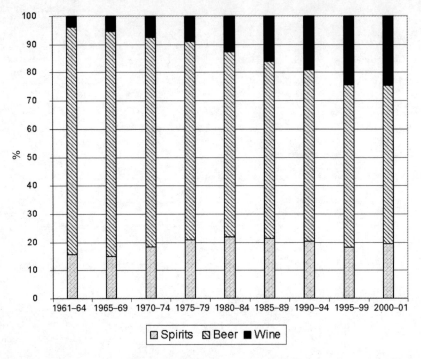

Source: Anderson and Norman (2003, Tables 70–74).

*Figure 7.2   Shares of wine, beer and spirits in total alcohol consumption,
            UK, 1961–2001*

largest bodega). These purchases added to Allied Domecq's previous wine
sector purchases, which include sizeable interests in Chile. While there are
only a few of these multinational drinks companies, their acquisitions have
lasting effects and are part of a worldwide trend which sees the gap between
small and large enterprises growing, with very few organizations occupying
the middle ground.

  Despite its predominantly post-production orientation, the UK wine industry has, for centuries, been a highly influential force on the world wine market.
The 1990s have seen further radical changes to the UK wine market with the
advent of flying winemakers, the joining of the EU, and burgeoning domestic
production. The metamorphosis of the industry continues today with multi-
sector global corporations, which arose in the 1970s and 1980s, bringing
producers and agents from around the globe together under the one corporate
banner.

CONSUMER TRENDS

Growing per capita consumption, paired with negligible domestic wine production, ensures that the UK is an attractive market for wine-exporting countries to pursue. Imports grew steadily over the 1990s (Figure 7.3), continuing the trend since the 1960s. The wine imported by the UK four decades ago was priced well above the global average, but with the growth in demand for lower-priced wine the UK average import price is now very much closer to the global average, as reflected in the convergence of the volume and value trends in Figure 7.4.

The highest rate of wine consumption within the UK is concentrated around the greater London area, but with the strengthening of economic centres in the north of England these areas are now also increasing their levels of wine consumption.

The heaviest purchasers of wine in the UK are 35–54 year olds (Mintel, 2000). The last decade has seen wine consumption by this segment grow steadily, and it is predicted that this growth will continue, with population increases for this age group predicted to grow into the next decade.

Gaining attention from marketers within the industry are female wine consumers: because more women are now in the workforce, they have a higher disposable income than in previous generations. Female wine consumption is beginning to mirror male consumption, in terms of situation and products consumed. The transition of pubs and bars from male-dominated establishments to unisex areas is influencing women's consumption patterns in following those

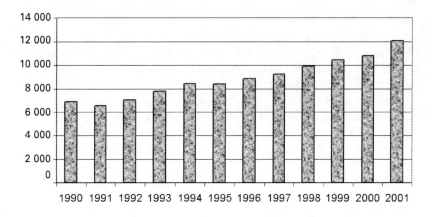

Source: Anderson and Norman (2003, Table 27).

Figure 7.3   Wine imports, UK, 1990–2001 ('000 hl)

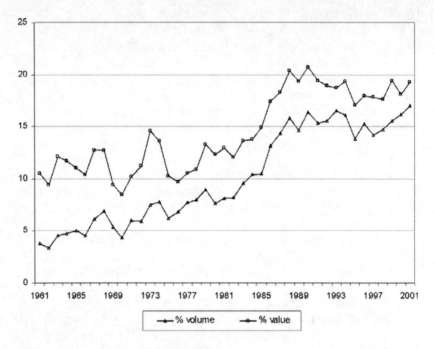

Source: Anderson and Norman (2003, Table 84).

Figure 7.4   UK share of world imports of wine, 1961–2001

of men, particularly in regard to drinking as part of socializing after work. Unpublished research shows that the trend of women drinking after work is not unique to the UK market, with similar trends being noted in Australia, Japan and France. It is likely that the increased patronage of female wine consumers in the on-trade has driven the small amount of growth experienced by this sector of the industry.

Although producers have focused their attention on the young female market, many of the products have been unsuccessful, being seen as patronizing by the target market. Also, the segment has gained the attention of beer and spirit manufacturers, whose ready-to-drink products and boutique beers have the advantage of single-serve packaging. Even so, wine's share of total alcohol consumption in the UK has been rising steadily (Figure 7.2).

The highly publicized enforcement of drink driving laws has been credited with changing the way in which alcohol is consumed. It is anticipated that the legal blood alcohol limit in the UK will be reduced from 80 mg to 50 mg as is currently enforced in other parts of Europe. Further changes to wine consumption can be expected although it is likely that they will be in the context of where wine is consumed, rather than how much, as drinking habits change to accommodate the changes in blood alcohol limits. As drink driving laws have been visibly enforced over the past decade, the future impact of reductions to the lower alcohol blood levels is expected to be minimal.

Increases in the standard of living in the second half of the 1990s have been credited with increasing the value of wine sold in the UK. There has also been an increase in consumer knowledge of wines. The Wine and Spirit Education Trust (WSET), which for many years has been responsible for training the UK wine industry, has seen increasing numbers of the general public undertaking their education courses. A growing number of students from outside the wine industry are sitting exams for the WSET Diploma, an award involving two years' part-time study (Fattorini, 1994). Increased wine knowledge and interest has led consumers to expect a wider variety of products to be at their disposal, and UK retailers have responded by sourcing wine from around the globe.

A trend that has yet to be capitalized on is the increasing demand for wine in 1.5 l packaging. In the USA, where supermarket sales also dominate the retail market, 1.5 l bottles or magnums of wine are the fastest-moving size package. This phenomenon seems to be a result of the stigma attached to bag-in-the-box packaging, sales of which have been in decline for at least a decade. Despite the connotations of inferior wine associated with the bag in the box, it is potentially the best packaging of bulk wine, because it minimizes spoilage once the product is opened.[1] Moves to introduce other wine-packaging innovations such as stelvin caps (screw caps) in the past had met with similar resistance by UK consumers, but that has begun to change.

The French paradox, which has had a major impact on many national wine markets, appears to have had little impact on the British wine consumer. Historically, UK consumer demand appeared to be more sensitive to price changes than health concerns or other influences. From the marriage of Henry II to the twentieth century, taxes and duties – designed to protect the domestic brewing industry – have influenced the British palate. The former strength of the breweries has waned, however, and is not as strong in today's alcoholic beverages industry. Indeed, with British multinational organizations now among the largest wine producers in the world, the wine industry has much increased its lobbying power. In addition to the growing strength of the wine sector, membership of the EU tempers any decisions to change excise duties or tariffs to favour the brewing sector.

WINE RETAILING

Off-trade

Sainsbury's became the first supermarket to acquire a licence to sell liquor, in

1962, and it was soon followed by other stores (Burnett, 1999). The introduction of supermarkets to the wine retail market drastically reshaped the UK off-trade. In the 1980s and 1990s sales of wine in the off-trade increased dramatically. Drink driving laws, the popularization of wine, a rise in home entertainment, the availability of high-quality, inexpensive wines from the New World, and the economic recession all contributed to increased wine consumption at home and hence sold at off-licences. By 1993 the off-trade accounted for 85 per cent of all wine sold in the UK (EIU Retail Business, 1994). Sales of wine through supermarkets have increased from 55 per cent of all wine sales in 1990 to 72 per cent in 2000.

Enjoying higher margins than other alcoholic beverages (approximately 30 per cent for wine as opposed to 5 to 10 per cent for beer and spirits), and accounting for approximately 45 per cent of all alcoholic beverages sold in the off-trade, wine represents an important category for the supermarkets. The supermarkets' promotion of wine as part of the evening meal has helped to popularize what had traditionally been a drink just for the upper classes. Wine has become an important category for the supermarkets, and multinational alcoholic beverage companies are beginning to concentrate their efforts to capitalize more on this market. Recent years have seen them divest their interests in the breweries so as to focus on wine and to a lesser extent spirits.

Heightened competition between supermarkets and wine specialists has seen the merging of many smaller specialists. While many of these mergers have been in the form of buyouts, they have enabled specialist retailers to create economies of scale. By 1999, two major groups emerged in the wine specialist retail market: Thresher and Victoria Wine merged to form the First Quench Group, and Parisa acquired Greenall Cellars.

In previous years, acquisitions of retailers have not only been by other retailers. For example, Seagrams acquired the Oddbins retail chain in 1984. The acquisition of retail chains by some multinational wine companies necessitated similar actions by competitors in order to provide retail outlets to champion the companies' portfolios of brands. Unlike the USA, the UK permits vertical integration within the industry, and indeed integration has been ongoing in the UK trade throughout the last century. Although vertical integration is not unusual within the UK industry, the current scale of this integration is unprecedented. The latter part of the 1990s has seen a reversal of some of the wine shippers with regard to their participation in the retail sector, and some multinationals have divested their retail interests. While there are no legal constraints on producers acquiring retailers, such investments may represent a conflict of interest, thereby negatively affecting other functions in the organization.

Supermarkets have also pursued strategies of vertical integration within their supply chains. In the early 1990s supermarkets began to source and ship wine directly from producers, with their buyers placed as far away as Australia. Supermarkets are now buying grapes, hiring a winemaker and producing wine under their own labels to increase their margins (as they have in the past with numerous other products). This vertical integration has enabled supermarkets to drive wine retail prices down, intensifying price wars with high-street wine specialists. Flying winemakers have been instrumental in this vertical integration, allowing supermarkets to buy the expertise necessary for wine production. In 1995, wines made by two flying winemakers, sourcing fruit from four different countries, accounted for 10 per cent (by volume) of Sainsbury's wine sales. Despite criticism from some wine journalists, who find these wines simplistic and one-dimensional, the wines offer a reliable and affordable product for their target customers, the average wine consumer.

Another trend emerging among wine specialists is their move to convenience retailing in an effort to differentiate themselves from the supermarkets. A recent Mintel report found that although supermarkets were the primary retail outlet for wine purchases for 72 per cent of respondents surveyed, only 33 per cent of secondary wine purchases were at a supermarket (Mintel, 2000). Results indicate that customers are using the wine specialist and small licenced grocers for their top-up purchases. Location strategies for wine specialist retailers have sought to capitalize on convenience as the key factor in the patronage, forming tie-ups with petrol station forecourt retailers and convenience store operators (just-drinks.com, 2001).

On-trade

The off-trade has been growing at the expense of the on-trade. Traditionally, wide choices of wine have not been available through public houses in the UK. With the growing interest in wine, this absence of good wine in on-trade establishments may have aided the growth in off-trade sales. Responding to the growth in sales of wine in the off-trade, many on-trade establishments extended their wine offerings, resulting in some growth in on-trade sales of wine in the early 1990s. A good indication of the popularization of wine in the UK is seen in the number of pubs now carrying a wider variety of wines.

The young adult market is an important consumer segment for the on-trade, and many alcoholic beverage producers are targeting this group. Beer and spirits dominate the products in the on-trade market, but New World wines are growing in popularity. Commentators believe this trend will continue with the trend of dining out, among young adults (Datamonitor, 1999). Wine's association with food will no doubt ensure its preference among consumers dining out, however, this is a small portion of the on-trade market. Single-serve products such as beers and the oxymoronic alcoholic soft drinks will continue to dominate this market.

Off-shore and Illegal Trade

As a result of rises in excise duty paid on imported wine, excise duties in the UK are currently much higher than in other EU countries (some of which impose no excise duty on such products). The creation in 1993 of the European Single Market has meant that British cross-channel shoppers can bring back effectively unlimited stocks of wine for their personal consumption. Such is the impact of these changes that supermarkets such as Sainsbury's and Tesco have opened branches in Calais, France in an attempt to stem the losses in their domestic wine sales. Although it is predominantly retailers in southeast England who are hardest hit by these new laws, these regions are also home to the majority of England's wine consumers. Some estimates place losses to the UK retail trade as high as £190 million per year in sales.

Even though some retailers have chosen to counteract the problem of cross-channel shopping by expanding operations off-shore, the loss of sales to cross-channel shopping and smuggling continues to plague UK wine retail. In the 2000 Mintel wine retailing survey, 6 per cent of respondents reported that they primarily purchased their wines duty free or abroad, and 10 per cent reported these as their secondary outlets for wine purchasing (in both cases these are increases on previous years). On 30 June 1999, after almost a decade of debate, duty-free shopping was abolished for intra-EU travellers. However, this has only gone part way to solving the cross-channel shopping problem. The cause and incentive for these activities remains the inequity of wine excise duties with those of neighbouring countries. The UK wine industry is ongoing in its lobbying for UK excise duties to be brought in line with other European countries. While the industry is yet to see any fruit from its labours, reductions to excise duties would appear inevitable. Indeed, the EU has announced their intention to 'abolish all differences in tax duties across the 15 EU member states' (Diston, 2001). Should excise duties and hence the incentive for smuggling be reduced, reported consumption of wine, beer and spirits in the UK will rise.

HOW WILL CHANGES IN RETAILING AFFECT WINE IMPORTERS?

When Threshers and Victoria Wines merged to form First Quench, management changed its merchandising strategies. To streamline inventory, any products not stocked by both wine merchants were discontinued. What impact does this have on the global industry? A major problem faced by exporters to the UK is the ability to supply sufficient quantities of wine to ensure year-round availability to customers. The sheer volume sales of any one stock-keeping unit (SKU) in the supermarkets prohibits many producers from contemplating supplying these retailers. Even smaller chains, such as Oddbins, require guarantees of around 1000 cases, or a container equivalent. Such quantities are greater than many small wineries' annual production. The growing size of many wine specialists creates problems for many small to medium producers seeking to export their wines to the UK.

Countries such as France, with more developed domestic markets, appear to have systems in place to cope with the changing face of UK retail. Despite the seeming rigidity of Appellation Controllée regulations, some advantages are fostered by such industry systems. From a marketing perspective labels are more frequently associated with *négociants* than individual growers and so, provided the grapes within the classification are available, production of particular 'brands' can be increased by the addition of more growers. Such structures are either not present or underdeveloped in New World wine-producing countries. It follows that smaller wineries seeking to export to the UK may need to approach the market collaboratively. Cooperatives or similar associations may be able to pool resources to reach the minimum quantities required when supplying the UK market.

Internet Retailing

Internet retailing has received much attention in recent years but, despite the overwhelming level of publicity this retail channel has received, 'e-tail' accounts for very little retail overall. In the UK as in other countries, e-tail remains a weak force in retail. E-tail has seen retailers forming strategic alliances: Oddbins and Sainsbury's on-line retail venture was one such alliance. But after initial enthusiasm has come the realization that, even without the shop front, e-tailers face many of the same costs as brick-and-mortar retailers, such as holding inventory and promotion of the site. One of the dangers with Internet retail is that it will cannibalize the retailer's brick-and-mortar sales. Retailers have realized the greatest success by using the Internet to provide another service to their current retail offering similar to home deliveries and credit facilities. This channel is thus unlikely to have a major impact on future wine consumption.

WINE EXPORTS

The UK's wine exports comprise British wine and wine re-exported. The latter is largely a product of wine brokerage firms, which are not uncommon in the UK. The wine brokerage market is perhaps an unusual, but not surprising

feature of the UK wine industry, given its history in the shipping and broker-
ing of wines. While wine brokers in other parts of the world tend to focus on
the sale of excess wines from one market to the next, wine brokers in the UK
offer services more similar to the wine auction houses acting as procurement
agents for high-quality wines. More of the world's wines are probably available in the UK than in any other country. Wine brokers are able to supply
smaller amounts of rarer wines to markets which do not receive these wines,
and often act as parallel exporters. The volume of export sales is only a tiny
fraction (one-twentieth) of UK import volumes, though, and as the costs of
selling wine internationally decrease, UK shippers will find themselves
competing more directly with producers.

UK WINE PRODUCTION

UK winemaking enjoyed a rebirth during the 1990s. Wales and England dominate domestic wine production, producing wine under the relatively new classification of English and Welsh table wines. Domestic wine production in the
UK has been characterized by small producers (less than two hectares) who do
not rely on the vineyard as their primary source of income, but the 1990s has
seen the entry of some large-scale ventures such as Denbies' 100 ha vineyard
(Dorking) and Chapel Down Wines (Kent) sourcing fruit from 200 ha of vineyard (Unwin, 1991b; English Wine Producers, 2001). Many UK producers
lack formal training in viticulture or oenology, which often magnifies the
handicap of difficult ripening conditions.

Wines produced are predominantly white, and accordingly the major varieties planted in England and Wales are Müller-Thurgau, Seyval Blanc and
Reichensteiner (Robinson, 1994). While the 1980s saw production of much
sweet wine, current trends have seen drier more aromatic styles favoured by
producers (Robinson, 1994). Recently, some promising sparkling wines have
also been produced.

Problems with ripening have led to wildly fluctuating yields; latest figures
place the 1999 vintage at 13 000 hl, an increase on the previous two vintages
but half that of the 1996 vintage. Unpredictable yields not only pose problems
for producers seeking to generate a profit from their vineyards but also create
problems for the establishment of brands in the marketplace. A constant presence is necessary not only to remind consumers of the product but also to
ensure placement in retail outlets. UK wines are yet to enjoy a loyal following
of consumers.

The major impediment to winemaking in the UK is the EC regulation
prohibiting the use of hybrid[2] vines in the production of wine. A form of quality control, EC regulations dictate the demarcation of vineyards, the addition

of wine-based products not originating in the specified region, the making of quality wine outside the quality region concerned, the maximum levels of naturally occurring and total alcoholic strengths, the acidification/de-acidification and sweetening of wine; the wine varieties, the cultivation methods and yields, the winemaking methods, and the assessment of quality (Unwin, 1991b, p. 144). It is possible for winemakers to produce wine outside these regulations, but compliance is necessary for the wine to be included in the classification system. Such forms of quality control are necessitated by the UK's membership in the EU.

Other limitations resulting from compliance with the UK Quality Wine Scheme are constraints on the area able to be planted and the UK's overall production (currently less than 25 000 hl per annum). These limitations, together with the prohibition on hybrid vines, seem set to contain the UK's wine production at current levels. Despite the seeming enormity of the task, English and Welsh winemakers are continuing to lobby for the inclusion of hybrid vines in the Quality Wine Scheme. However, since other wine-producing member states, including France, Italy and Spain, would gain little from the introduction of hybrid vines, it seems unlikely that wines produced from hybrid vines will be included in any EC classifications.

In addition to producing wines from grape material grown in the UK, there is also a long history of wine made from grape concentrate imported into the UK. In such instances the resultant wine is referred to as British wine as opposed to English or Welsh table wines (Robinson, 1994). British wines are predominantly fortified and sometimes flavoured with fruits and spices. While such a practice is not uncommon in other countries, production is significantly larger in Britain than elsewhere, with strong brands such as Harveys of Bristol and Stones Ginger Wine.

LESSONS FOR INTERNATIONAL MARKETS

Acknowledgement of the long history of the UK wine trade provides observers with a greater understanding of their current industry. The UK market is highly developed, and part of the ongoing prosperity of the UK wine trade is due to the supporting associations that have emerged as the market developed. Wine education continues to be an important factor in the ongoing prosperity of the UK industry, with the level of education available for the post-production functions of the wine industry being unparalleled in other countries. Historically, the Worshipful Company of Distillers and Vintners was the city guild which regulated trade of wine into and within the UK. Today their influence is through their role as industry educators. Most members of the UK wine trade train and sit exams with the Wine and Spirit Education

Trust (WSET). Although such educational programmes are available around the world, UK industry participation in the WSET training is unprecedented elsewhere. WSET courses encompass wine production and appreciation and provide the preliminary training for individuals wishing to undertake training for the prestigious Master of Wine.

LOOKING TO THE FUTURE

Changes under way in the UK signify growing prosperity for the UK industry, in particular for shippers and merchants. Consumption trends show that the UK consumer is trading up as well as consuming more wine. While this is good news in itself for the industry placed in the context of declining world consumption, these trends reinforce the UK's position of power within the global marketplace. While legal blood alcohol levels for drink driving seem set to fall, it is doubtful that these reductions will have any major impact on the volume of wine consumed because most consumers have already changed their consumption patterns.

Recent announcements to equalize taxes and duties among EU member countries will further strengthen the UK market. Smuggling and cross-border shopping have been escalating in the UK, and the abolition of duty-free shopping has done little to improve this situation. The Wine and Spirit Association estimated in their 2001 Annual Report that smuggling and cross-border shopping of wine increased 120 per cent over the previous three years and are estimated to have lost the Exchequer £220 million in 1999 (WSA, 2001). The impact of these activities has been so great as to prompt some UK retailers to open outlets across the channel. Changes in taxation and duties will return some of these sales to the UK and may see a 'paper' increase in the consumption of wine. More importantly, it is likely that this will further strengthen the relative position of off-trade retailers within the market.

With predicted changes favouring the off-trade, there needs to be a concerted effort to maintain wine's presence in the on-trade. On-trade establishments are used by the global wine industry to introduce and gain exposure to brands. Although the on-trade market may generate less revenue for some suppliers than the off-trade, the value of this channel is in the brand equity it is able to build. Increased competition from other alcoholic beverages will see marginal wine drinkers change from wine to other single-serve beverages, particularly in public houses. The global wine industry has been slow to target this market (unlike the spirit producers, who are enjoying increased prosperity in this market).

Increased competition can also be expected when targeting the female market. Increases in the numbers of women in the workforce have meant that these consumers have a greater disposable income than in previous generations and wine producers are not alone in identifying the potential of this market. To the advantage of the wine market is the acceptance of wine within this consumer segment. In 1999 wine accounted for 51 per cent of the volume of all alcoholic beverages consumed by females, a share that is predicted to grow to 56 per cent by 2004.

In 1999 on-line sales accounted just for 0.5 per cent of the volume in the off-trade market, with an estimated 40 on-line wine retail sites servicing the UK market (Euromonitor, 2000). The future of this channel is a part of ongoing brick-and-mortar concerns, where current retailers' infrastructures can be utilized. As in other countries, on-line retail has failed to live up to expectations and, as in other countries, the UK has been the scene of many dotcom bombs, among these wine e-tailers. Convenience has been cited as a key reason for European customers to shop on-line. In the UK, Internet retailers are finding that this is not a sustainable competitive advantage. Off-trade retailers are opening outlets such as those in petrol station forecourts offering convenience without the risk associated with Internet transactions.

Overall, the UK will continue as a leading market for wine exports in the world. There will be increased competition for shelf space as retailers consolidate and export producers focus on this large and growing wine market.

NOTES

1. Trends that seemingly go against technological advances are by no means unusual in the wine market, where intangible attributes are often as important as tangible attributes.
2. Known in the EC as 'inter-specific crosses', hybrid vines are a cross between *Vitis vinifera* (the traditional wine-growing grapevine) and other *Vitis* species. Unlike *vinifera* varieties, hybrids frequently show greater tolerance of disease and adverse climatic and soil conditions (Robinson, 1994). Claims that hybrid vines produce inferior wines have resulted in such vines being banned by the EC (Unwin, 1991b; Robinson, 1994).

REFERENCES

Anderson, K. and D. Norman (2003), *Global Wine Consumption and Trade, 1961 to 2001: A Statistical Compendium*, Adelaide: Centre for International Economic Studies.
Burnett, J. (1999), *Liquid Pleasures: A Social History of Drinks in Modern Britain*, London: Routledge.
Datamonitor (1999), 'Alcoholic Drinks: Targeting the Young Adult Market', Datamonitor, UK.
Diston, S. (2001), 'Europe: EC to Re-think Alcohol Tax Policy' (www.just-drinks.com, accessed on-line 25/9/01).
EIU Retail Business (1994), *Market Survey 1: Table wines, part 1 & 2*, London: Economist Intelligence Unit.

English Wine Producers (2001), 'The History of Grapes and Wine in Britain',
    (http://englishwineproducers.com/, accessed online 6/9/01).
Euromonitor (2000), *Wine in the UK*, London: Euromonitor.
Fattorini, J. (1994), 'Professional Consumers: Themes in High Street Wine Marketing',
    International Journal of Wine Marketing, **6** (2), 5–13.
Mintel (2000), 'Wine Retailing, Retail Intelligence', Mintel UK, July.
Robinson, J. (1994), *The Oxford Companion to Wine*, London: Oxford University
    Press.
Unwin, T. (1991a), *Wine and the Vine*, London: Routledge.
Unwin, T. (1991b), 'UK Wine: From Table Wines to Quality Wine?' *Journal of Wine
    Research*, **2** (2), 143–50.
WSA (2001), *WSA 2000/ 2001 Annual Report*, London: Wine and Spirit Association.

8. The Nordic countries

Jan Bentzen and Valdemar Smith

Traditionally, the Nordic countries have been characterized as spirits- and beer-consuming countries as these two beverages have been by far the most popular alcoholic drinks through the centuries. Wine has only been consumed in very modest quantities in these northern, climatically rather cold countries until a few decades ago. For obvious reasons wine production is not possible or efficient in the Nordic countries and this has influenced drinking behaviour. But from the 1960s wine consumption suddenly increased in all Nordic countries and during the next three decades wine has become a widespread, popular beverage – to the point of per capita consumption levels (measured in pure alcohol) surpassing those of spirits. Beer is now the most common alcoholic beverage in all five Nordic countries, but in a few years wine may well be the most popular alcoholic beverage in one or more of the Nordic countries.

While the drinking patterns in the Nordic countries have evolved – or converged – towards continental European behaviour, in the wine-consuming countries of southern Europe beer has gained popularity in recent times. Hence a much more uniform pattern of alcohol consumption is seen today among Western European countries. The present chapter analyses this historical shift in the drinking behaviour in Nordic countries – that is, wine consumption becoming widespread and probably substituting for spirits and/or beer. As no wine production takes place in these countries, the focus of analysis is on the levels and patterns of wine consumption and on wine prices, imports and taxation. The Nordic countries include Denmark, Norway, Sweden, Finland and Iceland. The last, however, is included only in some parts of the chapter due to a lack of data and the minor importance of its wine consumption (Iceland having a population of just 270 000, compared with 9 million in Sweden and about 5 million in each of the other three countries).

The first section presents long-run trends in wine consumption, then recent developments are analysed in more detail, including examining the price, taxes and the retail systems, particularly the state controlled systems of Norway, Sweden, Finland and Iceland. A comparative analysis of retail prices for some selected, specific wines is then provided to illuminate differences between a liberal system concerning alcohol policies, as in Denmark and the

141

more restrictive systems of the other Nordic countries. Some forecasts of likely trends of future wine consumption in the Nordic countries also are presented.

LONG-TERM WINE CONSUMPTION TRENDS

There is no long-run tradition of wine drinking in any of the Nordic countries. Until the 1970s wine was considered a luxury good consumed regularly only by a small part of the population. As with other alcoholic beverages, wine has usually been heavily taxed. That means there are relatively good statistics on alcohol consumption, with Norway and Sweden's per capita consumption levels for specific beverages going back to the 1850s. Before World War II, less than 0.2 litres of alcohol p.a. were consumed per person as wine in the two countries. Figure 8.1 presents data on wine consumption (litres per person aged 15 years and above) from 1955 for Denmark, Norway and Sweden, from 1960 for Finland, and from 1980 for Iceland. The 1970s was the decade with the most remarkable break in long-run trends in Nordic wine consumption. For most of the twentieth century before then, per capita wine consumption levels were similar among the Nordic countries.

Denmark – the country that is part of continental Europe and has always had liberal alcohol policies compared to other Nordic countries – was the first to adopt a stronger preference for wine while Norway and Iceland, the countries with the most restrictive alcohol policies, are lagging most.

The reasons behind these increases in wine consumption are rising living standards, the opening of these economies, and the Nordic propensity to travel to the climatically more comfortable southern Europe, where it is difficult not to acquire a taste for wine. With no wine production (apart from fruit wines) taking place in the Nordic countries, consumer preferences or habits for wine had to be adopted from outside, whereas spirits and beer have always been produced in all Nordic countries and have for centuries been integrated into the food and drinking culture.

The changes in drinking patterns since the mid-1950s are shown in Table 8.1, along with those for France. They show the increasing shares for wine and the sharp declines for spirits in Norway, Sweden and Finland. Today, beer is still the most popular drink in all Nordic countries, but this may change in the future if the present trends in beverage shares continue. Despite the dramatic decline in per capita consumption of wine in France over recent decades, wine's share in the Nordic countries is still barely half the French share.

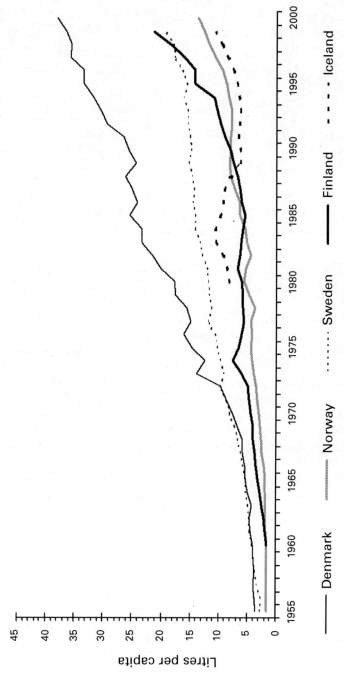

Note: [a] The data are calculated as litres per capita for the part of the population aged 15 years or above. For Finland the consumption data relate to light wines, excluding both 'long drinks' and cider.

Sources: See list of references.

Figure 8.1 Wine consumption per capita, Nordic countries, 1955–2000 (litres per capita, 15 years+)[a]

Table 8.1   *Shares of wine, beer and spirits in total alcohol consumption,*
              Nordic countries and France, 1953–2000 (%)

	1953/55			1973/75			2000[a]		
	Wine	Beer	Spirits	Wine	Beer	Spirits	Wine	Beer	Spirits
Denmark	11	78	12	17	64	19	39	49	12
Norway	9	42	49	10	47	43	30	51	19
Sweden	7	29	64	17	37	47	35	44	21
Finland	12	37	50	15	41	44	24	50	26
Iceland	–	–	–	–	–	–	21	49	30
France	82	5	13	74	12	14	63	15	22

Note: [a] 1999 for Sweden, Finland (includes 'long drinks') and Iceland; 1998 for France.

Sources: Nordström (2001); NTC (2000), *Statistical Yearbooks* of Denmark, Norway, Sweden,
Finland and Iceland (various issues).

THE NATIONAL RETAIL SYSTEMS

In all Nordic countries except Denmark, state monopolies in alcohol production, trade and sales were established at the beginning of the twentieth century,
although with some exemptions for beer. This was seen as the political solution to a long historical problem of heavy spirits drinking and its associated
health and social problems. Spirits production is still a state monopoly in
Norway today, but in Sweden, Finland and Iceland the state monopolies are
now confined to just retail sales of alcohol (again with some exemptions for
beer), with licences used to regulate the production and wholesaling of beer,
wine or spirits. In all the Nordic countries, heavy taxation of alcohol consumption generates considerable fiscal revenues while reducing the health and
social problems it can cause.

In Sweden the retail system of alcoholic beverages is organized by the
state-owned monopoly 'Systembolaget', which operates more than 400 shops
or local agents in 575 communities. The monopoly concerns spirits, wine and
strong beer. Light beer is available in other shops too, and the Swedish breweries have the right to sell strong beer (above 3.5 per cent alcohol) directly to
restaurants. At the retail level spirits, wine and strong beer may only be sold
to persons aged 20 years or more. The very restrictive alcohol policies and
control systems have a long history in Sweden, but it was not until the introduction in the 1920s of the so-called 'Bratt System' – a ration book for each
individual regulating the amounts of alcohol bought – that the selling of wine
was regulated. The Bratt System was later abandoned in the 1950s, and now

there are no quantitative restrictions on the amounts of wine individuals may buy.

Since the Systembolaget is a state monopoly with a policy of supporting 'a healthy drinking culture', it does not strive to attract customers to the shops. But it considers wine to be more healthy relative to spirits and so, since the 1950s, some effort has been devoted to the objective of making customers substitute wine for spirits. In this way the official alcohol policy may have boosted wine's share of alcohol consumption, despite an otherwise restrictive retail sales system. During the 1954–94 period Systembolaget had an effective monopoly not only in retail sales but also in quantities sold to, for example, restaurants. The latter part of the monopoly ceased in 1995 when Sweden joined the European Union, and now approximately 200 licenced, private import companies are selling wines to Systembolaget restaurants, hotels, and so on.

EU membership was expected to involve problems for the sales monopoly in the more market-oriented community. The EU Court of Justice ruled in 1997 that Systembolaget was not incompatible with an EU membership as the system was created due to public health considerations and was not found to be discriminatory between foreign and Swedish products. But a gradual liberalization of personal imports of (cheaper) alcoholic beverages has taken place, and a direct result of EU accession was the disappearance of monopolies in import/export, wholesaling and production of spirits.

The Norwegian system, 'Vinmonopolet', is quite similar to the Swedish system and was also established as an effort to control a widespread misuse of spirits or 'aqua vitae'. The annual per capita consumption of spirits reached peak levels in 1875 of 5 and 10 litres of pure alcohol for Norway and Sweden, respectively (although they may have been even higher in the first part of the nineteenth century). In the 1920s there was a short period of a ban on spirits and strong wines but, probably due to Norway's fish exports to wine countries, the ban did not include ordinary wines. Norway is not a member of the EU, but due to trade agreements – and the country's general unilateral liberalization of international trade – the state monopoly was split up in the mid-1990s and today Vinmonopolet is only a retail sales monopoly. It operates through about 160 shops in total, up from 101 in 1991. The low density of alcohol stores combined with harsh geographical conditions (mountains, forests, a lot of snow in the wintertime, and so on) together provide an effective barrier for people to buy alcohol – as they do to a lesser extent in Sweden, Finland and Iceland.

In Finland and Iceland similar systems – today named 'Alko' and 'ATVR', respectively – were established along the lines of the Swedish and Norwegian systems. After a prohibition period the state monopoly was initiated in 1932 in Finland, one of its purposes being to prevent profit-making from alcohol.

When Finland joined the EU in 1995 it was forced to liberalize the state-run alcohol system. Today, Alko is purely a retail sales monopoly, following the sale in 1999 of the restaurant wholesale business, and it operates through nearly 300 shops selling spirits, wine and beer (in the last case the monopoly relates to beer above 4.7 per cent alcohol content). Alko is directly owned by the Ministry of Social Affairs and Health. The Icelandic system is a spirits, wine and tobacco retail sales monopoly. It gave up the monopoly in importing and wholesaling alcohol at the end of 1995, with licence holders not allowed to operate the latter activities.

Denmark has always adhered to liberal, market-oriented systems, and the temperance movement has been relatively weak there compared to neighbouring countries. Taxes have been applied mainly for fiscal purposes, and there have been no impediments to alcohol consumption except for a minimum age of 18 years for sale in restaurants and a recently introduced limit of 15 years for the purchase of alcohol from retail shops. After the Danish accession to the EU in 1972, free trade and harmonization of tax systems have contributed to a rapid and continuous increase in wine (and other alcohol) consumption (Figure 8.1). This stark difference between Denmark and the other Nordic countries in both the level and rate of growth in consumption of wine from the early 1970s demonstrates the effectiveness of the Nordic state-monopoly systems in restraining alcohol consumption.

Finally, in Greenland and on the Faeroe Islands – both parts of Denmark but with home rule systems allowing independent alcohol policies – retail sales of alcohol are strictly regulated (again with some exemptions for light beer, also produced on the Faeroe Islands). Since the populations of these two countries are only 50 000 persons each, they are not included in the present analysis.

RECENT DEVELOPMENTS

Consumption of Wine

During the 1990s wine finally became established as a popular good, entering the consumption bundle of most Nordic households. In Denmark, red wine is now the consumer item among foodstuffs and beverages on which consumers spend most money. The market for wine in Denmark is by far the biggest among the Nordic countries, even compared with Sweden, where the size of the population aged 15 years or more is two-thirds above the Danish level.

Wine consumption data at the turn of the century are presented in Table 8.2. For each country the table shows the total consumption of wine as reported by the national official bureau in charge of alcohol statistics. It also reports the amounts sold by the state retail sales monopolies as reported by

Table 8.2   Wine consumption, Nordic countries,[a] 1999 and 2000 ('000 hectolitres)

		1999		2000
Denmark (population 15+: 4.3 million)				
Statistics Denmark		1588		1650
VSOD	Strong 30		Strong 30	
	Light 156	1588	Light 162	1650
Norway (population 15+: 3.6 million)				
Statistics Norway		449		488
Vinmonopolet	Strong 12		Strong 13	
	Light 385	397	Light 419	433
Sweden (population 15+: 7.2 million)				
Alkoholinspektionen		1401		na
Systembolaget	Strong 60		Strong 8	
	Light 1193	1253	Light 1240	1298
Finland (population 15+: 4.2 million)				
Statistics Finland, Stakes	Strong 44			
	Light 393	437		na
Alko	Strong 4247		Strong 43	
	Light 35988	402	Light 372	415
Iceland (population 15+: 0.2 million)				
Statistics Iceland		23		na
ATVR	Strong 2		Strong 2	
	Light 16	17	Light 17	19
Total Nordic countries (population 15+: 19.6 million)				
Statistical Yearbooks		3898		na

Note: [a] The data for Finland exclude cider and 'long drinks'. For Denmark the data from VSOD draw from Statistics Denmark. The population in 1000 persons, aged 15 years or above, is given in parentheses.

Sources: *Statistical Yearbooks* of the respective countries; Alkoholinspektionen (2000); and websites of VSOD (Denmark), Vinmonopolet (Norway), Systembolaget (Sweden), Alko (Finland), ATVR (Iceland).

those companies. For Denmark the information from VSOD (the wine and spirits organization in Denmark) relies on information from Statistics Denmark. It is clear that the Danish and Swedish wine markets are by far the largest and that these countries make up approximately 75 per cent of total wine sales in the Nordic countries. The consumption of strong wine – that is, 'fortified wine' with between 15 and 22 per cent alcohol – represents only a small share of the wine market except in Iceland and Finland, where the share is slightly above 10 per cent.

The four state monopolies are shown in Table 8.2 to have an average market share of approximately 90 per cent, the remaining share being held up by licence holders selling directly to hotels, restaurants, and so on.

The quantities in Table 8.2 only represent the official registered consumption of wine and so do not take into account wine imported by tourists or ship/aircraft crews, border trade, illegal home production, smuggling, and the like. There is a widespread border trade going on among Nordic countries because the tax rates, and hence retail prices, differ considerably between Nordic countries (and Germany, towards which the Danish border trade is directed). Table 8.3 shows the import allowance quotas. Denmark is the only country which has given up quantitative restrictions for both wine and beer (but for spirits there is still a 24-hour rule and a limit of 1.5 litres of spirits). The quotas refer to surface travel; the allowances are stricter when travelling by air.

For the EU member countries (Denmark, Sweden and Finland), tax-free trade was abolished from 1998 and the intention is to liberalize import quotas of alcohol on private travellers. Iceland and Norway continue to have the most restrictive alcohol policies and these will probably continue in the future as they have no plans to join the EU and thereby be forced to accommodate to the alcohol standard of continental Europe.

There is little information on the magnitudes of border trade and illegal

Table 8.3   *Travel import allowance quotas for wine, Nordic countries, 2001 and 2004 (litres per person)*

	Denmark	Norway	Sweden	Finland	Iceland
Year: 2001					
Light wine	No limit	2	26	–	1
Fortified wine	No limit	1	6	1	1
Year: 2004					
Light wine	No limit	2	90	90	1
Fortified wine	No limit	1	20	20	1

Source: SVL and VBF (2001).

smuggling/home production of wine. The Norwegian wine and spirits importers organization (VBF, 2001) estimates the border trade in wine to be 2.6 million litres from Sweden and 1.5 million litres from Denmark, which corresponds to 10 per cent of total wine consumption published by Statistics Norway (see Table 8.2). The Swedish and Norwegian wine and spirits importers' organizations (SVL and VBF, 2001) report that the black market share is estimated to be around 30 per cent for Norway, Finland and Iceland, 24 per cent for Sweden (only table wine) and 18 per cent for Denmark. Since a big part of this legal and illegal border trade takes place among the Nordic countries, it does not affect the overall size of the wine market represented by the sum of the consumption figures in Table 8.2, that is, 3.9 million hectolitres in 1999 or 20 litres per capita.

Prices and Taxation

Focusing on prices, the experiences in Denmark, Norway, Sweden and Finland have been somewhat different. In general, real prices of alcoholic beverages have declined in Denmark over the past 25 years, whereas real prices in the other Nordic countries have remained more or less stable or increased weakly. The Danish real price index for wine declined by more than 10 per cent during the last two decades, while it has risen by about 10 per cent over that period in Norway and even more so since 1993 in Sweden (Figure 8.2).

The decline in Danish real wine prices is partly due to changes in the Danish excise system on alcoholic beverages, which has been implemented as a per litre tax with different rates for beer, wine and spirits. Until Danish membership of the EU in 1972, tax rates in absolute figures were increasing. However, because of the new open European market, major tax cuts were necessary. Accordingly, there was a tax cut of 75 per cent on wine while the tax rates on beer and spirits were fixed in absolute terms. During the late 1970s and first part of the 1980s, taxes on beer, wine and spirits were readjusted upwards as part of fiscal policy, but were eventually lowered in the 1990s in order to complete the harmonization of the Danish tax level to the EU level. This suggests that more attention has been paid to fiscal considerations and EU obligations when deciding alcohol taxes than to health and social arguments. By the mid-1990s, nominal taxes on beer and wine in Denmark were back down to their 1970 levels, and the real tax revenue from Danish alcohol excises were 58 per cent less in 1993 than in 1972.

Norway and Sweden both decided not to enter the EU when Denmark did in 1972, leaving both countries free to formulate their own tax on alcoholic beverages. In Sweden real alcohol prices were relatively constant during the 1960s, but they have been increasing since the early 1970s. Until recently fiscal considerations have been of great importance to the Swedish taxation of

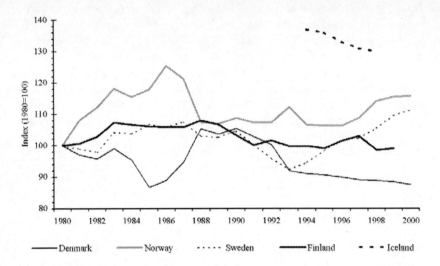

Note: ^a The consumer price index is used as a deflator in all cases. For Iceland only data representing the short time span 1994–98 are available.

Sources: *Statistical Yearbooks* of the respective countries; databases from Statistics Denmark and Statistics Sweden; Stakes (2000).

Figure 8.2   Indices of real prices of wine, Nordic countries,^a 1980–2000

alcoholic beverages. Since 1972 the tax revenue from alcohol has increased by more than 300 per cent (amounting to US$2 billion in 1995), and profit from the Swedish state monopoly on the sale of alcoholic beverages adds to that fiscal revenue.

To some extent the comments on the experience of Swedish real prices of alcohol also apply to Norway and Finland. In Norway the revenue from taxation of alcohol increased by nearly 400 per cent in current prices from 1972 to 1993. However, total alcohol consumption fell by 5 per cent over the same period, suggesting that the tax incidence on alcoholic beverages as a whole has increased in Norway. For Finland, historically the revenue from alcohol taxes has been relatively important, making up as much as 10 per cent of all state taxes in the early 1990s. Since then this share has decreased, but is still markedly higher than in any of the other Nordic countries.

The rates of wine taxation in the Nordic countries, presented in Table 8.4, are scaled progressively according to alcohol content in all cases except Finland. The last column in the table presents comparable tax equivalents in euros per litre of wine. Iceland and Norway have some of the world's highest taxes – rates that are five to eight times Danish levels even though the latter

Table 8.4   Wine taxes, Nordic countries, 2001

	Tax in national currency per litre[a] (for the alcohol strengths shown in parentheses)	Euro per litre equivalent of 12% wine tax
Denmark, DKK	10.15 (>15%) 7.05 (6–15%) 4.50 (<6%)	0.945
Norway, NOK	3.65 per % volume per litre (<22%)	5.348
Sweden, SEK	45.17 (>15%) 27.50 (8.5–15%)	
	18.98 (7–8.5%) 13.80 (4.5–7%)	3.036
Finland, FIM	14.00	2.355
Iceland, ISK	52.80 per % volume per litre (<22%)	8.052

Notes: [a] Exchange rates as of August 2001 are as follows (expressed as national currency per US dollar). Euro: 1.10; DKK: 8.18; NOK: 8.89; SEK: 10.35; FIM: 6.53; ISK: 98.64.

Source: SVL and VBF (2001).

are higher than in most other European countries. Finland and Sweden have rather similar levels of taxes, but still much higher than Danish wine taxes. Since 1995 alcohol taxes in Finland also have been set according to alcohol content – indicated by lower taxes on beer and higher taxes on spirits compared to the wine tax reported in Table 8.4.

It has been possible to sustain relatively high excises on alcoholic beverages in Norway, Sweden and Finland due to a system of very restrictive quotas on imports for personal use from other countries (border trade). After joining the EU, Sweden and Finland (like Denmark) were allowed an exception to the general EU rules. However, harmonization to EU standards will have to be carried out by 2004. Norway, having decided by referendum to stay outside the EU in 1972 and again in 1994, has no legal problems in relation to its high alcohol tax, but it is having increasing problems concerning border trade with both Denmark and Sweden.

Wine Imports by Country of Origin and Import Prices

The major European wine-producing countries, France, Spain and Italy, have a combined market share between 50 and 70 per cent in the Nordic countries (Table 8.5). The most preferred in Denmark and Norway are French wines, while Spanish wines have the highest market share in both Sweden and Finland (where French and Italian wine are equal second in importance). Germany has approximately the same market share in all Nordic countries, the vast majority of which is white wine. Finland's geographical – and until recently also political – proximity to Russia and Eastern Europe helps explain the fact that 15 per cent of the wine sales from Alko are from Bulgaria,

Hungary or Romania. Wines from Chile seem to have been well accepted by the Nordic populations, especially in Norway, where Chile has a market share similar to Spain and Italy.

As widespread wine consumption is a relatively new phenomenon in the Nordic countries, the non-European wine-exporting countries are relatively unknown to consumers in general and so there is plenty of scope to increase their market shares. Australian wines seem to perform well in Norway and Sweden, and there is no reason to believe that the market share in Denmark should stay at a low 2 per cent level in the future. The same is true for the USA and South Africa, which have been relatively most successful in Sweden and Finland.

Notice also that the market shares of red wines and white wines differ very much among the Nordic countries, where Finland has an unusually high share for white wine (56 per cent – see bottom of Table 8.5).

The differences in wine imports by country of origin may be related to supply conditions, for example the number of specific brands available in the retail monopolies. Denmark is completely liberalized concerning the brands

Table 8.5 *Import market shares by country of origin, Nordic countries, 2000 (retail market share in %)*

Source	Denmark VSOD	Norway Vinmonopolet	Sweden Systembolaget	Finland Alko[a]
France	39.6	24.9	14.2	13.7
Spain	21.0	13.4	27.3	21.4
Italy	10.9	16.1	15.8	13.6
Chile	7.9	16.1	7.0	8.7
Germany	6.4	8.8	7.8	7.2
USA	2.2	1.5	4.3	4.8
South Africa	2.9	1.7	4.1	3.0
Australia	2.1	6.1	5.1	2.3
Portugal	2.1	2.5	3.7	1.0
Argentina	1.7	0.5	1.0	1.6
Bulgaria	0.5	1.7	2.1	1.8
Hungary & Romania	0.0	0.0	2.9	13.2
Other countries	2.9	6.7	2.6	7.8
Red wines	74.0	77.0	61.0	44.0
White wines	26.0	23.0	39.0	56.0

Note: [a]1999.

Sources: VSOD (Denmark), Vinmonopolet (Norway), Systembolaget (Sweden) and Alko (Finland).

and numbers of wines appearing on the market, but in the other countries the monopolies exert some market influence. Figure 8.3 presents a scatter plot between the market shares of the wine-exporting countries and the number of brands offered in the retail monopolies for these countries. The positive relationship found in Figure 8.3 may be bi-directional in causation. On the one hand, the number of brands in the shops will influence what is actually sold, but on the other hand the specific market shares and accompanying number of brands may also simply reflect the preferences of consumers. For example, the many Chilean wines sold in Norway may simply mean that consumers have developed a strong preference for these wines.

Information on the import prices of wine can be derived from Eurostat statistics on international trade. For EU countries, import and export data are recorded in both volumes and values. Hence average import prices can be calculated with a detailed breakdown for region-specific wine brands. Due to the Intra-stat system the international trade flows are recorded for the exporting country and the corresponding importing country, but information concerning the country of origin is not recorded or available. Therefore, French wine exports to Sweden may in fact be re-exports of Spanish wine. This is an important caveat to the trade statistics and in connection with the construction of wine prices, the Eurostat sources only have information in the cases where an EU member country is involved. With these qualifications, Table 8.6 exhibits the country-specific import prices of wine.

The average wine prices in Table 8.6 are not easily interpreted as many

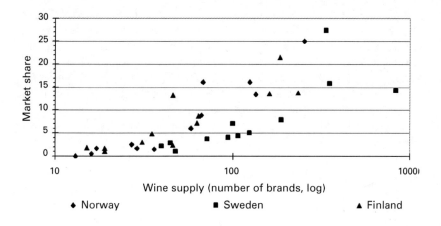

Sources: See references.

Figure 8.3 *Relationship between market shares and number of brands, Finland and Sweden, 2000*

Table 8.6　*Average import prices of EU wine into Nordic countries, 1993*
and 1999 (euro per litre)[a]

Exporting country	Red wine					White wine				
	DK	NO	SW	FI	IC	DK	NO	SW	FI	IC
1993										
France	1.83	1.22	1.49	1.42	2.13	1.48	1.60	1.68	1.81	2.48
Spain	1.54	1.14	1.63	1.06	3.81	0.91	0.65	1.46	0.51	2.75
Italy	1.53	1.00	1.21	1.29	1.61	1.21	2.48	1.07	0.78	1.50
Portugal	1.17	1.62	1.57	1.99	2.46	1.58	1.83	1.66	1.60	–
Germany	1.22	0.75	1.16	0.99	1.50	0.83	1.28	1.59	1.04	2.44
1999										
France	2.51	2.16	2.32	2.89	3.16	1.66	2.59	2.34	2.79	3.68
Spain	1.85	2.95	2.15	2.36	4.94	1.49	1.89	1.85	1.38	3.00
Italy	2.88	2.81	1.89	2.96	3.13	2.08	3.13	2.48	1.71	2.97
Portugal	1.72	2.14	1.95	2.30	2.41	2.01	2.03	3.90	2.22	–
Germany	1.20	1.23	1.08	2.21	–	0.90	1.45	1.66	1.47	3.37

Note:　[a]For Denmark the '1999 prices' relate to 1998 due to missing information in the Eurostat source. Exchange rates are 0.86 ECU/US$ for 1993 and 0.94 euro/US$ for 1999.

Source:　Eurostat (2001).

factors influence them. For example, high alcohol taxation might induce cheap wine imports in order to keep retail prices reasonable. Consumer preferences – or drinking habits – may also influence the quality of wine imported. For example, Danish consumers might be willing to buy the more expensive wines because they have a relatively long tradition of buying French red wine. The prices of wine exported to Iceland seem to be systematically higher than for other countries, which may be caused by the extremely small quantities of wine imported, making Icelandic buying power smaller than that of other Nordic countries.

Information on non-European wine prices can be constructed from Eurostat data only if exports to an EU member are taking place. Therefore only for Denmark, Sweden and Finland can this information be obtained, and only for recent years because the latter two countries became EU members only in 1995. The available data for a selection of wine-exporting countries are reported in Table 8.7. They show Australian wines as being the most expensive and Eastern European wines the cheapest, but the overall variation in prices is not very high and certainly does explain the big differences in retail wine prices between the Nordic countries.

Table 8.7 Average import prices of red wine, Nordic countries, 1999 (US$ per litre)[a]

Exporting country	Denmark[c]	Norway	Sweden	Finland	Iceland
France	(2.81)	2.30	2.47	3.08	3.37
Spain	(2.08)	3.14	2.29	2.51	5.27
Italy	(3.23)	2.99	2.01	3.16	3.33
Chile	2.21	–	2.37	2.36	–
South Africa	2.69	–	2.11	3.05	–
USA	2.73	–	2.03	2.92	–
Australia	3.60	–	2.81	3.98	–
Eastern Europe[b]	1.64	–	1.51	1.76	–

Notes:
[a] Exchange rates between euro and the US$ are 0.89 and 0.94 for 1998 and 1999, respectively.
[b] Eastern Europe here includes only Bulgaria, Hungary and Romania.
[c] For Denmark the prices concerning France, Spain and Italy relate to 1998 due to missing information in the Eurostat sources.

Source: Eurostat (2001).

A COMPARISON OF RETAIL PRICES FOR SPECIFIC WINES

In order to compare the absolute price levels of wines sold in the Nordic countries, price data for a number of specific wines sold in these countries have been collected. The retail prices of wines are directly available from the state monopolies, and for Denmark price information is easily available from private shops and wine companies, for example via their web pages. For Denmark the price information relies on 'listing prices', that is, the usual market prices without any special discounts or 'special offers' involved. Hence the Danish price level for wines used in the following analysis is probably too high as many wines are often sold with considerable discounts. It is no easy job to pick out brands that are marketed simultaneously in all of the countries (especially French wines), but the information used to construct Table 8.8 – showing the relative price differences between the respective countries and Denmark – relies on prices of specific brands typically marketed in at least three of the countries. The price variation is also reported in Table 8.8, along with the number of brands used when calculating an average price level for each of the countries (measured as the percentage above the Danish price level).

Table 8.8   Retail prices of wines, Nordic countries, 2001 (% above the Danish price level, September simple averages)

Country of origin	Norway	Sweden	Finland	Iceland
France	85	1	20	82
Price variation (min; max)	(50;150)	(–8;19)	(5;61)	(52;123)
Number of wines ( )	(3)	(2)	(8)	(4)
Spain	57	2	14	46
Price variation (min; max)	(23;87)	(–10;33)	(3;32)	(20;65)
Number of wines ( )	(9)	(9)	(13)	(7)
Italy	63	0	15	67
Price variation (min; max)	(25;124)	(–18;27)	(–11;32)	(24;165)
Number of wines ( )	(5)	(7)	(8)	(5)
Chile	75	17	29	89
Price variation (min; max)	(–16;182)	(–14;95)	(7;98)	(64;115)
Number of wines ( )	(7)	(8)	(8)	(4)
USA	64	9	20	120
Price variation (min; max)	(37;88)	(–9;30)	(9;34)	(91;190)
Number of wines ( )	(4)	(8)	(5)	(4)
Australia	69	26	36	122
Price variation (min; max)	(11;120)	(–18;45)	(–6;85)	(68;183)
Number of wines ( )	(9)	(9)	(7)	(6)

Sources: See list of references.

There are relatively large variations in wine prices in Nordic countries, with Denmark generally having the lowest wine prices – which is consistent with the tax structure. Norway and Iceland have exceptionally high retail prices, also compared with Sweden and Finland, whose wine prices seem to have converged rapidly towards the Danish price level. For Sweden especially it is not difficult to detect wines that are sold by Systembolaget below the normal market prices in Denmark. There are also large variations concerning country-specific wines sold in a Nordic country. For example, one of the Chilean wines was found to be cheaper in Norway than in Denmark. Generally, the Spanish wines seem to deviate least across countries.

Table 8.9 gives information on the retail prices of specific brands (converted to US dollars for ease of comparison). The prices seem to vary considerably and not all price differences can be explained by standard economic reasoning. Iceland and Norway again show up with the highest prices, but in some cases Sweden is cheaper than Denmark even though the Danish wine market is usually considered strongly competitive. Traditionally,

Table 8.9   *Retail prices of specific wines, Nordic countries, 2001 (US$ per bottle in September at 10 September 2001 exchange rates)[a]*

Country of origin	Brand	Denmark	Norway	Sweden	Finland	Iceland
Australia	Rosemount Shiraz	7.3	11.4	8.9	12.2	14.7
Australia	Hardys Nottage Hill Cab. Sauv.–Shiraz	7.3	13.6	6.3	9.1	13.4
Chile	Sunrise Cab. Sauv., Concha Y Toro	5.5	10.2	6.5	6.8	10.1
Chile	Santa Rita 120 Merlot	6.1	11.4	7.0	8.1	13.1
France	Chateau de Seguin	7.1	–	7.8	8.6	15.7
France	Mouton Cadet Rouge	8.8	13.1	8.1	9.9	15.6
Italy	Masi Campofiorin Ripasso	10.6	13.7	9.4	12.0	14.2
Italy	Villa Antinori Chianti Classico Riserva	13.4	16.8	10.9	11.9	16.6
Spain	Faustino VII	7.3	11.4	7.4	8.4	11.1
Spain	Campo Viejo Reserva	9.7	13.7	9.4	10.4	13.4
USA	Gallo Cab. Sauv.	6.7	10.3	6.6	7.6	12.8
USA	Gallo Ruby Cabernet	5.1	9.6	5.6	6.8	10.1

Note: [a] The retail prices refer to normal or usual prices (September 2001) and therefore do not represent 'special offers' – especially for Denmark, where many wines are sold in supermarkets at 10–40 per cent below the announced 'market prices'.

Sources: VSOD (Denmark), Vinmonopolet (Norway), Systembolaget (Sweden), Alko (Finland) and ATVR (Iceland).

wine has not been sold very much via special wine shops in Denmark; instead
supermarkets have been the most usual outlet. Therefore price competition, no
supply restrictions and a great variety of brands characterize the Danish wine
market in contrast to the other Nordic countries. Were the actual (often
discounted) prices used instead of listed Danish prices as the comparator for
Tables 8.8 and 8.9, the differences between Denmark and the rest would have
been even more marked.

FUTURE TRENDS

The Nordic wine markets have been growing rapidly during recent decades,
but present per capita wine consumption levels are still well below those of
continental Europe, so there is considerable potential for further development.
The potential relates both to quantities consumed and the diversity of sources
of imports. For Denmark, Sweden and Finland, the year 2004 is crucial as their
travel restrictions on private alcohol importation must be harmonized to less
restrictive EU standards. This will put further downward pressure on wine
taxes in Sweden and Finland, and is a serious potential threat to profits of the
state retail sales monopolies.

   To obtain a forecast of wine consumption for the next three to five years,
the per capita consumption levels from Figure 8.1 can be used. Applying the
exponential smoothing technique to those data involves calculating the best fit
of the data using exponentially decaying weights on historical values. When
the resulting estimated relationship is used to forecast wine consumption to
2005, one obtains Figure 8.4. Only data from 1989 to 2000 are used because
information from the last decade seems most relevant for the present purpose.

   Finland shows up with the relatively highest growth potential, almost
reaching the projected Danish consumption level by 2005. If the Nordic countries approach the 40 litres per capita level they will be above the Greek
consumption level (36 litres per capita). Further increases beyond that are
unlikely, as increasingly expenditure is being directed towards higher-quality
premium wines.

CONCLUSION

Although the Nordic countries are very similar in many respects in their
history, culture, languages and lifestyles, they differ substantially with respect
to both alcohol consumption levels and drinking patterns. As no wine production takes place in the Nordic countries – due to natural and climatic conditions – only beer and spirits have historically and traditionally been part of the

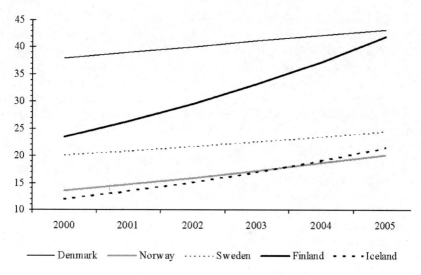

Source: Authors' calculations. Data from Figure 8.1 (and only from 1989) are used to forecast wine consumption by applying the exponential smoothing technique.

Figure 8.4   Projections of wine consumption per capita, Nordic countries, 2000–2005 (litres per capita, 15 years +)

food and drinking culture. During the last couple of decades this has changed remarkably as wine consumption has become both popular and widespread – especially in Denmark, but also in Sweden and Finland (while Norway and Iceland are still lagging somewhat behind).

In general, only Denmark has for decades adhered to liberal, market-oriented policies concerning the production and sales/consumption of alcoholic beverages, including wine. The other Nordic countries have in the first part of the twentieth century established state monopolies in order to control both production and sales of alcoholic beverages. Today, these monopolies only include retail sales of wine, spirits and (strong) beer, but these systems none the less still restrict the number of outlets, and their retail sales prices are relatively high for that reason (and because of relatively high taxation).

When compared with wine consumption in Denmark, there seems to be little doubt that in the other Nordic countries the monopoly systems have slowed down the introduction and dissemination of wine drinking. In 1995 Sweden and Finland joined the EU and therefore these countries have come under pressure to reform both alcohol taxation and travel import allowances. This has been happening in that wine prices in Sweden and Finland today are only slightly above Denmark's, whereas the wine prices in Norway and Iceland typically are still to be found in the range of 50 to 100 per cent above the level observed in Denmark. The market for wines in Denmark is very competitive, usually with prices no higher than found in the wine-producing countries of southern Europe. By contrast, the wine prices of the other Nordic countries seem to be distorted and not reflecting market conditions, even though some wines are found to be cheaper in Sweden than in Denmark. This can probably be related to the monopoly systems. This means that the year 2004 will be crucial as that is when travel regulations concerning alcoholic beverages among the EU countries are to be liberalized. This may also mark the end of the Swedish and Finnish retail sales monopolies, unless special arrangements are (again) negotiated.

The Nordic wine markets may all be characterized as 'emerging markets' in that wine consumption levels generally are low but strongly increasing, especially in Denmark, Sweden and Finland, and especially for non-European ('New World') wine producers who in most cases have held only small market shares to date.

REFERENCES

Alkoholinspektionen (The National Alcohol Board) (2000), *Alkoholstatistik (1995–1998 & 1999)*, Stockholm: National Alcohol Board.
Eurostat (2001), *Intra- and Extra-EU trade*, Brussels: European Commission.
Nordström, T. (2001), 'European Comparative Alcohol Study – ECAS', Report presented at the WHO European Ministerial Conference on Youth People and Alcohol, Stockholm, February 2001.
NTC (2000), *World Drink Trends*, London: NTC Publications Ltd.
Stakes (2000), *Nordic Alcohol Statistics (1994–1998)*, Helsinki: Stakes.
SVL and VBF (Swedish and Norwegian wine and spirits importers organizations) (2001), *Nordic Policies on Alcohol*, Stockholm: SLV and VBF.
VBF (Norwegian Wine and Spirits Importers Organization) (2001), *Norsk Grensehandel med vin og Brennvin 99-00*, VBF Rapport Nr. 1/2001, Oslo: VBF.

Other Statistical Sources

ALKO, Finland; www.alko.fi
ATVR, Iceland; www.atvr.is
Stakes, Finland; www.stakes.fi
Statistical Yearbooks for Denmark, Norway, Sweden, Finland and Iceland, various issues.
Systembolaget, Sweden; www.systembolaget.se
Vinmonopolet, Norway; www.vinmonopolet.no
VSOD, Denmark; www.vsod.dk

9. Eastern Europe and the Former Soviet Union

Nivelin Noev and Johan F.M. Swinnen

In the transition economies of Central and Eastern Europe and the Former Soviet Union, economic and institutional reforms have had important impacts on wine production, consumption, prices and policies. This chapter analyses the changes in grape and wine production, consumption and trade, as well as changes in policies and the industry's structure, and discusses how various factors are affecting the market and trade situation and outlook.

The transition countries account for a significant share of world wine markets. The ten Central and Eastern European Countries (CEEC-10) that have signed association agreements with the European Union (EU), several of whom are expected to join the EU this decade, currently produce somewhat more than 13 million hectolitres of wine or 4.6 per cent of total world wine production (Table 9.1). CEEC wine production is currently about 25 per cent less than the average level for 1984–88 (Figure 9.1). However, most of this decline occurred before 1990, since production in 1999 was slightly higher than in 1989.

The two other wine-producing regions in Eastern Europe are the Balkan Non-Associated Countries (BNAC-5),[1] four of which have emerged after the breakdown of the SR Yugoslavia, and some, mostly southern, republics of the Former Soviet Union (FSU). Four important FSU states (FSU-4), that is, Russia, Ukraine, Moldova and Uzbekistan, produced almost 6 million hl of wine in 1999, or 2.1 per cent of world wine production (Table 9.1). However, this is much less than their pre-transition levels: in 1992 they produced over 11 million hl of wine, 3.9 per cent of the world's total.

These three transition wine regions, taken together, produced 10.9 per cent of world wine output in 2001, compared with Latin America's 9.5 per cent and the USA's 8.6 per cent (Anderson and Norman, 2003).

At the country level in 1999, the most important wine producers are Romania (6.5 million hl), Hungary (3.3 million hl), Russia and Croatia (each 2.1 million hl) and Bulgaria (1.4 million hl). In most transition countries, wine production was quite volatile in the 1990s due to a number of factors discussed below. However, the fall in output in Bulgaria and the FSU was stronger than

Table 9.1 Production and exports of wine, Central and Eastern European wine-producing countries, 1999

Country	Production of wine in volume ('000 hl)	Share of world wine production by volume (%)	Export of wine by volume ('000 hl)	Share of world export of wine by volume (%)	Export of wine by value (US$ million)	Share of world export of wine by value (%)
Romania	650.4	2.29	29.3	0.46	22	0.16
Hungary	333.9	1.17	87.2	1.36	76	0.54
Bulgaria	139.4	0.49	74.0	1.16	75	0.53
Slovenia	68.8	0.24	14.0	0.22	4	0.03
Croatia	209.4	0.74	6.6	0.10	9	0.06
Serbia & Mont.	140.0	0.49	4.9	0.08	4	0.03
Macedonia	122.7	0.43	55.0	0.86	47	0.33
Albania	12.7	0.04	0.0	0.00	0	0.00
Bosnia and Herz.	6.0	0.02	2.2	0.03	1	0.01
Russia	214.0	0.75	0.8	0.01	1	0.01
Moldova	189.5	0.67	65.7	1.03	64	0.46
Uzbekistan	150.0	0.53	6.0	0.09	4	0.03
Ukraine	40.0	0.14	15.7	0.25	13	0.09
Georgia	154.0	0.54	13.2	0.21	24	0.17
Azerbaijan	37.5	0.13	3.6	0.06	1	0.00
Kazakhstan	19.1	0.07	0.2	0.00	0	0.00
Turkmenistan	18.0	0.06	6.0	0.09	181	0.13
Armenia	6.6	0.02	0.1	0.00	0	0.00

Region						
CEEC-10	13 223	4.6	2 188	3.4	193	1.4
BNAC-5	4 908	1.7	687	1.1	60	0.4
FSU-4	5 935	2.1	882	1.4	81	0.6
FSU	8 495	3.0	1 151	1.8	130	0.9
EU-7	182 058	64.0	47 538	74.3	10 947	77.7
EU-15	182 256	64.1	48 383	75.6	11 348	80.5
World	284 337	100.0	64 010	100.0	14 094	100.0

Notes:
CEEC-10: Bulgaria, Czech Republic, Estonia, Hungary, Lithuania, Latvia, Slovakia, Slovenia, Poland, Romania.
BNAC-5: Albania, Bosnia and Herzegovina, Croatia, Macedonia, Serbia and Montenegro.
FSU-4: Russia, Moldova, Ukraine and Uzbekistan.
FSU: without Estonia, Lithuania, Latvia.
EU-7: Austria, France, Germany, Greece, Italy, Portugal, Spain.

Source: Authors' calculations based on FAO data.

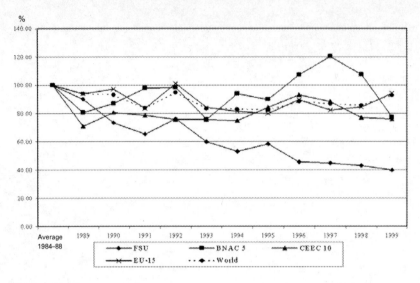

Notes:
CEEC-10: Bulgaria, Czech Republic, Estonia, Hungary, Lithuania, Latvia, Slovakia, Slovenia, Poland, Romania.
BNAC-5: Albania, Bosnia and Herzegovina, Croatia, Macedonia, Serbia and Montenegro.
FSU-4: Russia, Moldova, Ukraine and Uzbekistan.
FSU: without Estonia, Lithuania, Latvia.

Source: Authors' calculations.

*Figure 9.1   Change in production of wine, various regions of the world,
               1989–99*

in the other transition economies, and also continued throughout the 1990s. In these countries, wine production has declined by around 50 per cent over the past decade (Figures 9.2 and 9.3).

The wine sector (including grape producers at the farm level) was protected under the communist system. While government protection fell during liberalization, government interventions (particularly in some East European countries) increased again in the second half of the 1990s in the form of different measures, and will be altered further when some transition countries accede to the EU later this decade. With that in mind, this chapter first discusses the transition changes in consumption and production and how reforms have affected them, then analyses the restructuring of the production system and the wine chain and the impacts of those changes on wine trade, before discussing policy changes and the expected effects of integration of Central European countries into the EU.

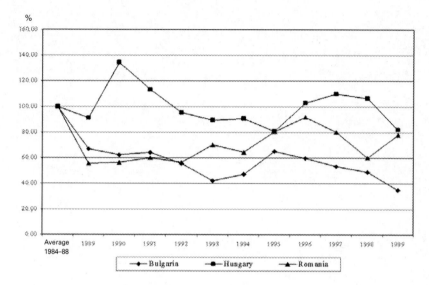

Source: Authors' calculations.

Figure 9.2 *Change in production of wine, Bulgaria, Hungary and Romania, 1989–99*

CONSUMPTION

In the late 1990s, wine consumption per capita ranged from over 40 litres in Slovenia, around 30 litres in Hungary and Romania, almost 15 litres in the Slovak republic to less than 10 litres in Bulgaria, Poland, the Baltic countries, Russia and Ukraine (Table 9.2). Consumption fell significantly in most countries at the start of the transition, particularly in those large wine-producing countries whose economies shrank most (Bulgaria, Ukraine and Russia). Hungarian official data also show declining domestic sales of wine, from US$1800 million in 1994 to US$1165 million in 1998, yet the volume data shown in Table 9.2 suggest an increase in wine consumption. These apparently conflicting data for Hungary may be explained by increasing amounts of wine being produced outside official plants and/or by consumers switching to lower-priced, lower-quality wines. The same may be true in Romania, where Euromonitor data show a decline in official sales of wine by 24 per cent in volume terms and by 42 per cent in value terms for the period 1995–99, in spite of the rise shown in Table 9.2. The latter may also reflect increased consumption by households producing their own wine. Similarly, in Bulgaria, the share of home-produced wine that is not captured by the official statistics

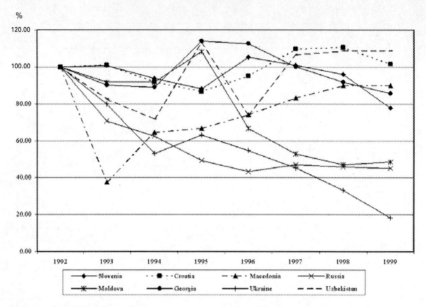

Source: Authors' calculations.

Figure 9.3   Change in production of wine, selected countries, 1989–99

is estimated at around 150–200 million litres per year, and thus approaches the
level of the official wine industry output.[2] The importance of home-produced
wine further rose during the transition due to increased numbers of subsistence
households, land fragmentation, the decline in real incomes as well as the
slowly implemented economic reforms.

Consumption and production of wine in Russia and some of the other
Former Soviet Union (FSU) countries is not as important as consumption and
production of strong alcohol.[3] Some estimates show that the decrease in
consumption of wine during the transition was offset by an increase in
consumption of strong alcohol. A specific factor influencing consumption of
wine and spirits in the FSU was the anti-alcohol campaign of the 1985–87
period and the subsequent liberalization following major political and socio-
economic changes. Alcohol consumption in Russia increased after 1993, when
reform had a dramatic impact on prices. For example, the real price of alcohol
declined by two-thirds in 1994 when average inflation (CPI) increased over
1200 per cent, but alcohol beverage prices rose by 'only' 420 per cent. This
caused a situation in which basic food products were several times more
expensive than a bottle of wine or vodka.

On average, data in Anderson and Norman (2003) suggest that consumption

Table 9.2 Consumption of wine per capita, selected CEECs, 1989–2001 (litres p.a.)

	1989	1990	1991	1992	1993	1994	1995	1996	1997	1998	1999	2000	2001
Bulgaria	16	15	12	14	13	10	9	8	9	9	n.a.	n.a.	n.a.
Hungary	23	28	29	30	32	29	27	30	32	32	n.a.	n.a.	n.a.
Latvia	n.a.	n.a.	n.a.	n.a.	n.a.	n.a.	6	7	4	6	n.a.	n.a.	n.a.
Poland	n.a.	n.a.	n.a.	n.a.	n.a.	7	7	7	7	8	n.a.	n.a.	n.a.
Romania	26	21	22	21	26	22	24	24	30	30	n.a.	n.a.	n.a.
Russia	10	10	9	6	6	8	10	6	6	6	7	8	8
Slovak Republic	n.a.	n.a.	n.a.	n.a.	n.a.	16	13	20	15	13	n.a.	n.a.	n.a.
Slovenia	n.a.	n.a.	n.a.	47	47	45	44	44	42	n.a.	n.a.	n.a.	n.a.
Ukraine	15	15	12[a]	12[a]	12[a]	12[a]	12[a]	8	7	6	n.a.	n.a.	n.a.

Note: [a] Average for the period 1991–95; n.a. = not available.

Sources: NSI (Bulgaria); Central Statistical Office (Hungary, Romania, Ukraine); EC (Slovak Republic, Slovenia); *World Drink Trends*, Anderson and Norman (2003) (Poland, Latvia, Russia).

Table 9.3   *Household consumption of wine and other beverages, by decile income groups, Bulgaria, 1998 (litres per capita)*

	Total	Decile groups									
		I	II	III	IV	V	VI	VII	VIII	IX	X
Soft drinks	20.3	8.6	12.1	15.0	16.6	18.7	18.8	22.0	25.3	28.9	36.5
Alcoholic drinks	21.1	7.1	10.4	13.0	14.7	17.5	19.5	23.3	26.9	32.6	45.6
of which:											
wine	9.2	2.6	4.6	5.6	6.3	7.6	8.2	10.0	11.7	14.7	20.8
beer	8.9	3.3	4.3	5.5	6.2	7.2	8.5	9.9	11.5	13.6	18.8
rakia	2.7	1.1	1.4	1.7	2.0	2.4	2.5	3.0	3.3	3.8	5.2
other	0.3	0.1	0.1	0.2	0.2	0.3	0.3	0.4	0.4	0.5	0.8

Source: National Statistical Institute, Bulgaria.

of wine per capita in Europe's transition economies decreased at the start of the reforms, but later recovered to the pre-transition level,[4] and that wine's share of total alcohol consumption continued to decline, as consumption of beer and spirits rose. Wine accounted for 26 per cent of alcohol consumption in the region in the 1970s, 22 per cent in the 1980s, 16 per cent in the 1990s, and 14 per cent in 2000–2001; and overall consumption of alcohol rose from 6.1 litres in 1985–94 to 7.8 litres in 1995–99 and to 8.2 litres in 2001.The decline in incomes and higher excise duties on wines shifted consumers' preferences towards beer as a cheap substitute, average consumption of which rose from 37 litres p.a. in the late 1980s/early 1990s to 50 litres in 2000–2001 (Anderson and Norman, 2003).

The strong income elasticity of demand for wine relative to other beverages even in transition countries with a tradition of wine consumption, such as Bulgaria, can be seen from official the data in Table 9.3 – although again these numbers should be interpreted with care given the large amount of home-produced wine in Bulgaria not counted in the official statistics.

PRODUCTION AND YIELDS

Grape and wine production, like the production of other commodities, has been severely affected by the political and economic reforms over the past dozen years. However, it is clear from Figure 9.1 that the wine output pattern has taken a different path in the three analysed regions in the second half of the 1990s. Wine output declined around 24 per cent in CEEC-10 and around 25 per cent in BNAC-5 between 1984–88 and 1993. Since then it has more or less stabilized in CEEC-10, while rising and then falling in BNAC-5. In contrast, wine production continued to fall in the FSU, to 43 per cent of the pre-reform level by 1998.

Wine and grape output development patterns, together with the development patterns of vineyards for the CEEC-10, FSU and BNAC-5, show how reforms affected differently the development in these sub-regions. Figures 9.4 to 9.6 illustrate the contrasting processes. The area remained fairly stable on average in CEEC-10, although this average hides important changes: Romania's vineyard area increased, Hungary's declined just 10 per cent, while Bulgaria's declined by one-quarter. The increase in Romania's vine area was mostly the result of an increase in low-quality hybrids, which in 1997 represented 45 per cent of total vine area, up by one-fifth over 1989 (Rusu, 2001). The decline in Bulgaria was largely due to the fall of the inflation-adjusted price of wine by 40 per cent and grape prices 60 per cent in 1991–92, and then remaining at those lower levels throughout the 1990s.

Vineyards declined sharply (by 27 per cent) between 1989 and 1993 in the BNAC-5, and declined only slightly afterwards. The decline resulted from the political changes in Yugoslavia and especially from the dramatic reforms in Albania in 1990–92. The area of vineyards in Albania declined by more than 70 per cent between 1989 and 1992, as a complete collapse of the collective farming system caused a radical decollectivization and fragmentation of

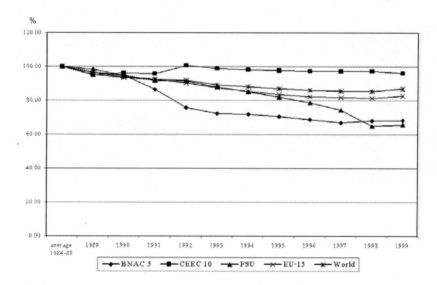

Source: Authors' calculations.

Figure 9.4   Change in area of vineyards, various regions, 1989–99

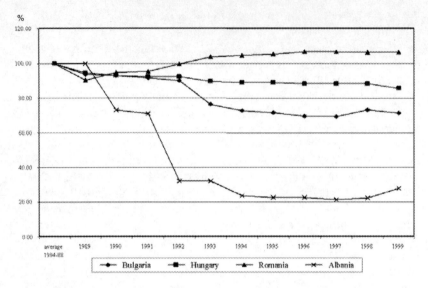

Source: Authors' calculations.

Figure 9.5   Change in area of vineyards, selected countries, 1989–99

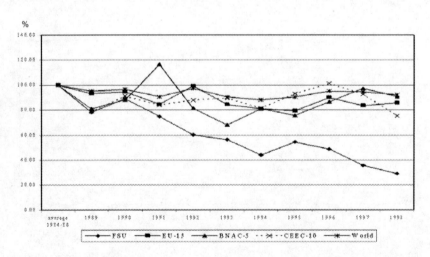

Source: Authors' calculations.

Figure 9.6   Change in production of grapes, various regions, 1989–99

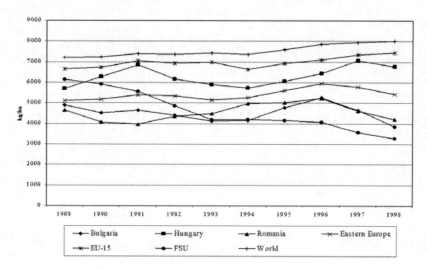

Source: Authors' calculations.

Figure 9.7 Grape yields, various regions, 1989–99

Albanian agriculture (Cungu and Swinnen, 1999). The only region where the wine area continued to decline after 1995 was in the FSU.

More than in any other development, the impact of the reforms can be seen from the evolution of grape yields. While yields are affected by climate and so on, the three-year moving averages in Figures 9.7 and 9.8 indicate diverging patterns. In those countries where economic and institutional reforms have been implemented thoroughly and effectively, grape yields are increasing, or have at least been recovering since the mid-1990s, while in those countries where this is not the case, yields are static or declining. This is also true within the CEECs, where Romania and Bulgaria are falling behind Hungary and Slovenia, as yields and growth after 1996 in the former countries suffer from delayed reform effects and structural constraints. By 2001 grape yields in Eastern Europe averaged 5000 kg/ha, which is considerably below the EU-15 average of 7900 kg/ha (Anderson and Norman, 2003).

FARM RESTRUCTURING

Grape production took place on large-scale cooperative and state farms under the communist regime, with the exception of Hungary, where about 68 per cent of the vineyards were private property at the beginning of the reform, and

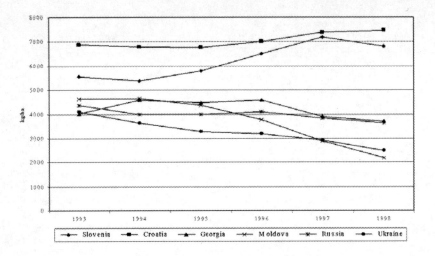

Source: Authors' calculations.

Figure 9.8   Grape yields, selected countries, 1989–99

the republics of the former Yugoslavia, where individual farms dominated under the communist regime.

With privatization and land reform, a major restructuring of the grape production system has occurred in several transition countries so that the majority of grape production currently occurs on much smaller family farms. For example, in Bulgaria, where cooperative farms dominated under communism, most grape production now occurs on (very) small-scale individual farms. The liquidation of the former communist cooperatives and the land restitution process disrupted the cultivation of vineyards and created a large number of absentee landowners and extreme land fragmentation. While former large blocks of vineyards continue to exist in most cases, the property rights are now spread among many landowners. However, many of the new owners do not cultivate the land properly and do not replant and replace the old and depreciated vines with new ones,[5] nor do they want to enter into co-operative arrangements. This affects neighbouring plants and reduces yields and the quality of the grapes. Hence there is now a tendency for wineries to purchase vineyards from those many new landowners uninterested in entering the agricultural business.

In Hungary, over 132 000 individual farms were involved in (some) grape production by 2000, according to official statistics, and small-scale farms accounted for 92 per cent of all grape-producing farms. In Slovenia there are about 34 800 individual farms involved in production of grapes whose average vineyard area is just 0.4 ha. Official statistics for Bulgaria show that there are around 23 000 grape producers for Bulgaria and more than 120 wine processors. However, in Bulgaria only 55 per cent of the wine grape production was purchased by the wineries in 2000, the rest being used in home-produced wine. Economic reforms led to an increase in subsistence farming not only in Bulgaria but also in Romania, Slovakia, Macedonia and especially in the FSU. In other transition countries where grape production was located on large state and collective farms under communism, such as in Romania, where grape growing is an important activity, grape production has also shifted to individual farms on scattered plots. By 1997, almost three-quarters of Romania's wine area was private property (Rusu, 2001).

The small individual farms typically use very labour-intensive production techniques. This creates specific problems in grape production if these farms need investments in human capital and in equipment and technology to upgrade their production techniques in order to produce at least the minimum quality required by wineries. Even then, fragmented farm structures are a problem for investors in wine processing, where there are high costs of grape collection in the absence of vineyard consolidation.

REFORM OF THE SUPPLY CHAIN

Wine companies were strongly co-integrated with grape producers (mainly large cooperatives) under the former central planning, but wineries had low levels of investment capital and knowledge about wine production. International trade in wine depended, then, on the decisions and acts of a capital monopoly trade organization, not at the winery level. After the reforms, the link between wine processors and grape farms was very disrupted in countries like Bulgaria, Albania and Romania, while it was more successfully maintained in countries like Slovakia, the Czech Republic and Hungary, where cooperatives were not so severely restructured or liquidated.

Like food-processing companies, wine processors had difficulties in accessing capital, especially during the first years of transition, because of the ongoing land and banking reforms accompanied by the decline in GDP and high inflation. Some of the wine producers were left with debts, and their situation was worsened by the loss of the East German and Russian markets. This is because previously the best wines were exported to the EU market while the low-quality product was sold in the FSU countries, Poland and East Germany.

There were payment delays, especially at the beginning of the reforms, when farmers received part of their money at the time of delivering the grapes and part a few months later, usually after the produced wine was sold by the wineries. This created disturbances and capital constraints in the wine chain,

174

The Old World

and induced farmers to reduce inputs. That caused a decline in grape supply and quality, and encouraged the shift to subsistence farming.[6]

PRIVATIZATION AND FOREIGN INVESTMENT

Various approaches of privatization of processing facilities have been followed, resulting in different market and industry dynamics during the transition period (Gow, 2000). For example, the Hungarian privatization procedure of selling off processing facilities to the highest bidder has given rise to a much more efficient restructuring and stronger inflow of foreign capital than other procedures followed by most CEECs and FSU countries (Swinnen, Dries and Gow, 2001). In general, the food industry has attracted much foreign direct investments (FDI). By 2000, more than 50 per cent of the assets in the Hungarian food and beverage industry was foreign property. By the end of 1998 major FDI in the Bulgarian food industry accounted for US$257 million or one-eighth of total FDI in the country by that time. By 2000, investments in the food industry accounted for 30 per cent of total FDI in the country. FDI in Bulgarian wine production increased from $17 million in 1998 to $81 million in 2000. Although most of the Romanian wine industry was privatized by 1999, foreign investment is still very low.

Different types of privatization methods applied in FSU countries resulted in large differences in ownership structure. For example, in Ukraine, where privatization favoured incumbent managers, 54 per cent of total assets were owned by managers in 1997, while enterprises in Russia and Moldova had more diversified ownership on average (Djankov, 1999). State participation in the management of enterprises has effectively constrained enterprise restructuring. In Hungary, a variety of wineries has emerged. In some cases, joint ventures (CANA and Eurobor, Hungary) and local management (Helvecia, Hungary) have retained past structures of integration through ownership and contracts. In cases where new ownership is not in full control, changes in the management may not occur, whereas in cases of complete buyouts or foreign control the wineries have vertically integrated through contracts, with no assurance that former suppliers will be retained (Hungarovin and Szekszard, Hungary).

In Slovakia, by April 1998 there were only 40 public companies among the 1289 registered companies in the food and drink sector. In Bulgaria, by the end of 2000, all wine-processing assets were private property, but only a few were owned by foreign companies. Most of the wineries stayed cooperative or were subject to managerial and employee buyouts in Bulgaria, Romania, and also in some FSU countries.

Because of the narrowing export market for Bulgarian wines, the process of restructuring started with the establishment of Boyar Estates after the merger between the foreign-owned Domaine Boyar and Vinprom-Rousse Seabord. This merger established a new structure with large market power, especially in the export of quality wine and domestic retailing. The new owners in 2000 possessed four large wineries in very favourable areas: two in the northern part and two in the southern part of the country. Most of the other large wine-processing companies are in a difficult economic situation, especially Gamza Suhindol. Further consolidation in the local wine markets may boost quality production and marketing, as is the case in other industries in transition countries, but it will also create more competition for the small local wine processors.

Some private wine companies are trying to set up technology adoption and credit facilitation programmes for their wine grape supplying farms.[7] With major capital market imperfections in most of the countries, such programmes can significantly affect farms' access to basic inputs and finance. For example, some companies provide loans for farms to invest in new plant or machinery, and assist them in getting access to better fertilizers, chemicals and other inputs, and in some cases even support their investments in land purchase. They even directly buy and supply the necessary inputs to the farms and guarantee the purchase of future production in the case of Damianitza, Bulgaria. Both foreign-owned and domestic wine companies implement such credit and investment programmes in order to guarantee their inputs, but it is not yet a widespread practice because of the difficult economic situation in most of the wineries.

Although data are difficult to obtain, foreign investors appear to be imposing higher quality standards. Their example is being followed by domestic investors who produce for Western markets, where market pressures from both consumers and competing wine suppliers are much higher than in East European markets.

FDI in the wine industry was hindered in most of the CEECs by several factors, such as general economic and institutional uncertainty; small domestic demand for high-quality products; tight state control on foreign capital and state preferences for domestic capital in the privatization process; lack of transparency in the general rules for investment and privatization; legal restrictions on FDI; unstable and not well-developed foreign markets for wine production; the predominant orientation of wine producers towards the FSU market and its unclear future; general uncertainty about the future of the former Yugoslavia; prohibition of sales of certain assets;[8] taxes levied on the sales of state assets; and excessive bureaucracy.

FDI in the retailing system, which could assist the promotion of wine on domestic markets, has increased rapidly in recent years. Furthermore, the direct sale of wine from local producers to consumers is increasing and the importance of media advertising and specialised magazines is rising, at least in Bulgaria and Hungary. Overall, distribution systems are slowly becoming more demand-driven, but inefficiencies remain at both wholesale and retail levels.

REFORM IMPACTS ON WINE TRADE

Moldova, Bulgaria, Hungary, Macedonia, Georgia and Romania are the largest wine exporters in the region, with Russia, Poland and the Czech Republic the largest importers (Table 9.4). Within the Former Soviet Union, Moldova, Ukraine and Georgia exported much wine to Russia. Since the

Table 9.4   Wine exports and imports, selected countries, 1992[a] and 2001 (US$ million)

	1992			2001		
	X	M	X–M	X	M	X–M
Bulgaria	202	2	200	59	1	–58
Czech Republic	3	13	–9	2	35	–33
Hungary	115	8	108	58	5	53
Poland	3	15	–11	0	150	–50
Romania	11	7	4	20	2	18
Slovakia	8	1	8	6	6	0
Slovenia	20	21	0	9	3	5
Croatia	18	4	14	11	5	6
Macedonia	21	0	21	28	0	28
Serbia & Montenegro	7	1	7	4	1	2
Georgia	4	0	4	27	1	27
Moldova	66	0	63	155	2	154
Russia	1	143	–137	1	242	–241
Turkmenistan	5	0	5	0	0	0
Ukraine	44	6	3	13	17	–4
Uzbekistan	6	0	6	4	0	4

Notes:
[a] 1992 for Bulgaria and Hungary = 1989; for Czech Republic and Slovakia = 1993; and for Romania = 1990.
X = exports; M = imports.

Source: (Anderson and Norman 2003) and FAO.

reforms, Ukraine exports' have not grown greatly, but Moldova's and Georgia's have, at 10 and 27 per cent p.a., respectively, in US dollar terms between 1992 and 2001. Almost all those exports still go to Russia, however, at prices between 40 and 60 per cent of the average for the world (Anderson and Norman, 2003).

Traditional Central European and Balkan wine-producing countries (Bulgaria, Croatia, Hungary, Macedonia, Romania, Serbia and Montenegro, Slovakia) are net exporters of wine. Changes in CEEC-10 exports of wine can be divided into three phases. During the first years of the reforms, exports declined sharply. After 1992 they recovered significantly, reaching a maximum in 1995. In the second half of the 1990s wine exports in volume and in value declined again (Figure 9.9).

Exports of wine from Hungary have been relatively stable since 1993, but exports from Bulgaria and Romania have been more volatile (Figure 9.10). The increase in Bulgarian exports between 1992 and 1996 was mostly to Russia at the expense of its share in the EU (Table 9.5).[9] The recent decline in Bulgarian wine exports (which represented about 30 per cent of the country's agricultural exports in 1999), as in wine production, followed restructuring and privatization in the wine sector in 1995 and the economic crisis in 1996–97, which was the most severe since the start of the reforms. The Russian crisis in 1998 further complicated export problems.[10]

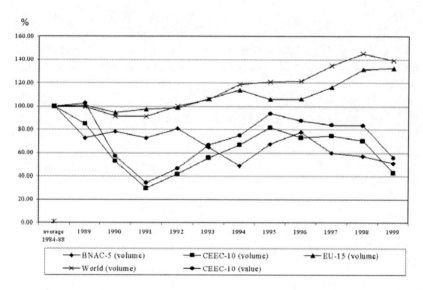

Figure 9.9   Change in volume and value of wine exports, by region, 1989–99

%

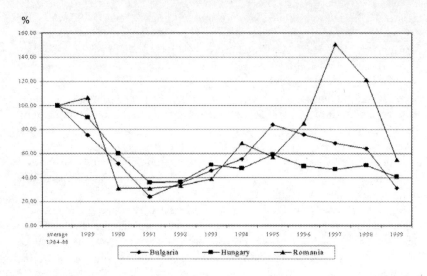

Source: Authors' calculations.

*Figure 9.10   Change in volume and value of wine exports, selected countries,
1989–99*

In contrast to trade developments with the EU, Bulgarian exports of bottled
wine to the FSU increased after 1992 until 1998, when the Russian financial
crisis effectively closed down that market, causing in turn major problems for
Bulgaria's domestic market. Improvements in grape processing and distribution have improved the quality and international competitiveness of the wine

*Table 9.5   Bulgaria's exports of bottled and bulk wine to various regions,
1993–2000 (% by volume)*

Exports to:	Bottled wine			Broached (bulk) wine		
	1993	1997	2000	1993	1997	2000
Western Europe	62	48	50	77	44	73
Central and Eastern Europe and FSU	30	43	43	8	18	8
USA and Canada	3	3	3	1	2	2
Japan	0	0	0	12	29	17
Other	5	7	4	3	6	0
Total	100	100	100	100	100	100

Source: Authors' calculations.

chains in Hungary and Bulgaria (as in some other CEECs), but much hard work still lies ahead.

Romanian exports of wine have never been strong, and in 1999 accounted for only 15 per cent of that country's wine output. In general, state enterprises still dominate in upstream and downstream industries and the country suffers from a lack of export specialization. Low-quality wines still dominate, with production and sales of white wine representing more than 80 per cent of total sales in 1999 (Euromonitor, 2001). Most of the wine exports go to Germany (40–50 per cent), although those exports have fallen by 76 per cent in the period 1986–99. A specific feature is the export of broached (bulk) wine that is bottled in Germany and sold with labels showing the Romanian origin of the wine (Gavrila, 2001). Considerable steps in quality improvements and marketing have still to be taken.

Although imports of wine (in volume and value terms) increased during the transition for the CEEC-10 and for the FSU also (before the financial crisis in Russia), they were not of high-quality wine. Parts of the imported production had been bottled in the country, possibly mixed with local wines and re-exported to third countries including FSU markets. In wine trade developments in Eastern Europe and the FSU, bilateral trade relations between neighbouring countries still play a special role (for example Macedonia and Bulgaria, the Czech Republic and Slovakia, Moldova and Romania, Moldova and Ukraine, Hungary and Slovenia, Georgia and Russia).

WINE POLICIES

Government intervention in the wine sector differs between countries. In several countries, such as Bulgaria, Romania and Hungary, there are no direct subsidies for grape producers and wine processors. Hence market requirements are the regulator. By contrast, in Slovenia from 2000 onwards, direct payments for grapes per ha (fixed at 294 EUR/ha) were introduced to make the policies consistent with the Common Agricultural Policy (CAP) of the EU. Because of administrative controls in the application of subsidies, a register of grape- and wine-growers has been set up to collect data on grape- and wine-growers' vine area, grape crop and wine crush.

In the Czech Republic, legislation is partly aligned with EU requirements concerning wine. Amendments to the Act on Viticulture have been introduced concerning oenological practices, requirements on imported wine, a vineyard register, conditions for production of quality wines and the labelling of individual types of wine, in anticipation of a new viticulture law. In Slovakia the completion of the vineyard register has been hindered by unclear land property rights and land fragmentation. Bulgaria has introduced a new Law on Wines and Spirits, and a Law on Vineyard Cadaster, which entered into force in 2000; it is also preparing secondary legislation. Even so, implementation of the legislation, and the link between the institutions and the local producers, remain weak.

After the Uruguay Round Agreement (URA), non-tariff barriers were dismantled through the tariffication process, and import licensing has been outlawed. This enabled Hungary to bind relatively high tariffs, but Romania has set the highest tariff ceiling bindings among the CEECs due to it obtaining 'developing country' status at the WTO. In Hungary, the tariff escalation, together with higher export subsidies for processed than primary products, provided significant protection not only for the food industry but also for wine.

EFFECTS OF EU ENLARGEMENT

When the CEECs join the EU from 2004 they will have to adjust their agricultural policies to the CAP as it stands at that time and thereafter. Wine trade and policy reforms in the CEECs depend on the association agreements with the EU, CEFTA and EFTA agreements, FTAs with third countries, other specific regional agreements (the Czech–Slovak Customs Union, the Baltic FTA, and so on, and bilateral agreements on economic development and protection of investments) within the CEE countries. In the CEFTA agreement, wine stayed in the third group of products for which no common agreement could be reached.

Extending the current EU wine policy to the CEECs raises a number of important challenges, none of which have obvious solutions. For example, if wine quotas and restrictions on vineyards are to be implemented, what is the relevant base period for the CEECs, given their specific communist and transition history? How can wine quotas be implemented in countries such as Bulgaria and Romania with their hugely fragmented grape-farm structures? What will be the impact on prices and supply and what will be the impact on trade, export subsidies and WTO commitments? What will be the effect of EU enlargement on prices of raw materials and on the trade performance of CEECs (for example, is trade diversion likely to occur)?

Turning first to the price effects, producer prices in CEEC are lower than EU prices due to current low levels of support and inefficiency of the downstream sector. The relatively high level of EU prices compared with world prices is another reason for the existing price gap, which has been diminishing for all CEECs since the early 1990s. Also, price differences among CEE countries are large as a result of their unequal economic development and the relatively high competitive wine market positions of Bulgaria, Hungary, Romania,

Macedonia and Croatia mask severe structural problems, especially in grape production.

Apart from differences in policies, quality differences explain a large part of the price gap. Furthermore, the relative EU–CEEC prices are also strongly affected by exchange rate developments, and revaluations of the CEEC real exchange rates since the mid-1990s have contributed to reducing nominal price gaps for agricultural products (Swinnen, 2002).

As far as the WTO is concerned, enlargement of the EU will be considered, in legal terms, to be the enlargement of a customs union, governed by the povisions laid down in GATT article XXIV (Tangermann, 2000). That article contains provisions for tariff bindings,[11] but not for the other commitments. In the 'precedent' of the northern enlargement of the EU in 1995, commitments on market access and domestic support and export subsidies were just added up, net of bilateral trade. Probably the same procedure will be followed with eastern enlargement, although this may require compensation to trading partners who are directly affected by the customs union – as was the case in the northern enlargement (Burrell, 2000).

Some CEECs were already GATT members when the Uruguay Round Agreement on Agriculture (URAA) was negotiated (Czech Republic, Hungary, Poland, Romania, Slovakia). These countries accepted schedules of quantitative policy commitments during the Uruguay Round, like other countries, but as the UR overlapped with their transition process, the starting conditions for these countries in the process of converting past policies into future WTO commitments differs from Western countries because finding a base period was a particularly difficult issue. CEECs were given the option to adopt tariff bindings essentially unrelated to past policies, similar to the way developing countries are treated. Other transition countries have negotiated their accession to the WTO since the URAA and have become members (Bulgaria, Estonia, Latvia, Slovenia) or are still negotiating (Azerbaijan, Belarus, Russia, Ukraine, Central Asian Republics). The fundamental nature of their agreement is similar to that of others. Hence their agricultural parts specify commitments on market access, export subsidization and domestic support. However, commitments and details differ quite significantly among the CEECs.

Most CEECs have implemented tariff bindings considerably above applied tariffs on wine imports. For example, Bulgaria chose tariff bindings of 40 per cent plus 80 ECU/hl in 1995, to be reduced to 25 per cent plus 51 ECU/hl in the end period. That is considerably higher than the EU-15 end-period bound tariff for wine of 32 ECU/hl. Romania opted for a base rate of duty of 350 ECU/hl for wine in 1994 that has to be reduced to a bound rate of 315 by 2006. Slovenia's base rate of duty for wines of 27 per cent in 1995 was reduced to 17 per cent by 2000, but it had a specific tariff of 245 ECU/ton in 1997 that was increased to 436 ECU/ton in 2000. These high tariff bindings have allowed the CEECs to increase tariffs significantly without creating conflict with WTO members.

Few problems are expected with EU enlargement in the area of domestic support since both the EU-15 and the CEECs still have considerable slack in their commitments. However, problems may arise with tariff bindings and export subsidies, not least because the CEECs and the EU-15 already have problems with export subsidies in some cases. The quantity reduction commitments on export subsidies reflect historical evolutions, including those during the central planning period. For Hungary the trend in the export commitments shows a reduction from 499 000 hl (ECU 4.8 million) in 1995 to 408 000 hl (ECU 2 million) in 2000 without waiver and to 408 000 hl (ECU 10.1 million) with waiver. The reduction for Bulgaria is not so significant and is from 99 000 tons in 1997 (ECU 1.6 million) to 87 000 tons in 2000 (ECU 1.3 million), while for Romania it is considerably lower: from 9250 tons in 1995 (Lei 65 million) to 8870 tons in 2000 (Lei 60 million), with a projected reduction to 7900 tons in 2004 (Lei 50 million). The reduction for Slovakian export commitments are from 9800 tons in 1997 (SKK 49 million) to 8700 tons in 2000 (SKK 38 million), while for the Czech Republic it is almost insignificant: from 4200 tons in 1997 (CZK 20 million) to 3700 tons in 2000 (CZK 15.6 million).

Finally, on EU accession, the low quality of CEEC grape production resulting in production of wines of low quality will continue to hold back the international competitiveness of most wineries in the region. One of the preconditions to sell in the EU market is the accordance of production standards with the quality, sanitary and hygiene regulations imposed by the EU. Certificates have to be mutually approved and issued by official certification agencies based on evidence that the wine has been produced in accordance with the ecological standards of the EU. It remains to be seen to what extent such technical barriers to trade will impede wine exports from Central and Eastern to Western Europe.

NOTES

1. Albania, Bosnia and Herzegovina, Croatia, Macedonia and Serbia and Montenegro.
2. Home production of wine is popular not only in Bulgaria, but also in the rest of the Balkan countries, as well in Ukraine, Moldova and Hungary.
3. According to the official statistics, production of vodka and liquor in the Russian Federation in 1999 reached 98 per cent of the pre-transition level in 1990. By contrast, production of grape wines remained relatively low during the last decade and in 1999 had only reached 24 per cent of the 1990 pre-reform level, while production of sparkling wines in 1999 was only 7 per cent of the pre-transition level in 1990.
4. Consumption of wine declined from 9.7 l/capita in the period 1985–89 to 8.6 l/capita in the period 1990–94, but later recovered to 9.5 l/capita in the period 1995–99.

5. In Bulgaria many vineyards are old: only 3 per cent are under five years old, 13 per cent are five to ten years old, 22 per cent are 10–15 years old, and 62 per cent are over 15 years old.
6. The position of farmers was worsened by the delay in the establishment of clear property rights and in the land reform. In Bulgaria and Romania the process continued for more than nine years, and while in Bulgaria by 2000 about 98 per cent of the agricultural land had been restituted, only 85 per cent was in Romania.
7. Improvements in technologies also started to appear in the FSU countries. For example, in five Moldovian wineries (Milestii Mici, Nisporeni, Stauceni, Ciadir-Lunga and Carpineni) new lines for sparkling wines have been built. Additionally, with credits granted by the EBRD and the Canadian company Garling, 24 wineries have been equipped and a new glass factory (US$28 million) is under construction. Investments of Penfold (Australia) and HDR (France) are also present, but administration problems and bureaucracy still impede foreign capital inflow.
8. In Ukraine, some equipment was still under mobilization reserve and the enterprise had to maintain it in case of war and could not sell it.
9. Bulgarian wine exports to the EU have fallen by one-half during the 1990s. More than 65 per cent of Bulgarian wine exports go to Moldova, the UK, Germany, Japan and Poland.
10. The low and unstable quality of Bulgarian wines makes it unattractive on foreign markets. Additionally, the chaos during the purchase campaigns, decreasing quality of grape production, and the disrupted marketing of the wines after privatization significantly reduced its wine exports. Wineries are full of wine of low quality that cannot be sold, which further reduces available storage space and hence new production.
11. Tariff bindings after enlargement must not, on the whole, be higher than the average of the individual members before enlargement.

REFERENCES

Anderson, K. and D. Norman (2003), *Global Wine Production, Consumption and Trade, 1961 to 2001: A Statistical Compendium*, Adelaide: Centre for International Economic Studies.

Burrell, A. (2000), 'The World Trade Organisation and EU Agricultural Policy', in A. Burrell and A. Oskam (eds), *Agricultural Policy and Enlargement of the European Union*, Wageningen: Wageningen Press.

Cungu, A. and J.F.M. Swinnen (1999), 'Albania's Radical Agrarian Reform', *Economic Development and Cultural Change*, **47** (3), 605–19.

Djankov, S. (1999), 'Ownership Structure and Enterprise Restructuring in Six Newly Independent States', *Comparative Economics Studies*, **41** (1), 75–96.

Euromonitor (2001), *The Market for Wine in Romania*, London: Euromonitor.

Gavrila, V. (2001), 'Economia Viticola a Romaniei – Adaptabilitate Din Perspectiva Aderarii la Uniunea Europeana', Working Paper, Institute of Agricultural Economics, Romanian Academy, Bucharest.

Gow, H. (2000), 'Restructuring the Agribusiness Sector and the Role of Foreign Direct Investment', in A. Burrell and A. Oskam (eds), *Agricultural Policy and Enlargement of the European Union*, Wageningen: Wageningen Press.

National Statistical Institute (Bulgaria) (2001), *Statistical Yearbook*, Sophia, various issues.

Rusu, M. (2001), 'State and Prospects of Horticulture in Romania', Working Paper, Institute of Agricultural Economics, Romanian Academy, Bucharest.

Swinnen, J. (2002), 'Transition and Integration in Europe: Implications for Agriculture and Food Markets, Policy and Trade Agreements', *The World Economy*, **25** (4), 481–501.

Swinnen J., L. Dries and H. Gow (2001), 'Dairy Markets, Policies, and Trade in Eastern Europe and the Former Soviet Union', PRG Working Paper No. 26, Department of Agricultural and Environmental Economics, K.U. Leuven, Belgium.

Tangermann, S. (2000), 'Widening the EU to Central and Eastern European Countries: WTO and the Perspectives of the New Member States,' in A. Burrell and A. Oskam (eds), *Agricultural Policy and Enlargement of the European Union*, Wageningen: Wageningen Press.

PART III

The New World

10. North America

Daniel A. Sumner, Helene Bombrun, Julian M. Alston and Dale Heien

The wine industry in the USA and Canada is new by Old World standards but old by New World standards. The industry has had several rebirths, so specifying its age depends on the purpose of the investigation. In the colonial and post-colonial period up through the middle of the nineteenth century, it was a relatively tiny industry with imports accounting for almost all of the still meager consumption of quality wine in the region (Winkler et al., 1962). There was gradual development in the latter half of the nineteenth century, but wine production in the USA and Canada only began to develop significantly with the expansion of the California industry early in the twentieth century (Carosso, 1951; Hutchinson, 1969). Then the industry needed to be recreated after the prohibition era from 1920 to 1932. More recently, in a sense, the industry was reborn again thirty or so years ago with an aggressive movement towards higher quality.

The geography of the industry is relatively simple. Despite some wine and wine grape production in Canada and most states in the USA, California is the location of more than 90 per cent of grape crush and about 85 per cent of the wine production in North America (Wine Institute, 2002). Therefore, most of the discussion of grape and wine production in this chapter focuses on California, while the discussion of demand and policy issues covers all of the USA and Canada.

The chapter begins with a brief outline of the history of wine production and consumption in the USA to roughly 1990. The expansion of the industry up to the prohibition era and the climb back after prohibition are the main parts of this story. We then turn to the demand side to consider recent data on wine markets, including information on demand by quality, and the domestic and import sources of wine consumed in the USA and Canada. Wine marketing regulations are complex and influence the pattern of demand, given state-by-state and province-by-province rules on wine retailing and wholesaling.

The third section reviews recent data on grape and wine production in the USA and Canada with specific attention to grape acreage and production by variety and region in California. We also examine grape prices by region and variety, and the consequences of the spread of grape pests such as phylloxera and Pierce's Disease. The next section also includes analysis of recent wine production patterns and the industrial organization of the wine industry, including vertical integration from grape production through wine production, and a brief discussion of exports. The final section reviews the most important economic and policy issues now facing the wine grape and wine industries in the USA and Canada and discuss how the industry is likely to evolve in the near future and over the longer term.

HISTORY

The wine industry and market in North America began as soon as there were sufficient European immigrants to drink, buy and produce wine. The abundance of native grapes suggested that wine could be produced successfully in North America. However, the expansion from nascent beginnings was slow. In the sixteenth century wine was produced in both Spanish and French colonies of North America successfully enough that the home-country industries blocked further development, which then stimulated wine production in the English colonies (Mishkin, 1966). In the seventeenth century attempts to establish *Vitis vinifera* in what later became the eastern United States failed, and grapes grown there even now are based on early native species (Winkler et al., 1962).

During the seventeenth and early eighteenth centuries vines and wine were spread throughout what is now Mexico and the southwest of the USA by Spanish soldiers and missionaries. Like much else in the history of the state, the wine industry in California was created by the establishment and spread of the missions (Conaway, 1992). Beginning in 1790 in San Diego, over the next four decades, Spanish missions moved up the coast bringing vines and winemaking abilities with them. The local grapes were of no use for winemaking, but a European-based variety known as 'Mission' did well, and became the basis of California wine production for many years (Hutchinson, 1969; Winkler et al., 1962). The mission vineyards and winemaking facilities fell into disuse and disarray when the Spanish were forced out after Mexico (which included California) became independent in the 1830s (Winkler et al., 1962).

California joined the USA as a part of the settlement of the war between the USA and Mexico in the 1840s. The California Gold Rush, beginning in 1849, hurried California to statehood in 1850. Then the wine industry expanded rapidly in a state that was experiencing a population and economic boom. In 1850, only 9462 hl of wine were produced in the USA. By 1860, US production had jumped to 56 775 hl, with California joining the major production states (Hutchinson, 1969). Most of this wine was very low quality, produced for consumption locally by miners. However, the production of quality wine also had its beginnings during this decade. In 1857, Colonel Haraszthy, the founder of Buena Vista winery in Sonoma, began propagating important European varieties in California.

The well-known phylloxera story from the nineteenth century also shows the interdependence between the American and European industries (Unwin, 1991). Grape phylloxera, which are root-destroying insects, are native to the Americas, where native *Vitis* species are rarely damaged by its feeding. European-based rootstock proved to be extremely susceptible to phylloxera during various attempts to develop quality wine production in North America, from Jamestown onward. Phylloxera were identified in California in 1873 and this hampered the development of high-quality wine production in California in the nineteenth century. Also, the phylloxera were unintentionally imported to Europe in the mid-1800s and about 75 per cent of the vines of France were destroyed within 30 years of the introduction (Winkler at al., 1962). Eventually it was discovered that root systems of American species could be grafted with *Vitis vinifera* scion cultivars to produce phylloxera-resistant plants that yield European varietal grapes (Granett and de Brenedictis, 1996).

From about 1875 to 1915, the wine industry in the USA and Canada developed rapidly in both quantity and quality. After depressions in the 1870s, and the battle with phylloxera, the industry gradually began replacing Mission grapes with higher-quality varieties (Gregory, 1912). By the 1904 to 1908 period, annual US wine production was about 1.55 million hl, with about 85 per cent produced in California. Annual production peaked in the 1909 to 1913 period at 2.01 million hl before declining back to about 1.55 million hl again from 1914 to 1918 as the movement towards prohibition began (Selden, 1941; Hutchinson, 1969; US Tariff Commision, 1935). The influx of about six million immigrants from wine-producing regions of Europe during the early part of the twentieth century contributed to both more demand and better-quality wine production. This immigration was halted by World War I and was not allowed to resume. Then prohibition shifted industry progress into reverse.

The 18th Amendment to the US Constitution, which implemented prohibition, had been ratified by 36 states in January of 1919. This prohibition against beverage alcohol other than for medicinal or sacramental purposes was law from January 1920 until 1933. The operative Section 1 read simply: 'After one year from the ratification of this article the manufacture, sale, or transportation of intoxicating liquors within, the importation thereof into, or the exportation thereof from the United States and all territory subject to the jurisdiction thereof for beverage purposes is hereby prohibited.'

The law allowed the production of wine for use in the home of the wine-maker; but there was also widespread illegal consumption of wine. Therefore, grape acreage did not fall, and some estimates suggest that overall wine consumption expanded during the 1920s (Hutchinson, 1969). California grape production was reported as about 0.71 million tonnes in 1910, with about 57 per cent crushed commercially. In 1920, production was 1.15 million tonnes, but only 13 per cent of these were crushed commercially. Then, after ten years of prohibition, in 1930 production had risen to 1.87 million tonnes, but only 4 per cent of these were commercially crushed in that year. Grape production remained relatively stagnant during the 1930s, with total output rising only about 10 per cent, to 2.04 million tonnes in 1940, but by then about 44 per cent of the California grapes were commercially crushed (California Crop and Livestock Reporting Service, various years). Most observers assume that much of the grape crop was home crushed and turned into wine during prohibition, but that wine production took place in home wineries. In addition, the California table grape and raisin industries developed rapidly in the first half of the twentieth century, and the expansion of these other markets for grapes would probably have reduced the share of grapes used for wine during the 1910 to 1940 period even without prohibition.

There is little question that the impact of prohibition on the commercial wine industry was dramatic. Almost all of the 700 commercial wineries that operated in California in 1920 were closed over the subsequent 12 years. This implied a major loss in capital investment and in human capital for the industry. Further, the development of the market for high-quality commercial wines was reversed (Tillitt, 1932; King, 1967). Lapsley (1996) discusses three explanations why, in the first years that followed repeal of prohibition, most wine was of poor quality. First, 80 per cent of California wine production was shipped as bulk to out-of-state bottlers who had their own labels. This reduced incentives for California wine producers to build a reputation for quality with consumers. Second, winemakers in the post-depression years were untrained and were producing wine in unsanitary conditions. Third, demand for grapes had been high all over the continent so that grape prices rose and during prohibition growers planted high-yielding, low-quality, thick-skinned grape varieties that could withstand transportation.

The role of prohibition in the development of demand for wine quality is not fully understood, but one apparent consequence was an emphasis during prohibition on production of sweet dessert wines that persisted after repeal (Lapsley, 1996). For example, in 1950, only 26 per cent of US consumption was table wine, most of the rest was sweet, high alcohol dessert wine. Lapsley points out that during prohibition, most wine drinkers were looking for high alcohol rather than traditional wine flavour. Moreover, he notes that the market for quality commercial table wine remained low, in part because some immigrant Americans continued to produce wine at home (from California grapes), thereby escaping high excise taxes. Finally, prohibition itself was the consequence of an anti-alcohol sentiment that would have had significant effects even without the 18th Amendment.

By 1950, annual US production of wine had tripled pre-prohibition quantities, with about 90 per cent of the total of 52 million hl produced in California. Consumption stood at about 3.5 litres per capita. Of this consumption, less than 5 per cent was imported (Table 10.1). At that time, three-quarters of imports were from France and Italy.

Several factors contributed to overall demand growth in the second half of the twentieth century. From 1950 to 1980, per capita wine consumption in the USA more than doubled, from 3.5 to 8 litres per capita. Although 8 litres is low by European standards, the growth in per capita consumption actually stopped and went into reverse in the 1980s. Population growth continued to contribute steadily to total demand. From 1950 to 1980, imports grew from less than 5 per cent to 22 per cent of consumption by 1980, and California continued to supply about 90 per cent of domestic production. In total, table wine consumption rose from about 1.36 million hl to about 15.1 million hl. Quality improved as well. From 1950 to 1980, the share of table wine (that is, still wine having less than 14 per cent alcohol by volume) in total wine consumption grew from one-quarter to three-quarters (Table 10.1).

The gradual upgrading of the quality of California wine is usually dated from the late 1960s or early 1970s. The coastal industry began expanding and the area planted to higher-quality varieties grew. The basis for this change was an expansion of wine awareness and consumption in the USA. However, a wine consumption boom in the late 1960s and early 1970s (per capita consumption jumped by 50 per cent from 1967 to 1971) gave way to sluggish

Table 10.1   Wine consumption, by type and source, USA, 1950–2002

Year	US consumption			From the US		From California	
	Litre/ capita	'000 hl	% table wine	'000 hl	%	'000 hl	%
1950	3.5	5 299	26	5 148	97	4 542	85
1960	3.4	6 170	36	5 791	93	4 883	79
1970	5.0	10 106	50	8 970	87	7 343	73
1980	8.0	18 168	75	14 156	78	12 490	69
1990	7.8	19 266	83	15 935	83	14 270	74
2002	7.9	22 523	89	16 892	75	15 090	67

Sources: Hutchinson (1969); Wine Institute, *Annual Wine Industry Statistical Surveys*; Wine Institute website, *Key Facts*, 7/31/01; *US Wine Market Impact Databank Review and Forecast* 1990 and 1998 Editions; USDA (ERS); and Anderson and Norman (2003).

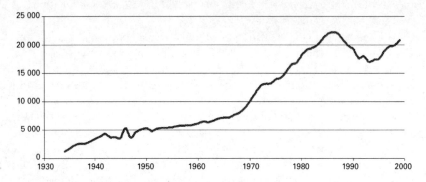

Source: Wine Institute, *Key Facts* (website).

Figure 10.1   Wine consumption in the USA, 1934–99 ('000 hl)

demand growth in the mid-1970s. And, when anticipated demand growth did not materialize, prices declined and a number of vineyards were removed.

After the plateau of the mid-1970s, US wine consumption and production began to pick up again. But that growth too was not sustained, and consumption peaked in the mid-1980s at 9.2 litres per capita, then declined gradually for a decade before moving back up again. By the start of the twenty-first century, per capita consumption had still not reached 8 litres per capita (Figure 10.1 and Table 10.2).

CURRENT WINE CONSUMPTION PATTERNS AND ISSUES

In this section, first we review the recent patterns surrounding wine consumption in the USA and Canada as a whole. Then we discuss data and issues related to the USA and Canada separately.

Table 10.2 shows that wine consumption in North America continued its decline from a peak in 1988 until 1996, when per capita wine consumption jumped from 6.5 to 7.6 litres. Since then, consumption has been steady, while total consumption grew slightly with population.

The changes in per capita consumption partly reflect shifts in the age distribution of the population. The huge baby-boom generation came of age in the 1970s and 1980s. The baby bust that followed meant that the share of the population entering maturity dropped during the late 1980s and early 1990s. However, much more than demographics drove the changes in US and Canadian consumption of wine from 1970 to 2000. The share of wine in the

Table 10.2   *Wine production and consumption, USA and Canada,*
            1988–2001

Year	Production ('000 hl)	Consumption ('000 hl)	Per capita consumption (litres)	Wine's share of alcohol consumption %
1988	18 612	23 326	8.6	14.0
1989	15 776	22 222	8.1	13.5
1990	16 307	21 630	7.8	13.0
1991	15 509	20 008	7.1	12.6
1992	16 877	20 288	7.2	12.7
1993	16 099	19 039	6.6	12.2
1994	17 850	19 341	6.7	12.4
1995	18 893	19 038	6.5	12.3
1996	19 210	22 479	7.6	14.1
1997	22 343	22 399	7.5	14.0
1998	20 875	23 103	7.7	14.2
1999	19 421	23 405	7.7	14.1
2000	23 812	23 747	7.6	15.0
2001	24 312	24 956	7.9	15.6

Source: Anderson and Norman (2003).

consumption of alcohol also dropped rapidly after 1986 and hit a 15-year low
in 1995 before rebounding strongly (Table 10.2).

Economists would expect price and income to play significant roles in wine
consumption, as with other goods. Available estimates of the own-price
demand elasticity for wine in the USA are based on data from the 1970s and
1980s. Leung and Phelps (1993) review two studies that report own-price elasticities for wine that range from –1.86 to –0.88, both based on aggregate cross-
section data. Heien and Pompelli (1989) found an own-price elasticity of
demand for wine of –0.55 using a household sample from the USA. These estimates all suggest substantial negative demand response to an increase in the
relative price of wine. The econometric evidence on income elasticities is less
well developed, in part because of confounding of income changes with demographic shifts and in part because of quality movements that are correlated
with income (factors that also affect estimates of price elasticities). To date,
separate elasticities have not been reported for high-quality versus low-quality wine, for red versus white wine, or for imports versus domestic wines.
Clearly there is room for significant empirical analysis to obtain better estimates of demand parameters in the wine market.

United States

There is a wide variation in the price of wine purchased in US food stores. In 2000, one-fifth of the wine volume sold for more than $7 per 750 ml bottle (Figure 10.2), accounting for 43 per cent of the value of wine sold in the US. This has been a rapidly growing segment of the market, its volume share being less than 7 per cent in 1980 (Gomberg, Fredrikson and Associates, 2000).

Dessert wine is now less than 7 per cent of wine consumption in the United States, with sparkling wine accounting for another 7 per cent. Of the table wine, red and white each comprise almost equal shares of about 40 per cent, and blush wine accounts for about 20 per cent of volume. For wine sold in food stores by grape variety, Chardonnay has a 19 per cent share and is easily the dominant white. White Zinfandel is the sole 'blush' varietal wine, commanding more than 1 per cent of sales, and itself has 13 per cent of volume. Merlot at 11 per cent and Cabernet Sauvignon at 9 per cent are the dominant reds (Wine Institute, 2001).

Wine consumption in the US totalled about 23 million hl in 2001, two-thirds of which was supplied by California, one-quarter was imported and the remaining 8 per cent was wine produced in the USA outside California. Of the imports, three-quarters used to come from Europe, with almost three-quarters of that from Italy and France. However, with the growth in imports from other

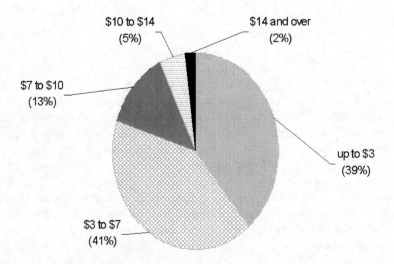

Source: Wine Institute, *Key Facts* (based on AC Nielsen/Adams 2000 survey).

Figure 10.2   Consumer purchases of table wine in food stores, USA, 2000 (volume shares)

New World suppliers, the share from France has begun to fall, and in 2002 was just 19 per cent by volume, behind Australia at 20 per cent and Italy at 36 per cent. Chile had a 9 per cent share, Argentina 2 per cent and South Africa 1 per cent (USDA website).

Important issues affecting the development of wine demand in the USA and Canada over the years ahead will include adjustments in state, provincial and local wine marketing regulations that discourage consumption by reducing consumer options and convenience of purchase. Alcoholic beverages are unique in the degree to which individual states have the authority to regulate marketing in the USA. For a typical product the interstate commerce clause of the US Constitution says, in effect, that commerce between states may not be limited except if there are compelling local reasons. (Conversely, the federal government may not regulate purely within-state commerce.) However, the 21st Amendment that reversed prohibition is usually interpreted as allowing states more leeway in regulating alcohol. Section 2 reads as follows: 'The transportation or importation into any state, territory, or possession of the USA for delivery or use therein of intoxicating liquors, in violation of the laws thereof, is hereby prohibited.'

In fact, individual states exercise substantial control over the marketing of alcoholic beverages, including sales through state-owned and operated stores. State authorities in states such as Pennsylvania and Utah are the sole importer, wholesaler, and retailer of alcoholic beverages in their boundaries. In general, many states have imposed regulations that make establishing national distribution systems more difficult, and severely restrict direct winery-to-customer shipments. Many of these restrictions favour local wine producers or local wholesalers and retailers to the detriment of the wine production industry elsewhere. Political attempts to reduce these restraints of trade face problems at the national level because of the interpretation of the 21st Amendment. Efforts to have regulations changed in state legislatures face the problem that politically powerful within-state interests often benefit from trade restrictions. Wine consumers have not yet become organized or effective enough to reform these restrictions.

Canada

Canadian wine consumption is a little over one-tenth that of the US total, with per capita annual consumption averaging 8 litres in recent years, similar to that in the USA. The Canadian table wine market is now split evenly between red wines and white wines after several years of rapid growth in the red wine share. Since almost all of the red wine is imported, this shift has affected the import share as well (Statistics Canada website).

Imports rose from about 55 per cent of consumption in the late 1980s to about 97 per cent of consumption in 2001. Even with this relatively small market share for domestic wine, a significant part of the domestic wine production in Canada relies on imported grapes or must, primarily from the USA. Wine imports into Canada derive from a variety of countries. In 2001, France accounted for 28 per cent, the USA and Italy each almost 20 per cent, Chile 13 per cent, Australia 7 per cent and Spain 3 per cent of imports. Import unit values in 2001 averaged just under US$2.50 per litre in Canada compared with US$3.80 per litre for the USA's imports (and $1.80 for its exports – see Anderson and Norman, 2003).

Regulation of wine sales is largely a provincial matter in Canada. 'The Importation of Intoxicating Liquors Act requires that liquor imported into Canada be brought in through a provincial or territorial liquor board. The provincial and territorial governments are also responsible for regulating and controlling traffic in intoxicating liquor for sale and consumption within their respective jurisdictions' (Treidlinger, 2001). The control of the sale of domestic and imported wines by the provincial government has tended to benefit wines produced in that province and to limit the selection available to customers. Provincial governments control the mark-up on wines and have tended to apply lower mark-ups on local wines. In response to NAFTA, they raised the mark-up on local or provincial wines rather than lower the mark-up on imported wines. All of these factors reduced the rate of growth of imports in Canada, which has none the less been rapid. The control over which brands are on offer may also make marketing particularly difficult for new suppliers. This may account for the still relatively small market shares for US and other New World suppliers in Canada (Heien and Sims, 2000). Anderson (2001) emphasizes, however, that trends in imports from the US into Canada were consistent with trends in imports into Canada from other New World suppliers such as Australia, Chile and New Zealand.

GRAPE PRODUCTION

The USA is a major producer of grapes used for fresh table consumption, dried consumption (raisins), and fresh or frozen grape juice, as well as wine. These multiple uses for grapes complicate the production picture, particularly because all four uses of grapes are important in some important regions, and for the most commonly grown variety, Thompson Seedless.

Grapevine area in the USA and Canada grew by 3.2 per cent p.a. from 1990 to 2001. The 2001 total of 432 000 hectares still comprises a tiny 0.2 per cent share of the total cropland in the region (Anderson and Norman, 2003). As grape area has expanded, so has total grape production (Figure 10.3), although yield per hectare has declined because the expansion in area has comprised lower-yielding wine varieties.

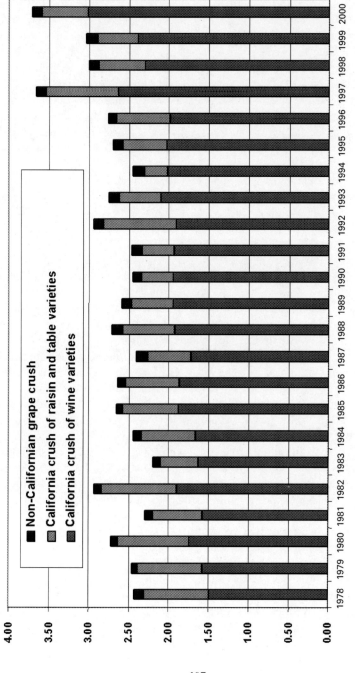

Source: Wine Institutes and CDFA.

Figure 10.3 Grape crush, USA and California, 1978–2000 (million tonnes)

The latest figures for grape production in the USA show an industry that is continuing to grow and to shift from other varieties of grapes toward wine varieties. Total US grape-bearing area was 382 833 hectares in 2000, up 10 per cent from 1998 (USDA, CASS). Of this, California accounted for 87 per cent of the total area, 4.5 per cent was in Washington, and 3 per cent in New York. The California share has been growing and almost all of this growth is in wine varieties (Figure 10.3). The bearing area of California wine-type grapes has grown by about 19 per cent in two years and now comprises 48 per cent of all the wine grapes grown in the USA. This underestimates the total wine use of grapes, however, mainly because a significant share of Thompson Seedless grapes (classified as a raisin variety) are used for crush and some of that for wine.

Grape yields in the USA vary widely, with the highest yields obtained from California raisin-type grapes. Average raisin grape yield in 2000 was 25 tonnes per hectare while overall average yield was 20 tonnes per hectare. California has the highest grape yields, but as we discuss below, there is wide variation within the state, and the high-yielding San Joaquin Valley dominates total production and average yields.

Total grape production in the USA was a record 6.9 million tonnes in 2000 and 5.9 million tonnes in 2001, 92 per cent of which was in California. The drop in total grape production in 2001 was caused in part by supply control measures introduced by the raisin industry in response to extremely low prices, but mostly by extremely low yields in California.

The regional breakdown of the grape crush in California is crucial to under-standing the wine industry in the USA. California is divided into 17 crush districts that range in grape price from the highest (Napa County on the North Coast), down to two large districts that comprise much of the Southern San Joaquin Valley. While there is heterogeneity within districts, there are much more distinct differences across districts.

The San Joaquin Valley produces about 60 per cent of the crush (Figure 10.4). About 25 per cent of the grapes crushed in the San Joaquin Valley are table grape and raisin grape varieties, whereas almost all of the grapes crushed in other districts are wine varieties. Further, about one-third of the total crush in the San Joaquin Valley is estimated to be used for grape juice concentrate. Some of that concentrate may be used for wine, for example blended in other states or Canada, or blended to make wine-like products; but most is used as juice.

Not only do varieties, yields and uses of grapes differ by region, but so too do grape prices even for the same variety. Over the decade to 2000, the price of all grapes used for crush in Napa County (the highest-priced crush district in California) averaged about eight times the price of grapes in the Southern San Joaquin Valley. Other districts range between these two (Figure 10.5). Lee

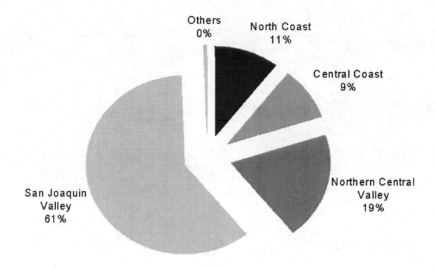

Note: ᵃ Total = 2 900 000 tonnes.

Source: CDFA/CASS (2001).

Figure 10.4   Regional distribution of grape crush within California, 2000ᵃ

and Sumner (2001) show that about 70 per cent of the variation in California grape prices can be explained by a set of fixed effects for crush district. On average they show that, even holding constant fixed effects for variety, the price of grapes in the Southern San Joaquin Valley averaged about $1212 per tonne lower than the average price in Napa County.

Variety is another quality factor affecting grape prices. From 1991 to 2000, the average price of Pinot Noir grapes was about seven times higher, and the average price for the more widely planted Cabernet Sauvignon grapes was about six times higher, than the price of Thompson Seedless grapes used for crush. Lee and Sumner (2001) show that variety alone accounts for more than 50 per cent of the variation in prices of grapes used for crush in California. But, given the correlation between crush district and variety, adding variety to a statistical model that already controls for district adds only about 7 per cent to the explanatory power. While the popular wine grape varieties such as Chardonnay or Merlot are grown everywhere, the low-priced varieties are only grown in significant quantities in the San Joaquin Valley districts. In 2000, the average prices of Chardonnay and Merlot grapes were $2151 and $2321 per tonne in Sonoma, respectively, but they were only $361 and $374 per tonne in the Southern San Joaquin Valley, respectively (CASS, 2001).

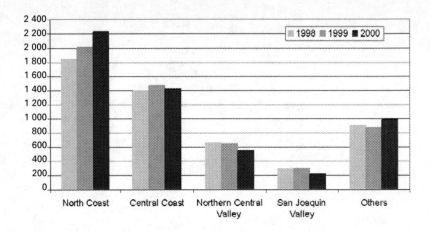

Source: CDFA/CASS (2001).

*Figure 10.5   Average price of crushed grapes in California by region,
                1988–2000 (dollars per tonne)*

There are also large variations within districts. For example, relatively
small quantities of Cabernet Sauvignon in Napa sold for double the district-
wide average in 2000. More surprising, prices also vary substantially in the
Southern San Joaquin Valley, where most observers say the product is more
homogeneous. The coefficients of variation of price in Napa and the Southern
San Joaquin Valley are both about 0.45 (Lee and Sumner, 2001). Some of this
price variation is likely to be explained by the timing of contracting on prices
(Goodhue et al., 2001).

The wine grape area in California has doubled in the past decade (Figure
10.6), but the regional breakdown of this growth is equally important. Lee and
Sumner (2001) show that from 1991 to 2000, the share of crush volume (for
the 15 varieties that account for 90 per cent of the crush) produced in the
coastal districts stayed constant at about 17 per cent. They also show that the
share of crush volume comprising the four high-priced varieties (Cabernet
Sauvignon, Chardonnay, Merlot and Pinot Noir) grew from 16 per cent to 35
per cent.

The remarkable growth in the production of wine grapes seems set to
continue for at least a few more years, especially in the coastal districts of
California. The California Agricultural Statistics Service collects data each
year on bearing and non-bearing grape area by variety and district.
Notwithstanding the well-known undercount of non-bearing area, the implied
growth rates in bearing area projected for the next few years are impressive.

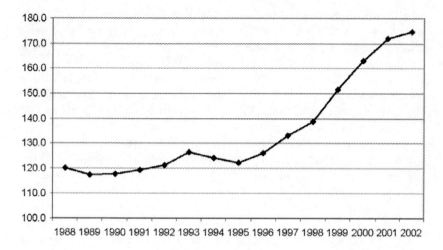

Source: Wine Institute (from CDFA/CASS, *Grape Acreage Report*, various years).

Figure 10.6   Bearing area of wine grapes, California, 1988–2000 ('000 ha)

The reported non-bearing area of six major wine varieties (Cabernet Sauvignon, Chardonnay, Merlot, Pinot Noir, Sauvignon Blanc and Zinfandel) grown in the coastal districts was 12 944 hectares in 1997, but was 50 per cent higher by 2000, when the non-bearing area was 30 per cent of the bearing area. The bearing area is therefore expected to grow by about one-quarter by 2003 simply as a result of the maturation of existing non-bearing acreage. Furthermore, there has been more planting of red than white wine varieties in the coastal districts. Therefore the proportional growth is even larger for red varieties, particularly Pinot Noir.

Unlike the coastal districts, reported non-bearing area in the Southern San Joaquin Valley declined considerably from 1997 to 2000, when it was about 9 per cent of bearing area. One reason for the small extent of non-bearing area is that growers anticipated that the high prices of the 1990s could not last.

The expansion in acreage in coastal districts is understandable looking at estimates of costs and returns being used in the industry. According to widely circulated budgets published by the University of California Cooperative Extension Service, the cost to establish a Chardonnay vineyard in Sonoma County in 1999 was about $32 000 per hectare. The major categories of cost are for trellising, planting and purchase of vines. Other costs include cultural practices and overhead costs in the first two years before marketable crops are harvested. Operating costs, including such items as irrigation, pruning, fertilizer, and harvest costs, were about $7500 per hectare. The assumed raw land value in this example, $85 000 per hectare, is important because it affects taxes, insurance and capital recovery. The overhead, including capital recovery, for such a vineyard is estimated to be about $15 500 per hectare for a total production cost of $23 000 per hectare. Returns are estimated in 1999 as 16 tonne per hectare at $1900 per tonne for total revenue of $30 000 per hectare (Smith et al., 1999). Thus, data circulated by the University of California suggest net revenue of about $17 000 per hectare above a normal return on capital and management.

Another supply variable has been disease. Since 1980 there have been two major pest insects affecting the California wine grape industry. In the 1980s the popular AxR1 rootstock began to succumb to attack by phylloxera. The infestation was found mainly in the North Coast, and the San Joaquin Valley. About 60 to 70 per cent of the vineyard area in Napa and Sonoma was to be replanted because of phylloxera (Sullivan, 1996). In the 1990s, a second major pest threat entered. Pierce's Disease has been in California for many years without causing widespread concern. Pierce's Disease can kill a vine in two years, but, until recently, infestations were relatively minor and the spread was slow. Nowadays, however, a new insect vector, the glassy-winged sharpshooter, is spreading the disease much more rapidly than before. Pierce's Disease has spread widely in Southern California, but has so far affected less than 1 per cent of the state's wine grape acres. The response has been to institute massive eradication and control measures to keep the pest contained and to fund substantial new research on an emergency basis to find an effective biological control to eliminate the insect. So far, there are several promising leads but no effective solution has been found.

WINE PRODUCTION AND SALES

Wine flows from grapes and transport costs for grapes or must are high. Therefore, most of the wine production in the USA and Canada occurs in California, where the grapes are grown. Although almost every state in the USA now boasts local wineries, these are generally relatively few and, with one or two exceptions, tiny, with a focus on direct retail sales to local tourists. The main exceptions are in Washington, Oregon and New York. In 2000, there were 2000 wineries in the United States, with about 850 in California. The numbers outside California have grown remarkably: there are now 122 wineries in Oregon, 153 in New York, and more than 170 in Washington (compared with just 19 in 1980). Despite many wineries in other states and in Canada, about 90 per cent of the wine produced in the USA and Canada is produced in California and that share has been gradually growing.

The California wine industry comprises a handful of relatively large firms, another couple of dozen firms that produce and market widely in the domestic and international markets, and several hundred wineries that produce mainly for the local market or for small national or international clientele. About 25 firms produce about 90 per cent of the wine. Half of the wineries in California are in Napa and Sonoma Counties, with most of the rest scattered throughout the coastal counties. The Central Valley, which produces most of the grapes, has some very large wineries, but comparatively few small wineries. Some larger firms produce and market under several winery-label names and may produce wines in several organizations managed somewhat separately from the corporate parent firm. Thus, there are many more wine labels in the market than actual wineries.

Gallo is by far the largest winery in the USA or Canada, producing about 6.3 million hectolitres of wine, or one-third of the total wine volume in California. Gallo produces and markets under many different label names and across the whole range of prices and qualities. The firm, headquartered in Modesto and with a long tradition in so-called jug wines, is established as the dominant player in the San Joaquin Valley. It is also a major producer of mid-priced varietal wines from grapes produced in coastal districts, and Gallo of Sonoma, the high-end label, has established itself as a significant producer of high-priced wines that sell for $25 per 750 ml bottle, and more.

Most wine producers in the USA and Canada also grow grapes, but the typical large winery buys most of the grapes it uses. The converse is also not uncommon. Some large grape-growers operate a small winery, but sell most of their grapes. The typical situation is for a winery to establish a contract with growers each year with the understanding that, subject to some quality rules, the winery will accept all of the grapes produced on the designated farm and the farmer will deliver all of their grapes to the winery (Goodhue et al., 2001).

In recent years exports have become important. As discussed above, both Canada and the USA are net importers of wine from the rest of the world, especially Europe. However, from 1990 there has been a rapid expansion of exports of wine from California to Canada, but also from the United States to the rest of the world. Wine export value has grown each year for the past decade and in 2002 totalled about $550 million. The major destinations are Canada, Japan and the UK, but significant shipments are also made to the Netherlands, Switzerland, Germany and Belgium.

One important characteristic of the export situation is the low export unit value of wine exports relative to the unit value of imports. In 2000–2002, the average US wine export unit value was less than $2 per litre, compared with around $4 for US imports.

PROJECTIONS

Most of the increase in grapes available for crush in the 1990s was in high-
end wine varieties (such as Chardonnay, Merlot and Cabernet Sauvignon)
planted in the San Joaquin Valley. These grapes and the wines they produce
do not receive high prices relative to the same varieties grown on the coast
(or in premium areas of Oregon or Washington State). However, they have
received substantially higher prices than Thompson Seedless grapes, which
are also grown for crush in the same region. Vineyards that were planted early
enough in the 1990s were able to capitalize on the relatively high prices in the
latter part of the decade and have probably already recouped the cost of vineyard establishment. More recent vineyard plantings will have a more difficult
time showing much return on the sizeable capital investment in vineyard
establishment. Low yields per hectare in 1998 and 1999 shielded the industry
from the full implications of this area increase, but the large crop in 2000
caused grape prices in the San Joaquin Valley to decline by more than 50 per
cent from 1999 to 2000. Beginning wine inventories going into the 2001
season added to available supply, and although yields were down in 2001,
prices reported were lower yet in 2001 than in 2000 and, in some cases, vineyards were left unharvested. This collapse was at least partially anticipated,
in the sense that the net increase in wine grape area in the San Joaquin Valley
stopped a few years ago.

There has also been a rapid expansion of wine grape planting in the coastal
districts. Average yields are lower and establishment and production costs are
higher in coastal districts, but grape prices have been much higher. For the
2001 harvest, prices in the medium-quality or medium-reputation regions in
coastal districts were lower than in recent years. This is especially true for
Chardonnay, the most important variety in the Central Coast and the most
important white wine grape in the state. This price decline occurred despite the
fact that yields were down in coastal districts in 2001. Planting of Chardonnay
slowed in the later 1990s and much of the new coastal wine grape area is in
red grapes, but that generalization is less true in the Central Coast counties
(Monterey, San Luis Obispo and Santa Barbara, for example) that have developed a reputation for quality Chardonnay grapes. And, given the large amount
of non-bearing vineyard area in coastal districts, further price declines seem
likely, at least outside the extreme high-price regions of Napa and Sonoma
Counties. The result is serious income pressure on some vineyards.

The wine grape area in Napa and Sonoma Counties has also expanded
rapidly and, based on the high proportion of non-bearing area, the expansion
of production will accelerate in the next few years. This expansion is not in the
core high-quality areas. For example, in specific American Viticultural Areas
such as Howell Mountain, Spring Mountain and some on the floor of Napa

Valley there is no room for expansion. Rather, the expansion has been on steeper slopes and in outlying areas of Napa and Sonoma Counties, where costs may be higher and reputations for quality are not yet established. Yield per hectare has also increased as new vines are being planted at closer spacing and with newer trellising systems that economize on expensive vineyard land. Prices of wine grapes in the premium-price region have so far remained immune to the glut facing the rest of the industry. For this to continue requires that the market for premium wine grapes be distinct from that for the lower-priced grapes and that demand for the premium grapes will continue to expand rapidly (discussed below). Industry practice and recent price movements suggest that wine demand does seem to be segmented by quality, which is associated mainly with where the grapes are produced. On this hypothesis, there is relatively little substitution between wine grapes grown in different geographically based quality segments of the market.

For 2001, crop yields were down significantly in the North Coast, so production will be down from 2000 despite an increase in bearing area. Our expectation is that prices for premium grapes have avoided the collapse experienced by the other parts of the industry, but that rapid price increases of the recent past may have ended. Further, given forward pricing provisions in contracts, it may take a couple of years before the most recent supply and demand conditions are fully reflected in average prices.

Against these forces for expansion of production are concerns about Pierce's Disease. The newly arrived glassy-winged sharpshooter is a much more effective vector for the disease than the native sharpshooter, and knowledgeable specialists are taking the threat to productivity of the grape industry very seriously. If this infestation were to carry forward unabated for the next few years in its move northward, the total size of the wine grape harvest could be seriously affected. This would raise prices, but that would come at the cost of substantial capital losses for many growers. Growers also face many other costs that have been rising, notably higher wage rates as hired farm labour supply tightens, and additional regulations on pesticide use.

The outlook for the demand side of the wine industry is equally complex. At the low-price end of the spectrum, grape juice that might be used for wine competes with apple juice and other sources of liquid sweeteners. These uses include drinks with and without alcohol content. This market for grapes as a food and beverage ingredient is huge, but only at very low prices that may not be much more than the cost of harvest. This market for grape juice concentrate is international, so supply conditions in Argentina, Brazil and other countries also affect prices in the USA. The grape-juice concentrate market provides no relevant demand support for higher-quality wine grape varieties (Chardonnay, Merlot and so on), even with the high yields and relatively low costs in the Southern San Joaquin Valley. If yields are normal, this part of the industry now faces a painful adjustment while demand growth catches up with the planting that occurred in the 1990s.

A recession began in the USA in March 2001. Increases in per capita consumption continue to be tiny and the quality upgrading that accompanies a maturing consumption base or income growth is hard to sustain, especially at relatively high wine prices. Further, consumption of high-end wine relies on the upper tail of the income and wealth distribution. This group did quite well relative to median incomes for two decades and was a major beneficiary of the stock market boom in the 1990s. Stock market growth has reversed and certain sectors with high average salaries (for example, high tech) have contracted recently. Thus the short-term demand prospects are not strong even at the upper end of the quality spectrum. Terrorist attacks on September 11, 2001 were a further shock to the wine industry, which is income-sensitive and relies on consumption away from home, including travel and tourism.

The other demand variables that are important in the United States and Canada relate to the regional and ethnic distribution of wine consumption. Wine consumers tend to be more urban or suburban, more from European immigrant populations, and more in the West Coast and northeast than in the south or the central regions of the country. Therefore, wine demand growth depends in part on growth in the upper tail of the distribution of incomes and wealth in the wine-consuming regions and populations. The rapid growth in Asian and Latin American immigrant populations has not contributed much to wine consumption.

The relatively low per capita consumption of wine in the USA and Canada may be seen as a great opportunity for potential demand expansion. It is certainly possible that favourable health news or some other demand shock could increase the demand for wine dramatically. Relatively little is spent on promotion of wine compared with beer or soft drinks, and it is possible that some promotional effort that has not yet been tried could pay large dividends.

Import competition is another important demand factor. Canada continues to import most of its wine from outside North America and thus there is potential for US exports to grow by successfully displacing European wine in Canada. However, New World imports, especially from Chile and Australia, are a growing force in the market for wine in the USA and Canada. The strong US dollar has recently tended to make US wine expensive relative to wines from elsewhere.

Export market growth, which has been important for a decade, also slowed in the new millennium. Part of export growth has relied on non-traditional wine markets such as in Asia, but the Asian financial crisis and lack of income growth in Japan have added to the difficulties of marketing there. The ability to expand by competing directly with European wines in their established markets such as Great Britain has also been important, although a strong US dollar has strengthened competition from the other New World countries.

The wine industry is still absorbing the new small and medium-sized wineries and grape-growers who sit alongside a handful of large wineries. Winery tourism is a major income contributor for smaller wineries, especially those located in scenic areas or convenient to population centres. Corporate ownership of larger wineries shifts occasionally, with international connections across the industry coming and going. The constant in the California industry is the important role of Gallo as by far the largest player, one that continues to be important in all quality categories.

The wine and wine grape industries in the USA and Canada are facing a challenging period over the next few years. Supply growth will continue while demand growth will be harder to sustain. The industry is differentiated, so some growers and wineries may do quite well, but it will not be an easy road in the near term for the sector as a whole. In the long term, however, the areas well suited to the production of high-quality, high-priced wine (such as the coastal districts of California or Oregon and Washington) and lower-priced, everyday wine (such as the Central Valley of California) will continue to be a competitive force in domestic and international markets.

REFERENCES

Anderson, K. (2001), 'On the Impact of the Canada–United States Free Trade Agreement on US Wine Exports', *Australian and New Zealand Wine Industry Journal*, **16** (1), 115–17.

Anderson, K. and D. Norman (2003), *Global Wine Production, Consumption and Trade, 1961 to 2001: A Statistical Compendium*, Adelaide: Centre for International Economic Studies.

California Agricultural Statistics Service (CDFA CASS) (2001), *California Grape Acreage 2000*, Sacramento.

California Agricultural Statistics Service (CDFA CASS) (2001), *California Grape Crush Report 2000*, Sacramento.

California Crop and Livestock Reporting Service (1956 and 1962), *California Fruit and Nut Crops, 1909–1955, and 1949–1961*, Sacramento.

California Crop and Livestock Reporting Service (1963–65), *California Fruit and Nut Crop Statistics, 1961–1962, 1962–1963 and 1963–1964*, Sacramento.

California Crop and Livestock Reporting Service (1968), *California Fruit and Nut Acreage, Bearing, and Non-bearing as of 1967*, Sacramento.

Carosso, V.P. (1951), *The California Wine Industry: A Study of the Formative Years*, Berkeley: University of California Press.

Conaway, J. (1992), *Napa: The Story of an American Eden*, Boston: Houghton Mifflin.

Fredrikson, J. (2001), *The Context for Marketing Strategies: a Look at the US Wine Market*, Ch. 5 in K. Moulton and J. Lapsley (eds), *Successful Wine Marketing*, Gaithersburg, MD: Aspen.

Gomberg, Fredrikson and Associates (2000), *The Gomberg–Fredrikson Report. WINEDATA Wine Pricing Report*, San Francisco.

Goodhue, R., D. Heien, H. Lee and D. Sumner (2001), 'Contracts, Quality, and Industrialization in Agriculture: Hypotheses and Empirical Analysis of the California Wine grape Industry', presented at the Econometrics VII Conference, St Helena, CA, 21–22 May.

Granett, J, and J. de Brenedictis (1996), 'California Grape Phylloxera More Variable than Expected', *California Agriculture*, **50** (4).

Gregory, T. (1912), *History of Solano and Napa Counties California*, Los Angeles: Historic Regional Company.

Heien, D. and G. Pompelli (1989), 'The Demand for Alcoholic Beverages: Economic and Demographic Effects', *Southern Economic Journal*, **55**, 759–70.

Heien, D. and E.N. Sims (2000), 'The Impact of the Canada–United States Free Trade Agreement on US Wine Exports', *American Journal of Agricultural Economics*, **82**, 173–82.

Hutchinson, R.B. (1969), California Wine Industry, unpublished PhD dissertation, University of California, Los Angeles.

King, N.L. (1967), *Napa County: An Historical Overview*, Office of Napa County Superintendent of Schools.

Lapsley, J.T. (1996), *Bottled Poetry – Napa Winemaking from Prohibition to the Modern Era*, Berkeley: University of California Press.

Lee, H. and D.A. Sumner (2001), 'Econometrics of Grape Prices in California: the Roles of Grape Supply, Location, Variety, Market Power and Contracted Quality Limits,' presented at Econometrics VI Conference, St Helena, CA, 21–22 May.

Leung, S.F. and C. Phelps (1993), ' "My Kingdom for a Drink . . .?": a Review of Estimates of the Price Sensitivity of Demand for Alcoholic Beverages', in M.E. Milton and G. Bloss (eds), *Economics and the Prevention of Alcohol-Related Problems*, Research Monograph No. 25, USDHHS, NIH Publication No. 93–3515, Washington DC: National Institute of Health.

Mishkin, D.J. (1966), 'The American Colonial Wine Industry: An Economic Interpretation', unpublished PhD dissertation, University of Illinois, Urbana-Champagne.

Selden, C. (1941), 'California's Wine Industry and Its Financing', unpublished Masters dissertation, Graduate School of Rutgers University, New Brunswick, NJ.

Shanken, M. (1998), *US Wine Market Impact Databank Review and Forecast*, M. Shanken Communications, Inc.

Smith, R., K. Klonsky and P. Livingston (1999), *Sample Costs to Establish a Vineyard and Produce Wine Grapes: Chardonnay–Sonoma County*, University of California, Cooperative Extension Service.

Statistics Canada (2001), 'Control and Sale of Alcoholic Beverage', *The Daily*, Thursday, 5 July, Statistics Canada website: www.statcan.ca/Daily, 9/14/2001.

Sullivan V. (1996), 'New Rootstocks Stop Vineyard Pest for Now', *California Agriculture*, **50** (4).

Tillitt, M.H. (1932), *The Price of Prohibition*, New York: Harcourt Brace and Co.

Treidlinger, M. (2001), Food Bureau, Market Industry Services Branch, Agriculture and Agri-Food Canada, interview, September.

USDA Foreign Agricultural Service (1998), *Canada Wine Annual Report 1998*, GAIN Report No. CA 8088, Washington, DC, 14 December.

USDA Foreign Agricultural Service (1999), *Canada Wine Annual Report 1999*, GAIN Report No. CA 9144, Washington, DC, 18 January.

USDA Foreign Agricultural Service (2000), *Wine Alcoholic Beverage Consumption in Canada*, GAIN Report No. CA 0093, Washington, DC, 28 June.

United States Tariff Commission (1935), *Report on Whisky, Wine, Beer and Other Alcoholic Beverages and the Tariff*, Report No. 90, Series Washington, DC: United States Government Printing Office.

Unwin, T. (1991), *Wine and the Vine*, London and New York: Routledge.

Wine Institute (2001), *Key Facts*, from the Wine Institute website as visited at www.wineinstitute.org/communication/statistics, (and earlier years).

Wine Institute (2002), *Annual Wine Industry Statistical Surveys*, annual issues, San Francisco: Wine Institute.

Winkler, A.J., J.A. Cook, W.M Kliever and L.A. Lider (1962), *General Viticulture*, Berkeley: University of California Press.

11. South America

William Foster and Alberto Valdés

EARLY HISTORY OF WINE IN CHILE AND ARGENTINA

Early chroniclers bestowed on a religious person, Don Francisco de Carabantes, the honour of having introduced the first vine to Chile in 1548, eight years following Pedro de Valdivia's conquest of the territory.[1] Details are scarce and some contend that Chile's first grapevines originated from Spain, some contend from the Canary Islands, and some have even argued that the vines grew from seeds in raisins, an important element in a happy sailing conquistador's diet. With more certainty we do know that Don Francisco de Aguirre planted the first vineyards in Copiapó in the central north of the country and enjoyed the first harvest in 1551. By 1554, large vineyards were already in the Central Valley, just outside the then small town of Santiago. Another priest, Juan Cidrón, is credited with bringing Criolla vine cuttings across the Andes from La Serena to the Argentine province of Santiago del Estero in 1556.

The use of cuttings first established the variety known as País in Chile, Criolla in Argentina and Mission in California. Whether this hardy variety originated in Spain or Italy is uncertain, but the evidence suggests that it came to Chile, and then to western Argentina, from Mexico via Peru. Due to its adaptability to adverse conditions and indifference to harvesting delays it was to become the most common vine cultivated for centuries. It continues to this day to be grown in significant amounts, primarily for inexpensive, popular wine consumption.

From Santiago, wine production expanded rapidly throughout the rest of Chile, from the semi-arid area region of Coquimbo in the north to the rainy coastal area around Concepción in the south. By 1594, the country was producing about 1.6 million litres, a respectable amount given the small population.[2] Governments being what they are, Spanish royal regulations were promulgated in vain to slow new plantings in the New World, and by 1654 official permission was required to begin new vineyards. The popular consumption of wine was considered so important that when 'scarcities' did develop, Santiago municipal authorities requisitioned wine from warehouses for mass distribution. Declaring wine an essential good, along with bread, salt, meat, potatoes and various other 'staples', authorities also fixed prices ostensibly to reduce year-to-year variation. Although the effectiveness of these price interventions is called into doubt by the data that exist from the seventeenth century,[3] it was not until the eighteenth century that fixed prices were set aside.

Although Sir Francis Drake intercepted what might have been the first Chilean exports of wine in 1578 (Johnson, 1989, p. 174), and Peru was receiving wine from north-central Chile in the 1600s, Chilean winemakers began to export wine in earnest probably only in the eighteenth century. Certainly the first reliable statistics are in reference to total exports during the period 1784–89 (Hernandez, 2000). Similarly, although winemaking was well established by 1600 in the semi-arid region of Mendoza in Argentina, it was almost entirely for local consumption until the eighteenth century, when small amounts of wine were shipped to Buenos Aires.

THE EMERGENCE OF THE MODERN WINE INDUSTRY

In 1830 Chilean winemaking began to change with the arrival of the Frenchman Claudio Gay. Gay began the first agricultural experiment station, introducing new varieties of food and ornamental plants from Europe.[4] But it was not until Silvestre Ochagavjá began to replace older rootstocks with finer French varieties in the early 1850s that the Chilean wineries began to make the turn toward European wines. Other winemaking enthusiasts, many of whom were businessmen and mining entrepreneurs, quickly began planting their own vineyards with Malbec, Merlot, Cabernet Sauvignon, Semillon and Riesling, and so established most of the large, successful wineries that continue to this day. Production of finer wines grew, French and other European experts were employed, and quality improved. Following the good reception of Chilean wine at the Vienna Exposition of 1873, exports to Europe first began in 1877, and gained over time some recognition in international exhibitions, especially at the Paris Exposition of 1889. As production rose from 51 million litres in 1875 to 110 million litres in 1883 to 275 million litres in 1903, the industry was pushed to search for foreign markets and became the principal exporter in South America (Hernandez, 2000).

A somewhat similar story of innovation occurred several years later in the Mendoza region of Argentina. In 1880 the French botanist Aimé Pouget introduced the first French varieties, followed four years later by the progressive-minded landowner Eusebio Blanco's publication of a book on how winemaking ought to be done in Mendoza. Blanco's civic-minded son-in-law, Tiburcio Benegas, later to be governor of the province, began improving all aspects of winemaking in the region, especially on his own estate, which he

planted with European varieties. When the first railway opened between
Buenos Aires and Mendoza in 1885, the commercial revolution in the
Argentine wine industry began. Whereas Chilean wineries, facing a small
domestic market, sought out customers beyond the country's borders, the
wineries of Mendoza had a larger home market of potential buyers centred in
Buenos Aires, consumers who, for whatever reason, were fond of drinking
wine in large quantities. Argentine per capita wine consumption at one point
exceeded 90 litres annually compared to a historical high of about 70 litres in
the case of Chile.

Despite the push for outside markets, during the first three decades of the
twentieth century Chilean exports probably never exceed 6 per cent of production (del Pozo, 1998). The country's good growing conditions and the availability of inexpensive imported technical talent led naturally to lower prices
and lamentations over a 'crisis of overproduction'. Taxes were also introduced
to discourage what by some legislators were thought to be socially destructive
drinking habits. The student of agricultural policies will not be surprised to
learn that as a response to depressed prices, vineyard owners and winemakers
sought the help of government to reduce the 'excessive' production plaguing
their balance sheets. At the First National Congress of Wine in 1933 the industry decried discriminatory taxes and the crisis of 'prices lower than costs' that
it had managed to endure since 1909. Wine producers, several of whom were
from the most aristocratic families of Chile, wanted to stop new vineyard plantations and implement other antidotes to the poison of overproduction. To this
end they enlisted the support of leftist legislators who saw wine as 'un veneno
para el pueblo' – literally, a venom for the people.

By 1939, laws were enacted to prohibit new vineyards, regulate transplant-
ing, and otherwise manage production so as to limit domestic consumption to
60 litres per capita annually. The legislation did reduce the hectares in production from 108 000 to 92 000 and produced a 10 per cent decline in the number
of vineyards. As prices rose, consumption per capita did indeed fall. The wine
sector avoided further low-price crises, but the protectionist environment of
the 1940s 'began the decadence of the Chilean wine industry in comparison
with the development of activities in the rest of the world'.[5] It was not until
after the fall of the Allende regime, and the turn toward open markets, that the
industry began, at first slowly, to re-establish its initial pattern of innovation.

RECENT HISTORY

Chile

From 1960 to 1982, although Chilean land in vineyards remained fairly stable (fluctuating between 105 000 and 113 000 hectares), production grew from 369 million litres in 1960 to a high of 610 million litres in 1982. Per capita consumption declined substantially during the two decades, from a high of 68 litres in 1962 to around 40 litres p.a. in the early 1980s. Exports began to increase from their initial insignificant levels, trebling in volume, but growing from under 1 per cent of production to just 2 per cent. More importantly, the average value of exports per litre increased by more than six times over the period, exceeding US$1 for the first time in 1980 (Table 11.1).

Between 1983 and 1991, hectares in vineyards and total production levels declined, while exports continued to increase as the steady decline in per capita domestic consumption accelerated. In response to better economic conditions and improved export prospects, wine-growers decreased their use of the traditional País and Semillon varieties. They replaced only a fraction of vineyards taken out of production with plantings of non-traditional varieties and increased their marketing focus in potential foreign markets. In the decade of the 1980s, wine grape area declined on average 6.8 per cent per year, wine production declined 6.3 per cent, and per capita wine consumption declined on average at 4.5 per cent per year. In 1991 production reached its lowest level in 30 years (282 million litres), but the US dollar value of exports increased almost fivefold. Per capita consumption continued its downward trend, so exports as a share of production rose from less than 2 per cent in 1982 to 25 per cent in 1991. Then in 1992 production levels reversed their previous trend and began to rise rapidly. While consumption fluctuated around 16 litres per capita, exports continued increasing until they represented half of total production.

With the recognition of the potential quality and profitability of Chilean wine exports came foreign investments and alliances between domestic and international firms, such as Rothschild, Robert Mondavi, Beringer Fetzer and Kendall-Jackson. Foreign and domestic investments have been both in terms of winemaking capacity and new vineyards. All new plantings have been non-traditional varietals, and most have been for red wines: Carbernet, Sirah, Carmenère, Pinot, and others aimed at improving quality, product mix and exports (Table 11.2). At present the area devoted to export varietals is twice what it was ten years ago. For 1999–2000, Cabernet Sauvignon represented 31 per cent of total land in wine grapes, Merlot represented 13 per cent, Chardonnay 8 per cent and Sauvignon Blanc 8 per cent. Notably, in the last three years, the once forgotten variety, Carmenère, has been growing in importance. Its area has risen from 330 hectares in 1997 to 2306 hectares in 1999. The success of Chilean Carmenère among wine enthusiasts over the last five years has led to the variety being a source of promised growth for many small and medium-sized producers.[6]

Table 11.1   Development of the wine sector, Chile, 1979–2001

Year	Wine grape area ('000 ha)	Prod'n (million l)	Cons'n per capita (l)	Exports (US$m)	Exports as a % of production	Exports as a % world export volume	Real domestic price (pesos/l)	Export price (US$/l)
1979	110	593	44	9	44	0	n.a.	0.3
1980	108	586	43	19	3	0	255	1.3
1981	105	594	41	15	2	0	217	1.5
1982	106	610	40	11	1	0	137	1.4
1983	98	520	39	9	2	0	94	1.1
1984	90	400	38	9	2	0	124	1.1
1985	75	450	37	10	2	0	104	1.0
1986	67	350	36	13	3	0	218	1.1
1987	67	400	32	17	4	0	238	1.2
1988	67	350	30	22	5	0	131	1.3
1989	66	400	28	35	7	1	102	1.3
1990	65	320	26	53	11	1	106	1.2
1991	65	282	23	85	25	1	247	1.2
1992	63	317	18	126	24	2	509	1.6
1993	62	330	13	135	23	2	436	1.5
1994	53	360	18	151	32	2	291	1.3
1995	54	317	15	182	41	2	199	1.4
1996	56	382	16	293	48	3	235	1.6
1997	64	431	13	412	48	3	405	1.9
1998	75	527	18	503	42	3	522	2.2
1999	85	428	17	528	49	3	541	2.3
2000	101	642	18	585	43	4	504	2.1
2001	n.a.	610	16	652	50	4	n.a.	2.2

Sources: Anderson and Norman (2003) and ODEPA.

Table 11.2   Area of wine grape vineyards, by variety, Chile, 1994–99 (ha)

Variety	1994	1995	1996	1997	1998	1999
Cabernet Sauv.	11 112	12 281	13 094	15 995	21 094	26 172
Merlot	2 353	2 704	3 234	5 411	8 414	10 261
Chardonnay	4 150	4 402	4 ,503	5 563	6 705	6 798
Sauvignon Blanc	5 981	6 135	6 172	6 576	6 756	6 564
Chenin Blanc	103	106	93	98	104	95
Pinot Noir	138	215	287	411	589	839
Riesling	307	296	317	338	348	286
Semillon	2 708	2 649	2 616	2 ,427	2 425	2 355
País	15 990	15 280	15 280	15 241	15 442	15 457
Carmenère				330	1 167	2 306
Sirah			19	201	568	1 019
Others	10 251	10 324	10 388	10 959	11 776	13 205
Total	53 093	54 392	56 003	63 550	75 388	85 357

Source: ODEPA.

With Chilean wine exports growing at more than 25 per cent p.a. in US dollar terms over the 1990s, Chile was one of the best performers among the New World exporters. Annual exports are now over US$600 million per year, exceeding that of the United States. Those exports are shipped to more than 100 countries and comprise bulk and bottled wine and recently relatively small amounts of sparkling wine and inexpensive table wine in tetra-pack. During the late 1990s, exported bottled wine grew about 10 per cent annually, while the volume of bulk exports declined, a shift that explains in part the increasing value per litre of export sales. In 1991 bottled wine represented 86 per cent of total value exported, bulk wine represented 12 per cent and the remainder was composed of sparkling wine and tetra-pack.

As in the case of Argentina, the United States and Britain are the largest importers of Chilean wine, each recently representing about 20 per cent of total export volume. Canada is also an important importer, acquiring 10 per cent. Unlike Argentina, there is less emphasis on exports to other South American countries in the area of table wines (although, interestingly, approximately 10 million litres goes to Argentina). Tetra-pack sales have grown but currently represent less than 1 per cent of volume and much less in terms of value. Chilean wineries are now principally interested in higher-priced markets in Europe and North America (slightly over 80 per cent of sales), but efforts have been made to export to Japan and other Asian countries. In 1998, Japan purchased 33 million litres, or 13 per cent of Chile's total shipments, a level comparable at the time to British imports. But in 2001, Japanese imports fell markedly, to less than 5 per cent of sales. At present there is little industry optimism that Japan will prove a high-growth market in the near future.

Per litre export prices have been rising rapidly for Chilean wine, from little more than US$1 in the 1980s to US$2.17 in 2001. This is due in part to the decline in bulk wine exports as a proportion of total sales, and to the rising quality of bottled wines exported. The mix of bottled exports is increasingly oriented toward high-value products, and industry leaders wish to double the proportion of high-valued wine in total exports. During 2001, wines costing over US$30 per case (US$2.50 per bottle) made up approximately 20 per cent of export sales. The industry target for these wines is to exceed 40 per cent by 2006 (*El Mercurio*, 3 October 2001).

The strides that Chilean wines have made in improving the average quality of exported bottled wines are illustrated in Figure 11.1, which demonstrates average prices and tasting scores from the Beverage Testing Institute for a random sample of US and Chilean wines for the vintage years 1991 through 1997. Not surprisingly, perceived quality is correlated with price. More important is the convergence of US and Chilean prices over time, due primarily to the fall in the average price of US wine. Chilean prices held steady although there was a slight increase in 1997, when there was also a convergence of perceived qualities of the two wines: the average tasting scores were nearly identical, 83 for US wines and 82.9 for Chilean wine.

Chilean wine export prices are negatively correlated with winery size due to the relatively lower emphasis on reserves and varietals of larger wineries. For example, the 120-year-old giant, Concha y Toro, the largest firm in the industry with total production of 100 million litres, dedicates only 3 per cent of its total product to reserves and 15 per cent to varietals. In terms of total exports, reserves of this company make up 5 per cent and varietals 25 per cent. Although less pronounced, this pattern holds for other large wineries. The four largest wineries together ship over 43 per cent of total Chilean exports, of which 62 per cent is in reserves and varietals. By contrast, wineries with production of less than 8 million litres only rarely have reserves and varietals making up less than 90 per cent of export shipments; for most of these firms higher-quality wines are 100 per cent of the firm's business (Larraín, 2001, p. 36.) These patterns of product mix naturally are reflected in per litre prices received by companies. Using survey data of 31 wineries, Foster, Beaujanot and Zúniga (2001) find that wineries that ship more than 3 million litres on average earn US$2.70 per litre, while those that ship less earn US$3.60.[7] The same survey data show that export growth performance also differs according to product mix. The largest firms (exports greater than 3 million litres), which place relatively more emphasis on lower-price wines, and the smallest firms (exports less than 1 million litres), which place relatively more emphasis on

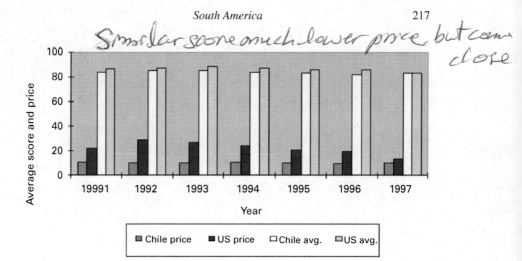

Source: Eyler (1999, Table 7).

*Figure 11.1   Average pricing and tasting scores, Chile vs USA, 1991–97
(all wines sold in the USA)*

very high-priced wines, have both been growing at approximately 7 per cent
per year since 1996. In contrast, medium-sized firms (between 1 and 3 million
litres of exports), which place more emphasis on medium-priced wines, grew
at 35 per cent per year.

Argentina

Argentina's per capita consumption experienced a similar decline to Chile's,
exactly halving in the last two decades, from 76 litres to 38 litres (see Table
11.3). Until recently, rising exports did not make up for the decrease in domestic consumption and consequently production fell. Again as in the case of
Chile, the land area in vineyards decreased by one-third between 1979 and
1990, when it stabilized at around 210 000 hectares. The major difference
between the two countries is that the U-shaped pattern of decline and rebound
of vineyards over the past 25 years that Chile experienced has yet to occur in
Argentina. And, given the recent stagnation of export volumes and the continued decrease in domestic consumption, an Argentine rebound is not imminent.
    Beginning with the economic reforms of the early 1990s, exports began to
rise, from under 2 per cent of national production before 1995 to an average
of 10 per cent in recent years. Argentina's share of world exports is still only
about 2 per cent. The stagnation is due in part to the appreciation of the
currency, which was tied directly to the US dollar. In contrast, wine exporters

Table 11.3   Development of the wine sector, Argentina, 1979–2001

Year	Area ('000 ha)	Prod'n (million l)	Cons'n per capita (l)	Exports (US$m)	Exports % production	Exports as % world export volume	Export price (US$/l)
1979	316	2 733	76	7	0	0	0.8
1980	320	2 427	76	6	0	0	0.9
1981	322	2 297	75	7	0	0	0.6
1982	324	2 728	74	6	1	0	0.3
1983	322	2 670	71	4	0	0	0.4
1984	306	1 963	66	6	1	1	0.2
1985	295	1 741	60	5	1	1	0.3
1986	284	1 952	59	6	1	1	0.3
1987	275	2 860	58	7	1	1	0.5
1988	268	2 452	56	7	1	1	0.6
1989	260	2 297	54	10	1	1	0.5
1990	210	1 775	54	19	3	1	0.5
1991	209	1 602	52	21	2	1	0.8
1992	209	1 700	50	24	2	1	1.0
1993	209	1 523	44	20	1	0	1.4
1994	210	1 975	43	20	1	0	1.3
1995	210	2 250	41	79	14	4	0.3
1996	211	1 606	41	84	11	2	0.6
1997	209	1 949	40	132	11	2	1.0
1998	210	1 544	39	188	9	2	1.7
1999	208	1 895	39	179	9	2	1.3
2000	209	1 684	38	157	8	2	1.6
2001	207	1 580	38	156	7	1	1.5

Sources: Anderson and Norman (2003) and INV.

218

in competing countries such as Australia and Chile have benefited from depreciating currencies.

The industry's optimism that began in the early 1990s, underscored by international investments[8] (including Chilean wineries) and foreign commentators' frequent references to Argentina being a sleeping giant in the wine trade, has perhaps been tempered in the last two years by the decline in both total export volumes and value. The most notable contributor to this decrease is the large reduction of Argentina's inexpensive wine sales abroad; but exports of finer wines have also shown a weakening in total sales value. The optimism that led investors to embark on the rapid and massive rebound of plantings seen in Chile has not prevailed in Argentina, yet leading Argentine wine-growers continue to increase plantings of 'international' varieties. More than one-eighth of the vineyard area is now devoted to the production of the exportable wine varietals. The Criolla and Cereza varieties, however, still make up about half of the country's vineyards, in contrast to Chile, where País now represents less than one-sixth of the wine grape area. Malbec, possibly the flagship of Argentina's export wines, represents nearly half of the land area going to finer varieties. The replacement of higher-yielding, lower-quality vines by varieties oriented toward higher-valued, export-quality wines has coincided with better vineyard management and the installation of more sophisticated processing facilities. Fine wines make up slightly half of export volume but over 70 per cent of export value. Table wines represent the bulk of the remainder, with some sparkling wines. The number of exporting wineries is increasing, which industry observers consider should lead to greater export growth in the next few years. In 1997 there were fewer than 15 exporting wineries and by 2001 there were 40.

The major single markets for Argentine exports of bottled wine are Great Britain and the United States. In terms of regions, more than one-third of all of the country's wine exports goes to Western European countries, but Britain is clearly the most important European market. In 2000, Britain imported nearly over 12 million litres, or about 17 per cent of the country's total exports, and 22 per cent of the total value of finer wine exports. North America received nearly 20 per cent of Argentina's wine exports. In terms of bottled wines, the United States ranks as the country's largest buyer, importing 27 per cent of the total value of higher-priced products. Canada, Brazil, Germany and Denmark imported lesser quantities of bottled wines, while Japan is the principal importer of bulk wines.

Argentine wineries place more stress on exports of lower-quality wines, especially in tetra-pack, than other New World exports. Inexpensive wines in general, significant in quantity but of much less value per unit, go mainly to Latin American importers, notably Paraguay, Uruguay and Chile and Brazil. The larger proportion of exports of lower-quality products accounts in part for

Argentina receiving the lowest average export prices among New World exporters. In 2000, for example, one-third of the country's export volume was composed of inexpensive wines, earning an average price of only US$0.61 per litre. By contrast, slightly less than half the export volume was fine wines, earning an average of 96 US cents. During 1995, the first year of Argentina's big breakout into world markets when 12 per cent of total production was exported, inexpensive wines made up 93 per cent of total exports for that year, an average per litre prices of just 34 US cents.

MORE ON DOMESTIC CONSUMPTION

As in other traditional wine-drinking countries, since the 1960s consumers in both Argentina and Chile have dramatically reduced their annual per capita intake of wine. Chileans have cut their alcohol consumption from wine by more than three-quarters, placing them in the same company as the British. The Argentines still rank as the eighth heaviest wine drinkers, double the consumption per person of Chileans, but one-third below the consumption level in France and Italy. In 1980 Argentina and Chile ranked fourth and sixth in the list of heaviest wine drinkers.

What factors contributed to the decline in per capita consumption in these two countries? Rapid economic development and the rise in per capita income in Chile certainly contributed to a change in the pattern of demand for alcoholic beverages. With the rising middle class, the nature of the workday for most Chileans changed as well. One might speculate as to the magnitude of the effect, but the increased incentives for punctuality and an attentive workforce almost certainly led to shorter, more temperate lunches and shorter, less celebratory evenings. The privatization of the largest beer producer led both to quality improvements in a lower-alcohol substitute for wine and to publicity campaigns to make the consumer aware of the purported advantages of drinking beer. Beer consumption has more than doubled since the early 1980s even though its price relative to wine remained fairly constant. In response to a fall in the relative price of the country's principal spirit, pisco, its consumption more than tripled. With import barriers lower, imported whiskey consumption also increased. At present, wine, beer and spirits contribute approximately equal shares to the total per capita alcohol intake in Chile.

In the case of Argentina, the change in wine consumption has been in the same direction as that of Chile. Beer consumption has increased at an average of over 6 per cent per year since the late 1980s. Spirit consumption has also increased, at about 3 per cent per year. Compared to Chileans, Argentines reduced their consumption of wine less dramatically, and substituted relatively more beer and less spirits. Of the total per capita alcohol consumption in

Argentina, wine still represents two-thirds compared with a little under one-half in Chile. As has been the case recently in other countries, Argentine consumers are tending to shift wine consumption to reds at the expense of whites.

Slightly over ten years ago, Johnson (1989, p. 468) offered an explanation of the difference in the styles of wine in Argentina and Chile. In the past, Argentine wineries produced rougher, sweeter wines, which were not the characteristics wineries now wish to produce for export markets. While there was room for much improvement, Chilean wineries by contrast produced wine in a style more suitable to export markets. He hypothesized that the reason for this difference was to be found in the size of the domestic markets of the two countries. Argentina had a much larger population whose tastes were derived from the large immigration of Italians. The industry initially oriented itself to this market, the size of which reduced incentives to improve quality, at least as defined by potential importers in the rest of the world. The preferences of Argentina's numerous and absorbent consumers tended and still tend to favour fruity wines, lower in tannins and higher in acidity.[9] To the winemakers in the isolated central-west, the proximity and size of the market in Buenos Aires and the rest of the country was hard to ignore. Chile, on the other hand, had a much smaller internal market, and the industry was more concerned with finding foreign buyers. Modern Chilean winemaking in its formative stages had early on adopted French ideas as to quality and had retained these standards even during the several decades of only modest exports before its breakout into world markets in the 1980s.[10]

Despite the still present discordance of tastes in domestic and export markets, Argentine wineries have managed to penetrate foreign markets and have moved to produce products that will compete with other exporting countries. The overall strategy of the industry has been to produce distinct styles of wine for domestic and foreign consumers. It is unknown to what extent this division of focus has led to lower scale economies in the planning, production and marketing of export wines or to slower export growth. But it is likely not to have enhanced export performance. Nevertheless, over recent years domestic consumption of premium wines has tripled and continues to rise, and there is likely to be a convergence in the design of export and domestic products.

GOVERNMENT POLICY

In the case of Chile, the only significant government policies affecting the wine industry directly are those related to certification and sanitary regulation. No explicit subsidies exist for exports or at the level of the grape and wine producer. There is an agency that promotes to some degree exports in trade shows, but this apparently has had little effect, especially in comparison with the private promotional activities of the large wineries and the wine export association. Certainly relative to export sales volume, expenses on publicity and marketing are low by international standards. Chilean wineries expend 2.5–3 per cent of sales value on marketing compared to the 5–6 per cent average in the case of competing industries in the rest of the world. Imports of wine pay a small tariff common to all imported goods, and all domestic wine sales are subject to an alcohol tax that is lower than that for spirits (with no differentiation between national wines and the few imports that enter the country). Argentina has a 23 per cent import tax on wine and gives a 10 per cent export rebate.

In terms of the effects of policies on the Argentine wine industry, the most important are not sector-specific but economy-wide policies, most notably the level of the exchange rate. The convertibility of the peso and the high value of the US dollar has been stymieing the export growth of Argentine wineries. Since 1994, the per litre price of Argentine export wines has shown the same pattern as that of US exports, albeit with greater percentage fluctuations. The flexible exchange rates of Australia and Chile, by contrast, have recently favoured exports. Both countries have increased exports as their currencies have depreciated and their per litre prices have risen as well.

CHILE PRICE BOOMS AND BUSTS

Over the past three decades, producer prices of grapes and wine have followed a cyclical pattern of booms and busts (Figures 11.2 and 11.3). During the late 1970s and early 1980s, paralleling an upsurge in the proportion of total production going to exports, prices rose strongly for grapes and intra-industry bulk wines. As exports declined in terms of both value and percentage of production, prices returned in the mid-1980s to their initial levels before the export surge, despite the trend downward in overall production. Again in 1985 exports began to increase both in value and as a proportion of production, and again the following year wine-grower prices showed dramatic increases, rising to a peak in 1992, only to fall dramatically over the next two years even though exports continued to rise. New plantings were coming on line, outstripping exports with growing supplies of grapes and bulk wine available to wineries. Growers, especially those producing Cabernet, enjoyed another boom beginning in 1993 as export growth rates jumped once more. This boom lasted about three years, but in 2002 growers have again seen collapsed prices that have fallen to their lowest real levels in ten years.

Apparent in Chile's pattern of booms and busts in wine-grower prices is the role of the growth rates of exports relative to the growth rates of production. During times of high stocks, competition among growers pushes the raw

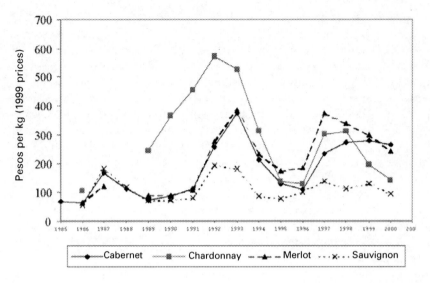

Source: ODEPA.

Figure 11.2   Real domestic prices of wine grapes, Chile, 1985–2000

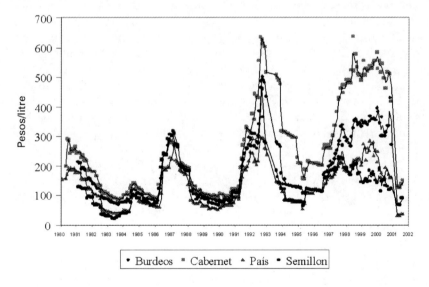

Source: ODEPA.

Figure 11.3   Intra-industry bulk wine real prices, Chile, 1980–2001 (local currency, September 1999)

product's price downward toward the breakeven cost of harvesting and processing. During times of faster-than-normal export growth, wineries bid prices to surprisingly high levels. During 1992–93 and again in 1998–99, a winery paid, for bulk wines acquired from other wineries, six times the price in 1995 or 2001. Intra-industry bulk prices are more volatile than grape prices, but the same pattern occurs in the raw product's price. For the 1999 season, Cabernet grape prices hit 320 Chilean pesos per kilo (roughly US$60/kg) – which exceeded the price for the 1997 season by 60 per cent. A kilo of Chardonnay grapes today would trade for 120 Chilean pesos (less than 20 US cents), but for the 1998 season prices stood at 300 peso (43 US cents), or 150 per cent higher that in year 2000.

One reason for the sharpness of the boom and bust cycle often mentioned by industry observers is the scarcity of storage facilities. In the next four to five years the wineries are projecting investments in bodegas of US$200 million, the largest share of which will be for storage by the larger firms with greatest emphasis on exports.

THE FUTURE

Slowing world economic growth and recent infamous events have left in doubt any optimistic scenario of robust expansion in international demand. Wine demand especially is sensitive to what takes place in sectors associated with tourism, hotels and restaurants, all of which have been negatively affected by consumers responding to discouraging economic and political changes in 2001–2002. Japan is in recession, economic activity in the USA and Europe is slowing, and at least at present American customers are travelling and spending less outside the home. In the short run the demand for wine will probably not grow at the rates that have recently sustained the rapid expansion of New World exporters.

As in other countries, for Chilean and Argentine wine-growers and winemakers such a slowdown comes at a time of increasing production – and decreasing prices – of wine grapes, and of heightened competition from international competitors. Of the New World exporters, Argentina is perhaps in the least envious position with declining domestic per capita consumption, internal economic woes, and the dollar convertibility of the peso. In Chile, the rapid expansion in vineyards and the effect of slower economic activity has already led to very low wine grape prices and a decrease in the rate of growth in export value. Given sales for the first eight months, total export value is expected to grow at only 3 per cent for 2001, considerably lower than the 9 per cent growth rate projected at the beginning of the year.

Although they are now growing more slowly, Chilean exports reveal some interesting shifts that might indicate what to expect in the next few years. After falling in importance for some years, the shipments of bulk wine increased substantially in 2001.[11] For smaller wineries there has also been significant growth. 'Emerging' wineries – the boutiques – that are members of Chilevid saw export sales of US$27.5 million in the year 2000 and an increase of more than 20 per cent in value and 50 per cent in volume in 2001. Moreover, several individual country markets that have typically demanded smaller quantities have shown surprises. During 2001, exports to Germany rose by 16 per cent, to Ireland by 37 per cent and to Russia over 200 per cent. In short, it is the larger-scale wineries that specialize in bottled wine for extensive sales that are likely to suffer most in the near future's economic environment. Wineries that take advantage of an abundance of inexpensive, quality wine, and wineries that specialize in small sales to niche markets, are going to be the relative winners.

Longer-term projections are for continued increases in wine grape production in Chile and for a continued conversion of vineyards in Argentina toward exportable varieties. Not long ago, there were expectations that in the next two to three years industry observers would see Chilean production rise to about 750 million litres. New plantings have slowed, however, and wine-growers are reducing yields, hoping to improve quality. Notwithstanding the slowdown in growth in the near future, over the next decade Chile's production could reach 900 million litres. This will require investments in storage facilities, which are now perceived to be a significant bottleneck in the processing chain. Argentina, on the other hand, will probably show little growth in production in the next few years but an improvement in average quality.

NOTES

1. Weakly supporting the conjecture that the grape is indigenous to Chile, one Abbot Molina reported seeing wild vines and black muscatel grapes growing near the town of Curicó.
2. This compares with the approximately 16 million litres produced in significantly more populous Peru some years later.
3. Yearly data from the accounts of the Hospital San Juan de Dios show that, between 1631 and 1637, the hospital regularly paid prices higher than those fixed by the Cabildo de Santiago (43 per cent higher on average). Only once, in 1635, did the official price exceed the price paid.
4. Within two decades the experiment station had 40 000 vines of 60 different varieties.
5. Hernandez (2000, p. 11), authors' translation.
6. As report in the Chilean press (*El Mercurio*, Revista del Campo, 1 October 2001), until recently Chilean wine-growers put little importance on the potential of Carmenère, a variety originating but now almost non-existent in Bordeaux. The perhaps embarrassing truth was that many of the ancient vineyards designated Merlot were in fact Carmenère and simply innocently (or not so innocently) misclassified. Until the mid-1990s, many growers were anxious to avoid discussing the topic of the lineage of their Merlots. But today a number of

wine-growers are hoping to capitalize on Carmenère's affinity for Chilean growing conditions, seeing the variety as a means to establish an insignia product, a particularly Chilean
quality wine that might parallel Malbec's role for Argentina and Shiraz for Australia.

7. Price differences are more striking among smaller wineries (exports of less than 1 million
   litres) once one controls for stated management priorities. The analysis of Foster, Beaujanot
   and Zúniga (2001) of the survey results reported in Zúniga shows that those small wineries
   placing the highest priority on quality received US$4.17 per litre in export sales but those
   putting a lower priority on quality received only US$3.06.

8. Moet-Hennessy entered Argentina in the1960s. Two notable recent international investors
   are Gallo and Drouhin.

9. One Argentinean commentator says of his compatriots' preferences: 'They like to smell old,
   damp wood.' (see www.argentinewines.com). The authors doubt that the randomly selected
   Argentinean would readily agree.

10. Moreover, many of Chile's élite families both affected European tastes and owned wineries.
    The benefits derived from the good opinion of one's family label among the aristocracy,
    many of which were winemaking rivals, undoubtedly contributed at least a small part to the
    maintenance of sophisticated standards (del Pozo, 1998).

11. Estimates in this paragraph are taken from *Estrategia*, 2 October 2001, p. 12.

REFERENCES

Anderson, K. and N. Berger (1999), 'Australia's re-emergence as a Wine Exporter: the
    First Decade in International Perspective', *Australian and New Zealand Wine
    Industry Journal*, **16** (6), 26–38.
Anderson, K. and D. Norman (2003), *Global Wine Production, Consumption and
    Trade, 1961 2001: A Statistical Compendium*, Adelaide: Centre for International
    Economic Studies.
El Mercurio (2001), 'Carmenere, una bendición', Revista del Campo (no. 1316), 1
    October, p. A10.
El Mercurio, 'El crecimiento del sector vitivinícola será muy bajo', Economía y
    Negocios, 3 October, p. B22.
Estrategia (2001), 'El 2002 el precio del vino no subirá', 2 October, p. 12.
Eyler, R.C. (1999), 'The International Competitiveness of the California Wine
    Industry', mimeo, Department of Economics, Sonoma State University.
Foster, W., A. Beanjanot and J.I. Zúniga (2001), 'Meeting Consumer Need:
    Competitive Priorities in the Chilean Wine Industry', Working Paper, Departamento
    de Economía Agraria, Pontificia Universidad Católica de Chile, September.
Hernandez, A. (2000), *Introducción al Vino de Chile*, 2nd edn, Colección en
    Agricultura de la Facultad de Agronomía e Ingeniería Forestal, Pontificia
    Universidad de Chile.
Johnson, H. (1989), *The Story of Wine*, London: Mitchell Beazley Publishers.
Larraín, C. (2001), 'Mecanismos de Coordinación Vertical: Caso de la Industria
    Vitivinícola Chilena', Tesis de Magíster (borrador), Departamento de Economía
    Agraria, Pontificia Universidad Católica de Chile, 28 September.
del Pozo, J. (1998), *Historia del Vino Chileno*, Santiago de Chile: Editorial
    Universitaria.

12. South Africa

Nick Vink, Gavin Williams and Johann Kirsten

Until 1997, the marketing of wine, like most sectors of agriculture in South Africa, was extensively regulated by statute. The 1924 Wine and Brandy Control Act pioneered statutory control of agricultural markets. However, whereas most of the 22 marketing schemes introduced under the Marketing Acts of 1937 and 1968 brought markets under state control boards, wine was regulated by the industry's own institutions. The state also provided few direct subsidies. The industry did benefit, though, from price support and import protection, which enabled it to pass costs on to consumers, and from favourable excise taxes, which favoured the distilling of grapes into spirits at the expense of sugar producers.

Like the rest of the agricultural sector of South Africa, the wine industry has been extensively deregulated in two phases over the past 20 years. The origins of the first phase can be found in the shift in monetary policy in the late 1970s and fiscal strategies in the 1980s, which undermined the complex structure of protection, price support and cross-subsidies on which the system of agricultural support was founded. Before 1994, the tax regime was changed, and a start was made to land reform, and to labour legislation and trade policies. The major change was the extensive deregulation of state agricultural marketing schemes within the framework of the Marketing Act of 1968 (Vink and Kassier, 1991; Francis and Williams, 1993; Vink, 1993, 2000; Kirsten and Van Zyl, 1996; Williams et al., 1998). One consequence was that statutory intervention lasted longer in the wine and sugar industries, which were not covered by the Marketing Act.

Then the government of national unity, elected in 1994, ushered in policies across the entire range of government activities. In agriculture, some tended to follow the direction of changes already under way (Williams et al., 1998; Hall and Williams, 2000). Major direct policy changes had to wait until after the National Party, and its Minister of Agriculture, Kraai van Niekerk, withdrew from the government in 1996. New policy initiatives included the land reform programme; laws protecting agricultural workers and labour tenants against eviction and extending their rights; liberalization of international trade and agricultural marketing; the Marketing of Agricultural Products Act, No. 47 of 1996; a new rural development policy; and institutional restructuring in the public sector. The purpose of the reforms was to correct the injustices of past policy, principally through land reform, to direct agriculture towards a less capital-intensive growth path, and to enhance its international competitiveness. The wine industry did not escape these changes. Future developments in the wine industry will be driven by policy reforms as well as by changes in domestic and global markets.

This chapter examines how the political, social and economic changes in South Africa affect the situation and future of wine farmers and those involved in the further processing, distribution and marketing of wine. The South African industry long shared characteristics with Australia, as both were predominantly producers of distilling and fortified wines for the first half of the twentieth century and then switched, initially to the production of table wines. Table wine exceeded fortified wine production for the first time in South Africa in 1953 and in Australia in 1968 (KWV, 1963, pp. 52–53; Osmond and Anderson, 1998, p. 48).

However, South Africa differs today from its competitors among 'New World' wine producers, including Australia, New Zealand and Chile, which all export a high proportion of their vintage: 41, 36 and 50 per cent respectively for 2001 compared with South Africa's 15 per cent (and Argentina's 7 per cent – see Anderson and Norman, 2003). Historically South Africa produced large quantities of cheap wine for the domestic markets, a legacy they share with Languedoc-Roussillon. This pattern of demand and supply constrains the capacity to adapt to a more differentiated international demand. South African producers thus face a considerable challenge in the wake of changes in global market conditions and in the South African policy environment if the country is to become and remain a force in global wine markets.

HISTORICAL LEGACIES

Bringing the Surplus under Control

Van Zyl (1993, p. 33) quotes a wine farmer as warning in 1918, at the beginning of a boom period for the industry, that he was 'bang dat 't te lekker gaan. Die surplus sal kom want men plant agter die prys aan' (he was 'frightened that it was going too well. The surplus will come [back] because one plants after the price'). These words summarize the legacy that the South African industry must escape if it is to succeed in the global marketplace, namely, to avoid excess production of poor-quality wine. Farmers took steps to address the problem, creating institutions, and specifically the Koöperatieve

Wijnbouers Vereniging van Zuid-Afrika (KWV), to manage the problem, but they never fully succeeded despite ever more sophisticated attempts to manipulate the market. Industry insiders persisted with arrangements such as guaranteed markets and fixed prices in periods of shortage and surplus as if farmers would voluntarily forego increased production in the boom years and not continue to expect assured markets and guaranteed prices when supply rose again ahead of demand.

The industry first reached maturity as a slave economy during and after the Napoleonic Wars, although the first vines had been planted and the first wine was made in the mid-seventeenth century. The number of vines planted increased from 15 million in 1808–10 to 32 million in 1823–25 (compared to 314 million vines in 2000). Between 1810 and the 1820s wine was the most important export commodity from the Cape, responsible for some 90 per cent of the Colony's exports. Under imperial preference policies, the duties payable on Cape wines were one-third of those levied on Iberian wines, their main competitor, and Britain became the largest market for the industry (Keegan, 1996).

When imperial preference was abolished in 1825, exports to Britain fell by 75 per cent, and the industry plunged into depression. Despite continued complaints about the quality of the wine, however, the industry revived sufficiently to export wine to the value of more than £120 000 annually to Britain in the late 1850s (Van Zyl, 1993). Then the industry had to face a new series of challenges during the second half of the nineteenth century. The 1860 trade treaty between Britain and France meant that by 1861 South Africa's wine exports to Britain had dropped to £8000. Then followed oidium and other diseases, and from 1885 the spread of phylloxera (Perold, 1936). Recovery from the ravages of phylloxera was slow, but local consumption did not rise to meet the expanding supply.

Farmers made several attempts to cooperate in the face of disaster. However, De Zuid-Afrikaanschse Wijnbouwersvereeniging (The SA Winemakers' Association) in Paarl in 1877 and the Paarlberg Wyn- en Brandewynmaatskappy Bpk (The Paarlberg Wine and Brandy Co. Ltd) in 1885, failed to survive more than a few years. In this period wine (and wheat) farmers organized politically against excise taxes to defend their economic interests (Giliomee, 1987). In 1905, a Committee of Inquiry reported that 'Large stocks held by producers and merchants are practically unsaleable, or saleable only in small quantities at unremunerative prices' (Cape of Good Hope, 1905). The government provided loans to finance the creation, under the Companies Act, of nine cooperative cellars to improve the quality of Cape wines (Malherbe, 1932, p. 9; Botha, 1966). In 1907, the Cape Wine Farmers and Wine Merchants Association (CFWWMA) was formed, with Charles Kohler as President. On 14 April 1909, a mass meeting of wine farmers protested against the excise tax. The Prime Minister, John Merriman, rejected these demands, blaming overproduction by the farmers for their plight (Kohler, 1946, pp. 74–6).

In 1913, the price for wine rose from £6 to £9 per leaguer (= 127 imperial gallons = 5.6 hectolitres). When the ostrich boom collapsed that year, farmers in the inland districts turned their irrigated fields from lucerne to vines. By 1918, there were 87 million vines, an increase of 25 per cent over seven years. Farmers had to sell their wine at the close of the season for whatever prices they could get in order to make space for the next vintage. In 1916 the South African government announced plans to increase excise duties. When the customary representations to the government failed to produce results, plans for a congress of wine farmers gained momentum. Kohler put forward plans for a cooperative of wine and brandy farmers, which would regulate the prices at which vine products were sold to the trade (merchants and manufacturers) by controlling the supply of grapes and wine.

KWV was initiated as a cooperative in 1916 and registered as a company in 1918. Its members had to sell all their wine through KWV and contribute a levy of 10 per cent on their sales. KWV would declare an annual 'surplus', which it would remove from the market. Some 90 per cent of the wine farmers in the Cape signed the constitution of KWV by the end of 1917. They insisted that they should not be prevented from planting more vines; Kohler realized that this would exacerbate the 'hideous nightmare' of surplus production (Kohler, 1946).

A few Stellenbosch farmers and most of the Constantia farmers refused to join. They argued that they had no need for such an institution, as they were producing a superior quality wine. Distillers and merchants and so on were opposed to the scheme from the outset. Kohler used the threat that KWV would enter the trade in its own right to secure their cooperation. Originally, this took the form of a five-year contract, which was signed at the end of 1917 (that is, even before the formal founding of KWV). The merchants agreed that they would buy only from KWV. The two sides reached a 'gentleman's agreement' in 1918. The manufacturing wholesalers ('the Trade') would distil and store the surplus on behalf of KWV who, in return, would not 'compete with the established wine or spirit trade or distilling of manufacturing interests in Africa south of the equator' (Kohler, 1924, p. 21).

In 1920, prices of wine rose to £30 per leaguer and then collapsed. In 1921, KWV signed a new agreement with a group of merchants. Between 1921 and 1923, members received £3 per leaguer for distilling wine. Merchants paid £9 in 1921–22 and £6 in 1923. The difference represented the 'surplus' of two-thirds or one-half. By the end of 1923, KWV could no longer sustain its control of the market. Constantia farmers had, in court, won their claim not to pay a 'surplus contribution' on sales of 'good wine' (K.W.V. v. Cloete, 1922

AD). Merchants could buy wine directly from farmers below the minimum price but well above what farmers would receive through KWV. At the end of 1923, the merchants withdrew from the agreement (Kohler, 1946, pp. 93–8; Van Zyl, 1993, pp. 35–7, 42–3). KWV had no way out other than to resort to a scheme for compulsory cooperation.

Smuts, the Prime Minister, agreed to such a scheme as long as it had support from the National Party opposition (Van Zyl, 1993, pp. 46–8; Kenney, 1981, p. 76) and overrode objections from the Constantia farmers and the Trade. The Constantia farmers succeeding in excluding wine not sold for distilling ('good wine') from control. Membership of KWV, registered in 1923 as a cooperative, and payment of levies were not made compulsory. The manufacturing wholesalers objected that the Bill sought to exclude them. It conferred a monopoly that enabled KWV to charge an artificially high price 'for wines to enable them to pay their members for the portion of the crop which is not required, and which will then become their property at no cost to themselves' (Cloete, 1924, p. 3).

The Wine and Spirits Control Act 5 of 1924 provided that the KWV would fix a minimum price for the sale of any wine for distilling, and that sales could only be made 'through or with the consent of' KWV. KWV was required to supply wine only in wholesale quantities and at a uniform price to 'any bona fide distiller, wholesale trader or cooperative society' for sale anywhere in southern Africa. Brandy sold after 1 June 1928 had to contain at least 25 per cent brandy pot-stilled for three years. The failure of KWV's attempt to control the production and marketing of wine and brandy led the government to extend statutory powers to enable the KWV to do so – and thereby save the KWV from liquidation (Drew, 1937, p. 9). The 1924 Act laid the foundation on which the institutional structure and patterns of production of the industry were built for the following 73 years.

Good Wine and Brandy Wine

KWV fixed the price of distilling wine to the merchants at £7 18s. 9d. per leaguer (1s. 3d. per gallon) and kept it there between the wars. It set the initial surplus deduction at 40 per cent. Wine production doubled from 95 211 leaguers in 1924 to 202 444 leaguers in 1934 and continued to rise. The largest increases in planting took place in the interior, irrigated districts of Worcester, Robertson and Montagu (Drew, 1937, Tables 1, 2, 5, expanded in Swart, 1944, Tables 2, 3, 5). Up to 1928, consumption of wines and brandies increased. Brandy was temporarily kept off the market by pot-stilling. By declaring generous 'surplus contributions', KWV was able to expand its distilling capacity and financial reserves, on which it drew to sustain prices between 1931 and 1933. KWV argued determinedly against the campaign for temperance that strongly influenced the 1928 Liquor Act. It wanted to expand the market by liberalizing liquor licences and the prohibition of sales to Africans and to extend to the Transvaal and Natal the *dop* system of providing free wine to farm workers (House of Assembly, 1926, pp. 733–70, 1054–69).

Imperial preference was re-established in 1919 and increased in 1924, opening access to the British market for the first time since 1861. In 1927, the KWV arranged to sell all its exports to the UK through Vine Products Ltd; they were mainly blended into 'British wine'. Brandy exports expanded to New Zealand and Canada. KWV fortified 'good wine', purchased from farmers, with surplus 'distilling wine' for export production. It was able to exclude merchants and farmers from the UK market for fortified wines because they had to pay the full price for distilling wine, which the KWV acquired and disposed of as part of the surplus. (C.C.W.E.S.A. v. K.W.V., *C.P.D.* 1934 and Drew, 1935–37, I, pp. 207–11; K.W.V. v. Bruwer 1936, *AD* 17 Aug. 1936). Exports increased from 26 104 bulk gallons in 1926 to 338 926 bulk gallons in 1929, and reached 2.2 million bulk gallons in 1939. However, exports did not keep pace with production and, over this period, only amounted to 51 per cent of the wine manufactured for export. The purchase of good wine for fortification helped to assure farmers of a sale and removed it from the domestic market, but it did so by incorporating it into accumulating stocks of fortified wine, which reached 11.5 million bulk gallons by the end of 1939 (Drew, 1937, Table 8; Swart, 1944, Table 9).

Domestic demand for good wine increased more slowly than production so that a rising share of the vintage had to be taken off the market as 'surplus' distilling wine. The fixed price paid to the producer for distilling wine was reduced from a peak of £5 0s. 6d. in 1928 to £3 3s. 6d. in 1932 and then increased slightly to reach £4 4s. 3½d. in 1939. The price paid by KWV and manufacturers for 'good wine' also fell from £7 7s. 0d. to £5 in 1939 and the gap between the two narrowed during the decade. Throughout the whole period, manufacturers had to pay a higher price for distilling wine than for 'good wine' (Drew, 1937, Table 2; Swart, 1944, Table 3). Most producers had little incentive to improve the quality of their wines and every reason to irrigate land, increase yields and stay with their tried and tested varietals. Production of quality table wines remained confined largely to Constantia, Stellenbosch and Paarl (Perold, 1936).

From 1929, the directors of KWV warned their members that continuation of surplus production would lead to a fall in producer prices. In 1931, they set up the first of a series of committees, and supported a bill in parliament, which sought to produce a scheme for discouraging surplus production. They all ran up against conflicts of interest between the established districts of Paarl and Stellenbosch and the expanding and irrigated districts of Worcester, Robertson and Montagu (State Archive Depository, K404; Drew, 1935–37, pp. 102, 179–84, 198–202; House of Assembly, 1932, pp. 3794–829) .

The 1934 Commission on Co-operatives and Credit argued that the KWV's minimum pricing policies had encouraged overproduction and discouraged quality, and objected to its refusal to discount the price of spirits for export to the UK. It recommended that a statutory board take control of distilling and also of good wine (Viljoen, 1934, pp. 16, 82–94). The appointment in 1935 of the Wine Commission by a new Minister of Agriculture, Deneys Reitz, kept the wine industry outside the 1937 Marketing Act. The Commission agreed that the buying of the surplus by KWV encouraged expansion of production and that a producer cooperative should not exercise statutory control over an industry. It decided that the only solution to the failure of partial control was to apply a comprehensive system of statutory control. This would have to fall under KWV, who had invested in the necessary cellar and distilling capacity. The Commission argued for minimum prices for 'good wine' and 'quality wine', opposed production quotas and suggested the creation of an advisory board (Drew, 1937, pp. 57–89, 104–5).

The Wine and Spirits Control Act 23 of 1940, introduced by W.R. Collins, Smuts's Minister of Agriculture, over the merchants' objections empowered KWV to set an annual minimum price for 'good wine', and for 'quality wine' of which wholesalers had to buy a minimum percentage. It made provision for production limits but did not introduce an advisory board or require KWV to discount sales of spirits for export (House of Assembly, 1940). Thus, KWV had maintained and extended its control of the industry, acquired the powers to set prices for distilling good and quality wine, protected its effective monopoly of the export market and secured, in principle, powers to limit production.

Regulation and Monopoly

Demand for brandy during the World War II solved the immediate problem of surplus disposal. Prices of good wine increased relative to distilling wine, and KWV withdrew from buying grapes for export production. Hence farmers needed access to cellars to produce 'good wine' (most of which was not very good at all). Farmers delivered grapes to their cooperatives, which took delivery and paid farmers from a pool in accordance with tonnage, sugar content, and possibly cultivar. The incentives to produce standard, high-yielding grape varietals on irrigated land continued. The number of cooperative cellars increased from six to 19 between 1939 and 1944, to 30 by 1950 and 46 by 1955. This initially suited the merchants to whom the cooperatives now supplied wine rather than grapes. The costs of new technologies, notably cold fermentation which was first introduced to South Africa in 1959, encouraged more farmers to join and form cooperatives, whose number rose to 69 by the end of the 1975 (Botha, 1966).

Wine production peaked in 1944 at 424 948 leaguers and only reached that level again ten years later (KWV, 1958, p. 16). KWV was able to raise the prices for distilling wine, and government increased the excise tax on brandy in 1942 (Kohler, 1944). A postwar shortage of wine allowed KWV to pay substantial bonuses to its members. In 1947, the supply had to be pooled between KWV, which got 25 per cent of the vintage, and the merchants, who shared the rest. In 1954, new laws were passed providing that, when supplies were rationed, the surplus should be between 15 and 25 per cent, thus enabling KWV to claim a share of the vintage to meet its export needs (Theron, 1954; Van Zyl, 1993, pp. 134–6).

From 1954 to 1963, increased production led to rising surpluses. Act 47 of 1957 made new provision for planting quotas, which were introduced in 1960. They were set above current output and expanded ahead of supply, and thus encouraged people to increase production to justify their quotas. A renewed shortage led to rationing of wine spirits in 1964 and to KWV acquiring an exclusive right to import distilling wine (Du Toit, 1960, p. 2; Deacon, 1980, p. 29; Van Zyl, 1993, pp. 141–3, 174).

A sharp increase in excise taxes in 1958 reduced brandy consumption but encouraged the demand for natural wines. In 1959, KWV increased the surplus declaration to 35 per cent and compensated producers by a sharp increase in the minimum price. Wholesalers responded by attacking KWV's unilateral right to fix powers and exclusive exports to the UK and demanded a commission of inquiry. They objected to direct sales at the minimum price by cooperative wineries and by 'pseudo-wholesalers' selling by the case to the public, thus excluding them from the distribution chain. They were not mollified by a law to 'load' the minimum price by the costs of bottling and storing wine (Steenkamp, 1967, pp. 168–77).

The expansion of demand for urban labour and the restriction of African migration to the Western Cape created a shortage of farm labour. This led both to increased use of prison labour and farm prisons, and to policies to improve conditions for coloured rural communities and to subsidize farm housing. In 1963, the supply of liquor to Africans was legalized and grocers were licenced to sell natural wine but not beer. The *dop* system was outlawed, in law if not in practice.

The system by which KWV unilaterally set uniform prices for distilling, good and even quality wines protected farmers' incomes but discouraged competition among buyers; and wholesalers' ties to retail outlets discouraged competition among sellers. This facilitated the process of concentration of control of markets for wines by Stellenbosch Farmers' Winery (SFW) and for spirits by Distillers. They sustained their domination of the market by building brand loyalty to familiar, established trademarks. In 1956, the country's three main breweries merged and in 1960 South African Breweries (SAB) took control of the Stellenbosch Wine Trust, which controlled SFW (Fridjhon and Murray, 1985, pp. 40–42; Van Zyl, 1993, pp. 226–9). Regulation of the industry facilitated monopolistic arrangements but also opened up bitter political contests for control of marketing arrangements between KWV and the Cape Wine and Spirits Institute, formed in 1967 to defend the interests of the 'Trade'.

The 'KWV Act', 47 of 1970 replaced and consolidated previous legislation. KWV no longer needed the support of two major parties and could rely on its links to the ruling National Party to secure political support for detailed amendments to Act 47 and its administration (Deacon, 1980, p. 52).

Legal regulation of standards of production of wine for the local and the export markets goes back to colonial legislation, consolidated in Act 15 of 1913 and in Act 36 of 1917 respectively. These and subsequent measures were consolidated in the Liquor Products Act 60 of 1989. The Agricultural Products Export Act, No. 36 of 1917, regulated the quality of wines for export. The Liquor Products Act, No. 60 of 1989 consolidated these measures (De Klerk, 1997).

The Plant Improvement Scheme, instituted by Act 53 of 1976, regulates the certification of material for the propagation of vines. In 1986 the Vine Improvement Association was established, with KWV, CWSI, the Western Cape Co-ordinating Vine Nursery Association and producer members from the wine cooperatives and independent estates. This led to revision of the Super grade scheme, whereby KWV had been the only institution certified to conduct plant propagation, to allow other participants. Full control over source material and certification, originally shared between the state and the Vine Improvement Board, was transferred to the Board in 1993.

Production quotas allowed rather than restricted an expansion of output far ahead of consumption, particularly in the irrigated Olifants and Orange River areas, where new distilleries were opened in 1977 and 1978. A wine of origin scheme, initiated by independent estate producers and Nietvoorbij (the industry research institute at Stellenbosch, now part of the Agricultural Research Council) was introduced in 1973; its provisions threatened to undermine the established trademarks of the major wholesalers (Van Zyl, 1993, pp. 198–210). Firms continued to complain that cooperatives were not prevented from selling directly to retailers.

Rembrandt acquired control of the renamed Inter-Continental Breweries (ICB) in 1973 to try to challenge SAB's domination in the beer market. In 1975, the government allowed SAB to take full control of SFW and changed the law to override a court challenge to this decision. In 1978, Rembrandt acquired all the shares in ICB and Oude Meester (Distillers); the government agreed to Oude Meester buying 49 per cent of Gilbey's and to Gilbey's acquiring the Rebel liquor chain contrary to its own rules. The 1979 beer (and the brief wine and spirits) war between SAB/SFW and Rembrandt (Oude Meester/ICB) was resolved by an agreement suggested by Fred du Plessis of Sanlam to Anton Rupert of Rembrandt. This separated the dominant beer interests from two leading wine and spirits companies (SFW and Oude Meester), which would be amalgamated. This could only be done with the approval of KWV (Deacon, 1980, pp. 53–5; Van Zyl, 1993, pp. 227–32).

In November 1979, the cabinet announced their approval of a restructuring of the liquor industry. SAB would again become a 'temporary sole supplier' of malted beer. SFW and Oude Meester (Distillers) would be amalgamated into Kaapwyn (CWD), in which Rembrandt, KWV and SAB would each hold 30 per cent of the shares; SAB and Rembrandt agreed to dispose of their retail interests (a step they did not take). Rembrandt then formed a joint holding company with KWV to control CWD. Objections from Union Wine were stilled when the minister allowed them to acquire 75 more retail outlets.

In 1982, the Competition Board belatedly accepted SAB's monopoly of beer as a *fait accompli*. However, it declared unlawful SAB's previous controlling interest in SFW, the integration of KWV as controlling body at primary level with SFW and Distillers, the combining of SFW and OM in CWD and the vertical integration of suppliers and off-consumption retailers. The Prime Minister chaired a cabinet committee that consulted Rupert and KWV and the Minister for Industry, Dawie de Villiers. It rejected the decisions of the Competition Board and upheld the cabinet's previous support for the restructuring (Deacon, 1980, pp. 371–5; Competition Board, 1982; Fridjhon and Murray, 1985, pp. 136–43; 181–3; Van Zyl, 1993, pp. 229–35, 241–3).

Exports, mainly of fortified wines and brandies, were reduced by informal actions from 1963 and formal sanctions from 1985, and by the entry of Britain into the European Community in 1973. Declared exports fell by about two-thirds between 1964 and 1989 (Anderson and Norman, 2003), modified only by low-price export deals to Eastern Europe, which in 1983 amounted to 3.5 million hectolitres, over a third of the vintage. In the domestic market, vertical integration and market sharing under state auspices enabled liquor cartels, now in partnership with KWV, to dominate the beer, wine and spirits industries.

Regulation and Markets

Production continued to increase to reach a peak of 9997 hectolitres in 1992, while domestic demand stagnated and exports were blocked. But critical changes began to take place in the 1980s. State regulation and commercial monopoly slowly began to be undermined. These changes in turn created conditions that made possible the response of the industry to the opening of export markets in the 1990s and the collapse of the system of regulation. In 1980, six premium cultivars (Cabernet Sauvignon, Shiraz, Pinotage, Merlot, Sauvignon Blanc and Chardonnay) made up 6.5 per cent of the national vineyard. From 1980, producers began to shift production away from high-yielding to higher-value cultivars. By 1990, the six premium cultivars made up 12.5 per cent of acreage and, by 1995, 19 per cent of acreage and 42.5 per cent of new planting (KWV, 1981–90; SAWIS, 2003).

Production quotas did not reduce overall production levels but hampered independent producers of quality wines. In 1984 KWV conceded a limited market in quotas within wine regions. In 1991, a group of estate producers formed an action group to challenge quotas and the fines that accompanied them. In 1992, KWV agreed to suspend quotas. The task of regulating production was now transferred to the cooperatives. They were encouraged to define, limit and even charge for their members' rights to crush grapes (Welgemoed, 1992, 1993). The cooperatives now needed to discriminate more carefully in the prices paid to their members for different cultivars and for grapes, or even vineyards, or different qualities. These changes exposed conflicts of interests among cooperative members and brought into question the established arrangements for paying members for their produce.

Rather than consolidating their domination of the wine and spirits market, the manufacturing wholesalers saw their share of the market fall significantly from their initial 85 per cent to 65 per cent in 1991 and 49 per cent in 1996 (Ewert et al., 1998, p. 21). Cooperatives were threatened by KWV acquiring an interest in Kaapwyn and thus in a lower producer price for wine. Cooperatives and estate producers expanded their direct marketing of wines, despite pressures to sell their whole vintage or none to the wholesalers. In 1988, government announced the separation of CWD back into SFW and Oude Meester, without any change in ownership, and a plan to separate whole-sale and retail interests (Boonstra, 1988). From 1989, the CWSI renewed their complaints that cooperatives were able to undercut the minimum price in local markets, while KWV continued to use their statutory privileges to undercut them in export markets. In 1993, KWV insisted that the minimum price for good wine would continue. But it was undermined by arrangements that were designed to meet the complaints of wholesalers and allow cooperatives to take account of services by wholesalers in setting a lower delivery price (Marais, 1994a,b). The separate minimum price for good wine was suspended from 1995.

In the 1980s, the industry set up the Rural Foundation with government support to improve the social conditions of workers in the industry. An attempt by a few producers in 1989 to secure a commitment to a minimum level of wages and conditions was resisted by most estate producers and KWV.

KWV expanded production of grape juice and obtained a 25 per cent share in Ceres fruit juices in 1992, thereby acquiring a new way to dispose of much of the 'surplus' (Van Zyl, 1993, p. 255). Nevertheless, in 1992, the surplus pool still took up 45 per cent of the vintage, of which 20 per cent was used for concentrate (ibid., p. 270). International markets offered new opportunities for producers to export wines. The end of the white minority regime in 1994 led to a sharp increase in brandy consumption and renewed imports of distilling wine to enable KWV to meet demand. In 1993, KWV declared that it would not convert to a company under the 1993 Co-operatives Amendment Act. However, it provided for non-members to be eligible for election as directors (Van Zyl, 1993, pp. 290–91).

The regulatory mechanisms that KWV had built up could not be sustained. On 9 October 1996, KWV announced its intention to apply to the Western Cape Division of the Supreme Court to change from a cooperative to a company. The Minister of Agriculture, Derek Hanekom, asked the court to delay KWV's application to enable him to examine the future regulatory framework of the industry, to ask which assets acquired for KWV's regulatory functions were to be distributed among members, and to consider the unresolved issues of competition in the liquor industry. The Minister's intervention was initially supported by CWSI, even though KWV Investments owned a 30 per cent share in CWSI's two main members (SFW and Distillers). The Minister of Agriculture appointed a committee, chaired by Professor Kassier, Chair of the National Agricultural Marketing Council, to investigate the regulatory framework of the wine and distilling industry.

The Ministerial Committee included representatives from KWV, CWSI and the Department of Agriculture. Professor Vink was an independent member of this committee. KWV wished to maintain statutory provisions under its own control, failing which it preferred to leave matters to the market rather than come under the 1996 Marketing of Agricultural Products Act. CWSI was concerned that KWV would be able to use its accumulated assets to compete with the 'Trade' in the domestic market. The Committee completed its deliberations by the end of January 1997. Its report recommended that the industry be deregulated and that remaining statutory powers (for example levies to collect information and fund research; maintenance of quality standards) be placed under the control of a body that represented the whole industry (Kassier, 1997). These recommendations were largely acceptable to the Minister. KWV agreed to give CWSI due notice before entering the domestic market.

An initial audit concluded that KWV's performance of its 'statutory function did not contribute to their reserves' (Steyn, 1997). The Minister commissioned a further investigation, which found that 'the pooling mechanism contributed substantially to KWV's net asset wealth', which it estimated at

R803 million. It did not, however, establish that the state had any right to these assets. After negotiations, the Minister agreed to approve conversion of KWV. KWV confirmed that it would expand abroad and not enter the domestic market, although it was now no longer under any obligation not to do so. KWV also agreed to contribute R200 million over ten years and to provide services, valued at R227 million for five years, to the South Africa Wine Industry Trust (SAWIT), directed by nominees of the Minister and KWV. SAWIT established a Business Committee (Busco) and a Development Committee (Devco). The main function of the former is to provide funding for groups such as Wines of South Africa (the exporters' association), Winetech (the research funding arm of the industry), SAWIS (providers of information and systems services) and Vinpro (the industry extension service). Devco, on the other hand, is charged with responsibility for promoting 'development', including land reform and facilitating entry of new farmers who had been racially excluded in the past.

A draft Liquor Act, which sought to prevent any vertical integration of producers, wholesalers and retailers, was blocked by the constitutional court for treading on the powers of provincial governments. The Competition Board announced an investigation into KWV and its agreement with CWSI, and into SAB's beer monopoly (*Business Day*, 1, 4, 15, 18 July 1997). This investigation did not, however, materialize. Deprived of its assured supply of 'surplus' grapes and distilling wine, for which it in the past only paid after the sale of the final product and after deducting its own administration costs, KWV had to compete for supplies with cooperatives cellars (some of which have converted into companies), with the major wholesalers, and with new exporting firms. In 2000, KWV informed CWSI that they would not be bound by the undertaking to stay out of the domestic market. SFW and Distillers, in whom KWV still holds a 30 per cent share, re-merged, without opposition from the Competition Commission.

By the end of the twentieth century, therefore, the South African wine industry was no longer subject to the restrictive structures of regulation that had sustained farm incomes but inhibited innovation. Patterns of production had changed considerably over the previous two decades. But they have only partly escaped the industry's legacy of producing large quantities of standard, high-yielding grapes on irrigated vineyards to make large quantities of cheap wine for which demand is declining – even though prospects for premium cultivars and quality wines had become buoyant.

CURRENT PRODUCTION FEATURES

By 2002, wine producers in South Africa had planted 107 998 hectares of land to wine grapes. This represented an increase over 1992 of 17 per cent in the area planted. Total production, on the other hand, decreased by only 5 per cent, from an average of 851 million tons of grapes in 1991–93 to an average of 806 million tons in 2000–2002. It is this apparent anomaly between the rate of expansion in land used and of output that is the key to a deeper understanding of the South African wine industry, because the gross value of output from the South African wine industry grew from R594 million in 1989/90 to R2.1 billion in 2002, or by 3.5 times.

South Africa's wine farmers ran fifth in the world in terms of the average grape yield per hectare, well above Australia (15th) and France (18th). Table 12.1 shows the regional distribution of the vines planted in South Africa. These data show that the regions that produce the most wine grapes (Worcester, Olifants River and Robertson, respectively) also produce the highest yields per hectare, while farms in regions such as Paarl, Stellenbosch and Malmesbury produce lower yields.

Table 12.2 shows the composition of types of cultivars grown and planted in different regions. Only in Stellenbosch do the seven premium varieties make up more than 50 per cent of the wine produced, and does red wine constitute more than half of total wine production. Data from SAWIS (2003) for 2000 show that the cooperatives press only 44 per cent of the total Sauvignon Blanc crop, and 65 per cent of the Chardonnay crop, as opposed to

Table 12.1   Regional distribution of grapevines and of wine output, South Africa, 2002

Region	Number of vines (million)	%	Area ('000 ha)	%	% of total output[a]
Worcester	61	19.4	18	16.8	25
Paarl	55	17.4	18	16.3	10
Stellenbosch	54	17.2	17	15.9	7
Robertson	43	13.6	12	11.5	15
Malmesbury	37	11.9	15	13.7	7
Orange River	29	9.2	15	14.3	16
Olifants River	27	8.6	10	8.8	16
Little Karoo	9	3.0	3	12.8	4
South Africa	316	100.0	108	100.0	100

Note: [a] Measured in tons of wine grapes.

Source: SAWIS (2003).

Table 12.2   Cultivar composition of vines and wine grapes crushed, South Africa, 2002

Region	Planted to big 7 varieties (%)[a]	Production from big 7 varieties (%)	White share (%)
Worcester	34	17	77
Paarl	53	44	56
Stellenbosch	75	74	42
Robertson	47	32	80
Malmesbury	52	39	61
Orange River	2	1	97
Olifants River	37	19	85
Little Karoo	22	9	87
South Africa	43	24	77

Note: [a]Cabernet Sauvignon, Pinotage, Shiraz, Merlot, Pinot Noir, Chardonnay and Sauvignon Blanc.

Source: SAWIS (2003).

87 per cent of all white wines. Further, they press 37 per cent of the Cabernet Sauvignon, 45 per cent of the Merlot and 46 per cent of the Shiraz, compared to 62 per cent of all red wines. By contrast private cellars, which press only 12 per cent of the total crop, press 40 per cent of the Sauvignon Blanc, 26 per cent of the Chardonnay, 41 per cent of the Cabernet Sauvignon, 37 per cent of the Merlot and 44 per cent of the Shiraz. The Wine and Spirits Board certified only one-fifth of the 'good wine' production of South Africa in 1997, but that rose to one-third by 2000 and to 44 per cent by 2002 (SAWIS, 2003).

The current production structure of the industry is explained in Figure 12.1. This structure of production is changing rapidly at the same time as the area under vines has been increasing. In the South African circumstances the replanting of vines is arguably affecting the structure of output more than the expansion of the area under vines, although both are adding to the proportion of noble varieties in the total crop. This changing composition is shown in Table 12.3.

The additional 4031 hectares planted to red wines in 2000 and an extra 1900 in 2002 should be placed in the context of the small net increase in the total area planted to wine grape vines in those years. As of 2000, only 5837 of the 71 748 hectares (8 per cent) planted to white varieties are under four years old, while 14 649 of the 33 818 hectares (43 per cent) planted to red varieties are under four years old. The proportion of 'good wine' that has been certified by the Wine and Spirits Board was only 20 per cent in 1997 and has more than

PRIMARY PRODUCERS:[a] 4501		
	Tons	No. of producers
Primary producers: 4346	1–100	2173
	>100–500	1545
	>500–1000	404
	>1000–5000	223
	>5000–10 000	1
		4346

↓

CELLARS THAT PRESS GRAPES: 355				
Cooperatives:[b]	Private cellars, estates:	Private cellars, non-estates:	Producing wholesalers:	Total
66	83	1266	13	428

↓

BULK BUYERS: 104
Wholesalers (including producing wholesalers): 70
Exporters (non-producing): 34

Notes:
[a] Producers sell to producing wholesalers, wholesalers, retailers, the public and exporters.
[b] This does not take account of cooperatives that have recently amalgamated or converted into companies.

Source: SAWIS (2003).

Figure 12.1   Wine industry structure, South Africa, 2002

doubled since then (34 per cent in 2000, 44 per cent in 2002). This figure can be expected to continue to expand rapidly in the next few years.

The main reason for these shifts in the composition of production can be found in the changing relative prices of the products of the industry, reflecting changes in demand in domestic and export markets and previous planting decisions. Table 12.4 shows the relative producer prices for wine sold in bulk (that is, to wholesalers and exporters). Prices for red wine sold in bulk have

Table 12.3   Net change in area planted to different grape varieties, South Africa, 2000 and 2002

Region	Planted in 2000	Uprooted in 2000	Net change in 2000	Net change in 2002
Sultana	340	448	–108	–504
Chenin Blanc	191	2449	–2258	–1021
Colombar(d)	174	600	–426	–140
Sauvignon Blanc	160	117	43	234
Chardonnay	40	127	–87	76
Other white	83	3249	–3166	–1250
Total white	988	6990	–6002	–2605
Shiraz	1536	76	1460	477
Cabernet Sauvignon	1438	237	1201	880
Merlot	838	76	762	317
Pinotage	500	172	328	–80
Cinsaut	124	337	–213	–126
Other red	619	126	493	432
Total red	5054	1023	4031	1900
South Africa	6043	8013	–1970	–705

Source: SAWIS (2003).

continued to increase rapidly, while those for white wine, including the noble varieties, have increased very little in nominal terms over recent years. Although the price of wine sold in bulk as rebate wine (which is allowed a rebate on excise duties if it meets the prescriptions for the making of brandy) and as distilling wine for brandy has declined since 1998, it is still over 50 per cent higher than in 1992.

The prices for quality wines are already in decline. The problem for producers in future may be to sustain demand, at home and abroad, for South Africa's quality red wines so that their price can be maintained and even increased. When planting decisions must be made several years ahead of the prices at which the crop will be sown, farmers are always likely, with encouragement from merchants, to 'plant after the price' rather than to get ahead of an uncertain market.

Table 12.5 shows the trends in the prices of different grape varieties sold for the making of wine. Again, prices of red varieties have generally risen faster than those of white varieties.

Table 12.4   Average prices for bulk sales of 'good wine', South Africa, 1992–2002 (cents per litre)

Good wine	1992	1997	1998	1999	2000	2001	2002	2002/ 1997
Cabernet, Merlot, Shiraz, Pinot Noir, Pinotage	–	545	648	708	745	736	719	1.32
Other red	–	304	359	409	448	448	484	1.59
Chardonnay	–	381	392	373	307	328	396	1.04
Sauvignon Blanc	–	381	392	358	340	317	409	1.07
Chenin Blanc	–	–	–	168	166	157	215	n.a.
Other white	–	161	168	147	127	138	192	1.19
Fortified wine	–	206	228	225	201	208	233	1.13
Rebate wine for brandy	68	127	133	127	120	115	130	1.02
Distilling wine for wine spirits	40	80	85	73	65	63	75	0.94

Source: SAWIS (2003).

Table 12.5   Index of prices of various grape varieties sold for winemaking,[a] South Africa, 1997–2002 (2000 = 100)

Variety	1997	1999	2001	2002
Cabernet Sauvignon	59	89	101	101
Merlot	58	93	100	101
Pinotage	67	96	97	92
Cinsaut Noir	61	92	98	107
Pinot Noir	65	89	107	109
Shiraz	63	98	96	96
Other red	59	73	105	107
Chenin Blanc	104	129	99	100
Sauvignon Blanc	79	97	104	103
Chardonnay	92	107	101	107
SA Riesling	88	99	96	99
Colombar(d)	126	147	81	89
Hanepoot	141	154	87	110
Semillon	82	113	96	96
Other white	83	111	108	117

Note: [a] Excluding deliveries by members to cooperatives.

Source: SAWIS (2003).

THE DOMESTIC MARKET

South Africa's domestic wine consumption per capita grew little in the 1990s but there was rapid growth in the volume of exports at around 30 per cent per year. The share of domestic sales of wine sold in glass containers has decreased from above 40 per cent of the total to between 30 and 35 per cent over the 1990s. The proportion of sales of wine sold in foil bags (that is, of lowest-quality wine) has doubled from approximately 10 per cent to 20 per cent. At the same time the proportion of wine sold in conventional 750 ml bottles has increased from about 45 per cent of all wine sold in glass containers to above 50 per cent. Thus the domestic market seems to be becoming more differentiated, with growth in the sales of premium wines as well as the cheapest wine, but a decline in sales of the lower-quality wine categories in between. Also the growth in the value of imports has been only half of the growth in the volume of imports, suggesting that imports have been used to cover deficits in the lower-quality range of wines.

INSTITUTIONAL CHALLENGES

Institutions play an important role in the ordering of economic activity, and are a key factor in determining international competitiveness. One of the main consequences of the historical legacy of the South African wine industry is uncertainty about its future institutional structuring. Institutional change is being fostered in an attempt either to escape the heavy hand of the past or to meet the challenges of the future, and it is often difficult to discern which of these motives is the stronger. The case of the conversion of KWV from a cooperative to a corporate business in 1997 illustrates this dichotomy. Whereas the Board of KWV argued that these steps were taken in order to position the company as a major player in the export market, the government accused them of trying to privatize state assets. As was seen above, the conversion was allowed to proceed, but only after specific arrangements were made regarding the responsibilities of KWV towards the rest of the industry.

Figure 12.1 above shows that no single institution dominates the growing and processing of grapes in South Africa. While the wine cooperatives generally handle more grapes than independent wineries (whether estate or non-estate), only one (a cooperative) presses more than 10 000 tons of grapes per year.

Historically, the large players in the industry were the 'producing wholesalers'. This sector has changed considerably in recent years with the apparent withdrawal of Gilbey's South Africa from the wine business. As we have seen, the two largest firms, Stellenbosch Farmers Winery and Distillers Corporation,

were both part of CWD and retained the same owners when they were separated in 1988. They merged again in 2000 to form Distell. Ultimate control
over Distell and KWV now lies in the Rembrandt group of companies, and
further changes can be expected. The domination of the domestic markets for
wine and spirits by SFW and Distillers has not encouraged competition and
innovation in winemaking, which has tended to come from the relatively small
sector of independent estate producers.

New opportunities have seen the emergence of medium-scale exporting
concerns. These have been formed by the conversion of former cooperatives
(for example Simonsvlei); by a new enterprise formed by existing cooperatives (for example Stellenbosch Vineyards); by strategic alliances formed
between private producers (for example Winecorp); and by new enterprises
(for example Vinfruco).

Cooperatives continue to face the dilemma of adapting their institutional
forms to the opportunities created by an increasingly differentiated market, in
which the cheapest wines can now be supplied by imports. In some cases, the
costs of buying higher-quality grapes and producing wine to a higher standard
may not be rewarded by equivalent returns (Ewert et al., 1998, p. 21). It is
complex, costly and divisive to devise and implement systems for differentiating the prices of the grapes they buy. Companies can choose from which
farmers, and even cooperatives, they source their grapes. Cooperatives need to
satisfy their members' expectations that they will press their grapes. On the
other hand, they face the risk that members will sell their best grapes to
competing firms or will withdraw from the cooperatives. To survive in the new
environment, cooperatives need to balance these conflicting interests and
secure for their members visible returns to the profits realized through the sale
of wine beyond the price for the delivery of grapes (Ewert, 2000).

The rapid institutional change that has characterized the industry in the past
decade has come about as a result of strategies to adapt to the new trading
environment. A key feature of this environment has been the ability to exploit
new opportunities in the global market, and more institutional changes can be
expected as the industry consolidates its position in the international market.
A second key feature of the trading environment is the uncertain domestic
investment climate, especially among South Africa's large corporations, which
have tended to invest in foreign markets rather than in the domestic economy
since exchange control began to be relaxed.

A recent survey among independent winemakers in South Africa (Schildt
and Bosch, 2000) showed that, as expected, foreign-owned wineries were
more likely to have begun operations after 1991. Of the foreign-owned cellars,
73 per cent had their first year of production in 2000, compared to 55 per cent
of domestically owned cellars. The new foreign-owned operations were much
smaller than their domestic counterparts. Farms were smaller (50 per cent of

new domestic operations were above 70 hectares compared to 18 per cent of foreign-owned ones); and their cellars were also smaller.

Interviews with a large number of wine farmers and others close to the industry revealed that the general perception is of a higher level of foreign investment than is the actual case. The reason seems to be the number of Europeans who have moved to South Africa for various reasons unrelated to the wine industry but who have ended up investing in the industry. Local farmers tend to regard these as instances of foreign investment. This reinforces the point made above regarding the lack of evidence of large-scale corporate investment in the industry. This is supported by the investment intentions of foreign-owned cellars. The survey showed that most of the foreign-owned cellars plan to invest in tourist-related activities, while the priority for domestic investors is to upgrade their cellar technology.

STATE INTERVENTION

South Africa's agricultural sector policy is aimed at achieving three main objectives: redressing the inequalities and injustices arising from the apartheid policies of the past; ensuring a more just and equitable distribution of income in the industry; and enhancing the international competitiveness of the industry.

The wine industry subscribes to all three of these objectives through its 'Vision 2020 Strategic Agenda'. Yet the industry is caught in a situation similar to the rest of the agricultural sector. It has successfully weathered the effects of deregulation, and it has learned to cope with new and (in its experience) unusual types of state intervention, such as the challenge to the conversion of KWV as illustrated earlier. Yet failed reform policies, especially land reform, continue to cloud the investment climate. Many of these uncertainties are reflected in the depreciation of the currency, a change that neatly illustrates the nature of the Catch-22 faced by stakeholders in the industry. Whereas exporters welcome a depreciating currency, investors wish to realize their profits in international currencies. They know that the reason for the depreciation is a lack of faith in the future of the economy by foreign investors, accentuated by the seizure of land in Zimbabwe by President Mugabe and the so-called 'war veterans'.

It is for this reason that stakeholders in agriculture in general, and in the wine industry through the 'Vision 2020 Strategic Agenda', have now called for a more vigorous land reform programme. Land reform has proved to be difficult to realize and confronts particular problems in wine and in horticulture, where production requires high levels of capital investment and returns are only realized some years later. In the Western Cape in particular, farmers and agribusiness companies have used grants to fund the acquisition by workers trusts of shares in farm enterprises. These schemes can potentially enable workers to share in the returns from marketing fruit or making wine and not only from growing grapes and other fruit. They depend on the use of the farmer's or the company's capital, equipment, skills and access to markets and must therefore fit in with the farmers' objectives. They may enable employers to acquire additional land and water resources, as well as capital for the enterprise, and to raise productivity by restructuring incentives. Ownership of shares in the enterprise has, however, not contributed sufficiently to changed power relations between employers and employees. As there are no independent smallholders, these schemes 'do not look like land reforms', but the 'vision of independent small-scale production' may be 'inappropriate in high-value horticulture' (Humphries, 2000; Hamman and Ewert, 1999).

CONCLUSION

The South African wine industry has changed rapidly over the past decade as a result of renewed access to the global market as well as changes in domestic economic and social policies. On balance, the industry seems to have a bright future. Yet these changes have taken place in something of a policy and institutional vacuum, and there are questions about their sustainability. The state has played an ambiguous role in these developments. On the one hand it has supported those in favour of deregulation by seeing to the abolition of all statutory powers to intervene in the industry, and has put in place measures to support exporters. For its own part, it has not been able to implement new programmes such as land and labour reform successfully. As a result, the same stakeholders are driving the process of change in the industry, while new interest groups are still largely excluded from meaningful participation. It is unclear whether this will eventually lead to a collapse in investor confidence and a decline in the industry's ability to compete internationally, or whether it will result in new investments, funding innovation in production of wine for more differentiated markets. It is also unclear whether the required investment will be driven by large multinationals, South African or foreign based, and what complex relations of interdependence may emerge among corporate manufacturing wholesalers, cooperatives and their members, and independent estate and non-estate producers.

REFERENCES

Anderson, K. and D. Norman (2003), *Global Wine Production, Consumption and*

Trade, 1961 to 2001: A Statistical Compendium, Adelaide: Centre for International Economic Studies.

Boonstra, G. (1988), 'Gees van Deregulering in Drankmark' (Spirit of Deregulation in the Liquor Market), *Finansies & Tegniek*, 16 June.

Botha, T.C. (1966), 'Ko-operatiewe wynkelders in Suid-Afrika', unpublished M.Sc. (Landbou) thesis, University of Stellenbosch.

Business Day (1997).

Cape of Good Hope (1905), *Report of the Committee of Enquiry into the Wine and Brandy Industry*, G30.

Cloete, P. (1924), *Report of Select Committee on the Wine and Spirits Control Bill: Minutes of Evidence*, 13 February.

Competition Board (1982), 'Investigation into Restrictive Practices in the Supply and Distribution of Alcoholic Beverages in the Republic of South Africa', Report No. 10.

Deacon, I.B. (1980), 'The South African Liquor Industry – Structure, Conduct, Performance and Strategies for Future Action', unpublished Ph.D. thesis, University of Stellenbosch.

De Klerk, W. (1997), 'The Effect of Legislation on the Quality of South African Wines', *Wynboer*, January.

Drew, H. (1935–37), *Minutes of Evidence to the 1935–37 Wine Commission*, Cape Archives.

Drew, H. (1937), *Report of the Wine Commission*, U.G. 25, GP2680.

Du Toit, A.J. (1960), 'Die Voorsitter van die Direksie van die die K.W.V. . . . se Rede' (Chairman's address), 10 June.

Ewert, J. (2000), 'All Growers for Themselves! the South African Wine Industry in the Face of Globalisation', X World Congress of the International Rural Sociology Association, Rio de Janeiro, Brazil, 30 July–5 August.

Ewert, J., J. Hamman, N. Tregurtha, N. Vink, C. Visser and G. Williams (1998), *State and Market, Labour and Land: the South African Wine Industry in Transition*, University of Stellenbosch.

Francis, E. and G. Williams (1993), 'The Land Question', *Canadian Journal of African Studies*, **29** (3), 380–403.

Fridjhon, M. and A. Murray (1985), *Conspiracy of Giants: the South African Liquor Industry*, Johannesburg: Divaris Stein.

Giliomee, H. (1987), 'The Beginning of Afrikaner Nationalism', *South African Historical Journal*, **19**, 115–42.

Hall, R. and G. Williams (2000), 'Land Reform in South Africa: Policies and Prospects', paper prepared for International Conference on Southern Africa's Evolving Security Architecture: Prospects and Problems, organized by International Peace and Academy, New York, Gaborone, Botswana.

Hamman, J. and J. Ewert (1999), 'A Historical Irony in the Making? State, Private Sector and Land Reform in the South African Wine Industry', *Development South Africa*, **16** (3), 447–54.

House of Assembly (1926), *Report of the Select Committee on the Liquor Bill, Minutes of Evidence*, Pretoria: House of Assembly, 28 April, 21 May.

House of Assembly (1932), *House of Assembly Debates*, Pretoria: House of Assembly.

House of Assembly (1940), *Report of the Select Committee on the Wine and Spirits Control Amendment Bill*, Pretoria: House of Assembly.

Humphries, N. (2000), 'Land Reform in the Western Cape, South Africa. Policy and Practice', unpublished B.A. thesis, St Peter's College, University of Oxford.

Kassier, W.E.B. (1997), *Report of the Committee of Inquiry into Regulation of the Wine and Distilling Industries*, Pretoria: Ministry of Agriculture.

Keegan, T. (1996), *Colonial South Africa and the Origins of the Racial Order*, Cape Town: David Philip.

Kenney, R.U. (1981), *Abraham Perold: Wegwyser van ons Wynbou (Abraham Perold: Pioneer of our Wine Industry)*, Cape Town: Oxford University Press.

Kirsten, J. and J. Van Zyl (1996), 'The Contemporary Agricultural Policy Environment: Undoing the Legacy of the Past', in J. van Zyl, J. Kirsten and H.P. Binswanger (eds), *Agricultural Land Reform in South Africa: Policies, Markets and Mechanisms*, Cape Town: Oxford University Press.

Kohler, C. (1924), *Report of Select Committee on the Wine and Spirits Control Bill, Minutes of Evidence*, Pretoria: Ministry of Agriculture.

Kohler, C. (1946), *The Memoirs of Kohler of the K.W.V.*, London (arranged for publication by A. Joelson).

KWV (1958), *A Survey of Wine-Growing in South Africa, 1956–57*, Paarl: KWV.

KWV (1963), *A Survey of Wine-Growing in South Africa, 1963–63*, Paarl: KWV.

KWV (1981–90), *Statistics Survey* (annual), Paarl: KWV.

Malherbe, P. (1932), 'Die Oorproduksie van Wyn in Suid-Afrika' ('The Over-production of Wine in South Africa'), unpublished M.Sc. thesis, University of Stellenbosch.

Marais, P. (1994a), 'KWV Plan vir Groothandelaars (KWV Plan for Wholesalers), *Finansies & Tegniek*, 29 April.

Marais, P. (1994b), 'Wynbedryf Kook al Weer' (Wine Industry Cooking Again), *Finansies & Tegniek*, 29 July.

Osmond, R. and K. Anderson (1998), *Trends and Cycles in the Australian Wine Industry, 1850 to 2000*, Adelaide: Centre for International Economic Studies.

Perold, A.I. (1936), 'Historical Notes on the Cape Wine Industry', in KWV, *The Wine Book of South Africa*, Paarl: KWV.

State Archive Depository K150, *Evidence to the (Steenkamp) Commission of Enquiry into Co-operative Affairs*, Pretoria.

State Archive Depository K404, *Wine Commission. Recommendations by the [KWV] Commission re Limitation of the Production of Alcohol*, Pretoria.

SAWIS (SA Wine Industry Information and Systems) (2003), *South Africa Wine Industry Statistics 2003* (annual), Paarl: SAWIS.

Schildt, H. and J. Bosch (2000), *Results of a survey amongst independent winemakers in South Africa*, Department of Agricultural Economics, University of Stellenbosch.

Steenkamp (1967), 'Report of the Commission of Enquiry into Co-operative Affairs', Pretoria.

Steyn, D. (1997), *Preliminary Report on the Assets of the KWV*, Paarl.

Swart, H.C. (1944), 'Prys en Produksiebeheer in die Wynbou van Suid-Afrika' ('Price and production control in South African viticulture'), unpublished M.Sc. Agric. Thesis, University of Stellenbosch.

Theron, H.F. (1954), 'Address by the Chairman of the Board of the KWV', Paarl: KWV, 11 June.

Van Zyl, D.J. (1993), 'KWV 75 Jare', bound typescript, Africana Library, University of Stellenbosch.

Viljoen (1934), *Report of the Commission to Enquire into Co-operation and Agricuktural Credit*, UG 16.

Vink, N. (1993), 'Entrepreneurs and the Political Economy of Reform in South African Agriculture', *Agrekon*, **32** (4), 153–66.

Vink, N. (2000), 'Agricultural Policy Research in South Africa: Challenges for the Future', *Agrekon*, **39** (4), 432–70.
Vink, N. and W.E.B Kassier (1991), 'Agricultural Policy and the South African State', in M. de Klerk (ed.), *A Harvest of Discontent: the Land Question in South Africa*, Cape Town: IDASA.
Welgemoed, Z. (1992), 'Gevolg van Kwotasopheffing' ('Consequences of Lifting of Quotas'), *Landbouweekblad*, 17 April.
Welgemoed, Z. (1993), 'Groter Innames vanwee Kwotaopheffing' ('Larger Deliveries as a Consequence of the Lifting of the Quotas'), *Landbouweekblad*, 8 January.
Williams, G. and N. Vink (1999), 'Co-operation, Regulation and Monopoly in the South African Wine Industry, 1905–2000', in *Proceedings of I Symposión Internacional de Historia y Civilizacion de la Vid y el Vino, El puerto de Santa Maria*.
Williams G., J. Ewert and N. Vink et al. (1998), 'Liberalizing Markets and Reforming Land in South Africa', *Journal of Contemporary African Studies*, **16** (1), 65–94.

13. Australia

Kym Anderson

More than 100 years ago it was claimed that 'Many of the leading wine merchants of London and other important commercial centres admit that Australia promises to become a powerful rival in the world's markets with the old-established vineyards of Europe' (Irvine, 1892, p. 6).[1] The first *Yearbook of Australia* made a similar claim in 1908, but by the 1922 edition it added some comments on why that had not happened:

> The production of wine in Australia has not increased as rapidly as the suitability of soil and climate would appear to warrant. The cause of this is probably twofold . . . Australians are not a wine-drinking people and consequently do not provide a local market for the product, and . . . the new and comparatively unknown wines of Australia find it difficult to establish a footing in the markets of the old world, owing to the competition of well-known brands. Active steps are being taken in various ways to bring the Australian wines under notice, and it may be confidently expected that when their qualities are duly recognised the wine production of this country will exhibit a rapid development.

The Australian wine industry is at last fulfilling that earlier promise: since 1990 it has trebled its share of global vine area and raised its share of global export sales fivefold (Figure 13.1) – and that performance has stimulated other New World producers to follow Australia's example. This chapter explores the ways in which Australia achieved that take-off despite the fact that national and global wine consumption per capita overall has not been growing. It also compares Australia's growth record with that of other New World producers/exporters and then examines the opportunities and challenges for the years ahead.

HOW WELL HAS THE AUSTRALIAN WINE INDUSTRY PERFORMED?

In the decade to the mid-1980s, Australian wine exports were less than US$15 million per year and the country was a net importer of wine. By contrast the majority of Australian wine is now sold abroad (Figure 13.2) and in 2003

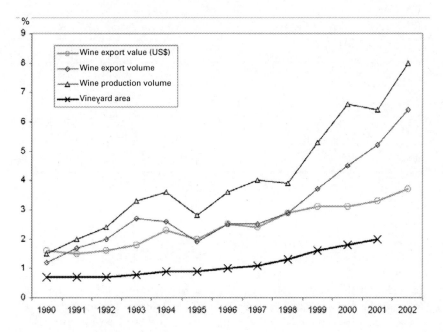

Source: Updated underlying data from Anderson and Norman (2003).

*Figure 13.1   Australia's share of global vine area, wine production, and
        wine exports, 1990–2002*

exports are expected to exceed US$1.5 billion, making Australia the world's
fourth largest wine exporter after France, Italy and Spain. Had 2003 not been
a low-yield season (because of a serious drought after a cold lead-up to the
2002 vintage), it would also have seen Australia pass Argentina to become the
fourth largest producer of wine. By 2003–2004, wine will be generating
almost as much export revenue for Australia as the three biggest farm export
items (beef, wheat and wool – see Table 13.1), and ABARE expects it to reach
AUD4.2 billion by 2007–2008. That converts to US$2.6 billion at the 2003
exchange rate, which is about what Italy exported and 50 per cent above what
Spain exported in 2001. ABARE's projections, based on recent plantings,
suggest that by 2007–2008 two-thirds of the volume of Australian wine sales
will be in foreign markets (Figure 13.2).

While Australia's wine exports have boomed several times in the past, in each
case those booms subsequently plateaued and the expanded acreage meant
grape-growers and winemakers went back to receiving low returns. Indeed the
industry's prospects were sufficiently dire as recently as 1985 as to induce the
government to fund a vine-pull compensation scheme to encourage grape-

Table 13.1   Value of five top agricultural exports, Australia, 1988–2003
(AUD billion)

	1988–89	1993–94	1998–99	2001–02	2002–03	2003–04[a]
Wool	6.0	3.4	3.0	3.7	3.8	3.3
Wheat	2.1	2.3	3.5	4.6	3.0	3.3
Beef	1.7	3.3	2.9	4.3	4.0	3.5
Dairy	0.6	1.3	2.3	3.2	2.7	2.2
Wine	0.1	0.4	1.0	2.1	2.4	2.9

Note: [a] Projected. The 2007–08 projection is AUD4.2 billion.

Source: Australian Bureau of Agricultural and Resource Economics, Canberra at www.abare.gov.au.

growers to move to alternative crops. Yet, like a phoenix, the industry has risen again and grown with renewed vigour: the acreage planted to vines has nearly trebled since the late 1980s (Figure 13.3), the real value of both wine grape and wine production has grown at more than 10 per cent per annum, and the real value of wine exports (in 1999 US dollars) has grown at 16 per cent per year.

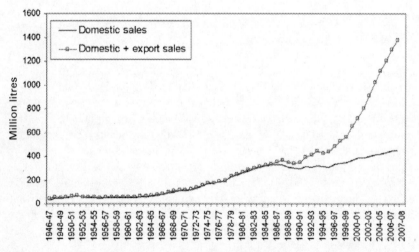

Note: [a] Export projections are from ABARE (2003); domestic sales projections assume the recent rate of growth of 2.5 per cent continues after 2002–2003.

Source: WFA/Winetitles (2003) and, for export projections, ABARE (2003).

Figure 13.2   Domestic and export sales of Australian wine by volume,
1946–2007[a]

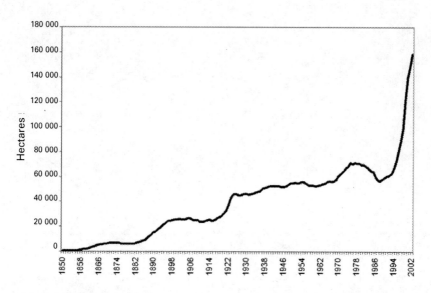

Source: WFA/Winetitles (2003).

Figure 13.3   Area of vineyards, Australia, 1850–2002

The long history of fluctuating fortunes raises the obvious question of whether Australia's current wine boom is to be followed by yet another crash, at least in wine grape prices if not in wine production and export volumes. Certainly enthusiasm to plant more red grapes plummeted after 1999, just as it did for Chardonnay after 1995 (Figure 13.4); but Chardonnay plantings increased again in 2002 and there is much discussion of the need to increase red plantings after 2003 in order to fully capitalize on the promotion efforts currently under way. The wine industry is thus still bullish, having in 1995 set itself targets of doubling annual exports to AUD1 billion by the turn of the century (since achieved) and of trebling the real value of wine production within 30 years (AWF, 1995). Others, aware of the boom–bust cycles of the past, still need to be convinced that this time the expanded demand is here to stay – at least long enough for growers to recoup a return from new plantings. To help resolve this difference in views, consider the features of Australia's previous wine booms.

On the one hand, it is difficult not to be sobered by the past. This is because, as is clear from Figure 13.3, each of the first four booms in the Australian wine industry finished with a plateau in vineyard area (and winery output) growth. These were periods when returns to grape-growers and often also winemakers were depressed for years because of the rapid growth in new plantings during

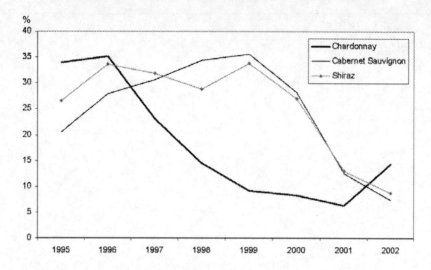

Source: Australian Bureau of Statistics, Catalogue No. 1329.0.

*Figure 13.4   Share of non-bearing vines in total vine area, by variety,
            Australia, 1995–2002 (%)*

the boom. Nor is this phenomenon unique to Australia. On the contrary, it has periodically been the case in grape and wine markets elsewhere in the world for at least two millennia.[2]

Yet, on the other hand, Australia's past history also is encouraging, because it shows the current boom to have several positive features that contrast with those of earlier booms. Some of these features are summarized in Table 13.2. The first boom, from the mid-1850s, was mainly driven by domestic demand growth following the gold-rush-induced trebling in Australia's white population in the 1850s. However, the wine produced from that excessive expansion was unable to be exported profitably, largely because of high duties on inter-colonial trade within Australasia plus poor marketing and high transport costs in exporting the rather crude product of that time to the Old World. Hence returns slumped quite quickly in that first cycle.

The second boom, from the 1880s, was due to a mixture of domestic and export demand growth, the latter involving better marketing and lower trans-port costs for what were higher-quality but still mostly generic bulk (rather than winery bottled and branded) dry red wines. The relatively open British market absorbed one-sixth of Australia's production early in the twentieth century, before World War I intervened. That boom was part of a general inter-nationalization of world commodity markets at that time – something that returned but in much-diminished form after that war.

Table 13.2 Booms and plateaus in the development of Australia's wine industry, vintages 1854–2003

Vintages	Boom/plateau/cycle no.	No. of years	Increase in vine area (% p.a.)	Increase in wine production (% p.a.)	Increase in wine export volume (% p.a.)	Av. share of exports in Australian wine sales (%)	Av. domestic per capita consumption (litres p.a.)
1854–71	1st boom	17	15.5	18.4[a]	14.1	1.8	n.a.
1871–81	1st plateau	10	-1.1	-0.6	-5.2	1.6	n.a.
1854–81	1st cycle	27	8.4	10.7	8.2	1.7	n.a.
1881–96	2nd boom	15	9.7	7.5	23.0	9.8	n.a.
1896–15	2nd plateau	19	-0.1	-0.4	0.4	16.5	5.1
1881–15	2nd cycle	34	3.9	3.3	8.7	14.4	n.a.
1915–25	3rd boom	10	7.0	12.7	4.5	8.5	5.8
1925–45	3rd plateau	20	0.9	0.1	-1.2	16.4	4.0
1915–45	3rd cycle	30	2.4	3.6	4.9	14.9	4.7
1945–68	Slow growth	23	0.2	2.1	0.2	5.4	6.2
1968–75	4th boom	7	3.3	6.2	-1.4	2.7	10.9
1975–87	4th plateau	12	-1.7	1.0	8.4	2.2	19.1
1968–87	4th cycle	19	0.2	3.1	2.5	2.4	16.0
1987–2003+	5th boom	>16	6.7	7.7	20.1	30.5	19.4

Source: Updated from Anderson and Osmond (1998, Table 1).

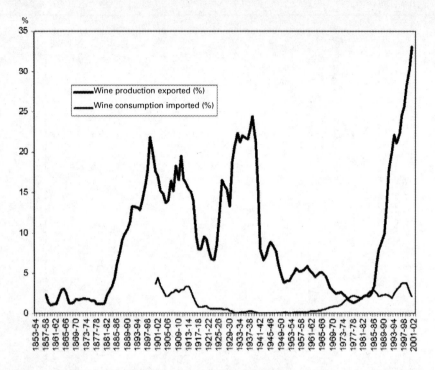

Source: Updated from Anderson and Osmond (1998, Table 3).

*Figure 13.5   Shares of wine production exported and wine consumption
              imported, Australia, 1856–57 to 2002–03 (3-year moving
              averages)*

The acreage boom induced by soldier settlement after World War I
provided the basis for the third boom, from the mid-1920s. That third boom
was helped by irrigation and land development subsidies, a huge fortified wine
export subsidy, and a new 50 per cent imperial tariff preference in the British
market for fortified wines. The decline in domestic consumption, induced by
the export subsidy and the Depression, added to wine exports in the 1930s –
which by then accounted for more than one-fifth of production (Figure 13.5).[3]
The subsequent removal of the export subsidy, and the huge hike in UK tariffs
on fortified wine in the latter 1940s, then caused a severe decline in export
orientation. As well, the return to normal beer consumption after war-induced
grain rationing kept down domestic wine sales growth. From World War I until
the late 1960s most wine grapes were destined for fortified wine or for distillation as brandy (Figure 13.6).

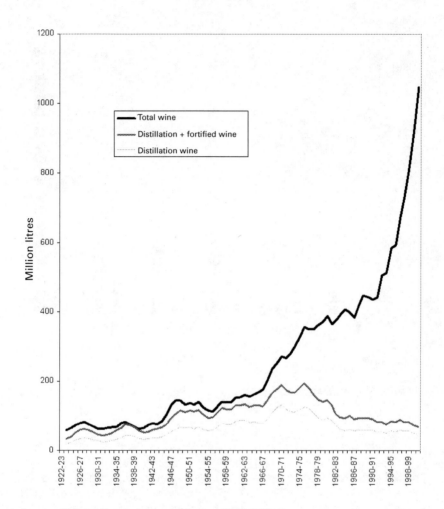

Source: Updated from Anderson and Osmond (1998, Table 4).

Figure 13.6   Composition of wine production, Australia, 1922–23 to
*   2001–02 (3-year moving averages)*

    The fourth boom, following two postwar decades of slow growth in the industry, was entirely domestic. It emerged as Australian consumer tastes became more Southern European, as licensing and trade practice laws changed with income growth, as corporatization of wineries led to more sophisticated domestic marketing and new innovations (including wine-in-a-box), and as Britain's wine import barriers rose again with its accession to the European

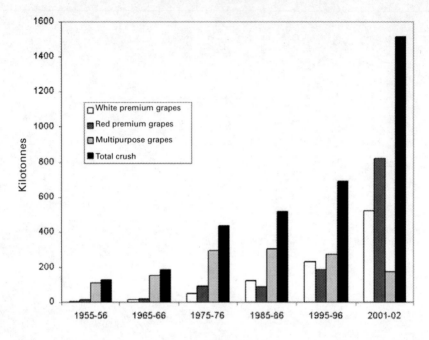

Source: Updated from Anderson and Osmond (1998, Table 7).

*Figure 13.7   Wine grape crush by variety group, Australia, 1955–56 to
                2001–02*

Community. Initially domestic demand grew for red table wine. Then the cask
or wine-in-a-box attracted a new clientele of white non-premium table wine
drinkers, causing Australia's per capita wine consumption to treble during the
fourth cycle (Table 13.2 and Figure 13.7). The economy-wide recession of the
early 1980s subsequently slowed demand growth and caused wine prices to
slump to the point that the Federal and South Australian governments intervened with vine-pull subsidies in the mid-1980s. As a result the area of vines
in 1988 was reduced to that of two decades earlier (Figure 13.3).

How does the fifth and latest boom, which began in the late 1980s, differ
from the earlier booms? One difference is that the current boom is over-
whelmingly export-oriented (Figure 13.2), since Australia's per capita wine
consumption has been static over the 1990s. This contrasts with the first and
fourth booms at least, which were primarily domestic. It also differs from the
interwar boom, when exports were more a way of disposing of soldier-settle-
ment-induced surplus low-quality wine grape production than as a pre-planned
development strategy.

Second, the current boom is mainly market-driven, which is not unlike the first two booms but contrasts markedly with the third (interwar) boom that evaporated once government assistance measures (the export subsidy and the preferential UK tariff) were withdrawn.[4] What triggered the growth in export demand for Australian wine was the change in liquor licensing laws in the United Kingdom in the 1970s, allowing supermarkets to retail wine to the postwar baby boomers (by then adults). By the mid-1980s supermarkets, dominated by Sainsbury's, Marks and Spencer, Waitrose and Tesco, accounted for more than half of all retail wine sales in the United Kingdom (Unwin, 1991, p. 341). Given also Australia's close historical ties with Britain, it is not surprising that Australian companies recognized and responded to this new market opportunity.[5] They were able to do so faster than EU suppliers because the latter have been hamstrung by myriad regulations and insulated from market forces by price supports.[6] To exploit this rapidly growing market required large volumes of consistent, low-priced branded premium wine. Land- and capital-abundant Australia had the right factor endowments to supply precisely that. High labour costs were overcome for larger firms by adapting and adopting new techniques for mechanical pruning and harvesting, thereby generating large economies of size, especially in warm, irrigated areas. That stimulated a number of mergers and acquisitions among Australia's wine firms that resulted in several large and four very large wine companies.[7] This has provided the opportunity to reap large economies of scale not only in grape-growing and winemaking but also in viticultural and oenological R&D, in brand promotion and related marketing investments, and in distribution, including through establishing their own sales offices abroad rather than relying on distributors or in enhancing their bargaining power with wholesalers or retailers.[8] The volumes of grapes grown and purchased from numerous regions by these large firms enable them to provide massive shipments of consistent, popular wines, with little variation from year to year, for the UK and now also North American and German supermarkets.[9]

Another major difference between now and the past is that the quality of wine output has improved hugely during the past decade or so, relative to the cost of production. Moreover, for the first time, the industry is in a position to build brand, regional and varietal images abroad to capitalize on those improvements in the quality of its grapes and wines. That image building has been partly generic, with the help of the Australian Wine Export Council's activities in Europe and elsewhere. It has also come from the promotional activities of individual corporations and their local representatives abroad as those firms became ever larger and more multinational via mergers and takeovers during the past dozen or so years. That promotion has been helped by being able to point to the legislated wine quality standards in the Australian Food Standards Code, and to the fact that Australian wines are still exceptionally good value for money in northern hemisphere markets, despite the real price increases of the 1990s. The depreciation of the Australian dollar during 1997–98 and again in 2000 has allowed overseas consumers and Australian producers to share the benefits: the unit value of Australia's wine exports rose from AUD2.80 in 1993 to AUD4.80 in 2000, a period when inflation averaged just 2 per cent per year.[10]

A fourth feature distinguishing the current situation is the health factor. An ever wider appreciation of the desirability of moderate over heavy drinking, and in particular of the possible health benefits of a moderate intake of red wine,[11] are ensuring that the consumer trend towards spending on quality rather than quantity of wine (Figure 13.7), and on wine in preference to beer and spirits,[12] will continue for the foreseeable future to boost wine demand both in Australia and abroad. The health factor has attracted many new consumers to red wine in particular, for whom Australia's relatively fruity, easy-drinking reds are especially attractive starters.

AUSTRALIA'S EXPORT-ORIENTED WINE GROWTH IN INTERNATIONAL PERSPECTIVE

How does the growth of Australia's wine production and exports compare with the growth of global wine consumption and expansions by other New World wine producers? How well is Australia penetrating traditional and new wine markets abroad, both absolutely and relative to other exporters? And to what extent is Australia upgrading the quality of its exports to different markets, again not just absolutely but relative to other exporters?

How Well is Australia Doing Relative to Other Wine Producers?

In terms of global wine production, Australia has always been a small player. Before the 1970s it accounted for less than 1 per cent of world production, and in 1992 its share was only 1.5 per cent. During the following decade the share rose, to 3.7 per cent, but on its own that statistic still makes Australia look rather insignificant.

In terms of exports, Australia was even less significant until the 1990s. As recently as the first half of the 1980s the country accounted, in volume terms, for only 0.2 per cent of global wine exports, the same as its share of global wine imports. The import share has changed little, but the export share has shot up to 6.4 per cent in volume terms and 8.0 per cent in value terms (Figure 13.1). In fact Australia's wine exports grew more than three times faster than the global average: at annual rates of 16 per cent in volume terms and 18 per cent in US dollar value terms over that period (Anderson and Norman, 2003).

That was sufficient to ensure the industry exceeded by 50 per cent its target of AUD1 billion of wine exports by 2000, helped by the strengthened US dollar that year.

Rapid though Australia's export growth has been, it has not been as fast as that for other southern hemisphere wine exporters, who as a group enjoyed a growth rate above 20 per cent p.a. Nor was it significantly faster than that for North America. It is simply faster than that for Europe, which is still the dominant exporter group. Certainly Australia's comparative advantage in wine has strengthened as Western Europe's has weakened somewhat, as has that of other New World wine exporters. Wine's share of merchandise exports has hardly changed for the EU at 2.1 times the global average, whereas for Australia that index rose from 1.3 in 1990 to more than 7 in 2002 – exceeding that of the European exporters for the first time (Anderson and Norman, 2003, Table 48).

What is striking are the different reasons for these high rates of New World export growth. Australia's exports grew rapidly because its production growth was much faster than its consumption growth. By contrast, in North America much slower production growth accompanied very little growth in the aggregate volume of consumption. Meanwhile, in South America production actually declined, but less so than domestic consumption, allowing exports to boom (Anderson and Norman, 2003).

The world's top ten wine exporters account for 92 per cent of the value of international wine trade, with Europe's economies in transition from socialism accounting for much of the rest (Anderson and Norman, 2003, Table 124). Of those top ten, half are in Western Europe and the other half are New World suppliers, led by Australia. Australia is the world's fourth largest exporter of wine in value terms, after France (alone accounting in 2001 for 41 per cent), Italy (17 per cent) and Spain (10 per cent). The share of France has dropped more than ten percentage points since the late 1980s, which with smaller drops for Italy and Germany has ensured that the shares of Australia and other New World suppliers have risen substantially.

If the European Union is treated as a single trader and so intra-EU trade is excluded from the EU and world trade data, the EU's share of world exports shows a much bigger fall, from 78 per cent to 58 per cent between 1990 and 2001 (Anderson and Norman, 2003, Table 42). With that adjustment, Australia moves to number two in the world, and its share of global exports rises from 4 per cent to 12 per cent. It is this fact, in spite of Australia's small share of global production, which has made Australia suddenly a much more significant player in the world wine market. Meanwhile, the share of the other main New World exporters (Argentina, Chile, New Zealand, South Africa and the USA) rose even faster, from 6 per cent to 22 per cent. That is, while Australia has done very well as an expanding wine exporter, it is not alone: the world

wine market as a whole is becoming more internationalized and far more
competitive, and most key New World suppliers are expanding their export
sales (albeit from a lower base) nearly as fast or even faster than Australia, as
is clear from Figure 2.5 in Chapter 2 of this volume.

How Well is Australia Penetrating Wine Markets Abroad?

Just as wine exports are highly concentrated, so too are imports. The ten top
importing countries accounted for all but 14 per cent of the value of global
imports in the late 1980s. Despite that concentration, the ten top exporters are
quite different in their penetration of those and other import markets. Australia
has concentrated on four English-speaking rich countries: the UK, the USA,
Canada and New Zealand. When these are depicted as shares of Australia's
total wine exports, it appears that Australia has not diversified its exports much
over the past decade: since 1993 those four countries have accounted for
between three-quarters and five-sixths of Australian sales abroad. Certainly
Australia has gradually increased its dominance as an importer in all four of
those markets, especially the UK and the USA. When sparkling wine is
excluded, Australia in 2003 looks like selling more wine to the UK and the
USA than to France in terms of US dollars, making it the top-ranked supplier
to the UK and second only to Italy in the USA. But Australia has achieved that
at the expense of its shares in continental Western Europe (most notably
Germany, the world's biggest importer of red wine) and in the emerging
markets of East Asia (Figure 13.8) – although sales to Germany trebled
between 1998 and 2001.

How Well is Australia Doing in Upgrading Wine Export Quality?

To see how different exporting countries are faring relatively, consider each
exporter's average price in 1990 and 2001. While France's strong position has
changed little, Australia along with other New World suppliers saw their average export price rise by 2.9 per cent p.a. in US dollar terms over those dozen
years. However, even though the Australian average unit export price rose at
2.3 per cent per year compared with the global average of 0.7 per cent, compla-
cency is not called for. The rise for Australia was exceeded by Argentina (7.3
per cent), Chile (5.8 per cent) and New Zealand (4.6 per cent – see Anderson
and Norman, 2003). Clearly, other exporters are striving to raise the quality of
their exports just as much as Australia, albeit from different bases.

Note, however, that the quality of wine exports varies markedly across
different markets. In 2002–2003 one-fifth of Australia's export sales to the UK
and more than half to Germany were at prices below AUD2.50 per litre,

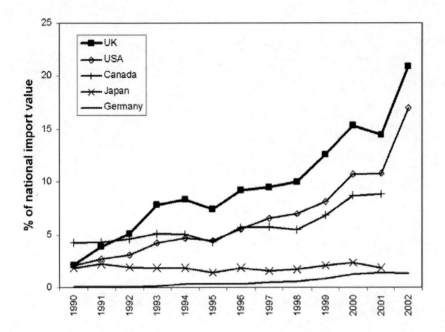

Source: Updated from underlying data for Table 98 in Anderson and Norman (2003).

Figure 13.8   Australia's share of the value of wine imports by selected importing countries, 1990–2002 (%)

whereas only 5 per cent of sales to the USA were in that category. By contrast, less than 5 per cent of sales to the UK were above $7.50 compared with 21 per cent for the USA and 38 per cent for Canada (Table 13.3). That table also shows that the US market has become Australia's No. 1 market in terms of value of exports as of 2003 (and even more so in terms of profitability to wineries).

Quality upgrading has also been taking place in Australia's domestic market. As recently as 1994, two-thirds of domestic sales of Australian wine were in soft packs ('bag-in-a-box') of two to five litres, whose retail price (including the 41 per cent tax) was as low as US$1.40 per litre. By 2002, that share was down to 54 per cent, and the average quality of wine in soft packs is considerably higher now than a decade ago. The average quality of Australia's bottled wine sold on the domestic market also has risen steadily since the 1980s. Hence even though Australia's per capita consumption has remained within a narrow band over the past quarter century (18 to 21 litres per year), expenditure has gone up substantially.[13]

Table 13.3   Australian wine export volumes to key markets, by price ranges, year ending June 2003 (%)

Price range (AUD per litre)	United Kingdom	United States	Canada	New Zealand	Germany	Total, all markets
<$2.50	20	5	8	49	55	19
$2.50–$4.99	53	45	17	31	35	45
$5.00–$7.49	23	29	37	14	8	24
$7.50–$9.99	3	15	28	4	1	8
$10.00+	1	6	10	2	1	4
Total	100	100	100	100	100	100
Average price (AUD per litre)	$4.12	$5.82	$7.10	$3.02	$2.66	$4.70
Share of Aust. export volume	40	28	5	6	4	100
Share of Aust. export value	35	35	7	4	3	100

Source: Australian Wine and Brandy Corporation.

WHAT ARE THE PROSPECTS AHEAD FOR THE WINE INDUSTRY IN AUSTRALIA?

Australia's grape and wine production is being increasingly oriented towards higher-quality products in response to the rapid growth in demand for premium relative to non-premium wine. However, Australian producers are acutely aware that other New World producers are also upgrading the quality of their product, as are numerous regions of traditional supplying countries (the south of France, Rioja and La Mancha in Spain, northern Italy, southeastern Europe). Meanwhile, global consumption in aggregate is declining slightly. What will be the net effect of those recent and prospective trends in grape and wine supply and demand on Australian grape and wine prices? The trend towards premium and away from non-premium wine production and consumption, together with the data on new plantings, provide enough information to attempt to project wine markets a few years into the present decade. That has been done recently using a 47-region global model of grape and wine markets that differentiates not only according to region of origin but also as between super-premium, commercial premium and non-premium segments of each market and each bilateral trade flow. A prototype model is described in Wittwer et al. (2003) and a more comprehensive version is presented in Anderson et al. (2003).[14]

The Anderson et al. (2003) projection has the volume of world wine consumption growing at less than 1 per cent per year from 1999 to 2005, but the premium segments (44 per cent of global wine output in 1999) grow at 3.7 per cent per year while that of non-premium wine declines slightly. Here attention focuses just on the results for Australia. They can best be summarized by showing how the projected numbers for 2005 compare with the recent trends depicted in the earlier tables and figures of this chapter and in Anderson et al. (2003). In short:

- Australia's domestic consumption continues to grow at just 1.2 per cent per year, but production growth accelerates to 8.7 per cent as more and more grapes from new vines enter the market, causing exports to grow at around 20 per cent per year (maintaining the high rate of recent years);
- Australia's share of global production rises from 3.0 to 4.0 per cent between 1999 and 2005, but its share of global export sales increases from one-nineteenth to one-twelfth;
- exports as a share of Australia's production expand to around 60 per cent in volume terms and just over 70 per cent in value terms (given that only premium wine is exported);
- Australia pulls even further ahead relative to the other New World wine exporters; and
- Australia catches up with France in terms of export sales to the UK.[15]

For the world as a whole, the model projects the 2005 price for non-premium wine to be virtually the same as in 1999 (in 1999 US dollars). This comes about because the decline in consumption is just matched by the decline in supply as producers upgrade the quality of their vineyards. The real prices of commercial premium and super-premium wines are projected to decline slightly (by 7 and 3 per cent, respectively), because supply growth outstrips the projected growth in demand for premium wines (Table 13.4). However, for wine in aggregate, the global average producer price rises, reflecting the fact that the average quality of the wine produced is rising.

What about producer prices in Australia? Without the planned expansion in promotion abroad of Australian wine, they are projected to decline, especially for commercial premium wine. With the additional promotion mentioned in note 14, they are projected to rise slightly for non-premium wine, remain about the same as in 1999 for commercial premium, and rise 9 per cent above 1999 levels for super-premium wine (Table 13.4), much of which may have already happened. But as more vineyards are upgraded, the proportions of Australian wine in those much higher-priced premium categories are rising. Hence the weighted average producer price of Australian wine is projected to rise in that scenario. The final row of Table 13.4 reports on a scenario in which

Table 13.4   *Projected changes in wine output and producer prices, world and Australia, 1999–2005 (% for the period, in constant US dollars)*

	Non-premium wine	Commercial premium wine	Super-premium wine	Premium grapes
Output				
World	−10	13	45	
Australia	−17	99	136	
Prices				
World average – base case	0	−7	−3	
Australia				
base case	−1	−12	−3	−8
with additional promotion by Australia	5	−1	9	−1
plus a halving of global economic growth, 1999–2005	−2	−5	2	−29

Source: Anderson et al. (2003).

the global economy grows only half as fast over the forecast period as in the base scenario (which was constructed before the downturn in growth expectations in 2001–2002). For premium wines, that slowdown sends commercial premium wine prices down another 4 percentage points, while super-premium prices would rise only 2 per cent instead of 9 per cent in the Australian promotion scenario.

Recall that this relatively rosy picture for the Australia wine industry is predicated on the assumption that a concerted expansion in promotional efforts abroad is successful in boosting the demand for Australian premium wines. What is needed for that to happen, and how else might the Australian industry improve its future competitiveness and reduce the prospects of a decline in profitability? It is bound to involve more investment not only in marketing but also in knowledge creation and dissemination and in lobbying for tax reform, all of which require a considerable degree of collaboration.

HOW COLLABORATION CAN IMPROVE PROSPECTS FOR AUSTRALIA'S WINE INDUSTRY

Standard neo-classical trade theory stresses the importance of resource endowments as the key determinant of comparative advantage (including in this case

climate, land with the appropriate *terroir*, sufficient water, and skilled viticulturalists and oenologists). For differentiated products such as wine, where
purchase decisions are to some extent driven by fashion (as determined by
advertising, the writings of wine critics/judges, food scares and so on), a
resource that is crucially important is information/knowledge (and the skills to
use it profitably).[16] Its generation, as well as its productive use, is to a considerable extent under the control of the industry's producers.

While acquiring and using information can be costly, it is gradually becoming less so − and it is becoming available more quickly, thanks to the digital
information technology revolution. To keep one's competitive edge in this new
economic environment, strategies are needed to obtain and make good use of
available information faster and at a lower cost than one's competitors, to
generate new information, and to cost-effectively disseminate information
about one's products to consumers and to governments wishing to tax it. The
information required relates not just to consumer demands but also to appropriate new technologies as they affect all aspects of grape-growing, winemaking and wine marketing.

Much of that information has a public-good nature. That, together with the
spillovers that can occur from private-firm generation of information through
such activities as promotion and technical research, means collaboration
between firms within the industry can have a high payoff. Hence critical deter-
minants of future competitiveness include improvements in efficiency not
only of individual firms (including through mergers and/or acquisitions and
better grower/winemaker liaison) but also via collaboration at the industry-
wide level. With that improved collaboration can come higher-payoff investments in generic marketing, in research and training and in lobbying
governments. We consider each of these in turn.

Collaboration and Firm-level Efficiency

Two levels of collaboration between wine firms are important: vertical (that is,
between the grape-grower, other input supplier, winemaker and wine
marketer), and horizontal. The various channels through which it can occur
include mergers, acquisitions and a range of other alliances.

As with so many horticultural products, the product only reaches the final
consumer after some time, in this case involving processing of wine grapes
and then marketing/distributing the wine. Many wine grape producers have
chosen to do some or all of those manufacturing and service activities themselves. But there are far more wine grape growers than there are wineries, with
the former heavily dependent on the latter to process their highly perishable
and virtually non-internationally tradable product. That dependence has not
been a problem during the past dozen years when wine grape demand has

grown much faster than supply. Indeed the shortage period has led to the widespread signing of long-term (often ten-year) contracts, providing wineries with security of supply in the 1990s and growers with greater security of demand into the next decade.(Should supply grow faster than demand in the next few years, the vulnerability of the non-winemaking grape-grower could return.) However, the increasing emphasis on producing and promoting consistent high-quality wine, and the fact that much of that quality is determined in the vineyard, has led Australia's wineries to improve their two-way relationships with contract grape-growers.[17]

Another form of vertical integration is occurring between winemaking and wine marketing. An example is e-commerce, which is lowering the cost, especially for smaller wineries, of using e-mail and the Internet to market their wines directly. One Australian firm even experimented in 2000 with selling its entire release by tender over the Internet. The exemption of small wineries from the Australian government's wine sales tax for own-marketed wines has added to the incentive to explore these new options. Another example is wineries getting involved in tourism, going beyond standard cellar-door activities to restaurant and entertainment services.

Turning to horizontal collaboration, New World wineries are beginning to diversify their markets abroad as their production grows. Knowledge about the various niches and the distributional networks in those foreign markets is expensive to acquire, however. Hence new alliances between Australian and overseas wine companies are being explored with a view to capitalizing on their complementarities in such knowledge. The purchase by the owner of Mildara Blass (Fosters Brewing Group) of Napa Valley-based Beringer, the alliance between Southcorp/Rosemount and California's Mondavi, BRL Hardy's absorption into the second-largest US wine company, Constellation Brands, and the purchase by New Zealand's biggest wine firm (Montana) of the second largest (Corbans) and Montana's subsequent absorption into Allied Domecq are all cases in point since 2000. These may achieve the desired result much more quickly than direct foreign investment, although that has been happening increasingly too. As well, in this era of floating exchange rates, cross-border operations can be a form of currency hedge; and ownership abroad can also serve as a form of insurance against a major disease outbreak (for example, phylloxera, Pierce's Disease) in the home country.

Horizontal mergers and acquisitions are also taking place domestically. A key objective is to get economies of scale not only in marketing but also in producing. This is especially important if firms wish to move beyond the boutique size and penetrate the large-scale (particularly supermarket) distribution networks. The most recent in Australia is the merger of St Hallett and Tatachilla to list a new firm, Banksia Wines, towards the end of 2000 (to which Hillstowe has since been added). Both Banksia and ultra-premium producer

Petaluma have since been taken over by the trans-Tasman/Japanese brewer Lion Nathan.

This trend is occurring in many industries as part of globalization. The value of cross-border mergers and acquisitions in particular grew at 25 per cent per year from 1987 to 1995, and since then they have grown at an average of 50 per cent (UNCTAD, 2001, p. 10). While that is likely to increase concentration in the wine industry, it should do little to reduce competition among winemakers, including in their purchase of grapes. A few left-behind wineries will be disadvantaged by the new alliances among more-progressive firms (as suggested by a model developed by Cassella and Rauch, 1999), but an alternative possibility is that even they could benefit as those merging ones improve their export performance. That could happen either by getting in the slipstream of the progressive firms' success abroad in promoting 'Brand Australia', or in supplying a less crowded domestic market while the merging firms focus on markets abroad.

More worried are Australia's specialist grape-growers. They are aware that the big wine corporations have valuable so-called 'knowledge capital' that is internationally mobile and hence tends to relocate to places where it can earn the highest rewards (Carr et al., 2001). During recent years Australia's grape-growers have enjoyed an exceptionally high proportion of the benefits of the growth in demand for premium wine, in the form of high prices for their grapes. Were those high prices to continue, large wine firms (which source three-quarters of their grapes from independent growers) may find it more profitable to expand their crushing capacity in lower-priced countries rather than in Australia in the years ahead – thereby causing wine grape prices to tend to equalize across countries, even though the grapes themselves are not traded internationally. Such developments help to keep profits of Australian-based multinational wine companies and targeted grape-growers abroad higher than they would otherwise be, while lowering profits to Australian grape-growers, other things equal. However, there is also the possibility that multinational wine corporations from abroad will invest in Australia, which would have an offsetting, positive effect on Australian grape-growers. Some of that happened in 2000 in response to the fall in the US price of the Australian dollar, and more still could occur as such firms seek a hedge against the possible spread of Pierce's Disease in California.[18]

Horizontal collaboration stimulated by the digital revolution is also occurring at the retail level. How are the savings from increased marketing efficiencies via supermarketing and e-commerce likely to be distributed between the consumer, marketer, winemaker and grape-grower? Wittwer and Anderson (2001b) explore this question with their global wine model. They suggest that in the short run the innovative distributors will gain most but that, over time, as competition among distributors drives down consumer prices, the gains will

be shared among consumers and producers. Given even further time, the benefits to producers will encourage increased plantings and winemaking capacity
and so consumers will end up with the lion's share of the benefits (all but one-
eighth in the empirical simulation experiment they report).

Collaboration at the Industry-wide Level

In addition to collaboration to improve the efficiency of grape-growing, winemaking and wine marketing at the firm level, the Australian wine industry
during the past decade has also enjoyed a high and envied degree of collaboration also at the industry level. The key motivations for that collaboration are
to internalize externalities and to overcome the free-rider problem of collective action. Efforts have traditionally been directed in three key areas: the
generic promotion of Australian wine domestically and especially overseas;
investments in research, education and training (and now also statistical information); and lobbying governments (most notably for lower taxes on wine
consumption at home and lower barriers to imports overseas). Maintaining and
expanding those activities requires a non-stop flow of deliberate and skilful
leadership, something that the Australian wine industry has been fortunate to
have in relative abundance compared with both other Australian industries and
the wine industry abroad. Nowhere was that entrepreneurial leadership more
noticeable than during the development through the Winemakers' Federation
of Australia of a shared vision for the industry called *Strategy 2025* (AWF,
1995). It was developed with nothing more in mind than providing a 30-year
vision for the future so as to stimulate a steady flow of investment. At the time
the targets in that document were considered by many observers as rather optimistic, since they involved a threefold increase in the real value of wine
production, 55 per cent of it for the export market. Getting half-way to those
targets requires having a crush of 1100 kt to produce 750 million litres of wine
at a wholesale pre-tax value of AUD3 billion (AUD4/litre). Yet so convincing
was that document, and so intense has been the subsequent investment (see
Figures 13.1 and 13.3 above), that the industry is virtually half-way towards
its 30-year targets – that is, in just six vintages.

Long-run strategic planning by firms and the industry is made easier with
an active system of producer organizations. The Australian wine industry has
an excellent system involving more than 80 organizations at the national, state
and regional levels, with a well-developed hierarchy of interaction between
them.[19] Among them is the Australian Wine and Brandy Corporation
(AWBC). One of its tasks is to ensure that exported wine meets the product
standards of the importing country, so that the reputation of the industry as a
whole is not jeopardized by any sub-standard shipments. Another is to super-
vise the Label Integrity Program. A third is to establish the regional boundaries

for the purpose of registering Geographical Indications. A fourth is to lobby directly and via Australia's Department of Foreign Affairs and Trade for greater market access abroad through a lowering of tariff and non-tariff import barriers. And very important has been its role, via its Australian Wine Export Council, to invest in generic promotion of 'Brand Australia'.

A further task for AWBC that has been expanded significantly of late is the systematic provision of strategic information on market developments at home and abroad. The smaller an industry, the less likely such data will be available at low cost. Yet for capital-intensive industries with long lead times and large up-front costs such as wine, information on planting intentions of others in one's own country and elsewhere is especially pertinent for those contemplating investing, given that full bearing may not occur until 5+ years after beginning to invest. The grape and wine industry recognized this and spent some of its R&D funds on commissioning (a) the Australian Bureau of Statistics to collect more information including on growers' planting intentions in the coming year, and (b) the Australian Bureau of Agricultural and Resource Economics to use that information each year to project supplies several years ahead (see, for example, Spencer 2002). In addition, each year the Winemakers' Federation of Australia organizes a Wine Industry Outlook Conference and the Winegrape Growers' Council of Australia organizes a National Winegrape Outlook Conference, so such projections information can be shared and discussed. In addition, the Australian Wine Industry Technical Conference held every third year keeps producers up to date on new technologies, as does the National Wine Industry Environment Conference (first held in 2000) and the Annual Wine Marketing Conference (first held in 2001). Also, the WFA's Wine Australia exhibition every second year is aimed at getting more wine information to new consumers.

MORE INVESTMENT IN RESEARCH, EDUCATION AND TRAINING

Australia has had a long history of investing in formal grape and wine research, education and training, dating from the establishment of Roseworthy Agricultural College (now part of the University of Adelaide) in 1883 and of its Diploma in Oenology in 1934, plus the creation of the Australian Wine Research Institute adjacent to the University of Adelaide's Waite agricultural research campus in 1955 (Halliday 1994. pp. 109–11). In that same Waite precinct, but involving several interstate participants as well, is a Cooperative Research Centre for Viticulture. And the industry since 1988 has had its own Grape and Wine Research and Development Corporation (called a Council until 1991). The GWRDC's current budget is over AUD15 million per year, and growing rapidly not only because output is expanding but also because in 1999 growers and wineries agreed to raise the research levy rate by more than one-third (and are planning to raise it again in 2004). The Federal government matches producer levies dollar for dollar up to a maximum of 0.5 per cent of the gross value of output (a limit yet to be reached).

Rankine (1996) claims that even though Australia has supplied less than 2 per cent of the world's wine until very recently, it contributes as much as 20 per cent of the global flow of research papers on viticulture and oenology. A more recent study of 1995 data suggested a somewhat smaller but still disproportionately large contribution (Hoj and Hayes, 1998, Figure 3). That latter study also showed that research as a percentage of gross national (GDP) product was considerably smaller for grapes and wine than for Australia's larger rural industries and for that of major manufacturers. Moreover, Australia as a whole spends only two-thirds as much as other OECD countries on R&D as a percentage of GDP. While that may not be sufficient justification for boosting R&D spending, it, along with recent cost–benefit studies undertaken for GWRDC, suggests that there will be a high payoff to both grape-growers and winemakers from raising grape and wine producer levies at least to the level of attracting the maximum dollar-for-dollar contribution from the government (Zhao et al., 2003).[20]

Formal education in viticulture and oenology has spread from the University of Adelaide first to Charles Sturt University and since then to other tertiary education institutions. Also, the University of South Australia and several other universities are adding to the pool of wine marketing courses. In addition, numerous Technical and Further Education (TAFE) campuses are offering viticultural training both for employees and for boutique vineyard/winery proprietors and hobby farmers. And many high schools in wine areas are offering grape- and wine-oriented material in their agricultural science courses. Notwithstanding all these programmes, the peak industry bodies believe much more effective programmes are possible. A recent strategic review of the issue (Andrews, 2000) recommends they establish an education and training steering committee to fine-tune the programmes to better meet the changing needs of the industry.

The payoff from investments in R&D is higher the more readily and rapidly new information is disseminated, trialled and adopted. That requires not only education and training but also – for ongoing lifetime learning – active journal, magazine and website publications, specialized publishers/ distributors, and regional, state and national associations of producers whose culture is to share new information, ideas and results of field experimentation.[21] The role of grower liaison officers employed by the wineries to interact with contract growers, in disseminating new information and helping to boost and appraise grape quality, has been considerable. Those officers now insist on the use of diaries to record irrigation, spraying and fertilizing activities, they encourage lower yields so as to intensify grape colour and flavours, and they help monitor baume (sugar) levels in the grapes. In short, 'precision viticulture' is being adopted as producers strive for quality improvements.

While Australia has been a leader in wine R&D investments and in the rapid adoption of new technologies, southern hemisphere and southern and Eastern European suppliers are seeking to catch up, including through international technology transfer. Australia is contributing to and benefiting from that in at least two ways. One is via Australian viticulturalists and winemakers exporting their services through spending time abroad as consultants (Williams, 1995; Smart, 1999). Another is via foreign investment by Australia's bigger wine companies in grape production, winemaking, and/or wine marketing and distribution in other countries. Such international technology transfers are not peculiar to the wine industry of course – it is part of the general contribution by multinational corporations to globalization. That in turn has been aided by reforms to restrictions on foreign investment and by the fall in air transport costs, and thanks to the digital/information revolution in communication costs. Smaller grape-grower/winemaker firms might be affected adversely in so far as the spreading abroad of Australian expertise in viticulture, winemaking and wine marketing eventually reduces the distinctiveness of 'Australian' wine in the global marketplace. However, there is the offsetting prospect that internationally engaged Australians will bring back new ideas that can be exploited to good effect in Australia.

Finally, on research, one of the more difficult priority-setting issues is to decide how much of the R&D budget to spend on GMO (genetically modified organisms), organic and biodynamic technologies. Food consumers, especially in Europe, have become far more sensitized in recent years to food safety issues, making it awkward to anticipate their – and their governments' – possible reactions to new products that might be generated using these different technologies. As recent work on GM feed crops has shown (Nielsen and Anderson, 2001), vastly different outcomes are possible depending on the nature of those consumer and/or government reactions. Given the international nature of these concerns, there may be a higher payoff than usual from collaborating with grape and wine researchers focused on these issues in the USA and other New World countries.

MORE INVESTMENT IN MARKETING

The other classic way to try to boost profitability is to promote one's product as different from and superior to what others produce. For Australian wine this has been done in two key ways since the 1980s. One is generic promotion abroad by the Australian Wine Export Council, particularly through its London-based Australian Wine Bureau. The other is corporate brand promotion. Both are becoming more cost-effective with the huge increase in the quantity and quality of Australia's exportable wine, and together they have greatly enhanced the reputation of Australia as a producer able to over-deliver quality value-for-money wines.

Marketing is something the industry may not have done well during its first 150 years which, as the opening quotation from the *Yearbook of Australia 1922* (p. 279) suggested, may partly explain why it had not revealed a strong comparative advantage in exporting premium wine in the past. But that is changing rapidly. For example, being acutely aware of the prospect of premium prices falling during the next few years from their historically very high 1990s levels – due in part to the spectacular success of its *Strategy 2025* – the Australian industry is turning its attention to the next steps in its strategy. One of them was launched at the Wine Industry Outlook Conference in November 2000: the *Australian Wine Marketing Agenda 2000–2010* (WFA and ABEC, 2000). That calls on firms to boost not only their own brand promotional efforts but also to support spending on 'Brand Australia' generic promotion.[22] Recent empirical research suggests there may well be scope for Australia to gain from generic promotion in the USA at least, as its wines have attracted lower prices than wines from Napa Valley that receive similar sensory ratings in magazines such as the *Wine Spectator* (Schamel, 2000).

National generic and brand promotion can be complemented by regional generic promotion. This is a more viable option now that the definition of boundaries for the various regions and sub-regions ('geographical indications') are being finalized. Thanks to the WTO's trade-related intellectual property rights agreement ('TRIPs'), Australia is now able to legally register and get its own geographical indications recognized globally. The payoff from exploiting that piece of intellectual property may be non-trivial: a new study by Schamel and Anderson (2003) finds that equally rated wines in sensory terms attract significantly different prices according to their regional origin within Australia, and similarly for New Zealand. Corporate brand advertising will still remain the dominant form of promotion, but regional branding will add to 'Brand Australia' as an additional and more specific means of generic promotion of the nation's wines. Domestically, too, the better definition of regions is leading to more information-sharing among producers within regions, and to better coordination with regional wine (and food) tourism activities.

An additional marketing tool is quality assurance. This strategy is as old as the ancient Greeks.[23] In Australia it takes the form of a Label Integrity Program to ensure the Australian wine and brandy quality standards in the Australian Food Standards Code are adhered to. That Code is partly as a consequence of the Australia–EU international wine agreement and partly because it was requested by the industry to assist the marketing of Australian wine abroad. The quality standards currently in place also apply to wine imported into Australia. These standards are not dissimilar to those in the EU or the USA (where more than two-thirds of the world's wine is produced, consumed and traded), and most wine-producing countries have seen virtue in legislating wine quality standards to regulate their domestic production and international trade in wine. Preventing consumer fraud has been one of the objectives of such regulation, since the damage to a national industry that follows exposure of fraudulent behaviour can be severe.[24]

A further marketing strategy involves diversifying the destinations for Australia's exports as more exportable production comes on stream. The current narrowness of that distribution is clear from the fact that four-fifths of its export sales are in English-speaking countries: two-thirds to the UK and the USA and another 11 per cent to Canada and New Zealand. The next largest market for Australian exports in 2003, Germany, accounted for just 3–4 per cent (Table 13.3), and all others are less than 2 per cent each and only 15 per cent in total.

Of course there are good reasons for low shares in some markets. One is that the types and qualities of wine that Australia exports may be not well matched with the types/qualities currently imported by some of the major importing countries. For example, France imports mainly low-quality wine (priced at barely one-quarter Australia's average export price), and the same is true for Europe's transition economies and, to a lesser extent, for the Netherlands and Sweden (Anderson and Norman, 2003). That is not the case in Japan though, yet Australia sells a very small proportion of its premium wine to Japan (while contributing a relatively high proportion of Japan's imports of other goods). This is probably because Australia is not perceived by the Japanese as a super-premium supplier, having exported relatively low-quality wine there in the early 1990s. Nor had Australia until very recently made much of an inroad into Germany, although Germany is the world's biggest red wine importer (and overall wine importer in volume terms, accounting for around 20 per cent of global wine imports). To date that has been because of insufficient premium red wine being available for export from Australia. As supplies expand over the next few years, the scope for high returns from further efforts in marketing and trade diplomacy in such countries will grow commensurately. Since the volume of Germany's red imports is around six times Australia's current premium red wine export volume, there is ample scope for that market alone to absorb all of Australia's expected output increase without reducing very much German imports from other countries (mostly France and Italy).

What about sales prospects in Asia's emerging economies? The claim that Asian food does not lend itself to wine as much as European food is difficult to sustain in the face of both contemporary and historical evidence. Recent efforts to match such foods with wine have been highly successful. And there is evidence that the élites of both China and India consumed wine centuries ago. China, for example, produced, consumed and traded grape wine with Persia as early as the first century BC, and Marco Polo noted that excellent wines were produced in Shansi Province for exporting all over Cathay (Johnson, 1989, pp. 20–21). And the Mogul empire in sixteenth-century India was supplied with wine from the High Indus Valley and Afghanistan (Johnson, 1989, pp. 106–8). It seems reasonable to expect, then, as incomes rise, and with this, access to refrigeration and air conditioning, that a gradual expansion in wine promotion in this food-revering region will yield a high payoff over the long term – vindicating the view of Stigler and Becker (1977) that prices and incomes together with product knowledge/information are the key factors affecting demand, not 'differences in tastes'. The speech in China by Premier Deng in 1997, affirming the health virtues of red wine consumption, like the *60 Minutes* TV programme in the USA in 1991 concerning the so-called French paradox, are stark reminders of how well-targeted information can alter consumption patterns overnight. Two cautionary points need to be made, however. One is that the biggest potential market in Asia in the long term, China, is likely to be supplied domestically to a large extent (having expanded its grapevine area rapidly in the 1990s and still having a very low share of its cropland devoted to vines). The other point to keep in mind is the relative smallness of that region's market, such that even a very rapid rate of import growth does not translate into huge volumes (as recent modelling shows – see Anderson and Wittwer, 2001).

Finally, more targeted marketing domestically may still have a high payoff, especially if it is targeted at younger adults, particularly females. After all, Australia's 20 litres per capita is still a long way short of the EU's 34 litres, where wine accounts for 45 per cent of all alcohol consumption compared with just 31 per cent in Australia (albeit up from less than 10 per cent in the 1960s).

MORE LOBBYING FOR LOWER WINE CONSUMER TAXATION IN AUSTRALIA

The consumer tax on wine is higher in Australia than in almost any other significant wine-producing country (Berger and Anderson, 1999). The introduction by the federal government of its so-called 'wine equalization tax' (WET) of 29 per cent, which came into force on 1 July 2000, is, together with the 10 per cent goods and services tax (GST) on wine, generating even more tax revenue from the industry than before the GST's introduction. The wine industry is lobbying for a reduction in the WET, at least for small and medium enterprises, to provide a cushion in the form of more domestic sales.

To get a feel for what impact that might have, Wittwer and Anderson (2002) analyse the impact of cutting Australia's tax on premium wine to just double the OECD average (leaving the non-premium rate unchanged so that, in volumetric terms, the latter tax is about the same as for premium wine). With such a tax cut consumer prices drop significantly for premium wine, by over $1.50 per litre, and domestic consumption of premium wine increases from 95 million litres to 107 million litres for red wine, and from 90 million litres to 102 million litres for white wine.[25] The impact on industry output is small, with the premium segment expanding by less than 0.5 per cent relative to the base case. This small change is due to the assumption that land in the wine grape industries and capital in all the wine grape and wine industries is the same in this as in the base scenario, leaving labour as the only variable factor within these industries. Importantly for producers, however, the volume of premium exports required to maintain the same total volume of sales as in the base case is significantly less in this scenario. That is, the amount of investment in promotion abroad over the next few years would not need to be as great if the imminent output growth coincided with a reduction in domestic wine taxation.

MORE LOBBYING FOR LOWER WINE CONSUMER TAXATION IN OTHER COUNTRIES

Import restrictions are commonly used to protect domestic producers of either wine or, as in East Asia, wine substitutes (beer and spirits). Import tariffs themselves are not very large except in East Asia (Berger and Anderson, 1999; Foster and Spencer, 2002). However, Old World fears of growing competition in the European and East Asian wine markets from New World suppliers could lead to the provision of more subsidies and protection via non-tariff import restrictions by the European Commission. Already recent subsidies to producers in the EU to help upgrade their wine industry are reputed to be of the order of US$2.3 billion.

There is also the possibility that technical measures are used to provide hidden forms of protection to the EU industry (as happened in Canada after the signing of the Canada–US free trade agreement – Heien and Sims, 2000). The EU's recent effort to have so-called 'industrial wine' distinguished from 'agricultural wine' (the former presumably referring to North American and Australian/New Zealand, the latter to European) would, if successful, provide a possible opening for another technical barrier to trade. Using their model of the global wine market, Wittwer and Anderson (2001b) explore the impacts of

a rise in technical barriers to EU imports of premium wine from the New
World; the results have the usual effects of such protection in the EU and elsewhere.

To avoid such outcomes, New World wine exporters need to develop ways
to make the most of the opportunity to become active participants, for the first
time as a group, in the next WTO round of multilateral trade negotiations.
While each of those suppliers alone is not a very big player in the world wine
market, their combined share of the value of global wine exports (excluding
intra-EU trade) is 31 per cent, which is a sizeable counterweight to the EU's
share of 60 per cent (Anderson and Norman, 2003). It thus makes sense for
them to form a coalition for the purpose of dealing with the EU, including in
multilateral negotiations. That was done recently, in the form of the New
World Wine Group that involves officials and wine industry representatives
meeting twice a year. Building up that new informal institution, by drawing on
the huge success during the Uruguay Round of the Cairns Group of like-
minded agricultural-exporting countries, is likely to have a high payoff during
and beyond the next round of WTO trade talks. Care is needed in fine-tuning
their requests to trade policy reforms abroad, however. Wittwer and Anderson
(2001b) note that their modelling of a reduction in the EU wine import tariff
generated some counter-intuitive results. In particular, since the EU tariff is
volumetric rather than *ad valorem*, its reduction encourages the consumption
and importation of non-premium relative to premium wines and so leads to
less rather than more sales from premium wine exporters such as Australia and
New Zealand.[26]

CONCLUSION

What should one answer to the person in the street who asks: has Australia
invested too much in vineyards in the past few years? The option value theory
of investment behaviour under uncertainty (involving waiting for more information on real price trends – see Dixit and Pindyck, 1994) helps us to under-
stand why Australia's vineyard area shrank in the mid-1980s and then
expanded only after the mid-1990s and despite little growth in real producer
prices since then. The slowdown in red plantings that began in 1999–2000
(Figure 3.4) also makes the same economic sense. As for whether Australia
overshot, the answer is the same as for all such economic questions: it
depends. The average price of Australian wine exports has stopped rising in
real terms, and the Anderson et al. modelling suggests that it is about to start
falling unless the industry boosts its marketing in response to the growing
supplies of premium wine at home and abroad. But the industry *is* doing a
great deal to reduce the risk of a slump in profits, and it has scope and plans

to do even more (for example, expanding its investments in promotion abroad and in high-payoff R&D). So long as its producers also remain attuned to the market and flexible enough to respond to exogenous shocks such as currency realignments, changes in consumer fashions, or disease outbreaks, its long-term prospects for continued prosperity look good. But, as anybody who has studied the history of the wine industry knows, the only thing that is really certain is that this is an industry characterized by great uncertainty and ever-fluctuating fortunes.

NOTES

1. Such an admission was not forthcoming from the French, however. At the international wine competition of the Vienna Exhibition of 1873, for example, the French judges, on hearing of the identity of the wines they had judged blind, are reported to have resigned when they learnt that a prize-winning Shiraz was not French but from the Colony of Victoria (Beeston, 1994, p. 62).
2. Johnson (1989, pp. 66–7) points to the example of the eruption of Mt Vesuvius in AD 79. Pompeii at the time was the Bordeaux of the world wine market. The burying of its vine-yards and cellars caused a huge hike in the price of wine, which stimulated plantings else-where. So great were the new plantings that a wine glut soon emerged, prompting Emperor Domitian in AD 92 to ban new plantings in Italy and to order the grubbing up of half of the vineyards in Rome's overseas provinces.
3. The share of production exported in recent years, shown in Figure 13.5, has been lagging the percentage of total sales abroad of Australian wine (shown in Figure 13.2) because produced wine – particularly as the proportion of premium reds rises – is spending longer in the cellar before sale by the winery. For 2001–2002, for example, the former indicator was 34 per cent and the latter was 52 per cent in volume terms and close to two-thirds in value terms.
4. In the present boom the only form of assistance offered and hence able to be withdrawn is the tax incentive to expand plantings via the tax-reducing accelerated depreciation allowance for some establishment costs (as applies to investment in many other indus-tries).
5. The timing of the initial export surge was helped by the devaluation of the Australian dollar in the mid-1980s, which was due to a sharp fall in international prices of Australia's coal, grain and other major primary export products. That devaluation, together with low domestic prices for premium red grapes at the time (due to a domestic fashion swing to whites from the mid-1970s – see Figure 13.7), increased substantially the incentive for investing in developing overseas markets for Australian wine. Other factors expanding foreign demand for Australian wine at the time were food safety scares associated with Chernobyl in April 1986 and scandals involving additives in Austrian and Italian wines (Rankine, 1996). Meanwhile, competition was minimal from South Africa, because of anti-apartheid sentiment, and from Argentina and Chile because their domestic and trade policies had for a long time discriminated against exportable agricultural products (and the wine style produced for their domestic market was heavier than that sought in the northern hemisphere – see Thompson, 2000). For a more formal accounting of the relative importance of various factors contributing to Australia's output boom since the latter 1980s, see Wittwer and Anderson (2001a).
6. Australia's share of the value of the UK's wine imports between 1990–92 and 2001 grew from 4 to 16 per cent, while the share of the four traditional West European exporters in UK imports fell from 75 to 63 per cent and that of Central and Eastern Europe fell from 2 to 1 per cent (Anderson and Norman, 2003). It is understandable that exports from the

economies in transition from communism have yet to be dramatic, given the myriad adjustment difficulties producers face in those countries. As for the EU producers, they have been slow to respond because the Common Agricultural Policy has insulated them from market forces, making it less profitable for them to respond to changes in consumer preferences. Specifically, the CAP in the past has provided such high prices for non-premium EU wine (largely destined for distillation, as its direct demand has slumped) that they did not find it worthwhile to make the considerable investments necessary to upgrade their product and to market it abroad.

7.   On the one hand, there has been a huge increase in the number of Australian wine producers (more than 1600 in 2003, compared with fewer than 200 in the early 1970s and 300 in the early 1980s – see Winetitles, 2003 and earlier issues), but most of them are very small. On the other hand, there have been numerous mergers and takeovers by larger firms to form even larger conglomerates (see Winetitles, 2003, p. 23 for a chronology of ownership changes since the early 1960s). The net result has been a substantial increase in firm concentration. Whereas in 1978 those crushing more than 1000 tonnes accounted for 17 per cent of wine firms, now they account for just 4 per cent of all wine firms. The top three producers in the late 1990s accounted for about 50 per cent of the annual vintage, of the number of bottles of wine sold, and of the value of domestic sales, and for 70 per cent of wine exports; for the top nine producers those shares are about 75 and 95 per cent, respectively (Osmond and Anderson, 1998, Tables 11 and 12).

8.   The corporatization of firms has helped in raising the enormous amounts of capital required for rapid expansion. In Australia the capital intensity of wine grape growing is about 50 per cent above that of other agriculture, and that of winemaking is more than one-fifth higher than that of other manufacturing. Australia's four biggest wine firms are listed in the world's top 20 producers of wine, but in terms of sales in 2000 they were ranked 6th (Southcorp/Rosemount), 7th (Beringer Blass), 11th (Pernod Ricard, strictly a French company but whose main wine holding is Orlando Wyndham) and 18th (BRL Hardy – which merged with Constellation of the USA in 2003). Southcorp/Rosemount and Beringer Blass in 2000 each had only 40 per cent of the sales of each of the world's top two wine firms (E. & J. Gallo of the USA and LVMH of France – see ABN–AMRO, 2001, p. 7) but after absorbing BRL Hardy, Constellation became No. 1 in 2003.

9.   Indeed some types (for example, Lindemans Bin 65 Chardonnay) were specifically developed for and only sold in those markets initially, being released in Australia several years later only after sufficient expansion in production of the required grapes.

10. Even after the recent AUD/US$ appreciation, the export price averaged AUD4.70 in 2002–2003. Those Australian consumers finding it difficult to adjust to the recent surge in domestic wine prices are none the less grateful for the very low prices they enjoyed for so long before the recent export take-off. Even the relatively high current prices are low by the standards of the Roman Empire: according to Unwin (1991, pp. 123–6) and Johnson (1989, p. 83), in the first century BC the price of a (roughly 22-litre) jar of standard wine exported from Italy to France was one Gaul slave!

11. Following the broadcast on US television in November 1991 of a *60 Minutes* segment on possible reasons for 'the French paradox' (concerning their superior health despite high levels of wine consumption), red wine sales in the USA shot up 61 per cent that month and have remained higher ever since (Heien and Sims, 2000).

12. Wine's share of total alcohol consumption in Australia has risen from less than 10 per cent before the 1960s to 31 per cent by 2001 (Anderson and Norman, 2003, Tables 24 and 75).

13. Hard direct evidence of the claim of quality upgrading domestically is difficult to obtain. However, indirect evidence can be found from winery turnover and export value data. In so far as the difference between those two is indicative of domestic expenditure on wine, it has risen from AUD49 per capita in 1991–92 to AUD96 in 1999–2000 dollars (inflated using the consumer price index).

14. That prototype version projected Australian producer prices for premium grapes and wine to fall by 9 to 12 per cent between 1999 and 2005 in 1999 US dollar terms if nothing exceptional was done to promote Australian wine abroad. However, the major marketing strategy launched by the Australian industry in November 2000 (WFA and AWBC, 2000)

is expected to counter that tendency. We therefore assume that, between now and 2005, consumers will show an increasing preference for Australian wines over those from other regions in response to that promotion boost, to the extent that the projected decline in the producer price of Australian commercial premium grapes between 1999 and 2005 is reduced from 11 per cent to almost zero.

15. When sparkling wine is not counted, Australia had surpassed France in value of imports to the UK by 2002–2003.

16. For a recent survey of trade theories in a growth context as applied to both standard and differentiable rural products, see van Berkum and van Meijl (2000).

17. See Hoole (1997) for the Orlando Wyndham experience and Steiman (1999) for Southcorp's approach. Southcorp introduced a system of rating the grapes from every plot of land and the wine that results using a sophisticated 30-point scale, and contract growers were paid accordingly. In turn, the wine point scores are used to determine under which label (and hence price bracket) a particular batch will be sold (Steiman, 1999, p. 130). Ways of measuring the quality of grapes delivered for crushing are improving too, so there will be less uncertainty about the appropriate bonus or discount that should be applied to the indicator price per tonne, and hence more incentive for growers to aspire to higher-quality production.

18. For an economic analysis of the distributional effects of both a change in the value of the US dollar and a spread of Pierce's Disease in California, see Wittwer and Anderson (2001c).

19. For this and all key aspects of the Australian Wine industry, see http://www.wineaustralia.com.au.

20. That recent benefit–cost study found that the current portfolio of GWRDC research projects is expected to yield a 9:1 benefit–cost ratio and that a sample of past projects yielded ratios ranging from 7:1 to 76:1 (McLeod, 2002). For more on Australia's levy-funded rural research and development system, see Brennan and Mullen (2001).

21. For a comprehensive listing of participants in the industry, and of the wide array of journals and magazines dedicated to grape and wine producer (not to mention consumer) information, see Winetitles (2003) and the websites www.winetitles.com.au and www.wineaustralia.com.au.

22. In addition to wineries, supporting industries are being asked to contribute. Nine key suppliers of inputs (ranging from corks and barrels to transport and label printers) became the inaugural Australian Wine Export Partners in late 2000.

23. Robinson (1994, p. 465) cites the case of the Greek island of Thasos which, as early as the second millennium BC, standardized the size of the amphorae and allowed exports only of wine sealed with the name of the magistrate as a guarantee of authenticity (a seal that was also used by other Greek states).

24. For example, following the scandal in 1985 involving Austrian wine being found to have been sweetened by a harmless but illegal additive, Austria's exports plummeted by four-fifths the next year (Robinson, 1994, p. 73).

25. In per capita terms, in the 2003 base case, premium consumption is 4.8 litres for red premium wine and 4.5 litres for white premium wine. These levels increase to 5.4 litres and 5.2 litres, respectively, in the wine tax cut scenario.

26. Another concern for trade negotiators is the Eastern enlargement of the EU. At present 12 countries are negotiating their accession to the EU, and no less than seven of them are among the 30 top wine-producing countries. It is hoped that such an enlargement will, for budgetary reasons, encourage the EU to lower its assistance to wine producers. But even that need not guarantee that the overall assistance to Europe's wine industry will fall.

REFERENCES

ABARE (2003), *Australian Commodities*, Canberra: Australian Bureau of Agricultural and Resource Economics, June.

ABN-AMRO (2001), *Global Wine Sector: Maturing With Age*, Sydney: ABN–AMRO.

Anderson, K. and D. Norman (2003), *Global Wine Production, Consumption and Trade, 1961 to 2001: A Statistical Compendium*, Adelaide: Centre for International Economic Studies.

Anderson, K. and G. Wittwer (2001), 'World's Wine Markets in 2005: Effects of Faster Asian Demand Growth', in *Proceedings of the 26th World Congress of the OIV, Adelaide, 11–18 October 2001*, Paris: OIV.

Anderson, K., D. Norman and G. Wittwer (2003), 'Globalization of the World's Wine Markets', *The World Economy*, **26** (5), 659–87.

Andrews, K. (2000), *Education and Training Review: Grape and Wine Industry*, Adelaide: Grape and Wine Research and Development Corporation.

AWF (1995), *Strategy 2025: The Australian Wine Industry*, Adelaide: Winemakers' Federation of Australia for the Australian Wine Foundation.

Beeston, J. (1994), *A Concise History of Australian Wine*, Sydney: Allen and Unwin.

Berger, N. and K. Anderson (1999), 'Consumer and Import Taxes in the World Wine Market: Australia in International Perspective', *Australian Agribusiness Review*, **7**, June (www.adelaide.edu.au/CIES/wine.htm#other).

van Berkum, S. and H. van Meijl (2000), 'The Application of Trade and Growth Theories to Agriculture: A Survey', *Australian Journal of Agricultural and Resource Economics*, **44** (4), 505–42.

Brennan, J.P. and J.D. Mullen (2001), 'Australia's Research Levy System', in G.H. Peters and P. Pingali (eds), *Tomorrow's Agriculture: Incentives, Institutions, Infrastructure and Innovations*, Aldershot: Ashgate.

Carr, D.L., J.R. Markusen and K. Maskus (2001), 'Testing the Knowledge-Capital Model of the Multinational Enterprise', *American Economic Review*, **91** (3), 693–708.

Cassella, A. and J.E. Rauch (1999), 'Autonomous Market and Group Ties in International Trade', CEPR Discussion Paper, London, February.

Dixit, A. and R.S. Pindyck (1994), *Investment Under Uncertainty*, Princeton, NJ: Princeton University Press.

Foster, M. and D. Spencer (2002), *World Wine Market Barriers to Increasing Trade*, Canberra: Australian Bureau of Agricultural and Resource Economics.

Halliday, J. (1994), *A History of the Australian Wine Industry: 1949–1994*, Adelaide: Winetitles for the Australian Wine and Brandy Corporation.

Heien, D. and E.N. Sims (2000), 'The Impact of the Canada–United States Free Trade Agreement on US Wine Exports', *American Journal of Agricultural Economics*, **82** (1), 173–82.

Hoj, P.B. and P.F. Hayes (1998), 'The Australian Wine Industry's Research and Development Effort and its Importance for Sustained Growth', in *Proceedings of the Tenth Australian Wine Industry Technical Conference*, Sydney, 2–5 August, pp. 10–15.

Hoole, B.J. (1997), 'Securing Supply Through Improved Grower and Processor Relationships: Orlando Wyndham Pty Ltd', D. Gifford, L. Hall and R. Collins (eds), *Competitive Performance: Case Studies on the Australia Agricultural Experience*, East Hawthorn: Morescope Publishing for DPIE.

Irvine, H.W.H. (1892), *Report on the Australian Wine Trade*, Melbourne: R.S. Bain.

Johnson, H. (1989), *The Story of Wine*, London: Mitchell Beazley.

McLeod, R. (2002), *Ex Ante and Ex Post Cost Benefit Analysis of the GWRDC's Project Portfolio*, Adelaide: Grape and Wine Research and Development Corporation.

Nielsen, C.P. and K. Anderson (2001), 'Global Market Effects of European Responses to Genetically Modified Organisms', *Weltwirtschaftliches Archiv*, **137** (2), 320–46.

Osmond, R. and K. Anderson (1998), *Trends and Cycles in the Australian Wine Industry, 1850 to 2000,* Adelaide: Centre for International Economic Studies.

Rankine, B. (1996), *Evolution of the Modern Australian Wine Industry: A Personal Appraisal*, Adelaide: Ryan Publications.

Robinson, J. (1994), *The Oxford Companion to Wine*, London: Oxford University Press.

Schamel, G. (2000), 'Individual and Collective Reputation Indicators of Wine Quality', Discussion Paper 00/09, Centre for International Economic Studies, University of Adelaide, March (www.adelaide.edu.au/CIES/wine.htm#other).

Schamel, G. and K. Anderson (2003), 'Wine Quality and Varietal, Regional and Winery Reputations: Hedonic Prices for Australia and New Zealand', *Economic Record*, **79** (246), 357–70.

Smart, R. (1999), 'Overseas Consulting: Selling the Family Silver, or Earning Export Income?' *Australian and New Zealand Wine Industry Journal*, **14** (4), 64–7.

Spencer, D. (2002), *Australian Grape Production and Winery Intake: Projections to 2004–05*, ABARE Report 02.2, Canberra: Australian Bureau of Agricultural and Resource Economics, December.

Steiman, H. (1999), 'Big, Bold and Booming: Australia's Southcorp Takes on the World with Penfolds, Lindermans and Others', *Wine Spectator*, **24** (12), 124–42.

Stigler, G.J. and G.S. Becker (1977), 'De Gustibus non est Disputandum', *American Economic Review*, **67** (2), 76–90.

Thompson, B. (2000), 'South America', in S. Brook (ed.), *A Century of Wine: The Story of a Wine Revolution*, edited by London: Mitchell Beazley, pp. 172–5.

UNCTAD (2001), *World Investment Report 2001: Promoting Linkages*, New York and Geneva: United Nations.

Unwin, T. (1991), *Wine and the Vine: An Historical Geography of Viticulture and the Wine Trade*, London and New York: Routledge.

WFA (Winemakers' Federation of Australia) and AWBC (Australian Wine and Brandy Corporation) (2000), *The Marketing Decade: Setting the Australian Wine Marketing Agenda 2000–2010*, Adelaide: WFA.

WFA/Winetitles (2003): *Vintage: the Australian Wine Industry Statistical Yearbook 2002*, Adelaide: Winetitles.

Williams, A. (1995), *Flying Winemakers: The New World of Wine*, Adelaide: Winetitles.

Winetitles (2003), *Australian and New Zealand Wine Industry Directory 2003*, Adelaide: Winetitles.

Wittwer, G. and K. Anderson (2001a), 'Accounting for Growth in the Australian Wine Industry, 1987 to 2003', *Australian Economic Review*, **34** (2), 179–89.

Wittwer, G. and K. Anderson (2001b), 'How Increased EU Import Barriers and Reduced Retail Margins Affect the World Wine Market,' *Australian and New Zealand Wine Industry Journal*, **16** (3), 69–74.

Wittwer, G. and K. Anderson (2001c), 'US Dollar Appreciation and the Spread of Pierce's Disease: Effects on the World Wine Market', *Australian and New Zealand Wine Industry Journal*, **16** (2), 70–75.

Wittwer, G. and K. Anderson (2002), 'Impact of the GST and Wine Tax Reform on Australia's Wine Industry: A CGE Analysis', *Australian Economic Papers*, **41** (1), 69–81.

The New World

Wittwer, G., N. Berger and K. Anderson (2003), 'A Model of the World's Wine Markets', *Economic Modelling*, **20** (3), 487–506.
Zhao, X., K. Anderson and G. Wittwer (2003), 'Who Gains from Australian Generic Wine Promotion and R&D?' *Australian Journal of Agricultural and Resource Economics*, **47** (2), 181–209.

14. New Zealand

Mia Mikić

The wine industry of New Zealand is a small industry from the national economy's perspective. Its contribution to GDP, total merchandise exports and
employment is still under 1 per cent.[1] However, this industry is a big achiever.
Twenty years ago, less than 1 per cent of the industry's production was exported;
in 2001 exports accounted for 36 per cent of produced litres of wine. Reliance on
imports also has increased dramatically: while in the late 1970s/early 1980s only
6 per cent of domestic consumption of wine originated from imports, in 2001 56
per cent of consumption was sourced from imports (Anderson and Norman,
2003). The focus of the industry has changed dramatically from being an import-
substituting industry to one where international trade, particularly exports, are
increasingly important. The industry has become globally oriented, with the
national market being seen as just an integrated part of the world market.
Consequently, import competition is no longer seen as threatening. Since the
number of wineries has steadily increased, competition is not only from imports
but also between domestic companies, whose number quadrupled over the past
two decades. None the less, the industry remains extremely concentrated as most
of the new wineries are small or boutique-sized producers.

The wine industry has had a multifunctional role in New Zealand. The
growth of the industry has impacted on a number of relevant social and
economic goals. The expansion of the wine industry has contributed significantly towards diversification of agriculture-based exports. Its expansion has
affected government revenues because the excise duty on wine has been
steadily increasing over the past decade. Not least importantly, the growth of
the industry is credited with having a positive social impact by allowing alcohol consumers to acquire more socially acceptable drinking habits. The focus
of this chapter, however, is on the role liberalization has played in the restructuring of the wine industry as well as on factors responsible for achieving the
industry's sustainable export-led growth.

NEW ZEALAND'S WINE INDUSTRY BEFORE THE 1990S[2]

Before 1990[3] we can identify three distinct phases in the development of the

wine industry with respect to the impacts of government policies (predominantly trade policy) on competition in the industry and its growth:

- passive import protection: the period from the establishment of the
  industry until the late 1970s;
- 'picking winners': the period preceding and including the Wine Industry
  Development Plan, from the late 1970s to 1986; and
- restructuring and early trade liberalization: the period of the Grape
  Extraction Scheme and trade liberalization, from 1986 to 1990.

Import Protection

The wine industry had received protection from import competition for a long
time up to the late 1970s. Tariff rates on wines (expressed as specific taxes)
before World War II included MFN (most favoured nation) rates, British preferential rates, and special preferential rates for Australia and South Africa. In
the late 1930s, for protectionist and balance of payments reasons, licences for
wine imports were restricted to half what had been imported in 1938, and by
1942 the surcharge on wine tariffs had increased to 50 per cent. The GATT
(General Agreement on Tariffs and Trade) MFN rates were set in 1948, but
import protection for the wine industry increased in 1958/59, 1962 and 1972
for various reasons, including the shortage of foreign exchange and emergency
protection against a wine glut in the international market. This protection of
the industry was consistent with New Zealand's high levels of protection
generally over that period.

Picking Winners

In the late 1970s the industry was 'hand-picked' for an assessment by the
Industries Development Commission (IDC), which marked a period of
special, mostly favourable, attention by the government (known as 'The Wine
Industry Development Plan to 1986'). The industry did not win everything it
lobbied for, however. For example, distribution was not fully deregulated, the
importing of grape juice was banned, and the level of protection granted was
not as high as demanded. Wine was exempt from import licensing, but was
subject to a complex tariff structure featuring tariff quotas, a tariff threshold
and composite tariffs.[4]

It is important to note that New Zealanders were not 'sophisticated' wine
drinkers (price was most important in their choice decision) and the supply of
domestic wine consisted mostly of cheaper varieties. Consequently, the deliberate setting of high tariffs on cheap imported wines was expected to result in the
cessation of imports of cheap wines, thus allowing an expansion by domestic

producers.[5] However, the implementation of the Plan resulted in overplanting of cheap grapes, causing a grape glut and oversupply of wine by the mid-1980s. A number of commentators and members of the industry stressed that the grape glut was partly caused by companies overreacting to changed signals under the Plan and miscalculating changes in domestic consumption. For example, the mid-term review of the Plan found that

> the problem arises from the industry's ability to divorce itself from market realities by relying on frontier protection. The result has been, inter alia, procedures for grape pricing which encourage risk aversion by favouring high and reliable yielding grapes, and the preservation of some uncompetitive vineyards, grape types, production processes and product lines. (p. 34)

While this statement was not true for all companies, it certainly correctly described the position of a large number of them including some large companies, which were threatened by bankruptcies.

Grape Extraction Scheme and Trade Liberalization

The Wine Industry Assistance Package announced in late 1985 offered a cash grant for the uprooting of grapevines amounting to NZ$6175 per hectare. By 1990 vines were pulled out from 1517 hectares and the resource base of the industry was significantly changed so that grape varieties used in the production of cheaper wines (such as Müller Thurgau or Palomino) became less represented. While officials judge this intervention by the government as especially successful, some commentators within the industry claim that the scheme had an adverse effect on the industry's development because it permitted much slower restructuring and prevented the exit of the least efficient and worst-managed companies by providing them with extra cash flow.

As part of the package, the government also looked at the level of protection granted to the wine industry by the tariff and quota regime originally imposed by the Plan. The regime was replaced by a tariff-phasing programme featuring the removal of punitive duties on cheap imports, the elimination of quotas by introducing progressively larger ones and the replacement of combined tariffs with a simple 25 per cent *ad valorem* duty on 1 July 1990.

In addition to direct assistance and import protection measures, competition in the domestic market was affected by a set of policies regulating the alcohol industry in general and the wine industry in particular. The development of these policies is briefly discussed below.

As part of the overall reforms, the government changed its ways of collecting revenue, and the excise duty on alcoholic beverages has frequently been increased. However, it has been imposed on both domestic and imported wine, implying no direct impact on competitiveness. WINZ (1992) claims, however, that high excise duties inhibit growth of the industry and indirectly affect its export potential. Although the burden of excise duty on table wine has been steadily increasing, there is no evidence on how strongly it discourages new investments in the industry. It is also claimed that high excise duties depress domestic demand. However, excise duties, being specific duties (for example, $ per litre), would affect more the lower-quality wines and thus would be helpful in the industry's plans to improve the average quality of wines offered in the market.[6]

Among other regulatory policies affecting wine, production and labelling requirements (PLR) and export certification had the greatest impact. PLR imposed on winemakers are established under the Food Act and Food Regulations 1984 and subsequent amendments. These rules are considered less rigorous than those in the more traditional wine-producing countries (see discussion further below).

Table 14.1 records the most important trade policy and regulatory changes and contrasts them with changes in wine consumption and production over a 40-year period. The increase in both consumption and production is definitely correlated to trade liberalization measures and also to the relaxation of domestic sale laws.

As a way of summarizing the pre-1990 developments, the following points are worth emphasizing:

- For the most part of its existence, the wine industry of New Zealand enjoyed border protection from import competition. That protection was particularly high during the Wine Industry Development Plan implementation period (1981–86) and it was biased in favour of cheaper (low-quality) wine production.
- Due to most members of the industry following the distorted price signals of the Plan, the early 1980s were marked by a glut of grapes and an excess supply of wine.
- Assistance in the form of the Grape Extraction Scheme in the late 1980s, plus global and sectoral trade liberalization, helped to create incentives for producers to switch from low-quality to higher-quality grapes and wines.
- Deregulation of the alcohol industry (distribution and sales regulation mostly) contributed to the expansion of the industry by lowering the costs of sales and boosting consumption. A combination of easier access to wine, exposure to better-quality wines while travelling overseas, increased immigration, and overall globalization had an impact on the change in tastes and domestic demand for wines in New Zealand in favour of better quality as well as higher per capita consumption (from 3 litres in the 1960s to 15 litres in 1990).[7]

Table 14.1 Trade policy and other regulatory changes affecting wine industry expansion, New Zealand, 1958–2001

Period	Wine consumption per capita in litres (year in parentheses)	Wine production, million litres (year in parentheses)	Trade policy and regulatory changes (year in parentheses)
1958–64	1.74 (1960)	4 (1960)	Higher taxes on beer and spirits (1958) Restaurants licenced (1960) Taverns licenced (1961)
1965–69	3.08 (1965)	8 (1965)	Restrictions on wine imports (1967)
1970–74	4.94 (1970)	19 (1970)	Theatres and cabarets licenced (1971)
1975–79	7.63 (1975)	24 (1975)	Bring your own restaurants licenced (1976)
1980–84	11.9 (1980)	43 (1980)	Import control removed (1981) Increase in sales tax on wine (1984)
1985–89	13.10 (1985)	60 (1985)	Grapevine extraction scheme (1985) Duties on wine imports reduced (1986)
1990–94	11.7 (1990)	54 (1990)	Further tariff reductions (1990–94) Supermarkets licenced to sell wine (1990) Wineries licenced to sell wine on own premises (1992)
1995–2001	8.7 (1995)	56 (1995)	Further tariff reductions (1995–2000) Customs and Excise Act (1996) Sale of Liquor Amendment Act (1999) ANZ Food Authority (2000) Review of wine legislation (in process) (2000) Mutual acceptance agreement on oenological practices (2001)

Source: Adapted from Workman (1994, p. 40) and updated by author.

DEVELOPMENTS SINCE 1990

While the wine industry in the 1950–90 period was never dormant, most of the qualitative and quantitative changes were more drastic during the last decade of the millennium (Figure 14.1). This period can be characterized as the phase of committed liberalization. The process of restructuring that began with the Grape Extraction Scheme and the redesign of the protection structure in the late 1980s was accelerated by further unilateral trade liberalization and domestic deregulation in the 1990s. By 1990, tariff quotas and specific tariffs were replaced by *ad valorem* tariffs which were to be reduced along a pre-announced path, from 25 per cent in 1990 to 5 per cent in 2000 (Figure 14.2).[8]

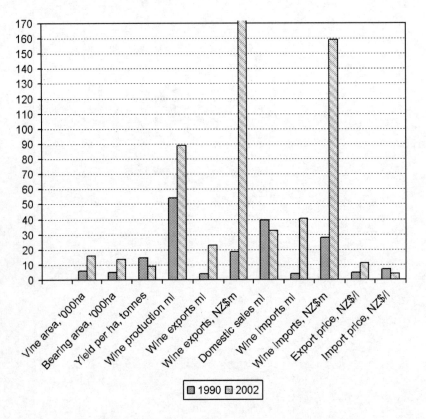

Source: Calculated by author from data in WINZ Annual Reports (2003).

Figure 14.1   Key indicators of the wine industry, New Zealand, 1990 and 2002

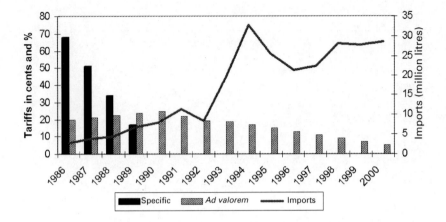

Source: Calculated by author from data in WINZ Annual Reports (2003).

*Figure 14.2   Wine import tariffs and volume of imports, New Zealand,
1986–2000*

Import barriers on the inputs used by grape-growers and winemakers (such as
cork, bottles, capsules, oak casks, chemical substances, and so on) have also
been adjusted in line with the overall liberalization. Therefore effective protection of winemakers may not have worsened relative to the pre-liberalization
period.

Imports as a share of total wine consumption have jumped from less than
20 per cent to more than 50 per cent in this period of liberal trade. Similarly,
exports have grown from 7 per cent of total production in 1990 to over 36 per
cent in 2001. Today, the domestic wine market in New Zealand is considered
to be freely accessible to overseas producers and, from the domestic producers' perspective, is becoming an integral part of the global wine market.

The value of total exports and imports reached US$143 million in 2001:
$83 million exports and $60 million in imports. Special circumstances of the
low value of the NZ dollar and increasing specialization in high-quality wine
are the most important contributors to the strong US dollar export growth rate
of 18.2 per cent p.a. in 1990–2001. In contrast, the volume of exports has
hardly moved: it grew at just 10.7 per cent p.a. as the quality of exports wine
rose and it became more widely appreciated. The most dynamic market for
New Zealand wine was the USA, but the volume of exports to the Netherlands,
Germany and Japan also grew although less dramatically (Table 14.2).

In April 2001 four New World wine-exporting countries – Australia,
Canada, the USA and New Zealand – signed a treaty on 'Mutual Acceptance

Table 14.2   New Zealand wine exports to key markets by export price, 2001

	UK	Australia	USA	Canada	Japan	Total all, markets
Total ('000 hl)	99.2	23.7	31.3	6.1	3.9	192.5
Share (%)	52	12	16	3	2	100
Total (US$m)	39.0	11.0	17.2	2.7	5.7	82.3
Share (%)	47	13	21	3	7	100
Average price (US$/litre)	3.93	4.62	5.48	4.34	5.41	4.33
White	3.67	4.67	5.16	4.41	4.44	4.07
Red	5.38	5.32	7.82	5.30	7.56	5.97
Average price of country's imports from all sources (US$/litre)	2.19	3.91	3.81	2.48	3.98	1.93

Source: WINZ (2003) and Anderson and Norman (2003, Table 51). The average US$/NZ$ exchange rate for 2001 was US$0.4203.

Agreement on Oenological Practices'. The Agreement removes non-tariff barriers to trade based on technical differences in winemaking practices for the signatory countries. Therefore wine sold in any of their domestic markets (implying it does not contravene the health and safety regulations of that country) would be automatically approved for sale in the markets of the other signatories. Other New World countries, namely Argentina, Chile and South Africa, are expected to join the treaty at a later date. This Agreement is seen in New Zealand as an 'insurance policy' for wine exporters as it covers the fastest-growing export market for New Zealand wines (the USA). However, to further reduce the extent of non-tariff barriers faced by New Zealand exporters, it would be necessary to sign a similar agreement with the EU.

Imports have been growing steadily during the 1990–2001 period (at 11 per cent p.a. in volume terms). The recent low NZ/US dollar exchange rate did not hurt because the Australian dollar was also low at that time and 70 per cent of imports were low-priced wines from Australia. Import volumes have continued to expand due to a shortage of New Zealand-produced wine for domestic consumption. This continuing shortage of locally produced wine is explained *inter alia* by the change from low-quality to high-quality grape varieties grown, causing average yields per hectare to decline at a rate of 6.4 per cent p.a. (average yield in 2001 was 5.1 tonnes per hectare compared with 14.3 tonnes in 1990). This shortfall in quantity has been compensated by the high quality of grapes and wines. The simple but reliable evidence of that is the movement of prices. The volume of wine production over the 1990–2001 period grew at just 2.6 per cent p.a. while the volume of exports grew at 13.6 per cent p.a. and its value in US dollars at 18.2 per cent.

The unit value of production exported has steadily increased through the decade from US$2.70 in the early 1990s to $4.33 per litre by 2001. By contrast, the average price of imported wine fell from more than $3 to $1.66 in the same period (Anderson and Norman, 2003). This indicates a permanent upgrade of wine production and exports. New Zealand wine producers are now recognized globally as producers and exporters of super- and ultra-premium wines, with the highest average export price of any wine-producing country (one-third above France in 2001, the next highest-priced exporter).

One of the lesser aspects of operation in the wine sector is New Zealand's wine legislation on labelling and certification. The lax requirements of the ageing Acts[9] have not been enforced by the Ministry of Health in the 1990s due to lack of funds (WINZ, 1999). Consequently many local and imported wines have been contravening the regulations. Export certification is required by all wine exporters and is issued by WINZ. Given that only a few wineries have invested in obtaining ISO certification, and the ridiculously low fines that the WINZ has been able to impose, quality control was in fact left to self-regulation of the industry with all the risks that entails. Given that new entry into the industry is still ongoing and that this may result in tougher competition, free-riding on the obvious success so far of self-regulation might become more prevalent.[10]

The legislative review overseen by the Ministry of Agriculture and initiated by the WINZ in February 2000 is now developing policy advice to government. The industry's motivation for a change in legislation was to secure a set of rules improving certainty, transparency and cost-efficiency of the current regulation. To achieve this the WINZ, which represents the industry, has proposed an amalgamation of current legislation in a single act tentatively called the Wine Act which will set standards for wine labelling, export certification, disciplinary actions for winemakers accused of breaching standards, and industry funding. The urgency to introduce this new legislation is being increased by other legislation coming into force in 2002 – the Australia and New Zealand Food Standards Code – because this new code does not provide coverage of vintage and varietal labelling.

The 1999 regulation (Sale of Liquor Amendment Act) that allowed for wine sales on Sundays and on a 24-hour basis had a positive impact on the industry and also on the attitude towards alcohol consumption in general. The outstanding area where the industry believes further progress in deregulation and liberalization could be made is the fiscal area. Given the pressure to create a surplus, the government has taxed the least elastic products most heavily (tobacco and alcohol) through excise taxation. In the past a combination of a policy of inflation indexation and *ad hoc* increases applied to excise duties on wine. This was considered by the industry as an unnecessary cost burden that also added to the uncertainty in which investors make their choices. The current policy of reliance on inflation indexation only is acknowledged by the industry as a positive contribution to an increase in certainty for wineries (see WINZ, 2001, p. 7). Nevertheless, the industry persists in its recommendations for the abolition of excise.

A few large-scale producers dominate wine production in New Zealand: throughout the 1990s four large companies accounted for around four-fifths of the industry's production and more than two-thirds of the industry's exports. On the New Zealand scene, wineries are classed in three categories: category I consists of small-scale producers (up to 200 000 litres per year); category II consists of medium-scale producers (with production levels anywhere between 200 000 and 2 million litres per year); and category III are large-scale producers (over 2 million litres per year). In the 1990s, the total number of wineries (members of the WINZ) increased by over 150 per cent. In 1990, of the total number of wineries, 90 per cent belonged to category I, 8 per cent to category II and 2 per cent to category III. Through the decade this structure has changed, reflecting an increase in concentration. In 2001 category I accounts for 93 per cent of all wineries, while medium-size wineries and large-scale wineries have dropped to 6.3 per cent and 0.7 per cent, respectively. In terms of their share in the total number of wineries, there are fewer wineries producing over 200 000 litres of wine. However, despite a reduction in the share of large-scale and medium-scale producers, they further increased their already dominant share of production, domestic sales and exports. In the 2000–2001 period mergers and acquisitions deepened the concentration as the number of players at the top fell by 25 per cent, leaving only three large companies to share the biggest slice of the domestic and export markets.[11] None the less, the domestic market still radiates dynamic competition. In particular, due to the high quality of New Zealand wines and the smallness of its supply, exports have accounted for an increasing share of most wineries' production. In a liberal trade environment this has allowed for a continuously increasing contribution of imports to supply the domestic market.

NEW ZEALAND'S EXPORT-ORIENTED WINE GROWTH FROM AN INTERNATIONAL PERSPECTIVE

This section provides more details on New Zealand exports and imports of wine. More specifically it addresses the following three questions: how does the growth of New Zealand's wine production and trade compare with the rest of the world and in particular other New World exporters; how well is New Zealand penetrating overseas wine markets; and how well is New Zealand upgrading the quality of its exported wine?

Unless a decimal point is used, New Zealand's shares of world production, consumption, exports or imports of wine are undetectable before 2000. However, New Zealand's share in the value of world exports rose steadily, from 0.1 per cent to 0.6 per cent between 1990 and 2001, a period when the traditional European producers' share of world exports fell from 77 to 67 per cent (Anderson and Norman, 2003). Thus the New Zealand wine industry has done very well compared with Old World traditional producers. In the 1980s exports averaged only 3 per cent of production, but by 2001 that had risen to 36 per cent, slightly ahead of France and Italy, not far behind Australia and Chile, and well ahead of the global average of 25 per cent.

Imports as a share of domestic consumption have also risen faster for New Zealand than for the world as a whole and even than for the USA. This is not because of a large rise in per capita consumption in New Zealand but rather a fall in production of lower-quality wine.

New Zealand's smallness on the global scene has both advantages and disadvantages. One of the disadvantages is that because of its limited supply, New Zealand cannot spread itself across all major importing markets. Instead, exporting needs to follow a very targeted and niche strategy to be effective. A starting point for such a strategy is the careful selection of core target markets.

Traditionally Australia and the UK market were the initial focus for New Zealand wine exports, so much so that its relative importance for New Zealand rose to be more than twice as high as the UK's (and even more so Australia's) share of world imports of wine (Figure 14.3). But from the mid-1990s an active strategy of market diversification has been employed by individual producers and by the WINZ through its export-promoting activities. Criteria used to identify markets with the best opportunities include historic and projected sales performance, consumption and distribution patterns and economic performance, and cultural affinity. Consequently export markets are segmented into two tiers: tier 1 markets (UK, USA, Australia), which account for about 80 per cent of export sales and will continue to absorb an increasing share in the next five years; and tier 2 (Canada, Germany, Ireland and the Netherlands), which all present good opportunities for growth but for various reasons have smaller shares than the tier 1 markets.

Of course there is a further layer of market segmentation within these two tiers. For example, within tier 1 the key markets lie in the metropolitan centres such as the southeast of the UK, the northeast of the USA, and Sydney and Melbourne in Australia.

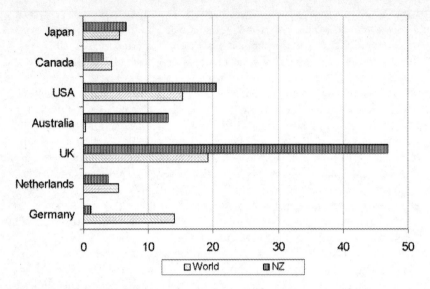

Source: Calculated from Anderson and Norman (2003, Table 100).

*Figure 14.3   Major wine importing countries' shares of global imports and
their share of New Zealand's wine exports, 2001 (%, based on
value in US$ million)*

What about changes in quality? Quality is always tricky to measure, especially in the case of wine where there are so many different varieties and
styles. A proxy index for the average quality of a country's wine exports, at
least in a willingness-to-pay sense, is the average export price. We have
already commented on the steady climb of the average price for New Zealand
wine exports, but here we want first to compare New Zealand's achievements
with other main wine exporters, and then to look at the main export markets
of New Zealand and how they differ in terms of price segmentation.

The unit value of wine exports rose over the 1990–2001 period by around
0.7 per cent p.a. for the world as a whole but by 4.6 per cent p.a. for New
Zealand – much faster than for any significant wine exporter except Chile (5.8
per cent), and well ahead of Australia (2.3 per cent – see Anderson and
Norman, 2003).

It is typical for wine exports to vary significantly in terms of quality across
different markets. Table 14.2 disaggregates New Zealand exports into several
key markets and shows the average price fetched in each one of these markets
in 2001. The UK market, where nearly half of New Zealand's exports still go,
pays relatively less than other key markets, but New Zealand wine fetches a
much higher price than the average price paid for total British imports

(US$3.93 compared with $2.19 in 2001). Most lucrative are the markets in the USA and Japan, where average unit values averaged almost US$5.50 in 2001.

PROSPECTS

Is the export-led growth of New Zealand's wine industry sustainable? There are several differentiating features of the New Zealand wine sector that will help the industry to continue to prosper despite the likelihood of downward pressure on international average prices at least in the middle part of the present decade.

First, New Zealand is small and will remain small in the global sense. The growth in vineyard area expected over the next few years is significant from a national point of view but will make almost no change to the global vineyard area.

In New Zealand, based on industry surveys (BNZ, 2000), it is anticipated that the production area will exceed 15 000 ha in 2004. MAF (2001) forecasts a steady increase in wine production in the longer term, to be accompanied by a considerable increase of new investment in processing capacity and market development.

A major increase in grape production is projected for the Marlborough region, which would cover around 43 per cent of the total area, followed by Hawkes Bay and Gisborne, together covering 38 per cent of the total. Looking at varieties, it is expected that Chardonnay and Sauvignon Blanc will remain the leading varieties, accounting for 39 per cent and 38 per cent of the total producing area of white varieties and 27 per cent and 26 per cent of the total production area in 2003, respectively.[12] Note that reliance on white varieties is slowly weakening, with 'bulk' varieties such as Müller-Thurgau and Muscat taking the biggest hit. The dominant red variety is Pinot Noir, which is projected to grow from 39 per cent of the red varieties' production area in 2000 to as much as 85 per cent. The second largest red variety will be Merlot, but the most dynamic growth is associated with Syrah and Malbec.

Second, New Zealand is steadily replanting with the aim of super- and ultra-premium wine production, because while a price fall is projected for standard medium qualities, it is not expected at the top of the quality scale for Pinot Noir and Sauvignon Blanc. As a result, New Zealand expects to continue to increase its market share in key importing countries. Table 14.3 presents projections of New Zealand sales in the top level of the three markets of tier 1 in year 2006. In terms of export prices, MAF (2001) forecasts only a slight fall in the medium term (Figure 14.4).

Continual quality improvements can only be achieved by innovating and perfecting vineyard and winemaking techniques to maintain their highly

*Table 14.3   Sales in super- and ultra-premium market segments in the UK,
the USA and Australia, actual 2000 and projected 2006*

	2000 actual			2006 projected		
	Million cases total	Million cases from NZ	NZ market share (%)	Million cases total	Million cases from NZ	NZ market share (%)
UK	11.5	1.1	9.6	18.2	2.3	12.6
USA	42.8	0.35	0.8	67.9	1.9	2.8
Australia	6.5	0.30	4.6	10.2	0.94	9.2

Source: McKenzie (2001).

distinctive, often unique character. Education and training for special skills at all levels of the vertical chain will become an important determinant of this ability to maintain high standards and to differentiate. Current educational capacity is limited, however, with only Lincoln University currently offering a postgraduate degree in viticulture.

New channels of distribution and new methods of marketing are being developed. E-commerce has been widely embraced by New Zealand wineries and there are many websites providing low-cost information, not only from sellers to buyers but also between producers and growers.

As a spillover effect from farm tourism, an extension of vertical integration is developing in the wine industry to cover wine tourism. It can be used for a wide range of activities aimed at improving profitability for wine producers such as supporting activities for developing brand recognition.

Third, New Zealand grape-growers and winemakers are embracing ideas for 'greening' the wine sector (Fairweather et al., 1999), where greening includes moves 'towards more sustainable/environmentally friendly production, or the auditing or branding of aspects of production that the market might perceive as "safe" or "green" ' (p. 2). This is not only important for exports, because local consumers too are becoming increasingly sensitive about the safety of food and the greening of production processes. New Zealand has developed the Integrated Winegrape Production (IWP) programme, which has already gained international legal recognition. The programme is still voluntary, but about 60 per cent of production is covered. As there are potentially adverse effects of partial coverage of this programme, more work is needed to use it as a powerful marketing tool. That requires maintaining its focus on environmentally friendly vineyard practices and nurture greening initiatives so as to capitalize on the increasing consumer demand for environmentally friendly products.

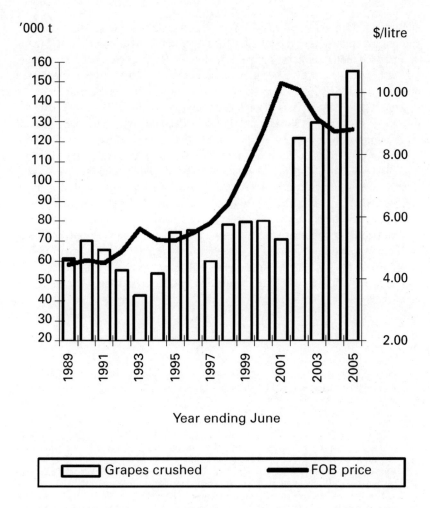

'000 t $/litre

Year ending June

Grapes crushed ▬▬▬FOB price

Source: http://www.maf.govt.nz/mafnet/publications/sonzaf/2001/2001–20.htm#P2344_121962.

Figure 14.4   Projections of wine grapes crushed and prices of wine exports,
New Zealand, 1989–2005

Fourth, the New Zealand industry is working continuously toward identifying finely defined niche markets. However, before that is possible, the cultivation of broader markets and the development of taste for New Zealand wine
is needed. WINZ has adopted generic export promotion under the logo 'Riches
of a clean, green land'. A collective promotion of the generic brand of New
Zealand wine helps the industry to achieve critical mass, economies of scale

and ultimately greater awareness. With this increased awareness, the task of gaining acceptance and recognition for individual New Zealand wine brands destined for niche markets is greatly facilitated. Relying on a generic brand is not without risk, however. As mentioned earlier, the lack of institutionalized quality control and 'free-riding' could easily damage the whole brand.

Finally, the industry has always been represented by at least two bodies – the WINZ for wine producers and the New Zealand Grape Growers Council representing grape-growers. In 2002 these two agreed to the formation of a unified industry organization that would work towards representing, enhancing and developing 'the collective brand "New Zealand Wine" for the benefit of all growers and winemakers' (WINZ, 2001, p. 8). The combined body, New Zealand wine growers, came into being on 1 March 2002. One of its most important activities is furthering research activity and complementing the IWP scheme with the development of a new standard for organic grape and wine production. In addition, as the process of improving the industry regulation is not finished, New Zealand Winegrowers will continue the WINZ activities in this area (including developing brands and intellectual property rights issues and lobbying for lower excise taxation).

NOTES

1. Most wine produced in New Zealand comes from grapes. For example in 2000, New Zealand produced around 60 million litres of grape wine and around 4 million litres of fruit and other non-grape wines (for example kiwifruit wine and cider) (MAF, 2000, p. 5). This chapter is concerned only with grape wine.
2. This section draws extensively from Mikić (1998).
3. Early (pre-1960) development of the industry could be credited to two distinct groups of producers in West Auckland and Hawkes Bay. Dalmatians, who ran the wine business as they were taught in their homeland, privately owned 90 per cent of vineyards in West Auckland. The vineyards were of small size and worked with family labour. Their businesses were vertically integrated, starting with the production of grapes through to bottling and ending with the sale of wine on the premises. In contrast, in Hawkes Bay there were fewer companies, expecting to benefit from large-scale production and specialization. These companies typically used waged labour, hired machinery at harvesting time, and used distribution channels for sales (Workman, 1994). Such diversity with respect to the types of producers inhibited the early development of the industry because of the inability of producers to agree on a unified body which would develop the industry's strategy and represent its interests with the government and the public. The Wine Institute of New Zealand (WINZ) was finally formed in 1975 as a self-regulatory and representative body of the industry.
4. Taken together, these protection instruments translated into *ad valorem* equivalent tariffs between 35 and 70 cent for imports under the quota and from 235 to 450 per cent for imported wine with a tariff threshold (for example, when the world price fell below a set level, a penalty tariff was applied – see Sanderson, 1998).
5. It was hoped that the elimination of imports would also allow the necessary time for restructuring within the industry, allowing for development of production of medium- to high-quality wines.
6. Moreover, empirically it has not been established how much demand is affected by excise taxation. Estimates typically produce relatively low price elasticities of demand for wine.

7. I am grateful to Irene Parminter for pointing out those societal factors.
8. New Zealand has kept discriminatory import policies with respect to the origin of wines, which take into account special relationships developed with certain economies over time. For instance, New Zealand has developed a free trade area with Australia (the ANCERTA – Australia New Zealand Closer Economic Relations and Trade Agreement) resulting in Australian wines being imported duty free. The same treatment is offered to potential exporters of wine from the Pacific Islands and the least developed economies, while developing countries (such as Chile) enjoy the opportunity to export wine to New Zealand at marginally lower rates than normal.
9. The Wine Makers Act (1981) and the Wine Makers Levy Act (1976).
10. Obviously there is a strong incentive to free-ride on high export prices by making one-off sales of low-quality wine. One does not need to emphasize how damaging this practice could be for the image of New Zealand wine in general. This is why export quality control cannot be left to self-regulation and market discipline.
11. For example, Montana Wines Inc. acquired Corbans in 2000, resulting in Montana controlling over 50 per cent of domestic sales. Allied Domecq in turn purchased Montana Wines Inc. in 2001 and Beringer Blass Wines Estates (part of the Australian Foster's Brewing Group) bought 51 per cent of Matua Valley Wines.
12. The projections on the growth of varieties are based on areas in production and not on planted areas (see BNZ, 2000, p. 7).

REFERENCES

Anderson, K. and D. Norman (2003), *Global Wine Production, Consumption and Trade, 1961 to 2001: A Statistical Compendium*, Adelaide: Centre for International Economic Studies.

Berger, N. and K. Anderson (1999) 'Consumer and Import Taxes in the World Wine Market: Australia in International Perspective', *Australian Agribusiness Review*, **7** (3).

BNZ (2000), *Wine and Grape Statistical Annual*, Winegrowers of New Zealand.

Fairweather, J. et al. (1999), 'The 'Greening' of the New Zealand Wine Industry', Research Report No. 7, Department of Anthropology, University of Otago.

IDC (1980), *The Wine Industry Development Plan to 1986*, Wellington: Industry Development Commission.

MAF (2000), 'Review of Wine Legislation', MAF Public Discussion Paper No. 22, November, http://www.maf.govt.nz/winereview/

MAF (2001), Wine, http://www.maf.govt.nz/mafnet/publications/sonzaf/2001/2001–20.htm#P2344_121962

McKenzie, A. (2001), 'Strengthening our Export Platform for Even Greater Growth', presentation of the Generic Export Promotion Scheme, WINZ.

Mikić, M. (1998), 'Wine Industry in New Zealand', published as *The Impact of Liberalisation: Communicating with APEC Communities*, Studies in APEC Liberalisation, Singapore: APEC Secretariat.

Sanderson, G. (1998), 'Tariff History – Wine Industry', mimeo, Wellington: Ministry of Commerce.

WINZ (1992), *New Zealand Wine 1993–2000*, Working Paper, Wine Institute of New Zealand, Inc., Auckland.

WINZ (1999) *The New Zealand Wine Industry: A Study and Development Plan*, Auckland: Wine Institute of New Zealand.

WINZ (2001), *Annual Report*, Auckland: Wine Institute of New Zealand (and earlier years).
WINZ (2003), *Annual Report*, Auckland: Wine Institute of New Zealand.
Workman, M. (1994), 'Geographic Orientation of the Wine Industry in New Zealand', unpublished thesis, The University of Auckland, pp. 94–127.

PART IV

Other Emerging Markets

15. East Asia

Christopher Findlay, Roger Farrell, Chunlai Chen and Dewen Wang

Wine consumption, production and trade in the East Asian markets of China, Japan, and the rest of Northeast and Southeast Asia are the focus of this chapter.[1] The region as a whole is a large consumer of grapewine in aggregate if not per capita, and now takes 4 per cent of total world consumption.

The main drivers of changes in the regional aggregates are events in China and Japan. China has by far the largest winemaking sector in the region even though its markets are still at an early stage of development. Immediate challenges relate to quality control and the impacts of WTO accession. China is close to self-sufficient in wine, but has the scope for a substantial two-way trade in wine products.

The Japanese market is at a later stage of development, although still with a relatively low consumption level per capita (3 litres p.a.). Japan imports most of its wine, but also appears to produce a large volume of wine 'made in Japan'. As in China and other Northeast Asian countries, this is the result of labelling laws that allow the blending of imported bulk (or semi-processed) wine with a small percentage of wine produced from domestically grown grapes.

These and related topics are examined in more detail in this chapter. The first section provides an overview of recent events in the region, while the following sections examine developments in the two key markets of China and Japan in more detail.

OVERVIEW OF THE REGION[2]

Consumption

Wine consumption in East Asia has been rising rapidly, albeit from a low base. The total rose from 3 million hl in 1990 to over 10 million hl in 2001, when East Asia accounted for 3.8 per cent of world wine consumption compared to 1.1 per cent in 1990. China is a major contributor to that growth, while Japan

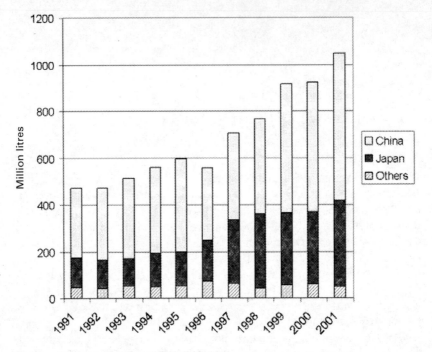

Source: Anderson and Norman (2003, Table 14).

Figure 15.1   Volume of wine consumption, East Asia, 1991–2001

has at least held its share of regional wine consumption (Figure 15.1). In 2001, China consumed 5.2 million hl, and consumption in Japan was 3.7 million hl. Consumption in the rest of the region is less than 0.6 million hl. By comparison, Australia and South Africa in recent years have each consumed around 4 million hl.

Per capita wine consumption remains low in East Asia, although it is increasing (Figure 15.2). In China, the level of apparent per capita consumption up to 2001 was still less than 0.5 litres per head but had grown rapidly over the 1990s. In Japan, consumption per head had remained at less than 1.5 litres up to 1997 but has doubled since then. Further comment on this change is offered below. Per capita consumption in the rest of Northeast Asia over this period was around 0.5 litres, but in Southeast Asia it was less than half that rate.

Wine's share of total alcohol consumption is still less than 1.5 per cent in China but is rising in Japan (from less than 3 per cent in the early 1990s to 7 per cent by 2001)[3] while falling in other Northeast Asia countries (currently around 3 per cent) and still less than 0.5 per cent in Southeast Asia.

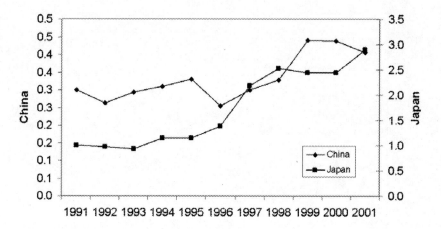

*Figure 15.2   Wine consumption per capita, China and Japan, 1991–2001
(litres per year)*

Production

In recent years China has produced just over 5 million hl of wine per annum,
which is close to its consumption level. Production in China had risen to this
level from well under 3000 hl before 1990. Significant changes on the supply
side in China have allowed this to happen.

Production of wine in Japan has more than doubled from 0.5 million hl in
the early 1990s to 1.3 million hl by the end of that decade. There is very little
grape production in Japan, unlike in China, and the origins of this wine, 'made
in Japan', are examined in more detail below. Anderson and Norman (2003)
report zero production levels elsewhere, although as in Japan and China there
may be some production in Korea based largely on imported bulk wines.[4]

Trade

The level of domestic production relative to consumption is mirrored by the
extent of reliance on the world market for wine supplies. As noted above, in
recent years China has shown a high level of wine self-sufficiency, and therefore a low import share of consumption. Japan is in the middle range, and the
other East Asian economies are heavily dependent on imports. The mix of
forms of wine imports varies among countries, as examined further below.

Figure 15.3 shows the region's shares in volume and value of world wine
imports. Both lines peak in 1998, then fall again, a consequence of the East
Asian financial crisis and of events in Japan which are outlined below. The

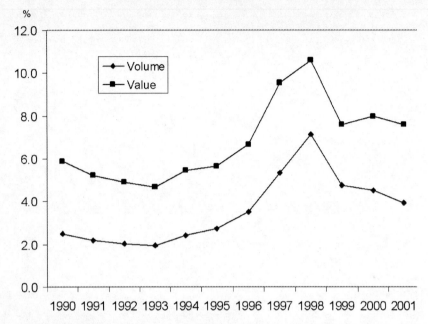

Source: Anderson and Norman (2003, Tables 34 and 43).

Figure 15.3   East Asia's share of global wine imports, 1990–2001 (%)

value share is consistently above the volume share for these economies, indicating that the region tends to import relatively highly priced wine. In 2001, the world average unit value of world imports was US$1.93 per litre whereas it was close to twice that for East Asia – although China has often imported bulk wine at less than $1 per litre.

FOCUS ON CHINA

Production

Since the dramatic economic reforms and opening up of China from late 1978, China's wine production has grown steadily, with the exception of some fluctuations in the late 1980s and mid-1990s. During the 20-year period 1978–98, China's wine production grew at an annual rate of 17.0 per cent. At that time, however, the wine produced was mainly low-priced and low quality (Wang and Sun, 1999).

Following the implementation of new production standards (first in 1984 and then revised a decade later), significant changes have taken place in China's wine production and its product structure. The production of low-quality wine (sweet products with less than half grape juice) dropped sharply, and made way for higher-priced, higher-quality, drier full-juice wines. Since 1995, dry wine production in China has been growing at an annual rate of 50 per cent, with dry red wine production growing faster than dry white wine. By the new millennium dry wine output accounted for more than 50 per cent of total domestic production (90 per cent of it red). This period also saw rapid development of new products, significant consolidation of winemaking enterprises, and also a rise in their profitability.

Total grape production in China has also grown rapidly. It now ranks sixth among all fruits, following apples, oranges, pears, bananas and peaches. In 1999, the vineyard area was 223 000 hectares and grape production was 2.7 million tons, nine times and 26 times the levels in 1978, respectively. Four-fifths of those grapes are used for table grapes, and the rest for processing. Processing grapes were split roughly 50:50 between wine processing and raisin production in 2000. These data indicate that even within the current plantings of the grape production sector, there is considerable scope to increase the wine crush. As markets for domestic dry red wine and dry white wine gradually mature, the volume of production which is managed under contracts between wine enterprises and grape-growers has increased rapidly and is now the norm for most wineries, which encourage grape-growers to plant varieties that match their demands for processing.

China's policy has been to encourage the expansion and development of the wine industry and to cut down production of traditional alcoholic beverages (grain-based beer and spirits). The target in the Ninth Five Year Plan (1996–2000) was 400 000 tons. Even though that target was not reached, the product structure, quality and technology changed considerably over those five years. In terms of quality, the National Quality and Technology Supervision Bureau reported that the share of wine products that met its standards was 85 per cent in 1995, 88 per cent in 1997, and 90 per cent in 1998.

The introduction of foreign production technology and equipment has helped China's enterprises to narrow the gap between domestic and international quality levels. In addition, China has also encouraged the industry to absorb and utilize foreign investment. At present, the types of foreign investment in China include 'fully foreign invested' enterprises (like Phoenix Liquor in Changli county, Hebei province), joint ventures (like Dynasty), joint share-holdings and technical cooperation. Joint ventures are mainly from France but Australia, Spain, Italy and the USA have also poured foreign investment into China's wine industry. The number of joint ventures was more than 20 in 2001.

Consumption

Features of China's consumption in aggregate terms were noted earlier in this chapter. Wine consumption before 1995 was mainly made up of non-full-juice and sweet wine priced at around 10 yuan per bottle (less than US$1.50). The target market was mainly rural areas as well as residents of small and middle-sized towns and cities. After 1995, with income growth and changes in consumption preferences of urban inhabitants, the consumption of full-juice wine priced in the range of 20–50 yuan rose rapidly, and the target markets are now concentrated in coastal areas in Southeast China as well as in big and middle-sized cities, where wine consumption is expected to grow at about 10 per cent per annum.

Trade

China is a now a net importer of wine. Since the surge in wine consumption in the large and medium-sized cities from the mid-1990s, the quantity of wine imports has increased dramatically. As shown in Table 15.1, imports and exports of wine were 0.7 and 2 million litres, respectively, in 1995. Since then, China has changed from being a net exporter to a net importer of wine. The quantity and value of wine imports increased quickly from 1996 to 1998, before decreasing. Figure 15.4 summarizes these data in terms of two ratios: net exports relative to exports plus imports, and the share of consumption imported. The latter rises due to the import boom in the 1990s but then falls back a little as domestic production grows from the late 1990s.

Table 15.1   *Volumes and values of wine imports and exports,[a] China, 1995–2001 (million litres and US$ million)*

Year	Imports		Exports		Net imports		Unit value of wine imports (US cents/litre)
	Volume	Value	Volume	Value	Volume	Value	
1995	0.7	2.2	2.6	4.4	−1.9	−2.2	314
1996	4.7	5.9	2.9	5.5	1.7	0.5	126
1997	37.6	35.6	2.8	6.0	34.8	29.6	95
1998	49.4	37.8	3.3	5.5	46.1	32.4	77
1999	44.4	34.3	4.5	5.5	39.9	28.9	77
2000	35.1	28.3	4.2	5.6	30.9	22.7	81
2001	28.5	17.5	4.1	6.0	24.4	16.5	61

Note: [a] Includes only grape wine and excludes products such as vermouth or wine coolers.

Source: China Customs Statistical Database.

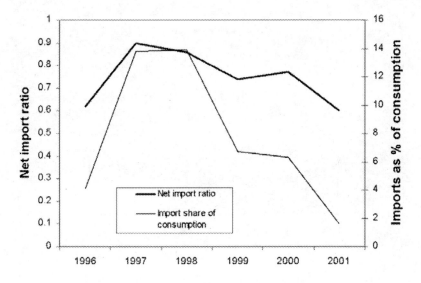

Source: Anderson and Norman (2003, Tables 29 and 36)

Figure 15.4 Ratio of net imports to exports plus imports and share of imports in consumption, volume based, China, 1996–2001

The decrease in net imports after 1998 also relates to an issue of quality uncertainty. Attracted by the brisk growth in the wine market, some enterprises imported grape juice and sold it as imported wine after simple processing, while others simply used false labels. According to a survey by the State Quality and Technology Supervision Bureau, two-thirds of the imported wines in the market in 2001 were fake (Xinhua Net, 2001). This has diminished consumers' confidence in the quality of imported wines and reduced demand for them.

Figure 15.5 shows the composition of imports since 1997 in terms of sparkling wines, bottled wine, bulk wine and grape juice for making wine. The striking feature of the chart is China's heavy reliance on imports of bulk wine (defined here as wine imported in containers of 2 litres or more).

In 2001 China levied a 65 per cent duty on foreign wine imports (except Champagne and grape juice for making wine, where the duty was 55 per cent). The *ad valorem* tariff rate is the same for bulk and bottled imports. In addition, wine is subject to a 10 per cent consumption tax and a 17 per cent value-added tax. The tariff plus the taxes increase the final retail price of a bottle of imported wine by approximately 120 per cent, which hurts demand more for expensive wines that for lower-priced ones. As a result of its accession to the

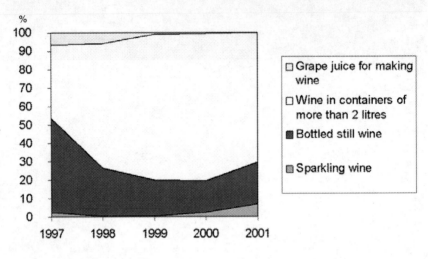

Source: China Customs Statistics.

Figure 15.5   Imports of wine by type, China, 1997–2001 (value shares %)

WTO, China has pledged to cut its wine tariff from 65 per cent to 14 per cent over the 2002–2006 period, and to allow any enterprise authorized to undertake foreign trade to import wine without a quota or licence.

China has demonstrated its capacity to export, but the unavailability of an original production certification system and the lack of uniform standards hinder the export of its high-quality products, like those produced by Changyu, Dynasty and Great Wall. For example, the European Union has listed China as one of the five prohibited countries because exporters are unable to describe the original production area. This is difficult to provide due to the absence of data on grapevine planting.

Challenges Ahead

China's wine industry faces a number of challenges as it integrates into the international market, adjusts to WTO accession, and works to satisfy the potential for growth in domestic demand. One is coping with fake products, inferior quality and variations in quality and in volumes of particular types of wines (which make it difficult to discern preferences of consumers).

Second, China's wine management system is far from integrated. Grape production, wine production and sales are regulated by different government management sectors. A system of wine quality control by grade and original production certification has yet to be established. China's wine production has two sets of standards: a state standard, and an industrial standard. The industrial standard has lower requirements for every index of wine production. According to the industrial standard, the original juice should not be less than 50 per cent grapes, which leaves loopholes for illegal winemakers to sell inferior or fake products and thereby tarnish the reputation of Chinese wine in domestic and international markets. Recently, many proposals have been made to terminate the industrial standard, aiming to standardize quality rules in China's wine industry.

Third, the structure of products is monotonous, mainly consisting of dinner wines. The availability of a variety of products within the wine group is necessary to encourage the development of consumption habits. Furthermore, the proportions of dry red wine and dry white wine have fluctuated, and labels of wines usually do not describe grape varieties or styles (for example fortified or sparkling wine).

Fourth, the relatively low quality of grapes grown in China inhibits quality improvement of Chinese wine. In recent years, due to the growth in red wine demand, the raw materials base for red wine has developed rapidly. Some regions rushed to invest in 'dry red wine' projects regardless of their natural and economic conditions, adding to the quality problem on the supply side.

FOCUS ON JAPAN

Consumption

Traditionally, beer, sake, shochu and whisky have been the most popular alcoholic beverages in Japan (Table 15.2). However, wine consumption has expanded in recent years, trebling its share of overall alcohol consumption since 1990. Red wine accounted in 2001 for about 60 per cent of sales, white wine for 30 per cent and rosé for the balance. The red wine share has risen rapidly, from just 30 per cent in 1994.

The main reasons for the increase in wine's popularity in the Japanese market appear to be a move towards Western consumption patterns, and increasing knowledge of wine as a product due to ongoing advertising campaigns and promotions by producers and importers. A very significant factor in Japan has been recognition of the apparent health qualities of wine, at least compared to beverages with a higher alcohol content. The Japanese media is generally recognized to have contributed to the 'wine boom' via the proliferation of stories about the beneficial effects of (particularly red) wine consumption. This perception has spread out from Tokyo towards regional areas.

Wine consumption has three main components in Japan: drinking at home, drinking in bars and restaurants, and wine for gift-giving. Prestige wines (typically French and German) tend to be purchased at department stores, while lower-priced wines are typically bought at neighbourhood shops for personal use.

Table 15.2   Consumption of alcoholic beverages, Japan, 2000

	Total annual consumption (million litres)	Share of total consumption (%)	Per capita consumption (litres)	Imports as % of consumption volume
Beer	5 832	57.7	58.2	1
Happoshu[a]	1 404	13.9	14.0	3
Japanese sake	1 067	10.6	10.6	0
Shochu wine	760	7.5	7.6	7
Liqueur	372	3.7	3.7	3
Fruit wine	298	2.9	3.0	54
Whisky	154	1.5	1.5	22
Others	213	2.1	2.1	4
Total	10 103	100.0	100.7	4

Note: [a] Sparkling low-malt beverage.

Source: JETRO (2001a) and National Tax Administration Agency.

The fall in the price of wine in recent years is likely to have contributed to an increase in home consumption. The entry of low-priced wine from Chile in particular drove down prices in all categories, although there is still a significant margin between prices of wine sold in the ordinary and premium ranges.

Production: 'Made in Japan'?

Japan is generally not considered to have a suitable climate for growing grapes. Total grape production in Japan is less than 300 000 tons per year, and 90 per cent of that output is sold as table grapes (USDA, 2000). Thus the main part of wine consumption in Japan is supplied by imports.

The largest Japanese domestic wineries are Suntory and Mercian, which have made large investments in equipment and Western expertise. Some wines carry the label 'Made in Japan' even though it means 'Bottled in Japan', since legally wine is considered Japanese wine if some part has been fermented domestically. JETRO (1998) notes that the term 'domestic wine' is commonly used in Japan, but it has no legal foundation. A domestic or Japanese wine is defined as having been fermented in Japan, even if all the raw materials are imported. Hence a Japanese wine could be produced from Californian grapes, Bulgarian grape juice concentrate or frozen must from France, as long as it was domestically fermented. The Japanese Winery Association (*Nihon Wainarii Kyoukai*) has adopted a slightly stricter voluntary labelling code, but it is unclear how widely this is used.[5]

The USDA estimates that 90 per cent of Japanese brands are made from imported bulk wine and grape must or concentrate.[6] Only 10 per cent of wine sold under a 'Made in Japan' brand is based exclusively on grapes grown in Japan. Japanese brands usually account for about 40 per cent of domestic sales.

Trade

Imports surged in 1998 and have since fallen, but by 2000 they were still 10 per cent higher in value terms than in 1997 and 60 per cent higher than in 1996 (Table 15.3). Bottled wine accounts for the bulk of imports in terms of volume (72 per cent) and value (76 per cent). Bulk wine is ranked second in terms of volume (15 per cent), while sparkling wine is ranked second in terms of value (16 per cent). Old World wine continues to dominate the Japanese market (Table 15.4).

The USDA attributes the boom in imports in 1998 to the red wine consumption boom that peaked a year earlier. Inventories thus accumulated in 1998 and have since been run down, with downward pressure on prices in Japan.

There has been considerable change in the sources of imports over the 1990s, but by 2000 the top three were France, Italy and the USA in terms of volume and value (Table 15.5). Demand for Old World wine is greater at the

Table 15.3   Value of wine imports by type, Japan, 1990–2000 (¥100 million)

Year	Imports for processing by Japanese wineries (bulk wine and grape must)	Imports of wine for direct wholesale or retail sale		
		Bottled wine	Sparkling wine	Wine coolers vermouth, sherry, etc.
1990	34	459	82	21
1991	38	340	77	17
1992	28	316	77	17
1993	20	218	60	13
1994	17	275	77	16
1995	30	318	94	22
1996	36	414	105	23
1997	60	611	123	25
1998	131	1454	134	29
1999	85	760	165	19
2000	45	670	144	22

Source: Calculated from Japan Tariff Association statistics.

Table 15.4 Sources of bottled wine imports, Japan, 1990–2000 (% by value)

Year	France	Other Europe	USA	Chile	Australia
1990	67.9	22.5	6.2	0.0	2.1
1991	63.0	26.1	6.8	0.2	2.2
1992	61.4	27.6	7.3	0.2	2.0
1993	59.4	28.7	7.9	0.2	2.2
1994	60.1	29.3	6.6	0.2	2.3
1995	59.5	30.1	6.8	0.4	1.8
1996	53.3	34.2	6.7	1.6	2.1
1997	57.0	28.1	6.2	3.5	2.1
1998	54.1	24.5	7.2	8.2	1.9
1999	56.4	24.2	10.2	3.7	2.6
2000	58.1	22.0	9.4	4.6	3.0

Source: Calculated from Japan Tariff Association statistics.

premium end of the market. Demand for French wine is supported by high visibility, while Italian wine's popularity is sustained by the large number of Italian restaurants in Japan. Without those advantages, German wine is losing market share. Imports from France are also distinguished by their very relatively high

Table 15.5 Volume, value and unit value of imported wines, by source, Japan, 2001

	Volume (million litres)	Value (US$ million)	Unit value (US$ per litre)
France	65	415	6.42
Italy	39	102	2.60
USA	29	51	1.74
Argentina	13	13	0.99
Chile	11	31	2.72
Spain	11	25	2.41
Germany	10	30	2.93
Australia	5	15	3.00
Bulgaria	3	2	0.61
All countries	199	792	3.98

Source: Based on data underlying Tables 96, 98 and 100 in Anderson and Norman (2003).

value per litre. The other top nine suppliers show unit values in the range of
US$3 to US$0.61 per litre (Table 15.5). The average value for all imports in
2001 was $3.98 per litre, since some high-priced bottled wine also comes as
re-exports from such entrepot countries as the Netherlands, the UK and
Singapore.

EU exporters account for about 70 per cent of Japan's imports, which
matches their share of world trade, while the share of New World wine suppliers – which was relatively high a decade ago – has not grown in line with their
expanding share of global exports and so in 2001 was only a little higher than
their share of world trade. This is captured in Figure 15.6, which shows the
trends in the intensity indices for various New World suppliers to the Japanese
market. The index in that figure measures the share of the supplier economy
in the imports of the focus economy, in this case Japan, relative to that
supplier's share of world exports. A value of the index greater than one shows
that the market share in Japan is higher than might be expected according to
the share of the exporter economy in the world market. Shown in the figure is
the downward trend for the so-called New World Wine Group (NWWG, which
includes Argentina, Australia, Canada, Chile, New Zealand, South Africa, the
USA, and Uruguay). The index value for Australia has been below that of the
group as a whole, and has also shown a steady decline. There are some success
stories within the group, however. The intensity values for the USA in the

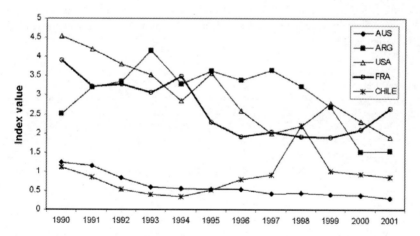

Note: ᵃ The index is defined as the share of the exporters' wine that is imported by Japan divided
by Japan's share of global wine imports, both in value terms.

Source: From the data underlying Table 103 in Anderson and Norman (2003).

Figure 15.6   Indices of wine import trade intensity,ᵃ Japan, 1990–2001

1990s have been above the NWWG level. Chile started from a position below
the group as a whole but in recent years has been at the same level or higher
than the group average.

Foreign Investment Strategies

Increasingly in the international wine industry there has been a series of mergers and acquisitions, leading to greater rationalization and globalization of
wine companies. Foreign investment has been used as a preferred method to
coordinate the acquisition and sale of wine and wine grapes (Pompelli and
Pick, 1999). Underlying international expansion through FDI is the motivation
of firms to internalize operations or activities that were previously performed
in intermediate markets, such as using an agent, by absorbing these operations
within the ownership and control of the firm (Caves, 1996). Another strategy
is to use FDI to gain capabilities, such as wine production knowledge, to
compete more effectively in a particular market (Dunning, 1980). Generally,
the decision to expand abroad through FDI is part of a sequence of marketing
steps which can be used to consolidate a firm's market share or resource base
(Johanson and Valhne, 1977; Craig and Douglas, 1996).

Supply chain management (SCM) is one aim of corporate mergers and
consolidations, as well as greenfield investments in the international wine
industry, as it is in other industries. Pompelli and Pick (1999), using surveys
of American investors, found that Beringer, Mondavi and Kendall Jackson
were leading investors, especially in France, Italy and Chile and Argentina.
The study noted that:

> US wineries are apparently motivated by pressures to innovate, to meet differing
> consumer needs, to reduce transaction costs, and to stabilise access to quality wine
> or wine grapes – and all of these pressures provide sufficient motivation for winer-
> ies to utilise SCM practices. [In practice] production flexibility and improved
> access to high-quality wine grape supplies were the primary motivations for inter-
> national investments.

According to Pompelli and Pick (1999), foreign investment was chosen by
some companies because of dissatisfaction with the effectiveness of contrac-
tual obligations in ensuring quality and the reliability of supply. On the other
hand, many wine companies did not invest overseas because they already had
access to a price-competitive, stable and adequate supply of domestically
produced wine grapes and possessed a sufficient portfolio of wines to be
competitive.

Such investments allow a more flexible response to changing consumer
preferences for types of wine and geographical sources, especially given the
need to place wines at popular price points. These measures integrate the

international supply management operations of wineries, overcoming actual or potential problems such as supply constraints or production gaps.

Japanese companies active in the domestic wine market have used a variety of strategies to remain competitive, given the comparative advantages of wine producers in other parts of the world. First, Japanese firms have become independent sales agents representing overseas wine or spirits producers in Japan. Others have used licensing arrangements, giving overseas producers a fee and royalties for the right to manufacture or market their product in Japan.

Another strategy has been to use FDI to secure raw materials (bulk wine and grape must) and proprietary knowledge of wine production. In some cases an interest in a wine producer was acquired to achieve a market presence in both the imported and domestic production segments of the market.[7]

Underlying the motivation for overseas investment by Japanese wine companies, such as Suntory, Mercian, Sapporo and others, has been the tariff regime for wine in Japan and a series of deregulation decisions of the Japanese government. The low duty on bulk wine and grape must provides an advantage to Japanese domestic wine producers to compete more effectively despite the slight local production of grapes for wine purposes. Clearly, a significant level of effective protection is accorded to the domestic industry. We discuss this effect in more detail below.

In contrast, there is a noticeable lack of investment in Japan by international wine companies in establishing production, marketing or distribution facilities. One key reason could be the established market position of a number of Japanese companies, which are dominant as both domestic producers and importers. These firms also dominate traditional distribution systems for wine in Japan, so newcomer suppliers of wine now distributed in those channels would consider the likely strategic responses of their previous partners to new investments in Japan.

Distribution Issues

Another market access issue has been the distribution channels in Japan, which vary according to the target market and price ranges of wines. The traditional channels for distribution were through a layer of specialist wholesalers and retailers. A couple of changes have led to adjustments in this system.

One force for change is retail deregulation in Japan, which has led to the establishment of larger retail outlets, including supermarkets. Sales of large-scale supermarkets in 1998 alone grew by 5.4 per cent to ¥6.2 trillion – or almost the GDP of New Zealand. These changes are causing the old liquor specialists to transform themselves into convenience stores.

Another force for change is the licensing system. Wine distribution is currently entirely regulated by the Liquor Tax Law, which requires whole-salers and retailers to have liquor licences.[8] Since June 1997 regulations on issuing liquor licences have been simplified, resulting in an expansion in the number of new liquor licences being approved. Further retail deregulation that removed restrictions on liquor outlets occurred in early 2001.[9]

To achieve national distribution, wine exporters or Japanese importers tend to choose a major Japanese liquor manufacturer or wholesaler with links to liquor outlets across Japan (Austrade, 2000). Suntory and Mercian are the two leading makers of domestic wine in Japan and are also the two leading wine importers, especially from France, Italy, Germany, the USA, Spain and Chile, as well as Australia.

These companies actively market their domestic and imported wine ranges on TV and in the print media. Leading independent importers include Jardine Wines and Spirits K.K., which sells Dom Perignon and other premium cham-pagne brands. Lower-priced wine importers include Nihon Shurai Hanbai, as well as a range of trading companies and smaller cooperatives. Itochu is an importer of wines from South Africa, for example, while Bukkan K.K. special-izes in Italian wine (JETRO, 2001b).

Another approach since retail sector deregulation is for large retailers such as supermarkets and department stores to import directly from overseas producers (JETRO, 2001c). A side-benefit of direct purchases by retailers is that wine promotions at department stores and smaller speciality stores are important ways to educate the Japanese consumer about different types of wine. Concerns remain, however, about the costs of distribution in Japan.

Trade Policy Issues

There is a complex structure of tariffs on wine imports into Japan. The tariff on still bottled wine imported into Japan is a combination of specific tariffs at the extremes of unit values and an *ad valorem* tariff over the middle range. The minimum duty is ¥67 per litre. Once the unit value of imports is large enough (at a value of ¥447 yen per litre), then the size of the tariff is determined by a 15 per cent duty on the cif (cost insurance freight) value, since at that value and above 15 per cent of the unit value exceeds ¥67. There is a cap on the tariff of ¥125, which applies from a unit value of ¥833 per litre and above.

There is also a gap between the bulk wine and bottled wine tariff. Bulk wine has a tariff of ¥45 per litre which remains constant over all unit values. In 2000, the average value of imports was ¥118 (US$1.10) per litre.[10] Bottled wine had an average value of ¥534 (US$4.95) per litre, which is over the ¥447 per litre threshold and so would have incurred duty at 15 per cent, equivalent to ¥80 per litre – almost twice the tax on bulk wine.

Currently wine consumption is taxed in Japan at a concessional rate compared to other alcohol. In early 2000 there was a proposal to increase the Liquor Tax on wine, happoshu (carbonated low-malt liquor) and shochu-enhanced sake by almost 100 per cent, but this has been deferred. In 2001 the Liquor Tax on wine was ¥56.5/litre compared to ¥222/litre for beer, while happoshu was levied at ¥152.7/litre (malt ratio 25–50 per cent) or ¥56.5/litre (malt ratio less than 25 per cent).

Importers of bulk wine might bottle and sell it under their own label, or leave the wine in a bulk form as, for example, house wine in restaurants. These strategies contribute to the relatively high share of Japanese brands on the domestic market. There is a significant margin between the cost of bulk wine and the price of wine at the bottom end of the market, for example for Chilean wine, or South African wine, so Japanese wine processing appears to have been quite profitable in recent years. But an offset to this incentive arises if it is valuable not to lose the identity of the brand that could occur in the process of bottling in Japan. Where this is so, incentives remain to import the established brands in bottled form. However, this situation poses a challenge for New World exporters who have not established a brand name. In this case, the Japanese companies who manage imports of wine are more likely to seek imports from these suppliers in bulk form.

A range of other regulations applies to imports, including rules on import notification for quarantine, labelling requirements, and rules on recycling of packaging. The Food Sanitation Law specifies allowable quantities of wine colouring agents and preservatives, as in other countries, and does not appear to be a significant barrier to imports.[11] However, under the Liquor Business Association Law, the Food Sanitation Law and the Measurement Law a wine may be labelled with Japan as the country of origin, even if all of the component materials (for example, grapes, must, bulk wine) have been imported.

These regulations also require that the labelling of wine sold in Japan should be in Japanese and indicate the product name, list of ingredients, alcohol content and country of origin.[12] Further work is required to establish whether these arrangements discriminate between foreign and domestic suppliers, and the significance of any burdens associated with differential treatment.

CONCLUSION

While East Asia accounts for a non-trivial share of world wine consumption, there is considerable diversity among the markets in the region, in terms of the levels of self-sufficiency, the nature of local production and the patterns and directions of trade in wine. This review of recent developments and current issues in East Asia has highlighted the relevance of a number of policy issues common to the region, including the development and application of process and product standards, the presence of tariff barriers, and impediments to trade associated with the distribution system.

Of particular interest are the impact of China's recent entry into the WTO and the implementation of China's commitment to cut tariffs. Also, the new Doha round of WTO negotiations could be a forum in which wine exporters raise the issue of the structure of Japan's tariffs and the biases it induces to import wine in bulk form. Changes in information and communication technologies will also create new opportunities to escape from some of the impediments associated with traditional distribution channels in these markets. Another feature of these markets to monitor will be the extent, patterns and contribution of foreign direct investment. Originating in either the wine-importing country or in its trading partners, foreign direct investment can complement trade in wine products.

The discussion also highlights the different experience of the New World suppliers in East Asian markets as compared to the Old World's. The data suggest that the New World's rate of penetration of East Asian markets, while still high in absolute terms compared to their share in world markets, has not been growing as fast as their shares in world trade. They face interesting challenges in establishing their brand names in the markets, in order to capture a larger share of returns to branding and production differentiation. Various policy impediments, including the structure of import tariffs, and labelling and other standards, make this more difficult and are important topics for further attention in the development of East Asian wine trade and investment strategies.

NOTES

1. The following categories of economies are used here (based on Anderson and Norman, 2003). 'Other Northeast Asia': Hong Kong, Republic of Korea, Taiwan. 'Southeast Asia': Brunei Darrusalam, Cambodia, East Timor, Indonesia, Lao PDR, Malaysia, Myanmar (Burma), Philippines, Singapore, Thailand, Viet Nam. 'East Asia' is the sum of these categories plus China and Japan.
2. All the data in this section are taken from Anderson and Norman (2003).
3. Total per capita alcohol consumption in Japan is estimated to be the same as that in Sweden and a little less than that in Canada. In sharp contrast to Japan's 7 per cent wine share, however, Sweden has a wine consumption share of over 30 per cent and Canada over 15 per cent.
4. For more commentary on the Korean market, see Shull (1997) and Brehm (2000).
5. See http://www.wineloverspage.com.
6. Domestic wine may consist of (1) wine produced from domestic grapes; (2) wine produced in Japan from grape must (mostly imported); (3) wine bottled in Japan and consisting of a blend of bulk wine with one of the above categories; or (4) a mixture of any of these categories (JETRO, 1998).
7. The Kirin Brewery of Japan has a 46 per cent shareholding in Lion Nathan, which is

Australia's second largest brewer. Lion Nathan is pursuing an expansion strategy into the wine industry and has begun by acquiring a number of premium wine companies in Australia, including Banksia and Petaluma.

8. A liquor vendor's licence is required to sell liquor in Japan (JETRO, 1998). A 1996 survey by the National Tax Administration Agency of liquor retail outlets found that 79 per cent of outlets were liquor stores, followed by convenience stores (12 per cent), mini-supermarkets of less than 500 square metres in area (3 per cent), supermarkets of more than 500 square metres in area (2 per cent), agricultural cooperatives (2 per cent), consumer cooperatives (2 per cent), and department stores (0.4 per cent).

9. The location and distance regulations that restricted new retail shops and the distance between liquor shops ended in January 2001 (JETRO, 2001a). A further population restriction will be phased out by 2003 so that a greater range of sales points will be able to sell wine.

10. Sparkling wine has a duty of ¥182/litre while fortified wine has a duty of ¥112/litre.

11. A wine importer may obtain a statement of voluntary inspection results by an official laboratory designated by the Ministry of Health and Welfare so as to exempt new imports of wine from being impeded by quarantine inspection when it enters Japan for the first time (JETRO, 2001a, p. 8).

12. Other information required includes the net content, preservative method, importer (or maker of domestic wines), distributor and whether carbonation has been used.

REFERENCES

Anderson, K. and D. Norman (2003), *Global Wine Production, Consumption and Trade, 1961 to 1999: A Statistical Compendium*, Adelaide: Centre for International Economic Studies.

Austrade (2000), 'Wine – Japan, Industry Overview', October, http://www.austrade.gov.au.

Brehm, D.A. (2000), 'Growing Demand for Wine in Korea Creates New Export Opportunity for US Producers', inspected 22 December 2001 at http://www.fas.usda.gov/info/agexporter/2000/December/growing.htm.

Caves, R.E. (1996), *Multinational Enterprise and Economic Analysis*, 2nd edn, Cambridge and New York: Cambridge University Press.

Craig, S.C. and S.P. Douglas (1996), 'Developing Strategies for Global Markets: An Evolutionary Perspective', *Columbia Journal of World Business*, **31** (1), 70–81.

Dunning, J. (1980), 'Towards an Eclectic Theory of International Production: Some Empirical Tests', *Journal of International Business Studies*, **11** (1), 9–31.

JETRO (1998), *Japanese Market Report, Regulations and Practices, Wine*, Report No. 15, March, Tokyo: JETRO.

JETRO (2001a), *Japanese Market Report, Regulations and Practices, Wine*, Report No. 54, March, Tokyo: JETRO.

JETRO (2001b), *Japanese Market Report, Regulations and Practices, Beer*, Tokyo: JETRO.

JETRO (2001c), *Market Report on Retail Food Distribution in Japan*, Tokyo: JETRO.

Johanson, J. and J. Vahlne (1977), 'The Internationalisation Process of the Firm', *Journal of International Business Studies*, **8** (1), 23–32.

Pompelli, G. and D. Pick (1999), 'International Investment Motivations of US Wineries', Mimeo.

Shull, P. (1997), 'South Korea: a Booming Market for US Wine Exports', from http://www.fas.usda.gov/info/agexporter/1997/south.html, inspected 22 December 2001.

USDA (2000), *Japan Wine Marketing Annual*, Foreign Agricultural Service, GAIN Report No. JA0527, Washington: US Department of Agriculture, December.

Wang Gongtang and Xuemei Sun (1999), 'Fifty-Year Development of Wine Industry in China', *Liquor-making Science & Technology*, **5**.

Xinhua Net (2001), 'The Domestic Brands Pitilessly Beat Overseas Brands in Wine Market', 3 July, 2001.

Index

Index

Index